ASP.NET 3.5 Social Networking

An expert guide to building enterprise-ready social
networking and community applications with
ASP.NET 3.5

Andrew Siemer

PUBLISHING

BIRMINGHAM - MUMBAI

ASP.NET 3.5 Social Networking

First published: December 2008

Production Reference: 1051208

Published by Packt Publishing Ltd.
32 Lincoln Road
Olton
Birmingham, B27 6PA, UK.

ISBN 978-1-847194-78-7

www.packtpub.com

Cover Image by Vinayak Chittar (www.visionwt.com)

Credits

Author

Andrew Siemer

Reviewer

Steven M. Swafford

Senior Acquisition Editor

David Barnes

Development Editor

Swapna Verlekar

Technical Editor

Gaurav Datar

Copy Editor

Sumathi Sridhar

Editorial Team Leader

Akshara Aware

Project Manager

Abhijeet Deobhakta

Project Coordinator

Leena Purkait

Indexer

Monica Ajmera

Proofreader

Laura Booth

Production Coordinator

Shantanu Zagade

Cover Work

Shantanu Zagade

About the Author

Andrew Siemer is the co-founder of the .NET user group VirtualDNUG.com, and is currently an architect/engineer at OTX Research. He has worked as a software engineer, architect, trainer, and author since 1998 when he left the Army. Andrew has provided consultancy to many companies on the topics of ecommerce, social networking, and business systems. He has worked with eUniverse (AllYouCanInk. com), PointVantage (MyInks.com), Callaway Golf (CallawayConnect.com), Guidance Software (GuidanceSoftware.com), *Intermix Media (FlowGo.com, Grab.com)*, and *FOX Interactive (AmericanIdol.com, FoxSports.com)* to name a few. In addition to his daily duties, he also conducts classes in .NET, C#, and other web technologies, blogs on numerous topics (*blog.andrewsiemer.com, socialnetworkingin.net* to name a couple), and works on fun new communities such as Fisharoo.com and GymEd.com.

I would like to first thank my wife Jessica Siemer. Without her love and understanding this project and all the others before it would not have been able to get off the ground, let alone get anywhere near completion! For this book project in particular though Jess gave me everything I needed to make it through to the end. My day to day successes in life would be nothing without you.

I would also like to thank Brian Loesgen from Neudesic for getting me started down the book writing path. He has been there for me time and time again keeping me headed in the right direction. And to the friends I made while at Intermix Media, Adam Wolkov and David Higbee. This book was inspired by our many early morning coffee and juice brain storming sessions. Thank you for igniting the initial spark to get this project started.

About the Reviewer

Steven M. Swafford began developing software in 1995 while serving in the **United States Air Force (USAF)**. Upon leaving the USAF, he continued developing leading edge solutions in support of the America's war fighters as part of the original USAF enterprise portal development team. His roots are now in central Alabama where he works as a software engineer developing Java and .NET based applications and web services. Steven's blog is located at `http://aspadvice.com/blogs/sswafford/`.

Steven credits his wife Su Ok and daughter Sarah for supporting and inspiring his ongoing passion for software development and the resultant challenges of life near the bleeding edge. He would like to thank Tim Stewart and Edward Habal who were his professional mentors and to this day remain close friends.

I would like to dedicate this book to my wonderful wife and my six monsters. They are my motivation to get up every morning and continue soldiering on.

Table of Contents

Preface

Social networking has become a driving force on the Internet. Many people are part of at least one social network, while more often people are members of many different communities. For this reason many business people are trying to capitalize on this movement and are in a rush to put up their own social network. As the growth of social networks continues, we have started to see more and more niche communities popping up all over in favor of the larger, all-encompassing networks in an attempt to capture a sliver of the market.

In this book, we will discuss the many aspects and features of what makes up the majority of today's social networks or online communities. Not only will we discuss the features, their purpose, and how to go about building them, but we will also take a look at the construction of these features from a large scale enterprise perspective. The goal is to discuss the creation of a community in a scalable fashion.

What This Book Covers

Chapter 1 gives you an overall structure of this book, that is, what a reader can expect from this book.

Chapter 2 helps you create an enterprise framework to handle the needs of most web applications. It discusses design patterns, best practices, and certain tools to make things easier. It also covers error handling and logging.

Chapter 3 covers registration process by means of an email verification system and a permission system to ensure security. It also touches upon password encryption/decryption techniques.

Chapter 4 covers the creation of a user's profile and an avatar in a manner that is flexible enough for all systems to use. In this chapter, we also implement some form of privacy to allow users to hide parts of their profile that they don't want to share with others.

Chapter 5 shows you how to implement friends, how to search for them, find them in the site's listings, and import your contacts into the site to find your friends.

Chapter 6 helps you create a full blown messaging system that will resemble a web-based email application similar to Hotmail or Gmail. We will also learn how to implement the Xinha WYSIWYG editor in a way that can be re-used easily across the site for complex inputs.

Chapter 7 covers details on how to build a generic media management system that will allow you to host video, photos, resumes, or any number of physical files with minimal tweaking. It also addresses the issue of multi-file uploads—one of the biggest limitations of many web programming environments.

Chapter 8 is all about Blogging. With search engines, users, and security in mind, we invest a part of this chapter to address an issue that plagues many dynamic websites—query string data being used to determine page output.

Chapter 9 discusses the creation of the core features of a message board—categories, forums, threads, and posts. Along with these features, the chapter also implements friendly URLs to make our content more suitable for search engine optimization.

Chapter 10 covers the concept of Groups. It focuses on how groups can be used to bring many different systems together in a way to start creation of sub-communities.

Chapter 11 helps us build three controls to allow our users to express their opinions about various content areas of our site—tagging, rating and commenting. Tagging control allows us to take in tag keywords as well as display all the tags for various levels of our site from specific records. Rating control allows us to configure many options per system object for individual ratings. And commenting control helps users to express very specific opinions regarding our content items.

Chapter 12 focuses on Moderation, that is, the means to manage community provided content using a very simple flagging tool. It also covers methods such as Gagging to deal with habitual rule breakers. Finally, it takes a look at what Cross-site scripting (CSS) is, and some measures that can be taken to address it.

Chapter 13 discusses some concepts to help you support a large number of users on your social network. It starts by looking at some key concepts of web farming. Then it goes on to discuss ways to create and search indexed data, methods to optimize data retrieval and content creation, and finally some mail queuing concepts.

Appendix A covers version control and ways to set up your database. It then moves on to various third-party and open source tools such as StructureMap, NAnt, ReSharper, and so on, which will help you create a stable development platform.

Appendix B discusses unit testing. It starts with NUnit and how it helps in the creation of unit tests. It then moves to NAnt and how it helps automate your building and testing processes. Finally, it explains CruiseControl.NET, and how it can help you finish off the automation aspects.

Appendix C contains entire SQL code from the book.

The appendices A, B, and C are not part of the actual book, but you can download them from Packt's website.

Appendix A is available at `//www.packtpub.com/files/4787-Appendix-A-Setting-Up-Your-Development-Environment.pdf`.

Appendix B is available at `//www.packtpub.com/files/4787-Appendix-B-TDD-and-Continuous-Integration.pdf`.

Appendix C is available at `//www.packtpub.com/files/4787-Appendix-C-SQL.pdf`.

What You Need for This Book

This book describes how to build a Social Network using ASP.NET, C#, and SQL Server. To use this book effectively, you will need access to a version of Visual Studio and SQL Server. Most of this book can be used with the various Express editions of Visual Studio and SQL Express, but you will find that having the Professional edition of Visual Studio will make your work flow more efficient. As we are not just discussing ASP.NET, but are instead more interested in what is needed for the features of social networking, there may be times when we turn to an open source solution. All the examples in this book will clearly point out where to get the needed software, and how to configure that software as we work through our examples.

Who is This Book For

This book is written for ASP.NET and C# developers who want to build an enterprise-grade Social Network, either for their own business purposes or as a contract job for another company. The book assumes you have prior experience of developing web applications using ASP.NET 3.5, C# 3.0, SQL Server 2005/2008, and Visual Studio .NET 2008; it focuses on topics that will be of interest to existing developers—not on providing step-by-step examples for each detail.

Conventions

In this book, you will find a number of styles of text that distinguish between different kinds of information. Here are some examples of these styles, and an explanation of their meaning.

Code words in text are shown as follows: "Create a new class in the `Core.Impl` directory called `ProfileService`."

A block of code will be set as follows:

```
if (profile != null && profile.ProfileID > 0)
    {
        attributes = _profileAttributeService.
                       GetProfileAttributesByProfileID
                       (profile.ProfileID);
        levelOfExperienceType =
                           _levelOfExperienceTypeRepository.
                           GetLevelOfExperienceTypeByID
                           (profile.LevelOfExperienceTypeID);

        profile.Attributes = attributes;
        profile.LevelOfExperienceType = levelOfExperienceType;
    }
```

When we wish to draw your attention to a particular part of a code block, the relevant lines or items will be made bold:

```
Account account = _accountRepository.GetAccountByID(AccountID);
Profile profile = _profileService.LoadProfileByAccountID(AccountID);
if(profile != null)
{
    account.Profile = profile;
}
```

New terms and **important words** are introduced in a bold-type font. Words that you see on the screen, in menus or dialog boxes for example, appear in our text like this:

"Click the **Test Connection** button to see if your settings are acceptable."

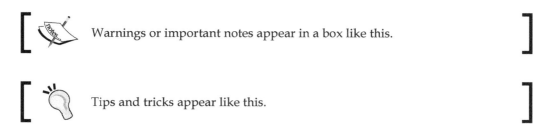

Warnings or important notes appear in a box like this.

Tips and tricks appear like this.

Reader Feedback

Feedback from our readers is always welcome. Let us know what you think about this book, what you liked or may have disliked. Reader feedback is important for us to develop titles that you really get the most out of.

To send us general feedback, simply drop an email to feedback@packtpub.com, making sure to mention the book title in the subject of your message.

If there is a book that you need and would like to see us publish, please send us a note in the **SUGGEST A TITLE** form on www.packtpub.com or email suggest@packtpub.com.

If there is a topic that you have expertise in and you are interested in either writing or contributing to a book, see our author guide on www.packtpub.com/authors.

Customer Support

Now that you are the proud owner of a Packt book, we have a number of things to help you to get the most from your purchase.

Downloading the Example Code for the Book

Visit http://www.packtpub.com/files/code/0956_Code.zip to directly download the example code.

The downloadable files contain instructions on how to use them.

Errata

Although we have taken every care to ensure the accuracy of our contents, mistakes do happen. If you find a mistake in one of our books—maybe a mistake in text or code—we would be grateful if you would report this to us. By doing this you can save other readers from frustration, and help to improve subsequent versions of this book. If you find any errata, report them by visiting http://www.packtpub.com/support, selecting your book, clicking on the **let us know** link, and entering the details of your errata. Once your errata are verified, your submission will be accepted and the errata added to the list of existing errata. The existing errata can be viewed by selecting your title from http://www.packtpub.com/support. And also take a look at the author supported site www.socialnetworkingin.net for follow up discussions and help regarding this book.

Piracy

Piracy of copyright material on the Internet is an ongoing problem across all media. At Packt, we take the protection of our copyright and licenses very seriously. If you come across any illegal copies of our works in any form on the Internet, please provide the location address or website name immediately so we can pursue a remedy.

Please contact us at copyright@packtpub.com with a link to the suspected pirated material.

We appreciate your help in protecting our authors, and our ability to bring you valuable content.

Questions

You can contact us at questions@packtpub.com if you are having a problem with some aspect of the book, and we will do our best to address it.

1
Social Networking

This book, as you might have guessed, is all about how to build a social networking site or a community site. In this book, we will take a look at a few well-known social networks and some not-so-well-known networks to get an idea of what features are popular out there. Then we will discuss the community that we will be building in this book. Once we have an idea of what others are doing and what our community will look like, we will dive right in to start building our own demo community.

What makes this topic so important

Social networking is all about developing connections or ties between friends and associates. While people have always networked with one another, the Internet has allowed us to do this in a global manner. Some great examples of popular social networks are Digg, LinkedIn, Facebook, and Twitter. Most people have heard of these services and many use them on a daily basis. These communities are able to generate income from advertising and additional paid services.

Large communities

`Digg.com` is an aggregator of information from other sites. They allow people to post links to interesting videos, blogs, news feeds, and other forms of media and content. This posting is then pushed to the top of their site based on how many others on the site also enjoy that post. Eventually, the posting will fall below the fold and fade into oblivion. The key with their site is that you are not actually viewing the body of the content on their site. This service is essentially a dynamic link *farm times ten*.

`LinkedIn.com` has taken the concept of a social network and polished it with a professional touch. With this service you can build a professional profile, connect with recruiters, connect with other professionals in your area, and most importantly, connect with everyone with whom they are connected. LinkedIn has really latched onto the power of the extended network concept.

`Facebook.com` originally started at Harvard University. This site was essentially a digital version of the book that the school gave to its incoming students so that everyone could get to know one another. This site is very much about building profiles and linking those profiles through an eavesdropping feature that Facebook calls "the wall". This feature essentially catches all the activity that your friends are performing on the site. The wall is another form of aggregation. Facebook is also well-known for its extensibility features in that it allows developers to create and host applications directly in the Facebook environment.

`Twitter.com` is what most would call a microblog. This site allows you to post very small blurbs to your blog which are then fed out to your subscribers (friends). This service is largely used for letting people know what you are up to. A great use of this feature is posting: "I am at such and such coffee shop. If anyone is nearby feel free to stop by and have a cup with me."

Niche communities

Communities listed in the previous section were some examples of large, very accomplished sites. There are far more examples of successful community sites that operate on a much smaller scale. Some of these include `Rockero.com`, `AnimeDates.com`, and `Ning.com`. While not as large or as well-known, these are very active communities that are able to generate a living by means of advertisements on their community.

`Rocker.com` (created by Jose Nava) is a community that is all about the Latino rock-and-roll scene. This site hosts news, articles, forums, and videos that are all about rock and roll! It has a fairly large following and is an excellent example of a niche site.

Your On-Line Source for Rock en Espanol!

search: [ ] GO

rockero
.com

login:

Forget Your Password?

Username : asiemer
Password : ••••••••

LOGIN

SIGN UP NOW!
It's fast, easy, and FREE!

register

HOME   ARTISTS   NEWS   MEMBERS   FORUMS   VIDEOS   CALENDAR

New Album From Jaguares

Jaguares, one of Mexico's legendary bands presents their newest material '45'. It's the bands first production after three years, time in which the band has also been successfully touring throughout Mexico, the United States, Central and South America. *More >>*

FEATURED ROCKEROS

koolrebel510   GreatWaffleVII   OldDominion

news:

: Juanes, Babasónicos y Belanova lideran nominacione... - 9/9/2008

: New Album From Jaguares - 9/9/2008

: The Ladies Of Latin Alternative Music - 7/19/2008

: Her Mood Swing Pays Off - 5/30/2008

: Babasonicos Mucho A La Venta - 5/27/2008

: Mexico's Cafe Tacuba plays Coachella music fest fo... - 4/28/2008

: Babasonicos Goes Mobile - 4/14/2008

: Babasonicos Estrena Hoy Su Nuevo Sencillo "Pijamas... - 4/8/2008

Featured Indie Artists

Animal3D

List more news

Submit news

calendar

Jaguares
Rainbow Ballroom
Fresno, California 93721
9/18/2008
8pm-1am

: The Mars Volta (9/18/2008)

forums

Rock en Español del 2000
porque la gente ya no cree en las nuevas bandas de rock en español? mi amigo me dice que ya no hay buen rock en español, que el bueno... read

more >>

members

bichiluz
Age : 22
Gender : F
Mexico

Rock En Espanol • **Latin Rock Bands** • **Latin Alternative News** • **Rockeros** • **Latino Forums** • **Spanish Rock Videos** • **Spanish Rock Concerts**

Friends : **Latin Music**   **Musica Mexicana**

Top Spanish Rock Artist / Bands

Cafe Tacuba	Zoe	Mago de Oz
Mana	Babasonicos	Andres Calamaro
Enanitos Verdes	Gustavo Cerati	Moenia
Jaguares	Rata Blanca	Julieta Venegas
Heroes Del Silencio	El Tri	Alejandra Guzman
Caifanes	Panda	Ataque 77
Belanova	La Ley	Fito Paez
Soda Stereo	Molotov	Bersuit
Juanes	Shakira	Ely Guerra
Enrique Bunbury	Los Fabulosos Cadillacs	Charly Garcia

Terms of Use • **Privacy Policy** • **Contact Us** • **Link To Us** • **Links** • **Chat** • **Latin Rock**

AnimeDates.com (created by Adam and Adrianne Wolkov) is a community that brings anime (Japanese cartoons) lovers together. This site puts a twist on the concept of dating in that it tries to bring anime followers together in an intimate way. They have actually had several from their community find the love of their life and get married as a result!

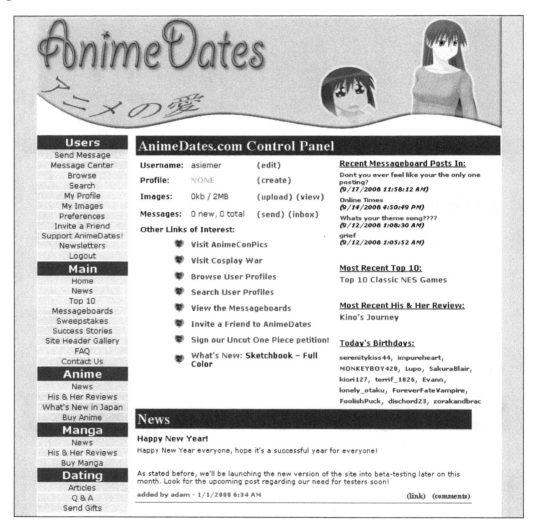

 During the writing of this book, AnimeDates.com was acquired by Mania. com. Congratulations Adam and Adrianne!

`Ning.com` is a community that allows you to build your own community in less than five minutes. This community by itself is large in that its users can create sub-communities that may also be large. But the point of this site is all about creating niche networks. An example of this is `http://userinterfacedesign.ning.com/`. This community allows its users to discuss the topic of user interface design.

Once I have my own social network, then what?

Everyone of my customers is gung ho about having his/her own social network. The customers think they have a better idea and can do a better job than the next guy. What they rarely consider though is that an even moderately successful community site is a lot of work. Some of the unknown requirements for any social network are listed here.

Customer service

In order to keep your site successful you must pay attention to your community. You need to keep your users happy by addressing their needs and by continuously making your site better. A social network is no different from any other business from your customers' perspective. They expect service of some kind or another. The better the service, the more your users will turn to you instead of the next guy.

If you have 5,000 users, you will have a fairly steady flow of communication between them and you. A user might report a broken feature on your site. They may want to shoot the breeze with you. They may need to report another user. They may want to suggest a feature. You need to stay responsive to your users.

It is said that a happy customer will tell a few of his/her friends about the good experience he/she had with your company. An unhappy customer, on the other hand, will tell everyone they know about the bad experience they had with your company. Keep this in mind! The more the users, the more this becomes important.

Content moderation

If you have a lot of users, you (or someone else) will have to manage their activities. They will be adding content to your site on a regular basis. You will need to protect your users from inappropriate content. This means keeping an eye on all of the content in your site. Also as your users will be able to interact with one another through your site, you will need to ensure that there are features that at the very least allow users to protect themselves from other users. If you don't have this sort of feature then you will need a way for your users to report other users to you so that you can deal with it.

If you don't do this, you could end up with at least two problems. You might have a user uploading adult content. This content might offend some of your users. These users could easily take you to court and create havoc for you (even if your terms clearly say that you are not responsible...blah blah blah). The other possible problem is that if a user is offended, he/she may not come back to your site. This may not sound bad, but a social network is all about its users after all!

Growing infrastructure requirements

With any successful site—and not just social networks—it is very important that you keep your infrastructure two steps ahead of your users' needs. If your site is all about video feeds, then you will be required to keep a watchful eye on your bandwidth capabilities and disk space. If either of these starts to fail, the user experience of your site will start to diminish or cease altogether.

If your site has a large number of users regardless of your topic, you will need to watch your web server's usage. You may be required to have your site hosted on many servers. Or you may need to upgrade the overall robustness of your servers to support the heavier demand.

If you are not capable of infrastructure management, it is certainly well worth your will to find someone who can take care of this for you. If you only need part-time care, you might turn to someone like `www.geeksontime.com`. They provide on and offsite care for infrastructure administration. And don't forget to backup all your data. If this is also not your thing, turn to an automated service such as `www.carbonite.com`.

Our social network—Fisharoo

In this book, we will discuss many of the common features that are required for a social network or community to succeed. We will discuss these features as they pertain to a community that I have long wanted to put up about salt water aquariums, their care, and about the people who are so invested in this hobby.

Unlike many books, we will not just discuss core concepts with demos in the form of snippets. We will build an entire working site from the ground up. And we will build our site in such a way that if by chance you become the founder of the next MySpace, you have a site that will form a great foundation for your community. With that in mind, this book will follow a common problem, design, and solution approach to building the site.

When I tell the story of how and why I want to build a community around the salt water aquarium world, I usually start by saying that salt water enthusiasts are very much like golfers. It is not a hobby where you buy a set of clubs and a few golf balls and then never return to buy anything else. You don't just take your new gear out to the course and proclaim yourself as being a golfer. Generally speaking, people buy a set of clubs, a funny hat and pants, some shoes, some balls, a glove or two. And work at golf a bit. Then they return to the local pro shop to find a better club, a funnier looking hat, perhaps different shoes, better balls, and so on. This repeats until they get to a point where they feel comfortable in their game and can call themselves golfers. Once they have reached this point, they still go to the pro shop forever in search of game improvements.

The salt water enthusiast is very much like a golfer. They buy their first salt water tank as a package with what they think is everything they need to set up a tank. They go home and set up their tank only to find out that the filter they bought was not big enough for their tank. Their lighting is not appropriate for their coral. Their filtration system is not appropriate for their fish. The live rock that they purchased contained a crab, which then started to eat all of their fish. And once the salt water tank is set up in a fashion that it is fairly self-sustaining (they are now a golfer so to speak) the owner wants to add new fish, maybe more fishes, have a bigger tank, and so on.

This social network will focus on helping new and old owners of salt water aquariums set up and take care of their salt water tanks. It will also help them to choose the right fish combinations. And, as it is a community, it will give them a place to go to give advice as well as receive it.

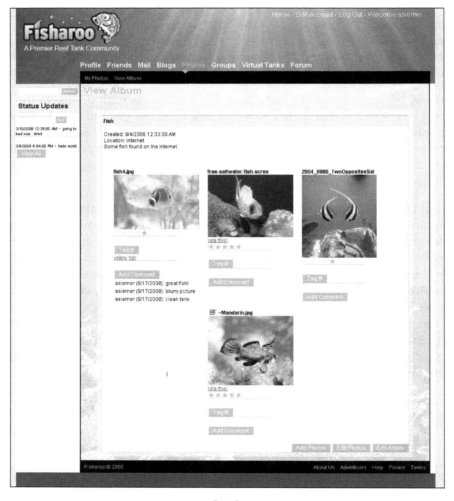

This book's approach

In each chapter I will attempt to follow a pattern to build a feature or set of features. We will start with the problem that the chapter addresses. We will then attempt to figure out a design that addresses the feature that we need to build. Finally, we will discuss what is needed to meet the design requirements.

Problem

In the problem section we will outline exactly what we need to do to achieve success for the chapter's topic. I will show you some screenshots of the finished product. And I will cover any major gotchas for building out the features.

Design

This section of each chapter is about defining what exactly we want from a feature or features. Here we will decide on and write down the physical requirements so that in the next section we can start to build out the feature set. Here we will start to look at what the database might look like, whether or not we need to make a page or two, or if a user control might work better, and if an open source tool might help us address our needs.

Solution

In the solution section of our chapters we will discuss how to implement all the requirements for each feature. This section will go deep into the actual code for implementing the feature from the database, out to the user interface. At the end of this section, you should have something that you can play with.

Features of our social network

Following are the desirable features that our social networking site will possess:

Accounts

I think that this section of the book is pretty much given on any data-driven site where you have users who are contributing to the site. If you need to know who your users are, then you need some way of tracking their accounts. Instead of showing you accounts from the pure ASP.NET way, this section will show you how to build your own accounting system from scratch.

This will include looking at the registration process where our users create their initial accounts. To make sure that we block bots and other programs from creating accounts in an automated manner, we will implement a CAPTCHA system and discuss some other options that are out there for this. We will implement an email verification system to make sure that our users actually are what they claim to be. With all this in place we will also discuss setting up a permissions system that we can build onto over time. And no chapter on account creation is complete until we discuss password encryptions (an often missed topic).

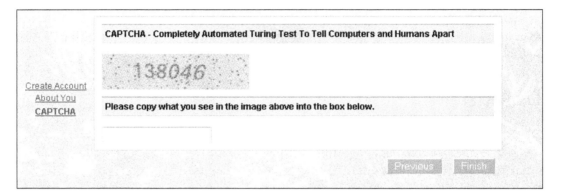

Profiles

A user's profile is really just an extension of his/her account. The difference being that the account holds the login information and the profile holds all the personal identifiers. It holds the description of the user, the user's attributes, and their photo (avatar). We will discuss creating a user's profile in a way that is flexible enough for all systems to use. We will also discuss how to handle creating an avatar in such a way that a user can upload a picture, and select from that picture only the part that they want to include in their avatar. As the profile contains a great deal of information about the user, we will also implement some forms of privacy to allow them to hide some bits and show others. Finally, we will discuss the creation of a personal page for our user that will allow them to have a vanity URL (www.site.com/AndrewSiemer) to send to their friends.

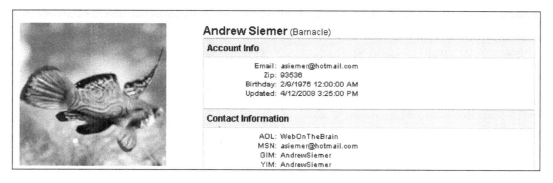

Friends

The concept of having friends in a community is the glue that keeps people coming back to your site. A friend is a user whom you have stated, whom you trust and allow seeing information about you, and about whom you are generally interested in knowing. Think of a friend as a connection, a colleague, and so on. Different terms describe the same concept for different community topics.

In this section, we will not only show you how to implement friends, but will also discuss how to search for them, find them in the site's listings, and import your contacts into the site to find your friends. We will also implement a microblog in the form of allowing your users to provide a status about where they are and what they are currently doing. This status will then show up on your microblog and your friend's microblog as an alert.

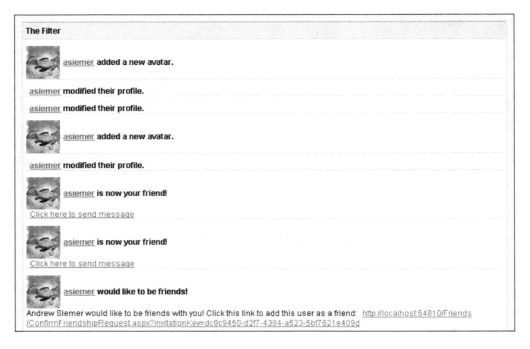

Messaging

Messaging is essential to any community site as it allows users to communicate with one another directly. This can come in many forms. You can send a message to a user, which is sent directly to the user via email. Or you can allow your user to send a message via the site, which is then stored in the recipient's inbox. A notification is then sent out to the recipient. This last form will be easier for you to manage as a site administrator.

In this section we will create a full blown messaging system that will resemble a web-based email application similar to Hotmail or Gmail. As part of our interface we will show a list of existing friends to send messages to. And we will learn how to implement the Xinha WYSIWYG editor in a way that can be re-used easily across the site for complex input.

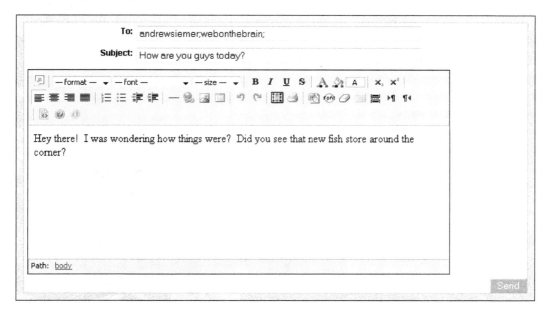

Media galleries

There are many communities that are very dependent upon media galleries. Some samples of this are YouTube or something similar. This is frequently the feature that can draw the largest percentage of your community back to your site. For that reason, it is very important to understand how to build a media system rather than an image gallery, video gallery, and so on. We will build a generic media management system that will allow you to host video, photos, resumes, or any number of physical files with a limited additional tweaking.

In addition to the media management system, we will take a look at addressing one of the biggest limitations of many web programming environments—multifile upload. ASP.NET is great at handling one file at a time. But when managing a photo gallery, for instance, you will find that you frequently have a handful or hundreds of photos to upload. Rather than create a Java-based or Active-X-based control, which may require some additional installations to your users' systems, we will look at a Flash-based implementation. The Flash player has a pretty large adoption rate, so our tool should load up with little or no problem. With this we will be able to browse to a directory and upload as many files as we want.

Blogging

Blogging is often a major feature in any community site as it gives those who enjoy speaking to the world a tool to do just that. On the other hand though, the output of your blog generates free content for those who are more on the voyeuristic side to read up and follow along with your blogs. One of the biggest benefits for a community with active bloggers is that you are acquiring a large amount of free content to feed the various search engine spiders with. This in turn will help you get your search ranking up, which will drive more traffic to your site, and will in turn grow your community.

With search engines, users, and security in mind, we will invest time to address an issue that plagues many dynamic websites—query string data being used to determine page output. Let's face it, from a user's point of view, seeing a bunch of variable names in the query string with random auto-generated record IDs and 32 character GUIDs is just not that user friendly and at times downright confusing. Add to this that search engines these days seem to be able to navigate some of this query string mumbo jumbo. But we are losing a key opportunity to optimize our site for keywords by spoofing URLs as though our keywords were directories. We will continue from our profile's example and extend our vanity URL support so that we can have something along the lines of `www.sitename.com/blogs/andrewsiemer/ 3may2008/my-article-name.aspx` (something of this nature).

Great Fish Article

Created: 9/18/2008 2:51:00 AM Updated: 9/18/2008 2:51:00 AM

Lorem ipsum dolor sit amet, consectetuer adipiscing elit. Pellentesque vel magna eget libero ullamcorper dapibus. Etiam a quam. Phasellus orci. Proin odio arcu, semper vitae, elementum sed, vehicula ultrices, mi. Praesent aliquet erat vel elit. Nunc placerat orci eget elit. Nunc imperdiet aliquam dolor. Quisque ligula. Praesent fringilla enim et orci. Mauris venenatis, ligula malesuada molestie fringilla, arcu mauris porta velit, a pellentesque elit tellus id mauris. Praesent ipsum. Fusce eget leo.

Ut quis lectus. Aliquam erat volutpat. Donec lorem. Praesent eleifend, lectus et interdum laoreet, augue odio auctor elit, vel ultricies ligula est et quam. Quisque bibendum, justo vitae elementum volutpat, ipsum dui ultricies lorem, sit amet dapibus purus erat nec velit. Ut dui. Aliquam vel nisi. Integer vehicula. Curabitur tellus leo, vehicula vitae, fermentum ut, venenatis fringilla, urna. Mauris in mi.

Duis metus felis, dapibus in, consequat eget, ultrices ut, orci. Pellentesque cursus interdum purus. Nullam dignissim nibh quis libero. Ut porttitor lacus ut nunc. Phasellus lectus. Cum sociis natoque penatibus et magnis dis parturient montes, nascetur ridiculus mus. Proin at mi eget justo viverra porta. Aliquam dapibus mi volutpat elit. Sed commodo porttitor sem. Nam facilisis molestie magna. Nunc ultrices, dui at congue interdum, velit nisi pharetra orci, in vehicula metus ante at risus. Morbi aliquam sem eget elit volutpat pulvinar. Suspendisse dignissim consectetuer nibh. Sed eget mauris. Nunc id sem vehicula mauris facilisis suscipit. Cras sollicitudin, massa vitae ullamcorper porta, purus felis dictum arcu, ac lobortis turpis pede et mauris. Praesent suscipit est.

Message boards

Everyone is well aware of what a message board or a forum is. For a social network, it is a disconnected form of communication where people can post something to discuss and others can happen across the posted item over time to add their two cents. Frequently in the developer world, you will have a community that is 100% focused around this sort of feature in the form of a technical help forum. For our site which centers on helping others figure out how to run a salt water aquarium, we will find this feature useful.

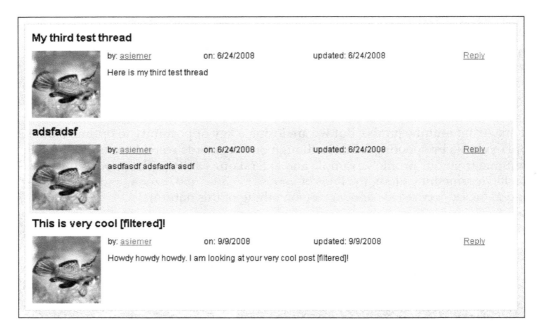

Groups

Groups to me are a form of containers for like-minded individuals. It allows a community to pool its resources. A group could comprise people who are interested in the same topic, people for or against a certain presidential candidate, or people representing a company. The common focus for a group is that when someone who is part of the group posts content to the site, all the members of that group are notified. If a user sends a message to a group, then all the members become recipients of that message.

In our site, we will support common concepts such as public and private groups. For private groups you will have to request a membership and should be granted access prior to getting into the group. We will also extend the group concept and provide all our groups with a private forum.

Comments

Commenting is just another way of allowing your users to interact with the content and other members of your social network. There isn't a lot that is special about the commenting concept. We will build out a custom user control to handle commenting any physical object in our system that has a supporting table behind it. This means that we can have comments on anything such as photos, videos, profiles, forum postings, blogs, and so on. To sum up, anything can have a comment!

Tags

Tags are very important to the navigation of your community. A **tag** is usually one or two keywords attached to some content or item in your site. This keyword may be attached to one or many items in the site by one or many users of the site. The more frequently the tag is applied, the larger its subscription base becomes. We can then show the tag in a cloud of other tags. This cloud would be sorted with the most frequently used keywords. Again, the more the keywords used, the larger they get displayed in the cloud.

We can then place a tag cloud in various places of our site such as the homepage, on a user's profile, or on a group's homepage. This will then act as a jumping off point for all of their most frequently tagged content. Usually, this promotes clicking around on the site. The more people move around on the site, the more likely they are to add tags of their own or some other form of content. This will give some activity to your community. We will build our tagging and tag cloud feature as another user control that can be attached to any object with a handful of different display types.

Ratings

Ratings are often a very important part of any community-supplied content site. This allows the whole community to be in charge of what content takes precedence on the site. While the ASP.NET AJAX Toolkit provides us with a rating tool, we will look at creating a custom rating tool. Our rating tool will not only use the AJAX rating tool but will also extend so that rather than apply a rating directly to an item, we can rate individual attributes of an item. All those ratings will then be rolled up, and that score will be the rating that is displayed for the actual item.

This feature will have the ability to be attached to any item in the site as well. Once built, this feature will really help us get the right content for our community. It also provides our users with the sense of belonging as they are now able to provide their opinion on just about anything.

Framework

Anyone can build a mom and pop community site with the features that we discussed. However, if you want to build a site that can grow with your community, we will want to start building it in a certain way from the beginning. For that reason we will follow a few design patterns and concepts upfront. We will use an n-tiered approach to build our site using Domain-driven Design, Test Driven Design, Model View Presenter, Factory Pattern, and Repository Pattern. We will also make use of the new LINQ to SQL tools that Microsoft has recently provided for us as well as a few great open source tool sets such as Lucene.NET, MemCached, StructureMap, and NUnit to name a few.

```
LuceneSearchService.cs  LuceneDiskCache.cs  Cryptography.cs  Log.cs  ContentFilterService.cs  MailMessageService.cs  FileRepository.cs

Fisharoo.FisharooCore.Core.Impl.LuceneDiskCache                                    LuceneDiskCache()

13  namespace Fisharoo.FisharooCore.Core.Impl
14  {
15      [Pluggable("Lucene")]
16      public class LuceneDiskCache
17      {
18          private const string INDEX_FIELD_NAME = "index";
19          private const string VALUE_FIELD_NAME = "object";
20          private Analyzer _analyzer;
21          private Directory _directory;
22          private string _cachePath;
23          private object _locker = new object();
24
25          public LuceneDiskCache()
26          {
27              _analyzer = new StandardAnalyzer();
28              _cachePath = Path.Combine(AppDomain.CurrentDomain.BaseDirectory, "cache");
29          }
30
31          public void Set<T>(string key, T value)
32          {
33              if(value == null)
34              {
35                  return;
36              }
37
38              lock (_locker)
39              {
40                  removeObjectIfExists<T>(key);
41
```

Scaling up

Once we have our core community built out, we will begin discussing some concepts to help you support a large number of users on your social network. We will start our discussion by looking at some key concepts to web farming. We will then discuss how to create and search indexed data with Lucene.NET. Next, we will cover how to optimize your data retrieval and content creation by implementing a caching farm inside your web farm using the new MemCached Win32 server. Then we can look at optimizing our email communications by implementing some form of mail queuing concepts.

```
39   public void ProcessEmails()
40   {
41       //make sure we are only processing this in one thread!
42       //otherwise we might lose emails
43       lock (this)
44       {
45           try
46           {
47               List<pr_MailQueue_SwapReceivingAndWorking_GetWorkingResult> results =
48                   new List<pr_MailQueue_SwapReceivingAndWorking_GetWorkingResult>();
49               using (FisharooDataContext dc = _conn.GetContext())
50               {
51                   results = dc.pr_MailQueue_SwapReceivingAndWorking_GetWorking().ToList();
52               }
53
54               foreach (var result in results)
55               {
56                   MailMessage mm = XMLService.Deserialize<MailMessage>(result.SerializedMailMessage);
57                   SmtpClient smtp = new SmtpClient();
58                   smtp.Send(mm);
59               }
60
61               using (FisharooDataContext dc = _conn.GetContext())
62               {
63                   dc.pr_MailQueue_MoveWorkingToHistory();
64               }
65           }
66           catch(Exception e)
67           {
68               Log.Fatal(this, e.Message);
69               return;
70           }
71       }
72   }
```

Summary

We have taken a look at some of the features that constitute a social networking site. We also looked at some examples of successful community sites and what their niche is. Next, we discussed the community that we will build and why we want to do it. Finally, we discussed what features we will build through the course of this book.

2
An Enterprise Approach to our Community Framework

We have all worked on a project that was supposed to be thrown together just to meet a current need. There wasn't ever supposed to be a need in the future for this application. It was meant to be just a simple down and dirty fix until you could get the next major version in place. Then you found yourself constantly adding features to this application. It continued to grow and grow uncontrollably. Had you known that this application was going to be so important and was going to be used so extensively, you would probably have built it differently. It is most likely that you would have designed your application with extensibility in mind rather than just hurrying to get the project finished and out the door!

A layered architecture versus a non-layered architecture

Not every application needs to be built in a heavily layered manner. Not every application needs to be overly extensible. Some applications need to be built quickly and simply for the sole purpose of getting them out the door. However, be careful not to build something simple when something flexible should have been built in its place. While you can easily grow an application that was built with growth in mind, extending an application that was built without growth in mind can be difficult, if not near impossible.

Knowing that our application is going to be a large undertaking that should last for some time, we need to design something that can be easily extended as the need arises. For that we will try to design this application with extensibility in mind. The easiest way to do that is to follow the general rule of maintaining "separation of concerns".

> **Separation of concerns** (**SoC**) is the process of breaking down your application into specific units of functionality in such a way that each unit only addresses the need of one concern with as little overlap as possible with other units in terms of functionality. Look here for more information regarding this topic: http://en.wikipedia.org/wiki/Separation_of_concerns

Layers

The easiest way to maintain SoC is to first break major areas of your application into layers. In most applications, this might be broken down into the presentation, business logic, and data access layers.

- Presentation: This layer would normally hold anything pertaining to the user interface of your application—the buttons, links, and other controls that a user would click on and interact with while using your application.

- Business Logic: This is where the rules of your application would live. This could be as simple as formatting the currency of a price in your product catalog to something more complex such as enforcing rules regarding data input.

- Data Access: The data access layer is responsible for connecting to a data source and interacting with the data that is stored in that location. This could be a database, some XML files, text files, or even a web service.

> There is a common argument amongst enterprise developers regarding the use of layers. It says something along the lines of "the more the objects in use, the more the resources in use". This is of course a true statement. However, the use of more resources in this case does come with a benefit in the form of greater flexibility in your application. Layers promote SoC as well, which directly benefits the developer as the physical code is easier to understand and work with.

I used to think that just these three layers were good enough and used them in several applications. However, I always found myself wanting more control in my application. Recently I worked on a project that expanded on these very common layers (into more layers of course) with the use of Domain-driven Design.

Domain-driven Design

Domain-driven Design (DDD) is not a methodology, framework, or technology, but more of a way of thinking practically. It is geared towards making software development move at a faster pace. It puts the focus on the domain and domain logic as it is truly the center of any application. Having a robust application and infrastructure wrapped around poorly designed domain logic is a problem waiting to happen.

The topic of Domain-driven Design is a vast one. To get you started in understanding the high-level concepts, I will outline the basics here. As we continue to build our framework and application, you will find some of the following principles applied.

 For more information about Domain-driven Design check out this website: http://www.domaindrivendesign.org.

Ubiquitous language

The concept of **ubiquitous language** is a simple one. It basically states that all individuals involved with a software development project—business owners, project managers, developers, that is, just about everyone—use the same language to describe the aspects of the software being developed. This reduces the confusion, which in turn increases the speed of overall development.

This concept is not just for discussion purposes. It extends to the actual naming of classes, methods, and more. Once this occurs all discussions will sound similar no matter who is involved with the discussion. When this is followed, and everyone is speaking the same language in all conversations, confusion is totally removed and there are no longer islands of expertise.

In the end, the domain and domain logic become more refined. The application is better for it!

Entities

An **entity** is an object in your application that maintains its state for the life of your application. This means that it can be rehydrated from an XML file, saved to a database, later loaded from that database instance, serialized, and sent across the network— resulting in the same object in all the cases. This is performed with the use of a unique ID. This could be anything from an auto-incrementing numeric ID, a GUID, a **Social Security number** (**SSN**), including anything that would be unique in your system.

An example would be a person in the US. In this case, we could use a person's SSN and each resulting person would be unique. When we look at all the people in the world, the SSN would no longer be considered a good form of unique ID as not all people in the world have one. So in this case, we would probably have to start looking at multiple properties of a person to define their uniqueness. We could take their birth date, last name, country/state, city, and so on. A combination of this information should result in a unique entity in your system. Entities are the most important objects of your domain.

Do all objects in an application need to be unique? Are all objects necessarily entities? Well, the answer is 'No'. In the next section, we will look at value objects as the answer to these questions.

Value objects

A **value object** is less important than an entity. It does not require an identity, and hence it can be easily created without being concerned to determine its uniqueness. We are more interested in what the item is rather than who it is. A value object should be immutable. If you need to modify the value object, toss it, and create a new one. But if you find that the object is not immutable, or can't exist without its own identity, it is most likely to be an Entity object.

To extend our person example from the Entities section further, we could make an "address" value object rather than have a person with properties of state, city, zip code, street or any other information pertaining to the address. The value object would then store information about state, city, zip code, street, and so on. This address object could then be part of a person. So you could say `person.Address. City`. Technically, this address could be shared for all the people in the same house. We don't care so much for the address itself, but for the fact that it is attached to a specific person.

Why do we need value objects? Value objects are important. They are not only a way of grouping bits of information as you saw in the above example. Being "lightweight" objects, they reduce the amount of resources used in an application. They also simplify an application in that value objects don't require uniqueness.

Services

As we discuss our application using the Ubiquitous Language (discussed previously in a separate section), we will quickly end up with a vocabulary of nouns (entities and value objects) and verbs (methods of those objects). However, not all the verbs that we end up with will easily fit into our defined entities and value objects. What do we do with these equally important but homeless verbs? They are obviously needed by the application. Do we stick them into one of our existing objects for lack of a better place to put them? Doing that would create clutter and confuse the objects making them difficult to use. So, the answer to the previous questions is 'No'. We would rather create a service.

A **service** is not an entity or a value object. Having said that, we have to create an object of some kind or another considering the fact that we are using an OOP-based language! So we create a service-based object that provides the needed action (verb) for our application. Take an e-commerce application for example. We might have a customer and a vendor wherein one of them needs to contact the other via email. Would it be appropriate to add a method to the customer object to send them email from the vendor to the customer? Would it be appropriate to add this method to the vendor object? It doesn't quite seem right in either object. So we could create an email service. Now when our customer needs to contact the vendor, or the vendor needs to contact the customer, either one can use the service to take care of the communication.

Modules

Even if you have never heard of or worked with Domain-driven Design, you will easily understand what a module is. A **module** is a group of features and functionality in your application. Modules are a way of organizing large and complex domain logic into smaller and more understandable units.

In this application, we will have accounts, blogs, picture galleries, and many other features. While we could easily create one vast library of code to cover all these features, it would be easier for us to create smaller units of code that specifically describe the features of each module separately. Obviously, we will have some overlap among modules as an account is used in both galleries and blogs. It would also be possible for blogs to reference an image in an image gallery. As you can see, not only do modules make your code easier to understand, they also help keep things decoupled as you have further refined your code into yet another container!

Aggregates

Up to this point we have discussed the idea that we must use a ubiquitous language to define our application's vocabulary. From that definition we will draw out entities and value objects. Where methods don't fit our entities or value objects, we can create services. And all these items can be grouped into modules. Now we are going to move on to how these items can be managed, created, and stored using aggregation, factories, and repositories.

With a complex application, we will have lots of objects to deal with. So far we have tried to reduce complexity by keeping things easy to understand by way of a well-defined vocabulary and by grouping that vocabulary into smaller containers. Also, we have tried to reduce complexity by stating that some objects need to be able to maintain the state across the application, while others do not.

What we have not yet discussed is how to maintain an object's life cycle. We know that they will be created, stored, passed around, and so on. But what about when it is time to completely erase one of these objects from the system? If we do not closely manage the usage of our objects, we could end up with objects randomly floating about our system for no reason at all. This in turn could create issues for us in the form of memory leaks resulting in a system crash.

For this reason, it is important that we plan for simplicity in how our objects interact with one another. Rather than have objects spin one another up haphazardly, it would be nice to have gatekeepers that we have to go through to gain access to other objects. For example, the only way for object Z to gain access to object B is through object A. This way when object Z is done using object A and object B, we can simply remove object A, and object B will go too.

An **aggregation** is a boundary that we can use with our objects. We discussed that our `person` object was an entity object, and that the address information was a value object. Let's extend this example to say that we would also have an object that handles the person's contact information, which could be phone numbers, email addresses, and so on. This too would be a value object. Rather than letting external objects directly access the address and contact information, we could force them to go through the entity object to read this data. Also, if an external object wanted to add a phone number to the list of phone numbers for a person, we could enforce that the only way to do this is through the `person` object rather than through the contact information object.

Following through with this concept further simplifies our domain logic in the form of breaking our class structure down into even smaller buckets of code. It is not only easier to work from a development point of view, but also simpler to manage how objects come and go in our application.

Factories

With all the simplicity that we are striving to achieve in our design, how can we limit the complexity that is involved in the creation of an object? It doesn't make sense to store that logic in the object that we are trying to create. It is one thing to put some simple logic in the constructor of an object and let the object make itself, but quite another when that object is an entity and itself has several value objects as part of its make up (an aggregate). In this case, we would want to stash the creation logic into something called a factory.

As we strive to keep the objects focused on their single concern it makes sense to have a person factory that would create a person, the person's address information, and contact information rather than have the `person` object know how to do these tasks, as well as how to be a person. To grasp the concept better, take the example of buying a TV. If you wanted a new TV, you would go to the local electronics store and purchase one. You wouldn't expect the vendor to give you a screen, a box, some electronics, a few cables, some plastic, a handful of buttons, and the directions to assemble your TV. You would walk down an aisle, pick a TV, purchase a box with a working TV in it, and go home. We should keep our objects working in the same order. Think of a factory as the electronics store, and your objects as the assembled TV. Your object should do what it does best, act like a person, and not worry about how to read genetic code and assemble cells.

Repositories

Now as we have understood that a factory's sole purpose is the creation of objects, what about the hydration of an already existing object? Perhaps we have a list of people stored in a data store. Should a factory be responsible for retrieving these people? In DDD, it is stated that this is the role of the Repository.

A **Repository** is an object whose purpose is specific to a single Entity object. For our purposes, we will have a `PersonRepository` object. This object would know how to get a person (or many people) based on certain well-defined parameters. It would also know how to persist `person` objects to a data store.

Note that I use 'data store', and not 'database'. A repository works closely with your application's infrastructure code. It should know how to work with all sorts of data stores that your application might know to work with. This could be a database, a web service, a collection of XML files, or any other data store. While your repository is intelligent enough to work with infrastructure code, the interfaces that it presents to other domain objects should be domain oriented and should be simple for the other domain objects to use.

Some examples can be passing in a social security number to hydrate a `person` object, or passing in a whole `person` object to be persisted to the appropriate data store. The clients of your repository should not be required to know anything about infrastructure code at all!

Model View Presenter pattern

I plan to follow a **Test-Driven Development** approach, that is, **TDD** (see Appendix B) while building this application. It is very easy to test our domain logic. It is not that easy to test the presentation layer of our web application if we stick with the simple `.aspx`/`.cs` approach that Microsoft gives us by default in Visual Studio. For that reason, we need to settle on a design that will allow us to test the presentation layer in as close to the same way as we would test any of our domain logic.

 At the time of writing this, Microsoft released its new **Model View Controller** (**MVC**) framework. While it is truly cutting edge, I couldn't introduce an unproven framework into this project at that time. Also, the way that the framework is set up would require more than simply learning about MVC for TDD purposes.

I have been using the **Model View Presenter** (**MVP**) pattern (also called Supervising Controller) to allow me to perform testing on my presentation layer for quite a while now. While I still find it a bit clunky, it is the best thing I have come across so far that allows me to perform my testing in an automated fashion. This pattern breaks down the presentation layer into three parts—model, view, and presentation. Each part has a specific responsibility.

Model

The **model** is a direct reference to your domain logic—the business logic layer so to speak. There is nothing more to be said! Think business layer!

View

The **view** is made up of the `.aspx` and `.cs` files of your webpage. These files are responsible for defining the physical items that a user interacts with in your website. They are also responsible for receiving the various events that a user raises while navigating through your site. The handled events should be immediately passed to the presenter rather than being handled in the view. It is the responsibility of the presenter to decide how to handle each event. The view is required to pass itself (by reference) to the presenter giving the presenter total control over the view.

This is where the topic of **Inversion of control** (**IoC**) comes up. We will discuss this more when we get into StructureMap. If you need more information about this topic now, look here: `http://en.wikipedia.org/wiki/Inversion_of_control`.

Presenter

The **presenter** is a separate class file. There should be one presenter file per webpage. The presenter is ultimately responsible for indirectly handling events fired by the view and directly controlling what the view displays. It is the only part of the presentation layer that can communicate with the domain objects (or the model).

Tests can be wrapped around the presenter object. While this is not a full test of the UI, it is a full test of the logic that the UI interacts with. This can get tedious sometimes. To make these tests go smoothly, plan on using a lot of mocked objects either with the NUnit framework, or with the RhinoMocks framework, or something similar.

 Look to Selenium (open source automation tool for executing scenarios against web applications) to provide full tests of your UI. It records physical interactions with your website and replays them in an automated fashion. I find this tool to be very useful for fairly static sites. If your site structure changes frequently, your tests will have to be updated frequently. At this point the value of this test suite may be lost! To find more about Selenium, go to `http://www.openqa.org/selenium-rc/`.

How it works

To quickly describe how this works from a programmatic point of view, let's think about loading a list of people. The view would contain something like a GridView or some other form of Repeater. On loading, the view would instantiate its presenter and pass a reference of itself to that presenter. This passes the control of the view to the presenter. The view then calls an `init` method in the presenter (which you define—call it what you like). The presenter is now responsible for initializing the page (loading the initial state of the page). The presenter works with our domain objects (the model) to get a list of people. The presenter then calls methods provided by the view and passes them to its newly acquired list of people. The view then attaches the list of people to the data source of a repeater and asks the repeater to bind on that list.

If someone were to click on a person in that list, the process would be repeated up through the view, into the presenter, over some domain objects, and back down to the view. This allows us to wrap our tests around the presenter, which is part of every interaction with the view and the model. As the presenter is removed from the page itself, it is easy to get to and interact with the outside web environment!

Read more about Test Driven Design in the *Appendix B* at the end of this book to understand its principles better.

Factory pattern using StructureMap

We discussed the factory pattern (under the Factories section) to help us in our efforts for loosely coupled objects of our application. We have also said that we plan to use a Test- Driven Development process. In order to achieve both of these easily, we will be using a framework called StructureMap. Get more information on `http://structuremap.sourceforge.net/Default.htm`. StructureMap is a dependency injection framework. Its primary goal is to help us to reduce the mechanical costs of good object-oriented design. It also helps us to have a more flexible application for testing purposes.

StructureMap is very easy to use. I have mostly covered how to get it set up in *Appendix A* at the end of the book. But if you don't want to read that now, I will give you a down and dirty here. Once you have downloaded the StructureMap files, add them to your `bin` directory. Then add a reference to the StructureMap in your projects. Add an XML file to your solution and share it amongst your projects calling it `StructureMap.config`. In that file, enter the following:

```
<?xml version="1.0" encoding="utf-8" ?>
<StructureMap>
  <Assembly Name="Fisharoo.FisharooWeb" />
  <Assembly Name="Fisharoo.FisharooCore" />
</StructureMap>
```

Now for every class that you create, add an attribute just above the class that looks something like this:

```
[Pluggable("Default")]
```

Once you have defined your class, you can define the interface that the class inherits from, open your interface, and add the following attribute.

```
[PluginFamily("Default")]
```

Once you have this in place, you can then write something along the following lines when instantiating a class:

```
IPerson person = ObjectFactory.GetInstance<IPerson>();
```

 Using interfaces like this is a good design regardless of other technologies such as StructureMap. It really helps to create a loosely coupled environment. Having said that, StructureMap relies heavily on the use of interfaces to define a PluginFamily. All members of the same PluginFamily are located through the process of reflection and grouped by the interfaces that they inherit from (example: `person` and `PersonStub` would both inherit `IPerson` and would therefore be part of the same PluginFamily). So in the interest of saving some space in this book, you can safely assume that for every class that has a pluggable attribute, you will need to create a simple interface that defines the default class. I will point out the interface usage, but will not discuss them in detail.

This instantiation says a lot. We no longer have a direct coupling between the `person` object and the client code using the `person` object. Instead, we have told StructureMap to go and load the default instance of a `person` object whatever that may be at the time we asked for it.

This decoupling is very nice. But once we have StructureMap woven into our application and we start writing our tests, we can now also tell StuctureMap which version of an object we would like to use at a specified time. For testing purposes, it is not always best to use our production objects. Perhaps the `person` object requires too many resources, or perhaps it relies on several other objects to perform its tasks. In that case, we may want to create a `PersonStub` class. This would be a lightweight class. It would of course conform to the `IPerson` interface in the same way that the production person does. The only major difference as far as StructureMap is concerned is that the attribute at the top of the class might look something like this:

```
[Pluggable("Stubbed")]
```

We have two ways to let StructureMap know that we want to use the `Stubbed` person rather than the `Default` person. We can programmatically specify it say while running tests. Or in case we have stubbed out a class for our development environment, to use something closely represents what we would have access to in production, we can specify what to use in the `StructureMap.config` file.

In the case of programmatic control, we can simply use the methods that are provided by the `ObjectFactory` class. We can use the `InjectStub` method to override the class to be used the next time it is called.

```
ObjectFactory.InjectStub(typeof (IPerson), new PersonStub());
```

The next time an `IPerson` is loaded by the `ObjectFactory` class, StructureMap will use the `PersonStub` class instead of the standard `Person` class.

That's great! But how do I revert StructureMap back to using the `Person` class once my testing is completed?

```
ObjectFactory.ResetDefaults();
```

This works well for testing purposes. But what about swapping something out in a more permanent way? In order to specify which class to use in the configuration file, you would enter something as shown in the following code snippet. Note that the `DefaultKey` has the `Stubbed` description.

```
<PluginFamily Assembly="Fisharoo.FisharooCore" Type="Fisharoo.
FisharooCore.Core.Impl.Person"
    DefaultKey="Stubbed" />
<!-- Default, Stubbed -->
```

Note that at the bottom, I have added a comment that defines the possible classes that can be specified.

The default key name doesn't have to be the word "Default", something that you are entirely in control of. You could use a different default tag for each class. We could have just as easily used `PersonDefault` or just `Person`. It is all in how you set it up. The interface's `PluginFamily` attribute defines the default key.

Repository pattern and LINQ

Earlier we had a high-level discussion on repositories. Now we are ready to dig in a little deeper. We know that repositories are all about providing a way for our domain logic to access resources in the outside world. We know that they can be used for web services, XML files, and just about anything else. In our case, we will discuss how to access data in a database using the new LINQ to SQL framework.

We haven't really touched upon anything related to the Fisharoo application so far, which means that we don't really have anything in the database for us to play with just yet. For that reason, I created a simple `Person` table for us to work with. It has the following fields: `PersonID`, `FirstName`, `LastName`, and `Email`. I then created four entries in the database for us to work with.

```
CREATE TABLE [dbo].[Person](
    [PersonID] [int] IDENTITY(1,1) NOT NULL,
    [FirstName] [varchar](30) NULL,
    [LastName] [varchar](30) NULL,
    [Email] [varchar](150) NULL
) ON [PRIMARY]
```

Next, I opened the `web.config` file and added a database connection to the `connectionStrings` section.

```
<connectionStrings>
   <add name="Fisharoo" connectionString="Server=localhost\\
sqlexpress;Initial Catalog=Fisharoo;User=USERNAME;Password=PASSWORD"
providerName="System.Data.SqlClient" />
   </connectionStrings>
```

I then created a data connection in Visual Studio. This is done by opening the **Server Explorer** window (**View | Server Explorer**) and right-clicking on the **Data Connections** node, and then selecting **Add Connection**.

In the **Add Connection** window, type in your server name and configure your login credentials (I used SQL Server Authentication).

Once you have all your information entered as you think it should be, click the **Test Connection** button to check the connections status.

Once your connection reports that it was successful, click **OK** to continue. Click **OK** again.

Now expand your new data connection until you see the tables. If you have created a `Person` table as I had described earlier, you should be able to see it under the Tables node.

Once you have your `Person` table situated, let's start building our data access layer. Navigate to **FisharooCore | Core** and create a folder named `DataAccess`. In that folder, create another folder called `Impl` (short for Implementation which is a bit wordy!). In your `Impl` folder, we will create two classes and one `dbml` file. The first class will be our Connection object (named `Connection.cs`), and the second file will be called `PersonRepository.cs`. Once you have those class files created, add a new `LINQ to SQL Classes` file. Call it `Fisharoo.dbml`.

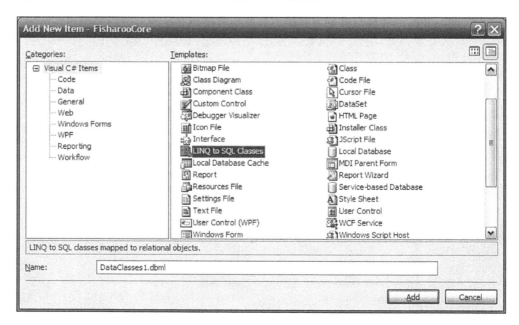

With the `Fisharoo.dbml` file still open, go back into your **Data Connections** and drag your `Person` table on to the design surface. Save that file.

 Once you have your table on the `Fisharoo.dbml` design surface, and you hit **Save**, Visual Studio creates a `FisharooDataContext` class and one class for every table that you have on the design surface. Each class that represents a table will have all the columns of the tables represented as fields and properties for that class. This will come in handy when you are using LINQ to perform your queries!

Once you save your `.dbml` file, you will have corresponding classes created for you. You can see them in the Class View (**View | Class View**).

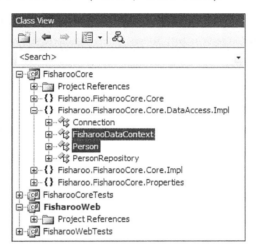

This takes care of the base framework for some demonstrations. Now, let's dig into those two class files that we have created. If you don't already have them open, open the `Connection.cs` file and the `PersonRepository.cs` file.

The Connection class gives us a way to encapsulate our DataContext creation. It has one method that returns the `FisharooDataContext` object. If we have other DataContexts to work with down the road, they could go here too.

```
using System.Configuration;
using System.Linq;
using System.Data.Linq;
namespace Fisharoo.FisharooCore.Core.DataAccess.Impl
{
    public class Connection
    {
        public static FisharooDataContext GetContext()
        {
```

```
FisharooDataContext fdc = new FisharooDataContext
    (ConfigurationManager.ConnectionStrings
    ["Fisharoo"].ToString());
return fdc;
        }
    }
}
```

There isn't much that is too fancy to explain here. Do you notice that we have references to Linq and Data.Linq? Without these in place, the repository that we are creating won't work. Also note that we are spinning up a new instance of our FisharooDataContext class with a reference to our connection string that we had put in the web.config file earlier.

Now, let's move over to the Person Repository. As the Person table that we created earlier is only for demonstration purposes, so is the repository. Here is that class.

```
using System.Linq;
using System.Data.Linq;
using System.Collections.Generic;
using StructureMap;
namespace Fisharoo.FisharooCore.Core.DataAccess.Impl
{
    [Pluggable("Default")]
    public class PersonRepository : IPersonRepository
    {
        public List<string> GetAllNames()
        {
            List<string> names = new List<string>();
            FisharooDataContext dc = Connection.GetContext();
            var persons = from p in dc.Persons
                          select p;
            foreach (Person p in persons)
            {
                names.Add(p.FirstName + " " + p.LastName);
            }
            return names;
        }
    }
}
```

Note that it has a StructureMap attribute so that we can swap it out later if we need to. As with all StructureMap classes (and for good design reasons) we have also inherited from an IPersonRepository interface, which clearly defines this class.

There is only one method in our repository now. It is responsible for simply selecting all the people in the `Person` table and returning a list of the first and the last names of those people. We have a list of type strings for the names collection, which will be returned at the end of the method. We then fetch our DataContext for our query. Once we have the DataContext defined, we can perform our query.

We declare a local variable with the `var` keyword. This allows us to declare a variable with a dynamic type. In this case, we will be selecting a collection of our Person classes. But we don't really know that for sure! Nor do we really need to know that. Let's look at the query.

```
var persons = from p in dc.Persons
              select p;
```

What this says is that we would like to select all the people from the `Person` table and return a collection of those people. It is very much like SQL. However, the reason we have specified `from` prior to anything else is so that **Visual Studio Intellisense** can be used. If we were to select the properties first, Visual Studio wouldn't really help us!

Technically speaking, this query is very much like a `SELECT * FROM table` type SQL query, which is just as bad in this environment as it is in the SQL environment! As this is only for demo purposes, I wanted to use the simplest query.

Once the query is executed, the `persons` variable is of type `IEnumerable`, which will allow us to iterate over it in a loop.

```
foreach (Person p in persons)
{
    names.Add(p.FirstName + " " + p.LastName);
}
```

In this loop, we will concatenate the first name and last name of each person and add them to our `names` collection. Once this is completed, we simply return that collection back to the user of this method.

The demonstration given here is very simple, as I didn't want to overwhelm you. It would get the idea across as to how the Repositories will work in this application, also touching upon the basics of LINQ.

Wrappers for everything!

In order to continue down the path of heavily abstracting all our objects, it is important to consider how coupled your application is to the .NET framework, or other frameworks, or third-party tools that you don't have control over. This may not seem important initially, but you will eventually find yourself in a place where the framework that Microsoft provides you with may not cut the mustard any more.

A quick example of this might be the caching objects that are provided. While these work great out of the box, they don't really scale well. What happens when you build a site that becomes so popular that you need to do everything possible to eek out that last bit of performance? The first response is usually to just go to a web farm. The next response is to add more boxes to the farm. The third response is to add more boxes to the farm…huh?

How often can adding more hardware to address performance issues be a standard response? At some point in time you will have to improve your application. If you could achieve a huge performance gain by swapping out the caching object, would you be able to? If you have references to the caching object scattered all over your code, you would have to go in and swap it out for your new third-party caching object. While this can be done, it would be tedious and error prone. A better option would be to stick to the principle of wrapping anything you don't personally control. If you create a cache wrapper that wraps the .NET cache object, you could easily and quickly swap out the MS cache object for something like MemCached.

I learned a saying in the Army that has served me well, and applies here too:

> *"It is better to have and not need, than need and not have!"*

Here, it is better to have wrappers around everything and not need to swap anything out, than need to swap everything out and have wrappers around nothing.

Configuration

For the configuration wrapper, we want to create something that is capable of returning a strongly typed item out of our configuration source. Of course, this configuration source will initially be the standard `web.config`. As the `web.config` only holds string values, our configuration object will be responsible for casting out the appropriate type.

```
using System;
using System.Configuration;
using StructureMap;
namespace Fisharoo.FisharooCore.Core.Impl
```

```
{
    [Pluggable("Default")]
    public class Configuration : IConfiguration
    {
        private static object getAppSetting(Type expectedType,
                                            string key)
        {
            string value = ConfigurationManager.AppSettings.Get(key);
            if (value == null)
            {
                throw new Exception(string.Format("AppSetting: {0} is
                                not configured.", key));
            }
            try
            {
                if (expectedType.Equals(typeof(int)))
                {
                    return int.Parse(value);
                }
                if (expectedType.Equals(typeof(string)))
                {
                    return value;
                }
                throw new Exception("Type not supported.");
            }
            catch (Exception ex)
            {
                throw new Exception(string.Format("Config key:{0}
                was expected to be of type {1} but was not.",
                key, expectedType), ex);
            }
        }
    }
}
```

As you can see, from the start I have included a StructureMap attribute so that we can easily swap out this object for a stub if needed.

```
[Pluggable("Default")]
```

Directly after that, you will notice that we have inherited from a Configuration interface. As this class doesn't currently have any public methods, this interface is currently empty! The goal of this class is to provide methods that can be called, which in turn will call the static getAppSetting() method. As we don't yet have any items in our configuration file, we don't have any public methods yet.

If we did have something to get to, we would make a method that looked similar to this:

```
public virtual int GetAuthCookieTimeoutInMinutes()
{
    int value = (int) getAppSetting(typeof (int),
        "AuthCookieTimeoutInMinutes");
    return value;
}
```

This method is basically providing a clean way for our domain objects to get to a configuration value as a specified type. Internally, the method calls getAppSetting, specifying the type expected and the name of the key to be fetched. It then casts the return value to that expected type and returns the value.

The getAppSetting() method itself currently communicates with the config file using the ConfigurationManager and gets the string value that was specified by the key that was passed in.

```
string value = ConfigurationManager.AppSettings.Get(key);
```

It then tests whether the retrieved value is null, and throws an error if it is.

```
if (value == null)
{
    throw new Exception(string.Format("AppSetting: {0} is not
                        configured.", key));
}
```

We then try to return the expected type. It is currently testing for an int or string value. If the expected type is int, then we attempt to use int.Parse on the value and return it. Otherwise, we try to return the string value.

```
try
{
    if (expectedType.Equals(typeof(int)))
    {
        return int.Parse(value);
    }

    if (expectedType.Equals(typeof(string)))
    {
        return value;
    }

    throw new Exception("Type not supported.");
}
```

If the expected type is not `int` or `string`, then we throw an error stating that the requested type is not supported. If anything in the initial `try` statement goes wrong, we throw an error stating that the key was not of the expected type.

```
catch (Exception ex)
{
    throw new Exception (string.Format("Config key:{0} was expected
                                to be of type {1} but was.not.",
                                key, expectedType),.ex);
}
```

As our application grows and we add items to our configuration file, we will extend this file and its interface to include one method per entry in the configuration file.

Cache

I like to have a cache wrapper so that we can immediately plan to cache items in our site. However, I know that down the road, the basic .NET cache implementation will not work in a high-traffic environment. I would prefer to use something like MemCached or something similar. However, we will discuss wrapping the basic `HttpContext Cache` object for now.

To get started, we need to add a reference to `System.Web` in our FisharooCore project (as it is an assembly project, which doesn't have that reference by default!). To do this, right-click on the project root, and select **add reference**. It may take a while, but eventually, the **Add Reference** window should pop up. Select the **.NET** tab, and scroll down till you encounter **System.Web**. Select that item and then click the **OK** button.

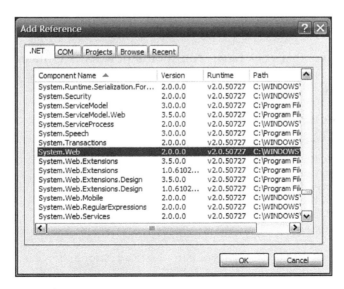

That will allow us to access the cache object in our assembly. Now, let's add a settings file so that we can set the default cache time out.

 I prefer that we add a settings file for this rather than make entries to our `config` file. The reason is that we can specify the type of each entry and programmatically access them via the `Settings` object.

In order to add this `Settings.settings` file, navigate to the FisharooCore project in Windows Explorer (not in Visual Studio). There, you should have a `Properties` folder. In this folder, create a new XML file called `Settings.settings`. Back in your Visual Studio environment, navigate to your FisharooCore project. Then, click the **show all files** button at the top of the **Solution Explorer** window.

You should now see your `Settings.settings` file. Right-click on that file and select **include in project**. Now click the **show all files** button again. The `Settings.settings` file should now be included and visible in your project. Double-click the file to open it in Visual Studio. You should see a window that somewhat resembles a spreadsheet! Type in the following information as you see it here:

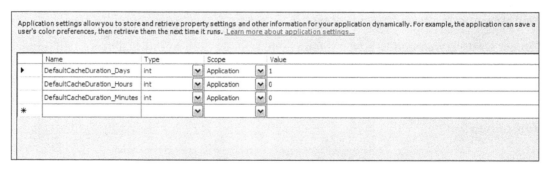

Application settings allow you to store and retrieve property settings and other information for your application dynamically. For example, the application can save a user's color preferences, then retrieve them the next time it runs. Learn more about application settings...

	Name	Type	Scope	Value
▶	DefaultCacheDuration_Days	int	Application	1
	DefaultCacheDuration_Hours	int	Application	0
	DefaultCacheDuration_Minutes	int	Application	0
*				

Once you have done this, click **Save**. You should now have a functioning `Settings` class to work with! Let's build our `Cache` wrapper now. Here is the code in its entirety.

```
using System;
using System.Collections;
using System.Collections.Generic;
using System.Web;
using System.Web.Caching;
using Fisahroo.FisharooCore.Properties;
namespace Fisharoo.FisharooCore.Core.Impl
{
    public class Cache
    {
        private static System.Web.Caching.Cache cache;
```

```
private static TimeSpan timeSpan = new TimeSpan(
    Settings.Default.DefaultCacheDuration_Days,
    Settings.Default.DefaultCacheDuration_Hours,
    Settings.Default.DefaultCacheDuration_Minutes, 0);
static Cache()
{
    cache = HttpContext.Current.Cache;
}
public static object Get(string cache_key)
{
    return cache.Get(cache_key);
}
public static List<string> GetCacheKeys()
{
    List<string> keys = new List<string>();
    IDictionaryEnumerator ca = cache.GetEnumerator();
    while (ca.MoveNext())
    {
        keys.Add(ca.Key.ToString());
    }
    return keys;
}
public static void Set(string cache_key, object cache_object)
{
    Set(cache_key, cache_object, timeSpan);
}
public static void Set(string cache_key, object cache_object,
                    DateTime expiration)
{
    Set(cache_key, cache_object, expiration,
        CacheItemPriority.Normal);
}
public static void Set(string cache_key, object cache_object,
                    TimeSpan expiration)
{
    Set(cache_key, cache_object, expiration,
        CacheItemPriority.Normal);
}
public static void Set(string cache_key, object cache_object,
                    DateTime expiration,
                    CacheItemPriority priority)
{
    cache.Insert(cache_key, cache_object, null, expiration,
                System.Web.Caching.Cache.NoSlidingExpiration,
                priority, null);
```

```
        }
        public static void Set(string cache_key, object cache_object,
                        TimeSpan expiration,
                        CacheItemPriority priority)
        {
            cache.Insert(cache_key, cache_object, null,
                    System.Web.Caching.Cache.NoAbsoluteExpiration,
                    expiration, priority, null);
        }
        public static void Delete(string cache_key)
        {
            if (Exists(cache_key))
                cache.Remove(cache_key);
        }
        public static bool Exists(string cache_key)
        {
            if (cache[cache_key] != null)
                return true;
            else
                return false;
        }
        public static void Flush()
        {
            foreach (string s in GetCacheKeys())
            {
                Delete(s);
            }
        }
    }
}
```

To get started, note that at the top we have several namespace references.

```
using System;
using System.Collections;
using System.Collections.Generic;
using System.Web;
using System.Web.Caching;
using Fisahroo.FisharooCore.Properties;
```

The most important ones to notice are the System.Web.Caching and the Fisharoo.
FisharooCore.Properties. The System.Web.Caching provides us with the object
that we are wrapping with this file. The Fisharoo.FisharooCore.Properties is
what gives us access to our newly created settings file.

The next thing to notice is that we have two static variables declared — cache and timeSpan. The cache object is a reference to the HttpContext.Current.Cache object. This is where we will be storing all of our cached items. The timeSpan variable is a defined TimeSpan, which will be used for the methods that don't provide a TimeSpan declaration, a default TimeSpan so to speak.

We then define a static constructor for our cache object. This basically means that our cache object is refreshed prior to any cache object being created. The exact time can't be determined but can possibly be done at the time that the assembly is loaded.

```
static Cache()
{
    cache = HttpContext.Current.Cache;
}
```

Now, we can get into our method definitions. We define a way to get something from the cache, get a list of keys currently in the cache, several ways to add items to the cache, a way to delete items from the cache, a way to see if a key is currently present in the cache, and a way to totally flush the cache. Let's look at each of these.

To get something from the cache we have a Get() method. This method simply requires a key value to be passed to it. We then use the cache implementation of Get() and return the value. Keep in mind that this could return the cached item or a NULL value.

```
public static object Get(string cache_key)
{
    return cache.Get(cache_key);
}
```

We then have a definition for getting a list of all the key values currently residing in the cache. This method returns a generic list of type string. The way it works is that we first define a keys List that we can add our keys to. We then declare an IDictionaryEnumerator and assign the cache.GetEnumerator() values to it. Once we have the Enumeration defined, we iterate through each item in the collection by checking the ca.MoveNext() method. With each iteration, we add the key value to our keys collection. We then return the keys collection.

```
public static List<string> GetCacheKeys()
{
    List<string> keys = new List<string>();
    IDictionaryEnumerator ca = cache.GetEnumerator();
    while (ca.MoveNext())
    {
        keys.Add(ca.Key.ToString());
    }
    return keys;
}
```

We then define several Set methods. This allows us to add items to the cache. Each method is a simple wrapper for all the Set methods that the cache object provides. All these methods require that a string key be provided along with the object that is to be cached. Some of them allow for various time-outs to be specified. Others allow you to additionally provide a priority for the cached items expiration. Here are the method declarations:

```
public static void Set(string cache_key, object cache_object)
    {
        Set(cache_key, cache_object, timeSpan);
    }

public static void Set(string cache_key, object cache_object,
              DateTime expiration)
    {
        Set(cache_key, cache_object, expiration,
           CacheItemPriority.Normal);
    }

public static void Set(string cache_key, object cache_object,
              TimeSpan expiration)
    {
        Set(cache_key, cache_object, expiration,
           CacheItemPriority.Normal);
    }

public static void Set(string cache_key, object cache_object,
              DateTime expiration,
              CacheItemPriority priority)
    {
        cache.Insert(cache_key, cache_object, null, expiration,
                System.Web.Caching.Cache.NoSlidingExpiration,
                priority, null);
    }

public static void Set(string cache_key, object cache_object,
              TimeSpan expiration,
              CacheItemPriority priority)
    {
        cache.Insert(cache_key, cache_object, null,
                System.Web.Caching.Cache.NoAbsoluteExpiration,
                expiration, priority, null);
    }
```

We then move to another simple method wrapper. This one provides a way to delete a cached item. It accepts the key to be deleted. The method then checks to see if the key exists and removes the key from the cache collection.

```
public static void Delete(string cache_key)
        {
            if (Exists(cache_key))
                cache.Remove(cache_key);
        }
```

The `Exists` method simply checks to see if an item is still in the cache collection. The reason for this method is that while items can be freely added to the cache collection, you can never count on them being there when you try accessing them the next time. The item could be removed or may not exist for several reasons:

- The item may have timed out and been removed
- It may have been pushed out of the collection due to the presence of many other new items added to the collection
- The collection may have been re-initialized intentionally, or due to some glitch in the system

This method returns a `true` or `false` value based on whether the key that is being checked exists in the collection or not. This only checks whether the key exists. It does not pull the item out of the collection and cast it to the appropriate type. The key value may exist while the item may not. For this reason, always check that your casted item is not null before using it!

```
public static bool Exists(string cache_key)
        {
            if (cache[cache_key] != null)
                return true;
            else
                return false;
        }
```

Now that we have all these nifty ways to add items, get items, and delete items, we need a way to clear the entire cache collection. This is easily accomplished by iterating through all the keys in the collection and calling `Delete` on each of them.

```
public static void Flush()
        {
            foreach (string s in GetCacheKeys())
            {
                Delete(s);
            }
        }
```

Session

The session object is another item that is frequently used in most web applications. That being said, it is also something that we can squeeze performance out of down the road. Even if performance wasn't an issue, the session object by itself does not really conform to the most basic of OOP principles. Rather than trying to cast an item out of thin air—or the `HttpContext.Current.Session`—it would be much better if we could call an object that returned the appropriate object for us. Here is the basic wrapper:

```
using System.Web;
using StructureMap;
namespace Fisharoo.FisharooCore.Core.Impl
{
    [Pluggable("Default")]
    public class WebContext : IWebContext
    {
        public void ClearSession()
        {
            HttpContext.Current.Session.Clear();
        }
        public bool ContainsInSession(string key)
        {
            return HttpContext.Current.Session[key] != null;
        }
        public void RemoveFromSession(string key)
        {
            HttpContext.Current.Session.Remove(key);
        }
        private string GetQueryStringValue(string key)
        {
            return HttpContext.Current.Request.QueryString.Get(key);
        }
        private void SetInSession(string key, object value)
        {
            if (HttpContext.Current == null ||
                HttpContext.Current.Session == null)
            {
                return;
            }
            HttpContext.Current.Session[key] = value;
        }
        private object GetFromSession(string key)
        {
            if (HttpContext.Current == null ||
```

```
                    HttpContext.Current.Session == null)
            {
                return null;
            }
            return HttpContext.Current.Session[key];
        }
        private void UpdateInSession(string key, object value)
        {
            HttpContext.Current.Session[key] = value;
        }
    }
}
```

Keep in mind that much like the cache object that was shown earlier, we would continue to extend this object to have specific methods that could handle some of the dirty work. Say we stored a person in the session as the current user. We could have a `GetCurrentUserFromSession()` method defined that would interact with our wrapper methods. It would retrieve the user and cast the object as a person. This is much better OOP-wise. Let's look at the wrapper.

Of course, the first thing to notice — as you will notice in most of our classes — is that this method is part of the StructureMap framework and has a `Pluggable` attribute defined.

```
[Pluggable("Default")]
```

You will then notice that the class inherits from `IWebContext`. This is so that we can use StructureMap to retrieve the appropriate class for us.

After that we jump right into the public method definitions. These are all pretty easy to understand and primarily work with the `HttpContext` object. We have a `ClearSession()` method that simply resets the session. After that, we have a `ContainsInSession()` method that takes a key value. It checks whether that key is present in the session and returns true or false. Next is the `RemoveFromSession()` method that takes in a key and attempts to remove that key from the session.

After our public methods, we have a few private methods left to build, namely, `GetQueryStringValue()`, `SetInSession()`, `GetFromSession()`, and `UpdateInSession()`. Before we discuss these methods, I need you to understand why they are private. We could make all of these public and they would work just fine. However, making them public would also mean that we would scatter the code about our application that directly interacts with the session. My preference is that we extend this object to provide more specific methods that work with these private methods, which in turn work with the session. This provides us a bit more encapsulation regarding the session interaction.

Let's have a look at these methods. The `GetQueryStringValue()` method takes in a key value and retrieves the item from the query string. The `SetInSession()` method allows you to pass in a key and an object. The object is then stored in the session under that key name. `GetFromSession()` does just that—it takes a key and retrieves that corresponding object. `UpdateInSession()` is very similar to `SetInSession()` with the exception that it assumes that a key already exists and updates the value that is currently stored there. This method will throw an error if a key does not exist. Therefore prior to using this method, you should check that your key exists in the session collection!

Redirection

From an OOP point of view, `Response.Redirect` is about as useful as the session object is (I'm starting to see a trend here). It simply provides a way of sending you from one place to another. It would be nice if we could work with it using methods. It would be even better if we could hide some logic in those methods if need be. Our initial wrapper is very easy.

```
using System.Web;
using StructureMap;
namespace Fisharoo.FisharooCore.Core.Impl
{
    [Pluggable("Default")]
    public class Redirector : IRedirector
    {
        public void GoToHomePage()
        {
            Redirect("~/Default.aspx");
        }
        private void Redirect(string path)
        {
            HttpContext.Current.Response.Redirect(path);
        }
    }
}
```

This class, like the others, uses StructureMap so that it can be used for stubbed out for testing later. Currently there are two methods—one an example, and another handling redirection. Let's look at the `Redirect()` method. It takes a path parameter and then uses the `HttpContext` object to redirect the user to the appropriate location. An example is the `GoToHomePage()` method. It asks the `Redirect()` method to send the user to the homepage.

Of course, this class can be expanded with as many new methods as needed to redirect for any purpose. We can extend this object to be a bit more versatile too. We can also perform all sorts of logic inside these methods prior to using the redirection, obviously without degrading the overall design and where actually required.

Email

Sending emails is one task that every website has to be capable of. How many emails you plan to send should certainly determine how you go about sending that email. As we do not yet know how many emails we plan to send, we will initially rely upon the tools that are provided in the .NET framework to send our email. Our wrapper looks like this:

```
using System.Net.Mail;
using StructureMap;
namespace Fisharoo.FisharooCore.Core.Impl
{
    [Pluggable("Default")]
    public class Email : IEmail
    {
        const string TO_EMAIL_ADDRESS = "website@fisharoo.com";
        const string FROM_EMAIL_ADDRESS = "website@fisharoo.com";
        public void SendEmail(string From, string Subject, string
                              Message)
        {
            MailMessage mm = new MailMessage(From,TO_EMAIL_ADDRESS);
            mm.Subject = Subject;
            mm.Body = Message;
            Send(mm);
        }
        public void SendEmail(string To, string CC, string BCC,
                              string Subject, string Message)
        {
            MailMessage mm = new MailMessage(FROM_EMAIL_ADDRESS,To);
            mm.CC.Add(CC);
            mm.Bcc.Add(BCC);
            mm.Subject = Subject;
            mm.Body = Message;
            mm.IsBodyHtml = true;
            Send(mm);
        }
        public void SendEmail(string[] To, string[] CC, string[] BCC,
                              string Subject, string Message)
```

```
    {
        MailMessage mm = new MailMessage();
        foreach (string to in To)
        {
            mm.To.Add(to);
        }
        foreach (string cc in CC)
        {
            mm.CC.Add(cc);
        }
        foreach (string bcc in BCC)
        {
            mm.Bcc.Add(bcc);
        }
        mm.From = new MailAddress(FROM_EMAIL_ADDRESS);
        mm.Subject = Subject;
        mm.Body = Message;
        mm.IsBodyHtml = true;
        Send(mm);
    }
    public void SendIndividualEmailsPerRecipient(string[]
        To, string Subject, string Message)
    {
        foreach (string to in To)
        {
            MailMessage mm = new
                MailMessage(FROM_EMAIL_ADDRESS,to);
            mm.Subject = Subject;
            mm.Body = Message;
            mm.IsBodyHtml = true;
            Send(mm);
        }
    }
    private void Send(MailMessage Message)
    {
        SmtpClient smtp = new SmtpClient();
        smtp.Send(Message);
    }
    }
}
```

As with all our objects, we have the StructureMap attribute in place that makes this a Pluggable class. The class itself inherits from our IEmail interface. Then, you will see a couple of constants declared — one for the websites receiving the email account and another for the websites sending the email account. (We could have used one variable for both, but a little flexibility never hurt anyone!) We then jump into our first method:

```
public void SendEmail(string From, string Subject, string Message)
    {
        MailMessage mm = new
            MailMessage(From,TO_EMAIL_ADDRESS);
        mm.Subject = Subject;
        mm.Body = Message;
        Send(mm);
    }
```

This method is one of the overrides for the SendEmail() method. This one is a bit different from the others in that it is used for the site to send email to another site rather than to a user. In that case, the user of this method will provide the email address that the message is from, the subject and the message. This method would be used in a 'Contact Us' page or a similar mail form. At the bottom of this method, you will see a Send() method call. This method spins up an SmtpClient and sends the email message as do each of the following methods.

The remaining SendEmail() methods are used in various ways for the site to send email to the users of the site. The first one allows single email addresses to be passed in for the **To, CC,** and **BCC** inputs.

```
public void SendEmail(string To, string CC, string BCC, string
                    Subject, string Message)
    {
        MailMessage mm = new MailMessage(FROM_EMAIL_ADDRESS,To);
        mm.CC.Add(CC);
        mm.Bcc.Add(BCC);
        mm.Subject = Subject;
        mm.Body = Message;
        mm.IsBodyHtml = true;
        Send(mm);
    }
```

The second method allows you to pass in an array for each email address input to specify multiple recipients.

```
public void SendEmail(string[] To, string[] CC, string[] BCC,
                     string Subject, string Message)
{
    MailMessage mm = new MailMessage();
    foreach (string to in To)
    {
        mm.To.Add(to);
    }
    foreach (string cc in CC)
    {
        mm.CC.Add(cc);
    }
    foreach (string bcc in BCC)
    {
        mm.Bcc.Add(bcc);
    }
    mm.From = new MailAddress(FROM_EMAIL_ADDRESS);
    mm.Subject = Subject;
    mm.Body = Message;
    mm.IsBodyHtml = true;
    Send(mm);
}
```

The next to last method allows us to iterate through each of the recipients and send one email to each recipient rather than have them all in one of the recipient lines.

```
public void SendIndividualEmailsPerRecipient(string[]
    To, string Subject, string Message)
{
    foreach (string to in To)
    {
        MailMessage mm = new
            MailMessage(FROM_EMAIL_ADDRESS,to);
        mm.Subject = Subject;
        mm.Body = Message;
        mm.IsBodyHtml = true;
        Send(mm);
    }
}
```

Finally, we get to the Send() method that is used by all of the other methods. This method is responsible for actually sending the emails. But before this method performs any action, we need to add the following section to our web config just after the configuration tag. It is responsible for telling the .NET framework how to connect to our mail server.

```
<system.net>
  <mailSettings>
    <smtp>
      <network
          host="serverHostName"
          port="portnumber"
          userName="username"
          password="password" />
    </smtp>
  </mailSettings>
</system.net>
```

Now, we can define the last method Send() as:

```
private void Send(MailMessage Message)
{
    SmtpClient smtp = new SmtpClient();
    smtp.Send(Message);
}
```

This configuration is very flexible in how it sends email. However, it still requires that the webpage be responsible for sending emails directly. This creates a page with lots of overheads given that there could be a lot of recipients to process, or a lot of network lag involved in the transactions.

The nice thing about having this wrapper is that we can easily create another class that implements the IEmail interface but uses a mail queue instead of requiring the page to send the email. This would allow the website to just create mail messages and put them in the queue, which is much faster than actually processing and sending the emails. We could then have a queue processor somewhere that would be responsible for sending our emails.

While I am sure that there will be other items that might need a wrapper, which we will come across, this small library should be good enough to get us started!

Error handling and logging

I don't think any "enterprise application" can truly be called "enterprise" if it doesn't handle errors well and notify someone to address them. In an ASP.NET site, there are basically two forms of errors—errors that you have caught, and the ones you couldn't. Pretty simple, right? Well, not so fast! Whether you have trapped an error or not, the user of your application is still going to end up with some form of disruption in their surfing experience. So we need a way to not only provide users with a smooth disruption but also to fix the disruption so that it doesn't happen again.

Error handling is the act of doing your best to trap expected or possible errors. It is also the act of not allowing ugly error messages to get in front of your customers. Logging is what we do with these errors so that we can fix them down the road.

Error handling

I am pretty sure that most of you are aware of how to catch an error using the familiar `try/catch/finally` syntax. To those of you who are not, it looks something like this:

```
try
{
    //code to run
}

catch (Exception e)
{
    //code to run when an error occurs
}

finally
{
    //code to run after the try or catch statement is complete
    //   ** this code is always executed no matter what
}
```

But what about errors those occur outside of the environment? What do you do then to prevent users from seeing some crazy geeked out error message? The easiest thing to do in a web environment is to tap into the `Application_Error` event handler using the `Global.asax` file.

To implement this, let's first add a `Global.asax` file to our FisharooWeb project. Right-click on the FisharooWeb project and select **Add | New Item** and select the **Global Application Class** item (leave the default name of `Global.asax`). Once this is added, we will want to take a look at the `Application_Error` method. This is the event that is raised when an unhandled error occurs. We want to do two things in this method:

- We first want to log what happened so that we can fix it
- Then we want to redirect the user to a friendly error page

We have not yet built the `Log` class, so for now, we will utilize the `Redirector` class that we built earlier.

To get started, make sure that you are in the `Global.asax.cs` file. At the top of this file ensure that you have at least these three `using` statements:

```
using System;
using Fisharoo.FisharooCore.Core;
using StructureMap;
```

Then, navigate to the already created `Application_Error` method and enter the following code:

```
protected void Application_Error(object sender, EventArgs e)
{
    //TODO: Add logging logic here.

    IRedirector redir = ObjectFactory.GetInstance<IRedirector>();

    redir.GoToErrorPage();
}
```

Note that I have entered a placeholder to remind us that we need to come back and add some logic for logging our errors somewhere. Then I used StructureMap to get an instance of `IRedirector`. As we currently have defined only one class, it will return the `Redirector` class. Earlier, we defined a `GoToHomePage()` method that simply sends users to the homepage (see the Wrap Everything section covered earlier for more on the Redirector). Now let's define the `GoToErrorPage()` method to handle this new redirection.

Open the `Redirector.cs` file and add the following method:

```
public void GoToErrorPage()
    {
        Redirect("~/Error.aspx");
    }
```

Don't forget to also add a method definition (void GoToErrorPage();) to the IRedirector interface!

As we are providing a way to send a user to an error page, we should also create an error page. Add a webform to the root of the FisharooWeb project named Error. aspx. For now, I have included a simple message in the body of the page. We can modify this later to something more explanatory.

```
<%@ Page Language="C#" MasterPageFile="~/SiteMaster.Master"
AutoEventWireup="true" CodeBehind="Error.aspx.cs" Inherits="Fisahroo.
FisharooWeb.Error" %>

<asp:Content ContentPlaceHolderID="Content" runat="server">
An error has occured!
</asp:Content>
```

Now, let's move on to how we can handle the logging section of error handling!

Logging

Logging can either be overly complex, or really easy. As I don't have loads of time on my hands, I usually opt not to reinvent the wheel whenever possible! So in this case, I will be using the log4net framework that provides an extensive set of tools for various forms of logging.

For more information regarding the log4net project look here: http://logging.apache.org/log4net/

To get log4net working, you will need to copy the log4net dll and the log4net. xml files into your bin directory in the FisharooCore project. Once it is there, add a reference to log4net. Then you will need to create a log4net.config file in the root of your FisharooWeb project or in the bin directory of the FisharooWeb project. Here is what our config file looks like:

For more information about log4net configuration, look here http://logging.apache.org/log4net/release/config-examples.html

```
<?xml version="1.0" encoding="utf-8"?>
<log4net debug="false">
    <appender name="RollingFileAppender" type="log4net.Appender.
RollingFileAppender">
        <file value="Logs/log4net.log" />
```

```
            <appendToFile value="true" />
            <rollingStyle value="Size" />
            <maxSizeRollBackups value="10" />
            <maximumFileSize value="1000KB" />
            <staticLogFileName value="true" />
            <layout type="log4net.Layout.PatternLayout">
                <conversionPattern value="%d [%t] %-5p %c - %m%n" />
            </layout>
        </appender>
        <appender name="ConsoleAppender" type="log4net.Appender.
ConsoleAppender">
            <layout type="log4net.Layout.PatternLayout">
                <conversionPattern value="%d [%t] %-5p %c - %m%n" />
            </layout>
        </appender>
        <appender name="OutputDebugStringAppender"
                    type="log4net.Appender.OutputDebugStringAppender">
            <layout type="log4net.Layout.PatternLayout">
                <conversionPattern value="%-5p %m - %c -%n" />
            </layout>
        </appender>
        <appender name="TraceAppender" type="log4net.Appender.
TraceAppender">
            <layout type="log4net.Layout.PatternLayout">
                <conversionPattern value="%d [%t] %-5p %c - %m%n" />
            </layout>
        </appender>
        <appender name="AspNetTraceAppender" type="log4net.Appender.
AspNetTraceAppender">
            <layout type="log4net.Layout.PatternLayout">
                <conversionPattern value="%d [%t] %-5p %c - %m%n" />
            </layout>
        </appender>
        <root>
            <level value="DEBUG" />
            <appender-ref ref="RollingFileAppender" />
            <appender-ref ref="OutputDebugStringAppender" />
            <appender-ref ref="ConsoleAppender" />
            <appender-ref ref="TraceAppender" />
            <appender-ref ref="AspNetTraceAppender" />
        </root>
        <logger name="StructureMap" additivity="false">
            <level value="WARN"/>
            appender-ref ref="OutputDebugStringAppender" />
            <appender-ref ref="ConsoleAppender" />
        </logger>
        <logger name="NHibernate" additivity="false">
```

```
        <level value="INFO"/>
        <appender-ref ref="AspNetTraceAppender" />
    </logger>
</log4net>
```

Now, we can create a class to help us interact with what `log4net` provides us. Here is the entire listing. It's a big one!

```
using System;
using System.Collections.Generic;
using System.IO;
using log4net;
using log4net.Appender;
using log4net.Config;
using log4net.Layout;
namespace Fisharoo.FisharooCore.Core.Impl
{
    public static class Log
    {
        private static Dictionary<Type, ILog> _loggers = new
        Dictionary<Type, ILog>();
        private static bool _logInitialized = false;
        private static object _lock = new object();
        public static string SerializeException(Exception e)
        {
            return SerializeException(e, string.Empty);
        }
        private static string SerializeException(Exception e, string
        exceptionMessage)
        {
            if (e == null) return string.Empty;
            exceptionMessage = string.Format(
                "{0}{1}{2}\n{3}",
                exceptionMessage,
                (exceptionMessage == string.Empty) ? string.Empty :
                "\n\n",
                e.Message,
                e.StackTrace);
            if (e.InnerException != null)
                exceptionMessage =
                SerializeException(e.InnerException,
                                exceptionMessage);
            return exceptionMessage;
        }
        private static ILog getLogger(Type source)
```

```
    {
        lock (_lock)
        {
            if (_loggers.ContainsKey(source))
            {
                return _loggers[source];
            }
            else
            {
                ILog logger = LogManager.GetLogger(source);
                _loggers.Add(source, logger);
                return logger;
            }
        }
    }
    /* Log a message object */
    public static void Debug(object source, object message)
    {
        Debug(source.GetType(), message);
    }
    public static void Debug(Type source, object message)
    {
        getLogger(source).Debug(message);
    }
    public static void Info(object source, object message)
    {
        Info(source.GetType(), message);
    }
    public static void Info(Type source, object message)
    {
        getLogger(source).Info(message);
    }
    public static void Warn(object source, object message)
    {
        Warn(source.GetType(), message);
    }
    public static void Warn(Type source, object message)
    {
        getLogger(source).Warn(message);
    }

    public static void Error(object source, object message)
    {
        Error(source.GetType(), message);
```

```
}
public static void Error(Type source, object message)
{
    getLogger(source).Error(message);
}
public static void Fatal(object source, object message)
{
    Fatal(source.GetType(), message);
}
public static void Fatal(Type source, object message)
{
    getLogger(source).Fatal(message);
}
/* Log a message object and exception */
public static void Debug(object source, object message,
                         Exception exception)
{
    Debug(source.GetType(), message, exception);
}
public static void Debug(Type source, object message,
                         Exception exception)
{
    getLogger(source).Debug(message, exception);
}
public static void Info(object source, object message,
                        Exception exception)
{
    Info(source.GetType(), message, exception);
}
public static void Info(Type source, object message,
                        Exception exception)
{
    getLogger(source).Info(message, exception);
}
public static void Warn(object source, object message,
                        Exception exception)
{
    Warn(source.GetType(), message, exception);
}
public static void Warn(Type source, object message,
                        Exception exception)
{
    getLogger(source).Warn(message, exception);
}
```

```
public static void Error(object source, object message,
                         Exception exception)
{
    Error(source.GetType(), message, exception);
}
public static void Error(Type source, object message,
                         Exception exception)
{
    getLogger(source).Error(message, exception);
}
public static void Fatal(object source, object message,
                                  Exception exception)
{
    Fatal(source.GetType(), message, exception);
}
public static void Fatal(Type source, object message,
                                  Exception exception)
{
    getLogger(source).Fatal(message, exception);
}
private static void initialize()
{
    string logFilePath =
    Path.Combine(AppDomain.CurrentDomain.BaseDirectory,
             "Log4Net.config");
    if (!File.Exists(logFilePath))
    {
        logFilePath =
        Path.Combine(AppDomain.CurrentDomain.BaseDirectory,
                 @"bin\Log4Net.config");
    }
    XmlConfigurator.ConfigureAndWatch(new
                                    FileInfo(logFilePath));
}
public static void EnsureInitialized()
{
    if (!_logInitialized)
    {
        initialize();
        _logInitialized = true;
    }
}
public static void EnsureInitializedForTesting()
{
    if (!_logInitialized)
```

```
        {
            OutputDebugStringAppender appender1 = new
            OutputDebugStringAppender();
            appender1.Layout = new PatternLayout("%-5p %m - %c -
                                                  %n");
            BasicConfigurator.Configure(appender1);
            TraceAppender appender2 = new TraceAppender();
            appender2.Layout = new PatternLayout("%d [%t] %-5p %c
                                                  - %m%n");
            BasicConfigurator.Configure(appender2);
            _logInitialized = true;
        }
    }
  }
}
```

This class is mostly bloated with overrides for logging messages in various ways. You will see Debug, Info, Warn, Error, and Fatal methods for logging both message objects and exceptions. Let's quickly step through this class to understand it.

Initially, you will notice several using statements. The most important are the IO, and the log4net references. One way of logging to the file system is to include the IO reference. Everything else is so that log4net will work appropriately.

```
using System;
using System.Collections.Generic;
using System.IO;
using log4net;
using log4net.Appender;
using log4net.Config;
using log4net.Layout;
```

The SerializeException() method provides a way to convert an Exception into a string. This has overrides that allow you to pass in an Exception or an Exception and a message. Both return the exception as a string.

```
        public static string SerializeException(Exception e)
        {
            return SerializeException(e, string.Empty);
        }
        private static string SerializeException(Exception e, string
                                                 exceptionMessage)
        {
            if (e == null) return string.Empty;
            exceptionMessage = string.Format(
                "{0}{1}{2}\n{3}",
```

```
            exceptionMessage,
            (exceptionMessage == string.Empty) ? string.Empty :
            "\n\n",
            e.Message,
            e.StackTrace);
        if (e.InnerException != null)
            exceptionMessage =
            SerializeException(e.InnerException,
                               exceptionMessage);
            return exceptionMessage;
    }
```

The next method we will look at is the getLogger method. It's responsible for
spinning up the log for you. It takes the type of the caller and returns the appropriate
log. You will see that most of the following methods use this method.

```
    private static ILog getLogger(Type source)
    {
        lock (_lock)
        {
            if (_loggers.ContainsKey(source))
            {
                return _loggers[source];
            }
            else
            {
                ILog logger = LogManager.GetLogger(source);
                _loggers.Add(source, logger);
                return logger;
            }
        }
    }
```

The next set of methods allows you to log a message object. There are two overrides
for each method name. One method allows you to pass an unspecified object and
a message while another requires a specific type and its message. You will see that
the first method simply does some dirty work to determine the type of object passed
in, and then calls the second version of itself. All these methods append to the log
through the getLogger method.

```
    public static void Debug(object source, object message)
    {
        Debug(source.GetType(), message);
    }
    public static void Debug(Type source, object message)
    {
```

```
        getLogger(source).Debug(message);
    }
    public static void Info(object source, object message)
    {
        Info(source.GetType(), message);
    }
    public static void Info(Type source, object message)
    {
        getLogger(source).Info(message);
    }
    public static void Warn(object source, object message)
    {
        Warn(source.GetType(), message);
    }
    public static void Warn(Type source, object message)
    {
        getLogger(source).Warn(message);
    }
    public static void Error(object source, object message)
    {
        Error(source.GetType(), message);
    }
    public static void Error(Type source, object message)
    {
        getLogger(source).Error(message);
    }
    public static void Fatal(object source, object message)
    {
        Fatal(source.GetType(), message);
    }
    public static void Fatal(Type source, object message)
    {
        getLogger(source).Fatal(message);
    }
```

The next set of methods is the same as the first set with the exception that they provide us with additional overrides that allow an exception to be passed in as well.

```
    public static void Debug(object source, object message,
                             Exception exception)
    {
        Debug(source.GetType(), message, exception);
    }
    public static void Debug(Type source, object message,
                             Exception exception)
```

```
{
    getLogger(source).Debug(message, exception);
}
public static void Info(object source, object message,
                        Exception exception)
{
    Info(source.GetType(), message, exception);
}
public static void Info(Type source, object message,
                        Exception exception)
{
    getLogger(source).Info(message, exception);
}
public static void Warn(object source, object message,
                        Exception exception)
{
    Warn(source.GetType(), message, exception);
}
public static void Warn(Type source, object message,
                        Exception exception)
{
    getLogger(source).Warn(message, exception);
}
public static void Error(object source, object message,
                        Exception exception)
{
    Error(source.GetType(), message, exception);
}
public static void Error(Type source, object message,
                        Exception exception)
{
    getLogger(source).Error(message, exception);
}
public static void Fatal(object source, object message,
                        Exception exception)
{
    Fatal(source.GetType(), message, exception);
}
public static void Fatal(Type source, object message,
                        Exception exception)
{
    getLogger(source).Fatal(message, exception);
}
```

Now we get to the `initialize()` method. This code is responsible for making sure that the logger is ready to go. First, it looks in the root of the website for the `log4net.config` file. If it doesn't find it there, then it checks in the `bin` directory for the file. The method then spins up the `XmlConfiguration` class. Here is that code:

```
private static void initialize()
    {
        string logFilePath =
            Path.Combine(AppDomain.CurrentDomain.BaseDirectory,
                    "Log4Net.config");
        if (!File.Exists(logFilePath))
        {
            logFilePath =
            Path.Combine(AppDomain.CurrentDomain.BaseDirectory,
                    @"bin\Log4Net.config");
        }
        XmlConfigurator.ConfigureAndWatch(new
                                        FileInfo(logFilePath));
    }
```

The `initialize()` method is called by the `EnsureInitialized()` method.

```
public static void EnsureInitialized()
    {
        if (!_logInitialized)
        {
            initialize();
            _logInitialized = true;
        }
    }
```

The `EnsureInitialized()` method first checks to see if the log has already been initialized by checking the `_logInitialized` flag. If the log has not be initialized, it calls the `initialize()` method and sets the `_logInitialized` flag to true thereby making sure to `initialize()` the log only once for every application startup.

Let's add this to our newly created `Global.asax` file in the `Application_Start()` method so that each time the application starts up we run through this initialization process.

```
protected void Application_Start(object sender, EventArgs e)
    {
        Log.EnsureInitialized();
    }
```

This basically states that when the application is first loaded, we want to make sure that our logging feature is set up and initialized correctly. If not, the application itself should fail entirely!

Now that the `log4net` wrapper is complete, all we have to do is send something to the log, which requires us to write the following code:

```
Log.Debug(this,"oops, something failed!");
```

Let's not forget to go back to our `//TODO:` in the `Global.asax.cs` file. Add this line where our `//TODO:` currently is:

```
Log.Error(sender,"Error caught by the Global.asax: " + e.ToString());
```

That should take care of our error handling and logging needs!

Summary

In this chapter, we have gone over creating an enterprise framework to handle the essential needs of most web applications. We have discussed design patterns, best practices, and some tools to make things easier. We also worked through some code to create wrappers for the basic framework classes that we will be using in our application. We discussed how we will approach our data access using some new technologies and existing patterns. Finally, we wrapped things up with a discussion on error handling and logging. This chapter should provide you with a solid foundation on top of which we can now begin to build our application.

3
User Accounts

Without people, your community doesn't exist!

For any community site to be considered successful, it must first have a group of dedicated users. The larger the community's population, the more successful it is considered to be. It would make sense then that we create a way for users to come to our site, create an account, and become a part of our community.

In this chapter, we will discuss many of the common features that are related to user accounts. This will include handling registration, authentication, permissions, and password security. We will also go over some basic tools such as password reminders, account administration, and CAPTCHA. This chapter will provide the foundation for our users upon which we will be able to build all of our other features.

Problem

With most sites these days, regardless of their purpose, you need to know who your users are. You might need to know this so that you can restrict where the users go on your site. Or you might need this information so that you can provide a dynamic experience to your user. No matter what your reason is to know who your users are, the task of identifying and controlling them has a few basic requirements.

In order to get to know our users, we will need a way to register them on our site. This would give us a footprint for that user, which we can use each time the user returns. The registration process is fairly straightforward most of the time. We need to capture the data that we are interested in (such as username, password, email, and so on). We need to make sure that we store their password properly so that their identification is safe not only from the other users of the site but also from the administrators and staff of the site. Also, given the amount of fraud and spam on the Internet these days, we need to equip our site with some form of intelligence to guard it from automated registrations. In another attempt to protect the site, we need to make sure that our users are providing us with valid information. We can do this by validating the email provided by them to check if it is a functioning account under their control. As part of the registration process, we also need to inform the user about our current terms and conditions so that they know the rules of our site up-front.

 When I refer to automated registrations, I am really describing the act of a bot (or program) that is used to create accounts with the sole purpose of posting advertisements to public areas such as message boards, blogs, and so on.

Once a user has successfully registered, we will need to provide them with tools so that they can identify themselves to us each time they return. Rather than require the users to authenticate themselves to us at each and every page view, we should provide a centralized login screen. Upon successful authentication, we can track that user through the site. Knowing that users frequently forget the information that they provided us with, we will need to offer tools to remind the users how to get into our site with a password reminder feature. After the users have authenticated themselves, we would need to define where a user can go and what they can do on our site with some kind of permissions based system.

Once the users are registered and authenticated, we will need to provide them with a way to administer their account data. In addition to the users being able to administer their own data, the staff that runs the site will also need tools to manage all the users and their data. In addition to managing user data, administrators should be able to control the users' permissions and update the terms and conditions.

Design

In this section, we will discuss the various aspects that are required to implement our new features. Once we are finished, we should have a good idea of what will be required from each area.

Registration

Registration includes the task of acquiring user information, allowing them to pick a username, password, and email verification. In addition, we will require that our users agree to our terms and provide verification that they are human and not a bot by reading our CAPTCHA image. Once we have all this information, we will create the user account and assign appropriate permissions to the account.

Accounts

While ASP.NET provides various pre-built tools for handling your users via the membership controls, I have decided to explore a custom way to handle our users with regards to logging them in, encrypting their passwords, and so on. You may ask why I decided to go this route. It's simple really; everyone has contributed a number of webpages and blog posts to the Internet as well as written a number of books regarding this topic. It seemed reasonable to me then that perhaps people might like to see if they can do it on their own. It's not that difficult really! Also, with custom logic comes more control.

To begin with, we need a way to describe our accounts. From the database point of view, it will be fairly simple. All we need is an "Accounts" table where we can hold a username, password, and a few other bits of information. This will look something like this:

Accounts	
PK	**AccountID**
	FirstName
	LastName
	Email
	EmailVerified
	Zip
	Username
	Password
	BirthDate
	CreateDate
	LastUpdateDate
	Timestamp
Fk1	**TermID**
	AgreedToTermsDate

While most of this information looks fairly normal (**FirstName**, **LastName**, **Email**, and so on), there are a few columns that may not make sense at first. You will see that I have added a **Timestamp** field to just about every table. This is important for smoothening your interaction with LINQ. While it is not required by LINQ, I find that LINQ works much better with it in place, when tracking changes across disconnected data contexts.

Password strength

Password strength is not only an issue for the account's security but also for the site owner. The weaker your user's password is, the more likely that someone performs a brute force attack on your site. If an account with a high-level permission (such as Administrator) is compromised due to a weak password, you will look pretty silly! It doesn't make much sense on your part to create a secure site in every other way and then allow your users to bypass all your efforts!

Having said that, forcing your users to have a strong password can become an inconvenience to your users. Believe it or not, there are many users who would prefer to have a password of "password". While I am not for letting your users become lazy, you do need to be aware that there is a chance that you will lose signups due to this requirement. It is up to you to decide how important a secure site is!

Terms and conditions

While terms and conditions are not a necessary requirement for a good site, this section is the place to cover the concept! We will create a simple way to manage your terms and conditions. Terms and Conditions are a legal thing. The legal aspect is not my strong suite, but building a system to house them is! Knowing that terms and conditions can change over time, it is important that you track which version of terms and conditions your users last agreed to. It is also important that you track when they agreed to them.

The database will look something like this:

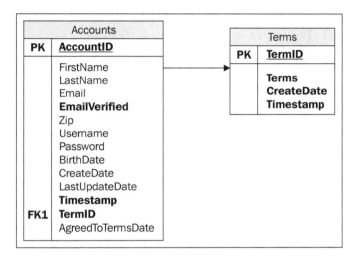

CAPTCHA

CAPTCHA, or **Completely Automated Public Turing test to tell Computers and Humans Apart**, is a form of challenge-response test to determine if the user of your site is a computer or human. Increasingly we are finding that people are writing bots to inject advertisements and other forms of SPAM into community sites to capitalize on the traffic of those sites. The bots sign up for an account, verify their emails, and start posting ads to our forums, blog comments, and so on. Hence we need a way to determine if the person registering for an account is a computer or a real human.

A CAPTCHA system does a fairly good job of determining this. These systems generate an image with an imbedded string that the registrant needs to read and copy into a text field. As there are currently no good algorithms for reading the obfuscated text out of the distorted image, we can feel pretty confident that the entity that is registering for an account is a human.

Here is an example of an image that will be generated by our system:

While our system could be very complicated, we will stick to a simple random number for our CAPTCHA string. Some systems use a table of words and present two words randomly paired. Either of these ways will work well enough, and random numbers are easily handled by .NET already.

Email confirmation and verification

There are several reasons to use email communications in our community. For example, this chapter will require registration confirmation and email validation.

When a user signs up at our site, we need to be able to let him/her know that the registration was completed successfully. This email will usually welcome a user to the site. It may also provide them with some frequently asked questions, a list of benefits received upon registration, and any other pertinent information that a user may need prior to using your site.

In addition to the registration receipt, we need a way to check whether the email address that the user has provided is a valid account (that it actually exists), and one to which the user actually has access. We will validate this by embedding a link in the email that the user will have to click. Once this link is clicked, we will assume that the email address is valid!

Security

Security is obviously one of the most important aspects of building a site. Not only should you be able to provide access to certain areas of your site to specific people, but more importantly, also be able to deny access to various people of your site. All sites have areas that need to be locked down. For example, one of the most important areas could be the administration section of your site, or paid areas of your site. Therefore, it is very important to make sure that you have some form of security.

Permissions

There are a number of ways to handle permissions. We could make something really complex by implementing a permission based system using permissions, roles, groups, and so on. We could even make it as complex as Microsoft's Active Directory system. However, I find that keeping something only as complex as your current requirement is the best thing to do. We can always add to the system as our needs increase.

Our permissions system will simply encompass a name (Administrator, Editor, Restricted, and so on). This permission name will then be statically mapped to each page (using the `Sitemap` file that .NET provides us!). As long as we keep our pages to serve a single functionality, this should always suit our needs. As this is a good design practice anyway, we shouldn't have any problems here. Of course, a user can have many permissions tied to their accounts so that they can traverse various sections of our site. Once this is in place, all we need to do is have a system that checks a user's permissions upon entering each page to ensure that they have the permission that the page requires.

The database structure for this will look like this:

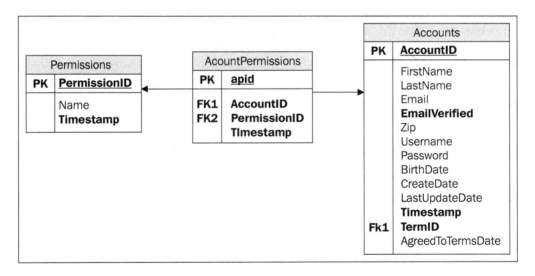

We will have a `Permissions` table, which relates to the `Accounts` table through the `AccountPermissions` table. This is a pretty straightforward and simple design.

Password encryption/decryption

While we could easily store a user's password in our database as plain text, it would not be a very responsible thing to do! Having a password stored in plain text not only leaves your user accounts open to someone who might hack into your system or database but also leaves them open to a possible attack from a disgruntled employee. These are good enough reasons to encrypt passwords prior to storing them in the database.

There is still an issue to discuss though. Do we have one way encryption, or do we also provide a way to decrypt our encrypted passwords? If we don't provide decryption facilities, then we won't be able to send reminder emails to our users who have their passwords. If we were creating a banking system, sending passwords via email would not be acceptable. However, as we are creating something slightly less confidential, the convenience for users to be able to retrieve their passwords without too much hassle is a great reason for decrypting the password and sending it to the user.

Logging in

Once a user has created an account, it is important for them to be able to re-identify themselves to us. For this reason, we will need to provide a way for them to do this. This will come in the form of a page that accepts a username and a password. Once they have authenticated themselves to us, we will need to make sure that they are still allowed to get into our site (if they are valid users).

Password reminder

A user will inevitably forget his/her password. As we require a strong password, and a fair number of users would rather not have a password at all, or would like to use the word "password' as their password, it is highly possible that they forget what they registered with. Not a problem! As we decided to use a two-way encryption, we will be able to decrypt their chosen password and email it to them. This way, our user will never be locked out for too long!

Manage account

In order to keep customer service calls to a minimum, we will need a way for our customers to manage their own accounts. Our customers will need a way to update most of the information they provide us. While we will not allow them to change their username, we will allow them to edit the rest. And when we allow them to change their email address we need to make sure that we force them to validate their new address.

Solution

Now, let's take a look at how we can go about implementing all the new features.

Implementing the database

We will start by implementing our database, and we will work our way up from there.

The Accounts table

The Accounts table will store all the base information for a user. Most of this is easy to figure out as they have indicative names (a sign of good design).

	Column Name	Data Type	Allow Nulls
🔑	AccountID	int	☐
	FirstName	varchar(30)	☑
	LastName	varchar(30)	☑
	Email	varchar(150)	☑
	EmailVerified	bit	☐
	Zip	varchar(15)	☑
	Username	varchar(30)	☑
	Password	varchar(50)	☑
	BirthDate	smalldatetime	☑
	CreateDate	smalldatetime	☑
	LastUpdateDate	smalldatetime	☑
	Timestamp	timestamp	☐
	TermID	int	☐
	AgreedToTermsDate	smalldatetime	☑

However, there are a few columns that may not be 100% clear at first glance. I will explain those here.

EmailVerified	This is a bit flag to let us know if a user's email address has been verified or not.
CreateDate	This is the date on which the record was created. It has a default value of GetDate().
LastUpdateDate	This is similar to the **CreateDate** with the exception that we should update it every time we update the record. This could be done with a trigger, or done programmatically.
Timestamp	As stated before, LINQ requires us to have a **Timestamp** so that we can easily use the Attach() method for persisting data to the database. There are other methods, but this requires the least amount of fuss.
AgreedToTermsDate	This is used to track the date on which the user agreed to the terms and conditions.

Here is the SQL that is needed to create this table. Be aware of the constraints that are added for the IDs and the various date fields.

The Permissions table

The Permissions table primarily acts as a lookup table for the various types of permissions. It holds the name of each permission with a unique ID.

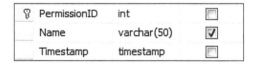

🔑	PermissionID	int	☐
	Name	varchar(50)	☑
	Timestamp	timestamp	☐

The AccountPermissions table

The AccountPermissions table allows us to create a many-to-many type of relationship between our Permissions and our Accounts. It simply holds a reference to a record at each end of the relationship.

🔑	apid	int	☐
	AccountID	int	☐
	PermissionID	int	☐
	Timestamp	timestamp	☐

The Terms table

The Terms table is a lookup for our terms and conditions. Also, it provides us with a historical view of the terms our customers have agreed to in the past.

🔑 TermID	int	☐
Terms	varchar(MAX)	☐
CreateDate	smalldatetime	☐
Timestamp	timestamp	☐

Creating the relationships

First, while you could work in a database without any enforced relationships, I wouldn't advise it. Secondly, you don't have all your database constraints clearly defined. So you might find yourself working with polluted data.

> Database constraints come in many forms. This could be a field-level constraint where you want to say that a date field must have today's date. Or it could come in the form that in order to have a Profile record you must have an already existing Account record. This is normally done with the use of a primary and a foreign key.

Also, LINQ prefers that the relationships are defined. In our architecture though, we won't be relying on LINQ in this manner. LINQ is not yet perfect with respect to this feature.

For this set of tables we have relationships between the following tables:

- Accounts and AccountPermissions
- Permissions and AccountPermissions
- Accounts and Terms

Implementing the data access layer

Now that we have our database defined for all the features required by this chapter, let's take a look at how we go about accessing that data! Keep in mind that this chapter will have a step that the other chapters won't have—we will actually be telling LINQ how to connect to our database so that it can generate Entity classes for us based on our table structure.

Setting up LINQ for the first time

In our `FisharooCore` project in Visual Studio, navigate to our `Core` directory. Once there, create a new folder and call it `Domain`. Let's add a file to the `Domain` folder by right-clicking on the folder and selecting **Add New Item**. The **Add New Item** window should pop up. Locate the `LINQ to SQL Classes` file and select it. Name this file `Fisharoo.dbml`. Click the **Add** button.

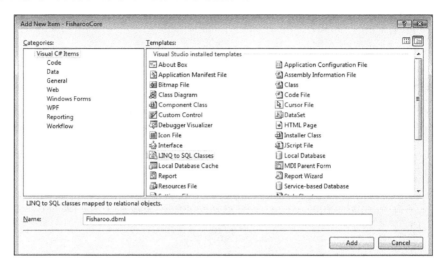

Once you have done this, you should have the **Object Relational Designer** open. This is a design surface that you can drag your database entities to. You can drag your stored procedures or tables to this surface from which LINQ will generate the appropriate classes.

In our case, we want LINQ to generate a class for each of the new tables that we have just created. To do that though, we first need to tell Visual Studio where our database is. Let's start this process by opening the **Server Explorer**. This is located in the **View** menu under **Server Explorer**. In this window, right-click **Data Connections** and select **Add Connection**. The **Choose Data Source** window should pop up.

Select **Microsoft SQL Server** and click **Continue**.

Depending on how your machine is set up, your configuration may be a bit different from mine. Make sure to enter the appropriate data into the **Server name** text field, which should be `localhost\sqlexpress` on a local development box provided that you used default settings when you installed SQL Express. Then choose the appropriate method for logging in to your server. I am using Windows authentication. You could also use an SQL Account. Finally, you can either enter the database name `Fisharoo` in the **Select** or enter a database name text field. You can also use the drop-down (which will use your previous entries to try and connect to your server to retrieve a list of databases).

Click the **Test Connection** button to see if your settings are acceptable. If your configuration is good, you should see an alert box pop up.

Click **OK** on the alert box and then once more to close this window.

You should now have your local `Fisharoo` database in your **Data Connections** window. You can open this database and expand the tables section to see our newly created tables.

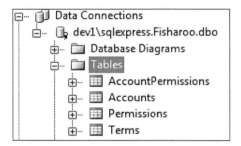

Once you have this connection configured and you can see your tables, you should be able to simply select all the tables and drag them on to your `Fisharoo.dbml` design surface.

Once you have dragged the tables to the design surface, you should see your four tables and the relationships between them defined.

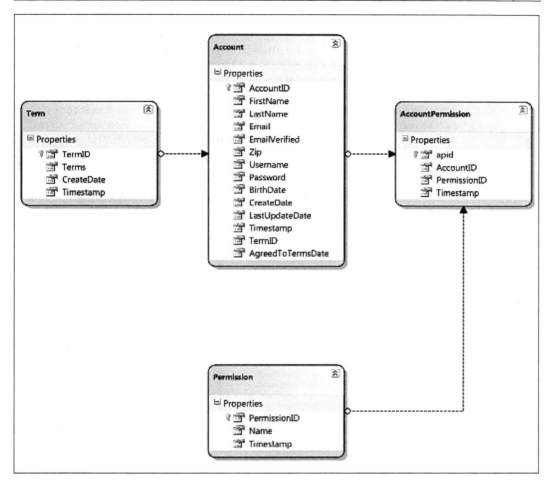

As we plan to manage the relationships between our data directly in our application rather than trying to get LINQ to do it, let's remove the relationships that have been defined for us. This will make working with LINQ a lot easier.

Why would you want to remove the relationships? Isn't LINQ supposed to handle the persistence of data based on the relationships defined here? Well, as it turns out LINQ to SQL is not 100% complete in the way that we would like it to be. Out of the box, it doesn't really work well in an n-Tier/disconnected architecture. But through several hacks here and there we are able to make it work the way we would like. I find that the easiest way to work with LINQ currently is to remove the need for LINQ to manage what is changed and where, as it pertains to objects and their children. We will touch upon this more as we start to use LINQ.

To remove the relationships, simply select all your relationships, right-click on one of them, and select **delete.** Your tables should now look something like this.

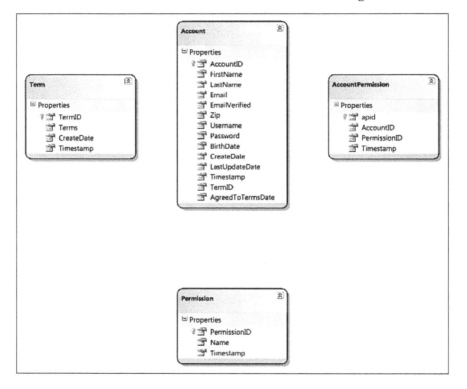

Once you save the `Fisharoo.dbml` file, Visual Studio will generate your Entity classes for you. You won't see these classes as files in your project. But we can see them in the class viewer. Open your class viewer by going into the **View** menu and selecting **Class View**. Then expand the `FisharooCore` project. Then open up the `Fisharoo.FisharooCore.Core.Domain` namespace. Here you should see a few things.

To start with, you should see a class for each table you put on the Fisharoo.dbml design surface. These are partial classes that you can extend by making an additional partial class of the same name in the same namespace (we will do this in a while). Do not edit the generated classes directly as your additions will get lost the next time you generate them!

The only other item here that you should see other than the classes that represent your tables is FisharooDataContext. This class handles all the LINQ facilities for your tables and classes. It tracks what changes you have made to your objects, what objects can be worked with, how you can query those objects, and so on. Any time we work with our LINQ classes or data, we will be going through the FisharooDataContext class.

A DataContext wrapper

Now that we know FisharooDataContext is used by LINQ extensively, let's look at how we can work with this DataContext wrapper in a way that fits our overall design by limiting the knowledge required to use the FisharooDataContext. We will create a Connection wrapper that will return the FisharooDataContext to the caller without requiring the caller to know what goes into its actual creation.

Start by creating a new class file in the FisharooCore project in the **Core | DataAccess | Impl** folder and call it Connection.cs. Here is how the class will look:

```
//FisharooCore/Core/DataAccess/Impl/Connection.cs
using System;
using System.Configuration;
using System.Linq;
using System.Data.Linq;
using System.Xml;
using Fisharoo.FisharooCore.Core.Domain;
using Fisharoo.FisharooCore.Properties;
using StructureMap;
namespace Fisharoo.FisharooCore.Core.DataAccess.Impl
{
    public class Connection
    {
        public FisharooDataContext GetContext()
        {
            string connString = "";
            //logic to retrieve your connectionString
            FisharooDataContext fdc = new
            FisharooDataContext(connString);
            return fdc;
        }
    }
}
```

This class is very simple. It is essentially just a wrapper to hide where you get your connection string as well as how the `FisharooDataContext` is spun up with the connection string that then returns a `FisharooDataContext` object. I did not show the logic for the retrieval of your connection string as that could be done any number of ways. You could use the `ConfigurationManager` class, store it in this file statically, and so on. The logic that I am using is more specific to my automated build process than it is directly to this project (you can see what I did though by opening this file in the code included with this book!).

Building repositories

Once we have a way to get to our DataContext, we can begin to look at how we work with the objects and data stored behind that DataContext. While we could just access our objects and the power of LINQ directly in our code, it would be very helpful down the road if we continued our layered approach by adding a Repository layer. A **Repository** provides us with a single place to go for our data (which doesn't necessarily have to be a database). Here are the layers that we currently have.

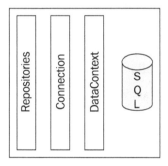

The repository layer is responsible for performing data access and data persistence. Each repository will be responsible for data related to a particular entity.

 Normally, when speaking in terms of Domain-driven Design, an Entity is considered to be something very important to the system. Unfortunately, as far as LINQ to SQL is concerned, every class that is derived from a table in your database is an Entity. While this is not true DDD, it is an unwritten law of LINQ currently! This does not mean that we are going to create a repository for something like the `AccountPermission` class that LINQ generated for us. That object is not a true entity in our design! It is simply a way for us to see related permissions for a given account.

So let's start creating our first repository by looking at the `AccountRepository`. Navigate to your FisharooCore project. Then open **Core | DataAccess | Impl** and create a new class there called `AccountRepository.cs`. Here is the code that goes into this file:

```
//FisharooCore/Core/DataAccess/Impl/AccountRepository.cs
using System;
using System.Collections.Generic;
using System.Linq;
using System.Text;
using StructureMap;
using Fisharoo.FisharooCore.Core.Domain;
namespace Fisharoo.FisharooCore.Core.DataAccess.Impl
{
    [Pluggable("Default")]
    public class AccountRepository : IAccountRepository
    {
        private Connection conn;
        public AccountRepository()
        {
            conn = new Connection();
        }
        public Account GetAccountByID(int AccountID)
        {
            Account account = null;
            using (FisharooDataContext dc = conn.GetContext())
            {
                account = (from a in dc.Accounts
                        where a.AccountID == AccountID
                        select a).First();
            }
            return account;
        }
        public Account GetAccountByEmail(string Email)
        {
            Account account = null;
            using (FisharooDataContext dc = conn.GetContext())
            {
                account = (from a in dc.Accounts
                    where a.Email == Email
                    select a).First();
            }
            return account;
        }
```

```
public Account GetAccountByUsername(string Username)
{
    Account account = null;
    using (FisharooDataContext dc = conn.GetContext())
    {
        account = (from a in dc.Accounts
            where a.Username == Username
            select a).First();
    }
    return account;
}
public void SaveAccount(Account account)
{
    using(FisharooDataContext dc = conn.GetContext())
    {
        if(account.AccountID > 0)
        {
            dc.Accounts.Attach(account, true);
        }
        else
        {
            dc.Accounts.InsertOnSubmit(account);
        }
        dc.SubmitChanges();
    }
}
public void DeleteAccount(Account account)
{
    using (FisharooDataContext dc = conn.GetContext())
    {
        dc.Accounts.DeleteOnSubmit(account);
        dc.SubmitChanges();
    }
}
    }
}
```

The first thing you will notice here is the references and attributes of StructureMap as well as the `IAccountRepository` interface. As we may want to swap this repository out during testing, these are important. Also, don't forget that the use of StructureMap allows us to easily ensure that coupling is reduced once we start using the Repository. This means that we could technically swap out the entire repository without requiring a change to our code.

For more on StructureMap, refer to the appendixes at the end of the book!

Then we have the declaration of the `Connection` class and a constructor for the `AccountRepository`, which initializes that `Connection` object for use throughout the rest of the `AccountRepository` class.

```
private Connection conn;
public AccountRepository()
{
    conn = new Connection();
}
```

Selecting accounts

Once our Connection object is ready for use, we can look at any of the methods from a generic point of view. Let's start with the first method defined in this class-`GetAccountByID`

```
public Account GetAccountByID(int AccountID)
{
    Account account = null;
    using (FisharooDataContext dc = conn.GetContext())
    {
        account = (from a in dc.Accounts
                    where a.AccountID == AccountID
                    select a).First();
    }
    return account;
}
```

This method is set up to retrieve an account with an ID. We first start out by defining our return variable (`account` in this case) outside the `using` statement.

```
Account account = null;
```

We then retrieve a `FisharooDataContext` inside a `using` statement (which ensures that the DataContext is disposed of once we are through with it).

```
using (FisharooDataContext dc = conn.GetContext())
{
...
}
```

We then move to the LINQ query itself inside the `using` statement.

```
account = (from a in dc.Accounts
                    where a.AccountID == AccountID
                    select a).First();
```

This looks very much like a standard SQL SELECT statement with a twist. We have to define the from statement first so that Intellisense can interrogate the collection we are working with. This allows us to work with our query as though we were working with any other collection of objects using dot syntax. We then define a where clause to restrict what is returned. Finally, we select the object that we want to use.

You will then notice that the entire query is wrapped in parenthesis. This allows me to chain methods on top of the result set. In this case, I am calling the First() function. This restricts my dataset to the first record returned by the query. As I know that there can only be one account associated with an ID, this should be acceptable here!

We could use var as the query result (inside the using statement) if we didn't know what to expect back from our query.

```
var account = [your LINQ query here];
```

var allows us to work with objects without having to know what they are and without having to declare them prior to using them. This is called an anonymous type. It is another widget used heavily by LINQ. The caveat to using an anonymous type is that it can only be used locally. So if your intent is to use the queried objects outside of the scope from which they were retrieved, you will have to do some form of casting, looping, or otherwise, to move them away from their anonymous status.

The GetAccountByEmail() and GetAccountByUsername() methods are almost identical in the way they function. So I am not going to explain them in detail.

Saving an account

Now that we have a way to select Account objects out of the database in various ways, we now need to consider how we are going to get the data into the database. This brings us to our SaveAccount() method.

```
public void SaveAccount(Account account)
{
    using(FisharooDataContext dc = conn.GetContext())
    {
        if(account.AccountID > 0)
        {
            dc.Accounts.Attach(account, true);
        }
        else
        {
            dc.Accounts.InsertOnSubmit(account);
```

```
        }
        dc.SubmitChanges();
    }
}
```

Now, we could have created two methods out of this one method. We could have had an `Insert()` and an `Update()` method. However, the only difference is in the one line of code between those two methods. So I chose to roll these two methods up and replace them with the `Save()` method.

As you will see, with all our Repository methods, we have wrapped the acquisition of the `FisharooDataContext` in a `using` statement. This makes our clean up automatic! (Technically speaking, that is!). Once we have our DataContext to work with, we interrogate the object that was passed in to see if it already has an `AccountID`. If the object does have an `AccountID`, it can't be new. If it doesn't have an `AccountID`, it must be new.

A new object is easy to work with. We simply call the `DataContext.CollectionOfObjects.InsertOnSubmit(ObjectToAdd)` method. In our case, it would be the `dc.Accounts.InsertOnSubmit(account)` statement. Then you will see a call to `dc.SubmitChanges()`. This tells the DataContext that it needs to persist all the changed data into the database — in our case it needs to save that new Account record.

Our code makes updating data look almost as easy as inserting new data. However, know that this is a simple example of updating data. Also know that this is only as simple as it is because we have removed some of the relationships from the DataContext! As far as LINQ is concerned, we are not supposed to attach old objects to a new DataContext. While this can be achieved, you have to remove all the child objects of the object you want to attach, attach the parent to the DataContext, then re-attach the children to the parent, and then call `SubmitChanges()`. And even then the persistence may not always work the way you would want it to!

So, our update logic seems very easy because we have implicitly made it so by removing the relationships in our DataContext. We are indirectly telling LINQ to SQL that it doesn't need to worry about complex relationships. It only needs to worry about locating the one object that is already in the DataContext and updating it with our new disconnected object.

One of the three overrides for the `Attach()` method allows us to attach our disconnected `Account` object to the Accounts collection in the DataContext and force it to update the object already in the collection with the new object.

```
▲3 of 3▼  void Table<Account>.Attach (Account entity, bool asModified)
asModified: True to attach the entity as modified.
```

This is achieved by telling the DataContext that the object that is being passed in is the modified version of the current original.

Again, after the DataContext knows what you want it to do with the data, we should call `dc.SubmitChanges();`.

Deleting an account

Now that we have a way to add accounts into the system it only makes sense that we would also want to know a way to delete an account, which is achieved with this method:

```
public void DeleteAccount(Account account)
    {
        using (FisharooDataContext dc = conn.GetContext())
        {
            dc.Accounts.DeleteOnSubmit(account);
            dc.SubmitChanges();
        }
    }
```

I think deleting an object from the DataContext is one of the easiest things to do! Simply locate the collection that you want the object to delete from, pass the object to be deleted to the `DeleteOnSubmit()` method, and then call `dc.SubmitChanges()`. It doesn't get any easier than that!

Adding permissions to an account

Adding a Permission? Shouldn't this go in a `Permission` repository or something? No, not really. In reality, we are not really adding a permission. We are creating a record in the non-entity table, `AccountPermissions`, to link a Permission to an Account. Recall that I had stated that we will not create non-entity repositories so that we can at least try and stick to DDD. So this leaves us to add permissions to accounts in the `Permissions` repository or in the `Accounts` repository. Adding permissions to the Accounts repository makes more sense to me!

The code is also pretty simple (you will find that this is a recurring statement!):

```
public void AddPermission(Account account, Permission permission)
    {
        using(FisharooDataContext dc = conn.GetContext())
        {
            AccountPermission ap = new AccountPermission();
            ap.AccountID = account.AccountID;
            ap.PermissionID = permission.PermissionID;
            dc.AccountPermissions.InsertOnSubmit(ap);
```

```
                    dc.SubmitChanges();
                }
            }
```

This method is going to simply link an `Account` object to a `Permission` object. To do this, it expects an `Account` and `Permission` object to be passed in. It then creates a new `AccountPermission` object and assigns the `AccountID` and `PermissionID` properties based on the objects that were passed in. This new `AccountPermission` object is then inserted into the `AccountPermissions` collection in the DataContext. Finally, the `SubmitChanges()` method is called.

If you think back to our DDD discussions (covered in the Appendices), Entity objects are important enough to recreate and track with a unique ID. Value objects are less important and can't (or shouldn't) exist without a parent Entity object. In this case, the value object, `AccountPermission`, can exist with Permission or an Account as its parent. While this is a true statement, the overall design can be simplified by stating that Accounts can have `AccountPermissions` and that Permissions can't. This makes keeping track of the objects easier when they only have one entry point into the world.

Now, having said that, I can think of a scenario where we might need to be able to say: "For this permission, show me all the related accounts." This might be useful in an Administration console. We will see that when we get there. We could just as easily run a query that says: "Show me all the accounts with this permission."

The other repositories

Now that we have had a fairly detailed look at the `AccountRepository`, I am going to quickly cover the remaining repositories. I will discuss some interesting points here and there, but for the most part, once you have seen one repository, you have seen them all!

Permissions repository

```
//FisharooCore/Core/DataAccess/Impl/PermissionRepository.cs
using System;
using System.Collections.Generic;
using System.Linq;
using System.Text;
using Fisharoo.FisharooCore.Core.Domain;
using StructureMap;
namespace Fisharoo.FisharooCore.Core.DataAccess.Impl
{
    [Pluggable("Default")]
    public class PermissionRepository : IPermissionRepository
```

```
{
    private Connection conn;
    public PermissionRepository()
    {
        conn = new Connection();
    }
    public List<Permission> GetPermissionsByAccountID(Int32
                                                AccountID)
    {
        List<Permission> returnPermissions = new
        List<Permission>();
        using (FisharooDataContext dc = conn.GetContext())
        {
            var permissions =    from p in dc.Permissions
                                 join ap in
                                  dc.AccountPermissions on
                                     p.PermissionID equals
                                     ap.PermissionID
                                 join a in dc.Accounts on
                                     ap.AccountID equals
                                     a.AccountID
                                 where a.AccountID == 1
                                 select p;
            foreach (Permission permission in permissions)
            {
                returnPermissions.Add(permission);
            }
        }
        return returnPermissions;
    }
    public List<Permission> GetPermissionByName(string Name)
    {
        List<Permission> returnPermissions = new
                                        List<Permission>();
        using (FisharooDataContext dc = conn.GetContext())
        {
            var permissions = from p in dc.Permissions
                               where p.Name == Name
                               select p;
            foreach (Permission permission in permissions)
            {
                returnPermissions.Add(permission);
            }
        }
```

```
                return returnPermissions;
        }
        public List<Permission> GetPermissionByID(Int32 PermissionID)
        {
            List<Permission> returnPermissions = new
                                            List<Permission>();
            using(FisharooDataContext dc = conn.GetContext())
            {
                var permissions = from p in dc.Permissions
                            where p.PermissionID == PermissionID
                            select p;
                foreach (Permission permission in permissions)
                {
                    returnPermissions.Add(permission);
                }
            }
            return returnPermissions;
        }
        public void SavePermission(Permission permission)
        {
            using(FisharooDataContext dc = conn.GetContext())
            {
                if(permission.PermissionID > 0)
                {
                    dc.Permissions.Attach(permission,true);
                }
                else
                {
                    dc.Permissions.InsertOnSubmit(permission);
                }
                dc.SubmitChanges();
            }
        }
        public void DeletePermission(Permission permission)
        {
            using(FisharooDataContext dc = conn.GetContext())
            {
                dc.Permissions.DeleteOnSubmit(permission);
                dc.SubmitChanges();
            }
        }
    }
}
```

In the `GetPermissionsByAccountID()` method of this repository, you will see an interesting LINQ query.

```
var permissions = from p in dc.Permissions
    join ap in dc.AccountPermissions on
        p.PermissionID equals ap.PermissionID
    join a in dc.Accounts on
        ap.AccountID equals a.AccountID
    where a.AccountID == 1
    select p;
```

This query introduces the concept of joining one set of objects with another set of objects exactly like you would do in SQL. In this case, we need to create a variable to reference each collection of objects.

 For all you SQL people out there, think of this as a table alias.

Examples of this would be `p in dc.Permissions`, `ap in dc.AccountPermissions`, and `a in dc.Accounts`. Once you have your collections to work with, you can then define the join parameters with `on p.PermissionID equals ap.PermissionID`. This query basically says, "Give me all the `Permissions` related to these `AccountPermissions`, related to these `Accounts`, where the `AccountID` equals the passed in `AccountID`."

Terms repository

```
//FisharooCore/Core/DataAccess/Impl/TermRepository.cs
using System;
using System.Collections.Generic;
using System.Linq;
using System.Text;
using Fisharoo.FisharooCore.Core.Domain;
using StructureMap;
namespace Fisharoo.FisharooCore.Core.DataAccess.Impl
{
    [Pluggable("Default")]
    public class TermRepository : ITermRepository
    {
        private Connection conn;
        public TermRepository()
        {
            conn = new Connection();
        }
```

```
public Term GetCurrentTerm()
{
    Term returnTerm = null;
    using (FisharooDataContext dc = conn.GetContext())
    {
        var terms = (from t in dc.Terms
                     orderby t.CreateDate descending
                     select t).Take(1);
        foreach (Term term in terms)
        {
            returnTerm = term;
        }
    }
    return returnTerm;
}
public void SaveTerm(Term term)
{
    using (FisharooDataContext dc = conn.GetContext())
    {
        if (term.TermID > 0)
        {
            dc.Terms.Attach(term);
        }
        else
        {
            dc.Terms.InsertOnSubmit(term);
        }
        dc.SubmitChanges();
    }
}
public void DeleteTerm(Term term)
{
    using(FisharooDataContext dc = conn.GetContext())
    {
        dc.Terms.DeleteOnSubmit(term);
        dc.SubmitChanges();
    }
}
    }
}
```

In the `GetCurrentTerm()` method of the `TermRepository()`, there is a new LINQ query statement item added.

```
var terms = (from t in dc.Terms
               orderby t.CreateDate descending
               select t).Take(1);
```

Here, you will see that we have an `orderby` clause introduced as well as a `descending` keyword. This allows us to take all the terms ever created and put the most recent ones at the top of the stack. We then introduce `Take()`, a new LINQ method. The `Take()` method takes a number in and essentially acts like the `TOP` statement in SQL. If you were to look at the SQL generated from this statement, you would actually see a `TOP` statement created.

Implementing the services/application layer

Some call this layer the **Services** layer. Others call it the "application" layer. They are one and the same. This layer should be relatively thin and lightweight. It is not supposed to hold any business logic or data access logic. It is more of a working layer that is responsible for keeping the business layer easier and cleaner to use. Often, it will combine several items from the business layer and several methods from the data layer to present an easy-to-use interface for a complex task.

Here is what our current layers look like with the addition of the **Services** layer:

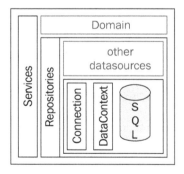

An example of this would be our `AccountService`. The `AccountService` provides a few simple methods that utilize several of our more infrastructure-oriented classes. Here is the code:

```
//FisharooCore/Core/Impl/AccountService.cs
using System;
using System.Collections.Generic;
using System.Linq;
```

```
using System.Text;
using Fisharoo.FisharooCore.Core.DataAccess;
using Fisharoo.FisharooCore.Core.Domain;
using StructureMap;
namespace Fisharoo.FisharooCore.Core.Impl
{
    [Pluggable("Default")]
    public class AccountService : IAccountService
    {
        private IAccountRepository _accountRepository;
        private IPermissionRepository _permissionRepository;
        private IUserSession _userSession;
        private IRedirector _redirector;
        private IEmail _email;
        public AccountService()
        {
            _accountRepository =
                ObjectFactory.GetInstance<IAccountRepository>();
            _permissionRepository =
                ObjectFactory.GetInstance<IPermissionRepository>();
            _userSession = ObjectFactory.GetInstance<IUserSession>();
            _redirector = ObjectFactory.GetInstance<IRedirector>();
            _email = ObjectFactory.GetInstance<IEmail>();
        }
        public bool UsernameInUse(string Username)
        {
            Account account =
             _accountRepository.GetAccountByUsername(Username);
            if(account != null)
                return true;
            return false;
        }
        public bool EmailInUse(string Email)
        {
            Account account =
             _accountRepository.GetAccountByEmail(Email);
            if (account != null)
                return true;
            return false;
        }
        public void Logout()
        {
            _userSession.LoggedIn = false;
            _userSession.CurrentUser = null;
            _userSession.Username = "";
            _redirector.GoToAccountLoginPage();
        }
```

```
public string Login(string Username, string Password)
{
    Password = Password.Encrypt(Username);
    Account account =
        _accountRepository.GetAccountByUsername(Username);

    //if there is only one account returned - good
    if(account != null)
    {
        //password matches
        if(account.Password == Password)
        {
            if (account.EmailVerified)
            {
                _userSession.LoggedIn = true;
                _userSession.Username = Username;
                _userSession.CurrentUser =
                    GetAccountByID(account.AccountID);
                _redirector.GoToHomePage();
            }
            else
            {
                _email.SendEmailAddressVerificationEmail(
                        account.Username, account.Email);
                return @"The login information you provided
                    was correct
                        but your email address has not yet
                        been verified.
                        We just sent another email
                            verification email to you.
                        Please follow the instructions in
                            that email.";
            }
        }
        else
        {
            return "We were unable to log you in with that
                        information!";
        }
    }
    return "We were unable to log you in with that
                        information!";
}
public Account GetAccountByID(Int32 AccountID)
```

```
    {
        Account account =
            _accountRepository.GetAccountByID(AccountID);
        List<Permission> permissions =
    _permissionRepository.GetPermissionsByAccountID(AccountID);
        foreach (Permission permission in permissions)
        {
            account.AddPermission(permission);
        }
        return account;
    }
    }
}
```

An example of this simplification comes in the form of the Login() method.

```
public string Login(string Username, string Password)
{
    Password = Password.Encrypt(Username);
    List<Account> accounts =
        _accountRepository.GetAccountByUsername(Username);

    //if there is only one account returned - good
    if(accounts.Count == 1)
    {
        //password matches
        if(accounts[0].Password == Password)
        {
            if (accounts[0].EmailVerified)
            {
                _userSession.LoggedIn = true;
                _userSession.Username = Username;
                _userSession.CurrentUser =
                    GetAccountByID(accounts[0].AccountID);
                _redirector.GoToHomePage();
            }
            else
            {
                _email.SendEmailAddressVerificationEmail(
                  accounts[0].Username,accounts[0].Email);
                return @"The login information you provided
                            was correct
                    but your email address has not yet
                            been verified.
                    We just sent another email
```

```
                                  verification email to you.
                        Please follow the instructions in
                                 that email.";
                }
        }
        else
        {
            return "We were unable to log you in with that
                            information!";
        }
    }
    else if(accounts.Count > 1)
    {
        throw new Exception("Account data corruption has
                            occured. There is more than one
                            account with the username: " +
                            Username + ".");
    }
    return "We were unable to log you in with that
                        information!";
}
```

It expects a username and a password. From there it fetches the users' accounts by their usernames. It makes sure that the password that was provided matches what we have on the file for that account. It then makes sure that the user has verified their email address, and finally logs the user in.

This method can be extended further to use additional repositories or other services for future needs. The signature of the method could still be just as simple without muddying up the design.

Extension methods

As you probably noticed in the Login() method just seen, we had our first introduction to the Cryptography class. However, this method is called directly from a string. How does that work?

 The subject of Cryptography is an extensive one, and is beyond the scope of this book. However, the Cryptography class that is included in this project is heavily commented if you want to understand System. Security.Cryptography.Rijndael a bit better! You can find that class here: FisharooCore | Core | Impl | Cryptography.

To start let's look at how we were able to call `Encrypt()` from a `string` variable. To achieve this is actually very simple. Although the `string` class is sealed, meaning that we can't technically extend it in any way that we are used too, we can use a new feature of .NET called "extension methods".

```
//FisharooCore/Core/Impl/Extensions.cs
using System;
using System.Collections.Generic;
using System.Linq;
using System.Text;
namespace Fisharoo.FisharooCore.Core.Impl
{
    public static class Extensions
    {
        public static string Encrypt(this string s, string key)
        {
            return Cryptography.Encrypt(s, key);
        }
        public static string Decrypt(this string s, string key)
        {
            return Cryptography.Decrypt(s, key);
        }
    }
}
```

An extension method allows us to extend a class without affecting the way that it would normally work. The way to do this is by defining a static method in a static class. The thing to notice is that the first parameter of the method starts with the target type, a `string` in this case. Therefore we have effectively defined an `Encrypt()` and `Decrypt()` method for the `string` class. Note that the only difference between this method and one you would normally write is the `this` reference preceding the first parameter.

```
public static string Encrypt(this string s, string key)
```

It's that simple!

Implementing the business/domain layer

As we are using the LINQ to SQL facilities that are now part of the .NET framework, our business layer has been greatly simplified for us. I can recall in previous applications different sorts of data access layers that required me to spend a great deal of time writing SQL in the database, connection logic, providers, and hydration and persistence logic for my objects. In addition to all that, I would still need to define my business objects. Of those objects, 95% of the logic was simply to shuttle data around in a more manageable manner.

Here is what our layers look like now:

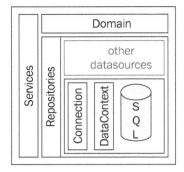

With LINQ to SQL so much of this has gone away! We now have fully generated classes that take care of shuttling our data around. But what happens if we need custom logic?

While we could simply add logic to the generated classes, this would not be the best route. The next time we make a change we will have to regenerate our classes. This would resort in the loss of all that custom functionality.

Fortunately for us the classes that are generated are partial classes. This means that we can make a new `partial` class file of the same name within the same namespace and extend our generated classes.

Here is our custom `Account` object, which extends the generated `Account` object.

```
//FisharooCore/Core/Domain/Account.cs
using System;
using System.Collections.Generic;
using System.Linq;
using System.Text;
using Fisharoo.FisharooCore.Core.Domain;
using Fisharoo.FisharooCore.Core.Impl;
namespace Fisharoo.FisharooCore.Core.Domain
{
    public partial class Account
    {
        private List<Permission> _permissions = new
                                        List<Permission>();
        public List<Permission> Permissions
        {
            get{ return _permissions; }
        }
        public void AddPermission(Permission permission)
```

```
    {
        _permissions.Add(permission);
    }
    public bool HasPermission(string Name)
    {
        foreach (Permission p in _permissions)
        {
            if (p.Name == Name)
                return true;
        }
        return false;
    }
  }
}
```

With this new `partial` class, we can now extend our existing generated `Account` class. I have added a few important features to the `Account` class. We now have methods for adding and checking permissions. We also have a property that returns a list of permissions.

This can easily be done for any partial class in our project!

Implementing the presentation layer

Most of the presentation layer is made up of very standard ASP.NET tools and principles. As this book isn't so much about how a button or label works, I will be focusing more on the nonstandard features of our site. We will look at building a scalable UI using the MVP pattern.

Model view presenter

To start with, let's discuss the overall architecture of our presentation layer. We have decided to use the MVP pattern. Information about this pattern can also be found under the separated names of Supervising Controller and Passive View.

The basic reason for this pattern is so that at the end of the day you can wrap a large percentage of your front end code with testing. It also allows you to easily swap out your UI without having to rewrite every aspect of the front end of your application. You will also find that this pattern significantly breaks up and compartmentalizes your logic, which makes working on the front end of your application more straightforward.

The MVP pattern in the ASP.NET world basically requires you to have four files (five if you are working in a web application project).

- The design or .aspx file
- Your code behind or .cs file
- An interface that defines the code behind (another .cs file)
- And a class (.cs) file called the presenter, which actually controls everything

Of course, the model portion of this pattern is generally referring to your domain objects that will constitute many other files!

The design file of course holds all your display logic such as a repeater, buttons, labels, and so on. It shouldn't have any server-side logic.

The code behind (or the view) is responsible for handling events from the page such as button clicks. It is also allowed to take care of simple display issues. The view also provides methods to the presenter to toggle the state of the various display items. When the page first starts up (generally on page load), the view initializes the presenter and passes a reference to itself, to the presenter. For every event that is triggered on the page, the view is simply responsible for informing the presenter so that it can decide what to do with the event.

The **View** passes a reference of itself to the presenter by way of the interface that defines the view. Using the interface for the type that the presenter expects, provides us with a decoupled structure. This is what allows us to easily swap out our UI if we so choose. As long as the UI implements the interface appropriately it can use the presenter.

The presenter is the acting controller in this scenario. Once it is spun up and has a reference to the code behind, it can actively decide how to handle events in the front end. The presenter is also the only part of our front end that is capable of interacting with our domain logic (or model).

Here is how MVP fits into our layers' representation:

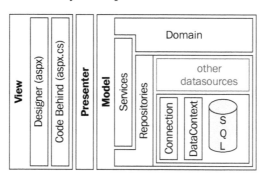

In the following sections, we will discuss the login process. This is more to illustrate how the MVP pattern works and less about ASP.NET, as the code itself is very simple.

View

We will start with the front end ASP.NET code. It basically defines a username and password text box and a button to click for login. It also has two buttons for simple navigational tasks—one to go to the recover password page and another to take you to the registration page.

```
//FisharooWeb/Account/Login.aspx
<%@ Page Language="C#" MasterPageFile="~/SiteMaster.Master"
AutoEventWireup="true" CodeBehind="Login.aspx.cs" Inherits="Fisharoo.
FisharooWeb.Account.Login" %>
<asp:Content ContentPlaceHolderID="Content" runat="server">
<div class="divContainer">
    <div class="divContainerRow">
        <div class="divContainerTitle">
            Please log in.
        </div>
    </div>
    <div class="divContainerRow">
        <div class="divContainerCellHeader">
            Username:
        </div>
        <div class="divContainerCell">
            <asp:TextBox ID="txtUsername"
                    runat="server"></asp:TextBox>
        </div>
    </div>
    <div class="divContainerRow">
        <div class="divContainerCellHeader">
            Password:
        </div>
        <div class="divContainerCell">
            <asp:TextBox ID="txtPassword" runat="server"
                    TextMode="Password"></asp:TextBox>
        </div>
    </div>
    <div class="divContainerRow">
        <div class="divContainerCellHeader">
             
        </div>
        <div class="divContainerCell">
```

```
            <asp:Button ID="btnLogin" OnClick="btnLogin_Click"
                    runat="server" Text="Log In" /><br />
            <asp:Label runat="server" ID="lblMessage"
                    ForeColor="Red"></asp:Label>
        </div>
    </div>
    <div class="divContainerRow">
        <div class="divContainerCellHeader">
             <br />
             
        </div>
        <div class="divContainerCell">
            <asp:LinkButton ID="lbRecoverPassword" runat="server"
                        Text="Forgot Password?" OnClick="lbRecoverPa
                            ssword_Click"></asp:LinkButton><br />
            <asp:LinkButton ID="lbRegister" runat="server"
                        Text="Register" OnClick="lbRegister_Click">
                                        </asp:LinkButton>
        </div>
    </div>
</div>
</asp:Content>
```

Normally I would not show you the interfaces in our application as they are very simple. But as the interface is very important to this pattern, we will make an exception this time! This interface is what the code behind has to conform to in order to be able to interact with the presenter.

```
//FisharooWeb/Account/Interface
namespace Fisharoo.FisharooWeb.Account.Interface
{
    public interface ILogin
    {
        void DisplayMessage(string Message);
    }
}
```

Here is the code behind for our application. Notice that it only handles display logic. It does not actually make any decisions. It defers all decision making to the presenter.

```
//FisharooWeb/Account/Login.aspx.cs
using System;
using System.Collections;
using System.Configuration;
using System.Data;
```

```csharp
using System.Linq;
using System.Web;
using System.Web.Security;
using System.Web.UI;
using System.Web.UI.HtmlControls;
using System.Web.UI.WebControls;
using System.Web.UI.WebControls.WebParts;
using System.Xml.Linq;
using Fisharoo.FisharooWeb.Account.Interface;
using Fisharoo.FisharooWeb.Account.Presenter;
namespace Fisharoo.FisharooWeb.Account
{
    public partial class Login : System.Web.UI.Page, ILogin
    {
        private LoginPresenter _presenter;
        protected void Page_Load(object sender, EventArgs e)
        {
            _presenter = new LoginPresenter();
            _presenter.Init(this);
        }
        protected void btnLogin_Click(object sender, EventArgs e)
        {
            _presenter.Login(txtUsername.Text, txtPassword.Text);
        }
        protected void lbRecoverPassword_Click(object sender,
                                               EventArgs e)
        {
            _presenter.GoToRecoverPassword();
        }
        protected void lbRegister_Click(object sender, EventArgs e)
        {
            _presenter.GoToRegister();
        }
        public void DisplayMessage(string Message)
        {
            lblMessage.Text = Message;
        }
    }
}
```

You will notice above that in the Page_Load() we initialize our presenter. Once we have the presenter spun up, we immediately pass a reference of the code behind to the presenter in the _presenter.Init(this) method call. You should also notice that there is a button-click event captured by the code behind. But all that this method does is notify the presenter that it needs to perform the Login() method and passes up the raw username and password values. Lastly, notice that the code behind does implement the interface with its DisplayMessage() method. As the presenter has access to the code behind class, it will be able to utilize any public method as it needs to.

Presenter

Here is the presenter code:

```
//FisharooWeb/Account/Presenter/LoginPresenter.cs
using System;
using System.Data;
using System.Configuration;
using System.Linq;
using System.Web;
using System.Web.Security;
using System.Web.UI;
using System.Web.UI.HtmlControls;
using System.Web.UI.WebControls;
using System.Web.UI.WebControls.WebParts;
using System.Xml.Linq;
using Fisharoo.FisharooCore.Core;
using Fisharoo.FisharooCore.Core.Impl;
using Fisharoo.FisharooWeb.Account.Interface;
using StructureMap;
namespace Fisharoo.FisharooWeb.Account.Presenter
{
    public class LoginPresenter
    {
        private ILogin _view;
        private IAccountService _accountService;
        private IRedirector _redirector;
        public void Init(ILogin view)
        {
            _view = view;
            _accountService =
                ObjectFactory.GetInstance<IAccountService>();
            _redirector = ObjectFactory.GetInstance<IRedirector>();
        }
        public void Login(string username, string password)
```

```
            {
                string message = _accountService.Login(username,
                                                        password);
                _view.DisplayMessage(message);
            }
            public void GoToRegister()
            {
                _redirector.GoToAccountRegisterPage();
            }
            public void GoToRecoverPassword()
            {
                _redirector.GoToAccountRecoverPasswordPage();
            }
        }
    }
```

Model

Note that the presenter doesn't take any time to connect to the domain layer or the model side of the house. In the `Init()` method it immediately sets up the objects that it needs to get its job done. If a page needs to display data on its initial load, this is where it would happen. Beyond the initialization of the presenter, you will notice that the presenter has three other methods: `Login()`, `GoToRegister()`, and `GoToRecoverPassword()`.

The `Login()` method handles the button-click event that the **View** passes to it. Note that even here we do not have a lot of logic to manage. The presenter is quick to pass off the responsibility of logging the user in to the `AccountService` object that we discussed earlier. It simply expects a friendly message back from the `AccountService` to describe how the login process went. As we know, if it gets a message back, it means that the login failed, otherwise the `AccountService` will redirect the user appropriately. Once the login is complete, the presenter uses the view's `DisplayMessage()` method to inform the user of its status.

The `GoToRegister()` and `GoToRecoverPassword()` methods simply utilize the Redirector object to send the user to the appropriate page on the site. While this may seem a bit extreme, remember that it follows the good design principles. If you follow this across your entire site, you will reap the following three benefits:

1. You can easily swap out the UI and expect the same results with minimum efforts.

2. As your redirection code is in one place, when several links use the same method to redirect to a location, you can change this redirection in that place and impact all the links across your site.

3. This aids the testability of your site!

Here are the added Redirector methods:

```
//FisharooCore/Core/Impl/Redirector.cs
. . .
        public void GoToAccountRegisterPage()
        {
            Redirect("~/Account/Register.aspx");
        }
. . .
        public void GoToAccountRecoverPasswordPage()
        {
            Redirect("~/Account/RecoverPassword.aspx");
        }
. . .
```

 I hope you are noticing that as each file is responsible for a very specific set of tasks, each file is also short and sweet. While this is a complex way of thinking about things, it is very nice to work with!

Registration page

I will admit that using the standard .NET controls to create an account is so much easier! Having said that, it was quite a bit of fun creating the registration page for this site. I ended up using a wizard control to display the various steps of the registration process. Our steps are as follows:

1   I always start by grabbing the email, username, and password of the users. There is validation in place for all of these. We want to validate their email addresses for their authenticity. We also want to make sure that their username conforms to some length rules. Then we allow them to enter their password and require them to re-enter their password to verify that what they have entered is what they meant to enter. And of course, all these fields are required!

```
//FisharooWeb/Account/Register.aspx
<asp:WizardStep Title="Create Account" runat="server" ID=
                                        "wsUsernameAndPassword">
    <div class="divContainerRow">
        <div class="divContainerTitle">
            Creating an account with us is a quick process!  Let's
                    get started by creating your login.
        </div>
    </div>
    <div class="divContainerRow">
        <div class="divContainerCell divContainerCellHeader">
```

```
            Email:
        </div>
        <div class="divContainerCell">
            <asp:TextBox ID="txtEmail" runat="server"></asp:TextBox>
            <asp:RequiredFieldValidator
                ID="valRequiredEmail"
                runat="server"
                ForeColor="Red"
                ControlToValidate="txtEmail"
                ErrorMessage="Please provide your email
                    address!">*</asp:RequiredFieldValidator>
            <asp:RegularExpressionValidator
                ID="RegularExpressionValidator2"
                runat="server"
                ForeColor="Red"
                ErrorMessage="This does not appear to be a valid
                            email address!"
                ControlToValidate="txtEmail"
                ValidationExpression="\w+([-+.]\w+)*@\w+([-
                                ]\w+)*\.\w+([-.]\w+)*">
                                *</asp:RegularExpressionValidator>
        </div>
    </div>
    <div class="divContainerRow">
        <div class="divContainerCell divContainerCellHeader">
            Username:
        </div>
        <div class="divContainerCell">
            <asp:TextBox ID="txtUsername"
                        runat="server"></asp:TextBox>
            <asp:RequiredFieldValidator
                ID="valRequiredUsername"
                runat="server"
                ForeColor="Red"
                ControlToValidate="txtUsername"
                ErrorMessage="Please provide a
                            username!">*</asp:RequiredFieldValidator>
            <asp:RegularExpressionValidator
                ID="valUsernameValidation"
                runat="server"
                ForeColor="Red"
                ErrorMessage="Your username must be at least 6
                            letters or numbers and no more than 30."
                ControlToValidate="txtUsername"
                ValidationExpression="^[a-zA-Z0-
```

```
                            9.]{6,30}">*</asp:RegularExpressionValidator>
        </div>
    </div>
    <div class="divContainerRow">
        <div class="divContainerCell divContainerCellHeader">
            Password:
        </div>
        <div class="divContainerCell">
            <asp:TextBox ID="txtPassword" TextMode="Password"
                    runat="server"></asp:TextBox>
            <asp:RegularExpressionValidator
                ID="RegularExpressionValidator1"
                runat="server"
                ForeColor="Red"
                ControlToValidate="txtPassword"
                ValidationExpression="(?=^.{5,}$)(?=.*\d)(?=.*\
                                        W+)(?![.\n]).*$"
                Display="Dynamic"
                ErrorMessage="Your password must be at least 8
                            characters long and contain at
                least one upper case letter, one lower case letter,
                one number, and one special character">*</asp:
                                RegularExpressionValidator>
        </div>
    </div>
    <div class="divContainerRow">
        <div class="divContainerCell divContainerCellHeader">
            Verify Password:
        </div>
        <div class="divContainerCell">
            <asp:TextBox ID="txtVerifyPassword" TextMode="Password"
                    runat="server"></asp:TextBox>
            <asp:CompareValidator
                ID="valComparePasswords"
                runat="server"
                ForeColor="Red"
                ControlToValidate="txtPassword"
                ControlToCompare="txtVerifyPassword"
                ErrorMessage="The passwords you entered do no match!"
                Display="Dynamic">*</asp:CompareValidator>
        </div>
    </div>
</asp:WizardStep>
```

2. The next step is to try and get some descriptive information about the users such as their first names and last names. When building a community site of any type, it is usually important that you also harvest their birthday and zip code or postal code. This lets you know what is appropriate for them and where in the world they are. There is validation in place to make sure that the date of birth they enter is a valid date and that the zip code is a valid format (for US). All these fields are also required fields.

```
//FisharooWeb/Account/Register.aspx
<asp:WizardStep Title="About You" runat="server" ID="wsWhoYouAre">
    <div class="divContainerRow">
        <div class="divContainerTitle">
            Tell us a little bit about yourself!
        </div>
    </div>
    <div class="divContainerRow">
        <div class="divContainerCell divContainerCellHeader">
            First Name:
        </div>
        <div class="divContainerCell">
            <asp:TextBox ID="txtFirstName"
                    runat="server"></asp:TextBox>
            <asp:RequiredFieldValidator
                ID="valRequireFirstName"
                runat="server"
                ForeColor="Red"
                ControlToValidate="txtFirstName"
                ErrorMessage="Please provide your first
                        name!">*</asp:RequiredFieldValidator>
        </div>
    </div>
    <div class="divContainerRow">
        <div class="divContainerCell divContainerCellHeader">
            Last Name:
        </div>
        <div class="divContainerCell">
            <asp:TextBox ID="txtLastName"
                    runat="server"></asp:TextBox>
            <asp:RequiredFieldValidator
                ID="valRequiredLastName"
                runat="server"
                ForeColor="Red"
                ControlToValidate="txtLastName"
                ErrorMessage="Please provide your last
                        name!">*</asp:RequiredFieldValidator>
```

```
                </div>
            </div>
            <div class="divContainerRow">
                <div class="divContainerCell divContainerCellHeader">
                    Birthday:
                </div>
                <div class="divContainerCell">
                    <asp:TextBox ID="txtBirthday" runat="server"
                            Text=""></asp:TextBox>
                    <asp:CompareValidator
                        ID="valDate"
                        runat="server"
                        ForeColor="Red"
                        ControlToValidate="txtBirthday"
                        Type="Date"
                        Operator="DataTypeCheck"
                        ErrorMessage="Please enter a valid
                                date!">*</asp:CompareValidator>
                </div>
            </div>
            <div class="divContainerRow">
                <div class="divContainerCell divContainerCellHeader">
                    Zipcode:
                </div>
                <div class="divContainerCell">
                    <asp:TextBox ID="txtZipcode" runat="server"
                            Text=""></asp:TextBox>
                    <asp:RegularExpressionValidator
                        ID="valZipcode" ControlToValidate="txtZipcode"
                        runat="server"
                        ForeColor="Red"
                        ErrorMessage="This must be a valid US zip code!"
                        ValidationExpression="^(\d{5}-
                            \d{4}|\d{5}|\d{9})$|^([a-zA-Z]\d[a-zA-
                            Z]\d)$">*</asp:RegularExpressionValidator>
                </div>
            </div>
        </asp:WizardStep>
```

3. The third step presents the terms and conditions. This is the one step that requires you to fetch some data for display. This data is retrieved from the `TermRepository.GetCurrentTerm()` (which we covered earlier). All the user needs to do here is read the terms (most of your users won't do this of course!) and check the box indicating that they agree with your terms.

```
//FisharooWeb/Account/Register.aspx
<asp:WizardStep>
    <div class="divContainerRow">
        <div class="divContainerCell">
            <asp:TextBox TextMode="MultiLine" Columns="40" Rows="10"
                         ID="txtTerms" runat="server">
                         </asp:TextBox><br />
            <asp:CheckBox ID="chkAgreeWithTerms" runat="server"
                    Text="I agree with the terms" />
            <asp:Label ID="lblTermID" runat="server"
                  Visible="false"></asp:Label>
        </div>
    </div>
</asp:WizardStep>
```

4. Finally, you should present some form of CAPTCHA so that we can make sure that the person signing up is a person and not a spam bot! You will notice that this appears to be very simple on the front end. The Image tag is simply calling JpegImage.aspx as its source. Here is the WizardStep. After that is the source code for the JpegImage.aspx page.

```
//FisharooWeb/Account/Register.aspx
<asp:WizardStep Title="CAPTCHA" ID="wsCaptcha" runat="server">
    <div class="divContainerRow">
        <div class="divContainerTitle">
            CAPTCHA - Completely Automated Turing Test To Tell
            Computers and Humans Apart
        </div>
    </div>
    <div class="divContainerRow">
        <div class="divContainerCell">
            <asp:Image runat="server"
                 ImageUrl="~/images/CaptchaImage/
                                   JpegImage.aspx" />
        </div>
    </div>
    <div class="divContainerRow">
        <div class="divContainerTitle">
            Please copy what you see in the image above into the
            box below.
        </div>
    </div>
    <div class="divContainerRow">
        <div class="divContainerCell">
            <asp:TextBox ID="txtCaptcha"
                       runat="server"></asp:TextBox>
        </div>
    </div>
</asp:WizardStep>
```

You will notice that the `JpegImage` page is using the Captcha and WebContext objects. This page generates a random number, which it then stores in `WebContext.CaptchaImageText`. It then instantiates and configures the Captcha object. The page then flushes its output and changes its content type to that of an image (image/jpeg). The page then saves the image to the output stream so that the image tag can render the image to the user.

```
//FisharooWeb/Images/CaptchaImage/JpegImage.aspx.cs
using System;
using System.Collections;
using System.ComponentModel;
using System.Data;
using System.Drawing;
using System.Drawing.Imaging;
using System.Web;
using System.Web.SessionState;
using System.Web.UI;
using System.Web.UI.WebControls;
using System.Web.UI.HtmlControls;
using Fisharoo.FisharooCore.Core;
using Fisharoo.FisharooCore.Core.Impl;
using StructureMap;
public partial class JpegImage : System.Web.UI.Page
{
    private Random random = new Random();
    private IWebContext _webContext;
    private void Page_Load(object sender, System.EventArgs e)
    {
        _webContext = ObjectFactory.GetInstance<IWebContext>();
        _webContext.CaptchaImageText = GenerateRandomCode();
        ICaptcha ci = ObjectFactory.GetInstance<ICaptcha>();
        ci.Text = _webContext.CaptchaImageText;
        ci.Width = 200;
        ci.Height = 50;
        ci.FamilyName = "Century Schoobook";
        Response.Clear();
        Response.ContentType = "image/jpeg";
        ci.Image.Save(Response.OutputStream, ImageFormat.Jpeg);
        ci.Dispose();
    }
    private string GenerateRandomCode()
    {
        string s = "";
        for (int i = 0; i < 6; i++)
```

```
            s = String.Concat(s, this.random.Next(10).ToString());
        return s;
    }
    override protected void OnInit(EventArgs e)
    {
        InitializeComponent();
        base.OnInit(e);
    }
    private void InitializeComponent()
    {
        this.Load += new System.EventHandler(this.Page_Load);
    }
}
```

Knowing that the code behind is really just a middle man responsible for passing data to and from the presenter, I am going to show you the code (because I hate not having all the code to look at!) but won't spend any time going over it.

```
using System;
using System.Collections;
using System.Configuration;
using System.Data;
using System.Linq;
using System.Web;
using System.Web.Security;
using System.Web.UI;
using System.Web.UI.HtmlControls;
using System.Web.UI.WebControls;
using System.Web.UI.WebControls.WebParts;
using System.Xml.Linq;
using Fisharoo.FisharooCore.Core.Domain;
using Fisharoo.FisharooWeb.Account.Presenter;
namespace Fisharoo.FisharooWeb.Account
{
    public partial class Register : System.Web.UI.Page, IRegister
    {
        private RegisterPresenter _presenter;
        protected void Page_Load(object sender, EventArgs e)
        {
            _presenter = new RegisterPresenter();
            _presenter.Init(this);
        }
        protected void wizRegister_ActiveStepChanged(object sender,
                                                        EventArgs e)
        {
```

```
            if(wizRegister.ActiveStepIndex == 1)
            {
                ViewState.Add("password",txtPassword.Text);
            }
        }
        protected void wizRegister_FinishButtonClicked(object sender,
                                                        EventArgs e)
        {
            _presenter.Register(
                txtUsername.Text,ViewState["password"].ToString(),
                txtFirstName.Text,txtLastName.Text,txtEmail.Text,
                txtZipcode.Text,Convert.ToDateTime(txtBirthday.Text),
                txtCaptcha.Text, chkAgreeWithTerms.Checked,
                        Convert.ToInt32(lblTermID.Text));
        }
        protected void lbLogin_Click(object sender, EventArgs e)
        {
            _presenter.LoginLinkClicked();
        }
        protected void wizRegister_NextButtonClick(object sender,
                                                    EventArgs e)
        {
            lblErrorMessage.Text = "";
        }
        public void ShowErrorMessage(string Message)
        {
            lblErrorMessage.Text = Message;
        }
        public void ToggleWizardIndex(int index)
        {
            wizRegister.ActiveStepIndex = index;
        }
        public void ShowAccountCreatedPanel()
        {
            pnlAccountCreated.Visible = true;
            pnlCreateAccount.Visible = false;
        }
        public void ShowCreateAccountPanel()
        {
            pnlAccountCreated.Visible = false;
            pnlCreateAccount.Visible = true;
        }
        public void LoadTerms(Term term)
        {
            if (term != null)
```

```
            {
                lblTermID.Text = term.TermID.ToString();
                txtTerms.Text = term.Terms;
            }
        }
    }
}
```

Now we get to the meat and potatoes of this page. Once we have gathered all the data, we need to process it. Enter the presenter (that was fun to say!).

```
using System;
using System.Collections.Generic;
using System.Data;
using System.Configuration;
using System.Linq;
using System.Web;
using System.Web.Security;
using System.Web.UI;
using System.Web.UI.HtmlControls;
using System.Web.UI.WebControls;
using System.Web.UI.WebControls.WebParts;
using System.Xml.Linq;
using Fisharoo.FisharooCore.Core;
using Fisharoo.FisharooCore.Core.DataAccess;
using Fisharoo.FisharooCore.Core.Domain;
using Fisharoo.FisharooCore.Core.Impl;
using StructureMap;
namespace Fisharoo.FisharooWeb.Account.Presenter
{
    public class RegisterPresenter
    {
        private IRegister _view;
        private IAccountRepository _accountRepository;
        private IPermissionRepository _permissionRepository;
        private ITermRepository _termRepository;
        private IAccountService _accountService;
        private IWebContext _webContext;
        private IEmail _email;
        private IConfiguration _configuration;
        public void Init(IRegister View)
        {
            _view = View;
            _accountRepository =
                ObjectFactory.GetInstance<IAccountRepository>();
```

```
    _permissionRepository =
        ObjectFactory.GetInstance<IPermissionRepository>();
    _termRepository =
        ObjectFactory.GetInstance<ITermRepository>();
    _accountService =
        ObjectFactory.GetInstance<IAccountService>();
    _webContext = ObjectFactory.GetInstance<IWebContext>();
    _email = ObjectFactory.GetInstance<IEmail>();
    _configuration =
        ObjectFactory.GetInstance<IConfiguration>();
    _view.LoadTerms(_termRepository.GetCurrentTerm());
}
public void LoginLinkClicked()
{
    IRedirector redirector =
        ObjectFactory.GetInstance<IRedirector>();
    redirector.GoToAccountLoginPage();
}
public void Register(string Username, string Password,
    string FirstName, string LastName, string Email,
    string Zip, DateTime BirthDate, string Captcha, bool
        AgreesWithTerms, Int32 TermID)
{
    if (AgreesWithTerms)
    {
        if (Captcha == _webContext.CaptchaImageText)
        {
            FisharooCore.Core.Domain.Account a =
                new FisharooCore.Core.Domain.Account();
            a.FirstName = FirstName;
            a.LastName = LastName;
            a.Email = Email;
            a.BirthDate = BirthDate;
            a.Zip = Zip;
            a.Username = Username;
            a.Password = Cryptography.Encrypt(Password,
                                               Username);
            a.TermID = TermID;
            if (_accountService.EmailInUse(Email))
            {
                _view.ShowErrorMessage("This email is already
                                        in use!");
                _view.ToggleWizardIndex(0);
            }
            else if (_accountService.UsernameInUse(Username))
```

```
                    {
                        _view.ShowErrorMessage("This username is
                                                already in use!");
                        _view.ToggleWizardIndex(0);
                    }
                    else
                    {
                        _accountRepository.SaveAccount(a);
                        List<Permission> permissions =
                _permissionRepository.GetPermissionByName("PUBLIC");
                        List<FisharooCore.Core.Domain.Account>
                            newAccounts = _accountRepository.
                            GetAccountByEmail(Email);
                        if(permissions.Count > 0 && newAccounts.Count
                                            > 0)
                        {
                            _accountRepository.AddPermission(
                                newAccounts[0], permissions[0]);
                        }
                        _email.SendEmailAddressVerificationEmail(
                                            a.Username,a.Email);
                        _view.ShowAccountCreatedPanel();
                    }
                }
                else
                {
                    _view.ShowErrorMessage("Your entry doesn't match
                            the CAPTCHA image.  Please try again.");
                }
            }
            else
            {
                _view.ToggleWizardIndex(2);
                _view.ShowErrorMessage("You can't create an account
                    on this site if you don't agree with our terms!");
            }
        }
    }
}
```

You will notice that most of this code is just more validation or navigation logic such as "did they agree with the terms?", or "did they enter the correct CAPTCHA?". Nothing fancy here!

The new thing here, which is somewhat interesting, is the mention of the `Email` object. You may recall when we built the `Email` object a while back. It provides us with the facilities to send an email in various ways. What we have done here is to extend the `Email` object so that it also encapsulates the messages that are sent by the system. Here is the new code for the Email object that allows us to send an email verification of the validity and ownership of an email address.

```
//FisharooCore/Core/Impl/Email.cs
    public void SendEmailAddressVerificationEmail(string
                                            Username, string To)
    {
        string msg = "Please click on the link below or paste it
          into a browser to verify your email account.<BR><BR>" +
                        "<a href=\"" + _configuration.RootURL +
                            "Account/VerifyEmail.aspx?a=" +
                        Cryptography.Encrypt(Username, "verify")
                            + "\">" +
                        _configuration.RootURL +
                            "Account/VerifyEmail.aspx?a=" +
                        Cryptography.Encrypt(Username, "verify")
                            + "</a>";
        SendEmail(To, "", "", "Account created! Email
                        verification required.", msg);

    }
```

Also notice that the link that is embedded here encrypts the registrants' username with a salt of "verify". This way we know who we are dealing with after they receive the email and follow the link back to our site (more about this in the next section).

In the Wizard's stepped environment, it is very easy to present small chunks of data like this without having too much coding overhead. While it is not as easy as the .NET membership widgets, I think it is quite a bit more flexible. Also, we can easily test this whole process now.

Email verification

We lightly touched upon this subject in the previous section. Basically, the registration process triggers an email to be sent to the newly registered user asking them to verify their email address. This process usually sends an email to the email address that the user provided us when they signed up. If the user can receive the email on their end, then we know that the email address is valid. If they can click on the link that is embedded in the email, then we know that they have access to the email as well. This doesn't necessarily mean that they own the account, but we can't really verify that, and hence we can't really worry about it.

The item we didn't cover above is the page that receives the click from the link in the email. This series of code is relatively simple. So to start, I am going to list all of the files in order of use (design, code behind, interface, and presenter). Then we can discuss it.

```
//FisharooWeb/Account/VerifyEmail.aspx
<%@ Page Language="C#" MasterPageFile="~/SiteMaster.Master"
AutoEventWireup="true" CodeBehind="VerifyEmail.aspx.cs"
Inherits="Fisharoo.FisharooWeb.Account.VerifyEmail" %>
<asp:Content ContentPlaceHolderID="Content" runat="server">
    <asp:Label ID="lblMsg" runat="server" ForeColor="Red"></asp:Label>
</asp:Content>
```

```
//FisharooWeb/Account/VerifyEmail.aspx.cs
using System;
using System.Collections;
using System.Configuration;
using System.Data;
using System.Linq;
using System.Web;
using System.Web.Security;
using System.Web.UI;
using System.Web.UI.HtmlControls;
using System.Web.UI.WebControls;
using System.Web.UI.WebControls.WebParts;
using System.Xml.Linq;
using Fisharoo.FisharooWeb.Account.Interface;
using Fisharoo.FisharooWeb.Account.Presenter;
namespace Fisharoo.FisharooWeb.Account
{
    public partial class VerifyEmail : System.Web.UI.Page,
                                       IVerifyEmail
    {
        private VerifyEmailPresenter _presenter;
        protected void Page_Load(object sender, EventArgs e)
        {
            _presenter = new VerifyEmailPresenter();
            _presenter.Init(this);
        }
        public void ShowMessage(string Message)
        {
            lblMsg.Text = Message;
        }
    }
}
```

```
//FisharooWeb/Account/Interface/IVerifyEmail.cs
namespace Fisharoo.FisharooWeb.Account.Interface
{
    public interface IVerifyEmail
    {
        void ShowMessage(string Message);
    }
}

//FisharooWeb/Account/Presenter/VerifyEmailPresenter.cs
using System;
using System.Collections.Generic;
using System.Data;
using System.Configuration;
using System.Linq;
using System.Web;
using System.Web.Security;
using System.Web.UI;
using System.Web.UI.HtmlControls;
using System.Web.UI.WebControls;
using System.Web.UI.WebControls.WebParts;
using System.Xml.Linq;
using Fisharoo.FisharooCore.Core;
using Fisharoo.FisharooCore.Core.DataAccess;
using Fisharoo.FisharooCore.Core.Impl;
using Fisharoo.FisharooWeb.Account.Interface;
using StructureMap;
namespace Fisharoo.FisharooWeb.Account.Presenter
{
    public class VerifyEmailPresenter
    {
        private IWebContext _webContext;
        private IAccountRepository _accountRepository;
        public void Init(IVerifyEmail _view)
        {
            _webContext = ObjectFactory.GetInstance<IWebContext>();
            _accountRepository =
                ObjectFactory.GetInstance<IAccountRepository>();
            string username =
                Cryptography.Decrypt(_webContext.
                                     UsernameToVerify, "verify");
            List<FisharooCore.Core.Domain.Account> accounts =
                _accountRepository.GetAccountByUsername(username);
            if(accounts.Count == 1)
            {
```

```
                accounts[0].EmailVerified = true;
                _accountRepository.SaveAccount(accounts[0]);
                _view.ShowMessage("Your email address has been
                                successfully verified!");
            }
            else
            {
                _view.ShowMessage("There appears to be something wrong
    with your verification link!  Please try again.  If you are having
    issues by clicking on the link, please try copying the URL from your
    email and pasting it into your browser window.");
            }
        }
    }
}
```

The reason that I listed out the code this way was to show you that all the logic is pretty much lodged in the presenter (as it should be!). Notice that we attempt to get the username from the WebContext (query string in this case) and decrypt it with our "verify" salt. Once we have this username, we attempt to retrieve the Account using AccountRepository.GetAccountByUsername(). If we got an account back, we toggle the Account.EmailVerified property to true and save it back into the repository.

Password recovery

This is another simple page that I can quickly show you the code for.

```
//FisharooWeb/Account/RecoverPassword.aspx
<%@ Page Language="C#" MasterPageFile="~/SiteMaster.Master"
AutoEventWireup="true" CodeBehind="RecoverPassword.aspx.cs"
Inherits="Fisharoo.FisharooWeb.Account.RecoverPassword" %>
<asp:Content ContentPlaceHolderID="Content" runat="server">
    <asp:Panel ID="pnlRecoverPassword" runat="server">
        <div class="divContainer">
            <div class="divContainerRow">
                <div class="divContainerTitle">
                    Please enter your email address below
                </div>
            </div>
            <div class="divContainerRow">
                <div class="divContainerCellHeader">
                    Email:
                </div>
                <div class="divContainerCell">
```

```
                          <asp:TextBox ID="txtEmail"
                                  runat="server"></asp:TextBox>
                  </div>
              </div>
              <div class="divContainerRow">
                  <div class="divContainerCellHeader">
                       
                  </div>
                  <div class="divContainerCell">
                      <asp:Button ID="btnRecoverPassword" Text="Recover
                              Password" runat="server"
                                  OnClick="btnRecoverPassword_Click" />
                  </div>
              </div>
          </div>
      </asp:Panel>
      <div class="divContainer">
          <div class="divContainerRow">
              <div class="divContainerCell">
                  <asp:Label ID="lblMessage" runat="server"
                      ForeColor="Red"></asp:Label>
              </div>
          </div>
      </div>
</asp:Content>
```

//FisharooWeb/Account/RecoverPassword.aspx.cs
```
using System;
using System.Collections;
using System.Configuration;
using System.Data;
using System.Linq;
using System.Web;
using System.Web.Security;
using System.Web.UI;
using System.Web.UI.HtmlControls;
using System.Web.UI.WebControls;
using System.Web.UI.WebControls.WebParts;
using System.Xml.Linq;
using Fisharoo.FisharooCore.Core;
using Fisharoo.FisharooWeb.Account.Interface;
using Fisharoo.FisharooWeb.Account.Presenter;
using StructureMap;
namespace Fisharoo.FisharooWeb.Account
```

```
{
    public partial class RecoverPassword : System.Web.UI.Page,
                                    IRecoverPassword
    {
        private RecoverPasswordPresenter _presenter;
        protected void Page_Load(object sender, EventArgs e)
        {
            _presenter = new RecoverPasswordPresenter();
            _presenter.Init(this);
        }
        protected void btnRecoverPassword_Click(object sender,
                                        EventArgs e)
        {
            _presenter.RecoverPassword(txtEmail.Text);
        }
        public void ShowMessage(string Message)
        {
            lblMessage.Text = Message;
        }
        public void ShowRecoverPasswordPanel(bool Value)
        {
            pnlRecoverPassword.Visible = Value;
        }
    }
}

//FisharooWeb/Account/Interface/IRecoverPassword.cs
namespace Fisharoo.FisharooWeb.Account.Interface
{
    public interface IRecoverPassword
    {
        void ShowMessage(string Message);
        void ShowRecoverPasswordPanel(bool Value);
    }
}

//FisharooWeb/Account/Presenter/RecoverPasswordPresenter.cs
using System;
using System.Collections.Generic;
using System.Data;
using System.Configuration;
using System.Linq;
using System.Web;
using System.Web.Security;
using System.Web.UI;
```

```
using System.Web.UI.HtmlControls;
using System.Web.UI.WebControls;
using System.Web.UI.WebControls.WebParts;
using System.Xml.Linq;
using Fisharoo.FisharooCore.Core;
using Fisharoo.FisharooCore.Core.DataAccess;
using Fisharoo.FisharooCore.Core.Impl;
using Fisharoo.FisharooWeb.Account.Interface;
using StructureMap;
namespace Fisharoo.FisharooWeb.Account.Presenter
{
    public class RecoverPasswordPresenter
    {
        private IRecoverPassword _view;
        private IEmail _email;
        private IAccountRepository _accountRepository;
        public RecoverPasswordPresenter()
        {
            _email = ObjectFactory.GetInstance<IEmail>();
            _accountRepository =
                ObjectFactory.GetInstance<IAccountRepository>();
        }
        public void Init(IRecoverPassword View)
        {
            _view = View;
        }
        public void RecoverPassword(string Email)
        {
            List<FisharooCore.Core.Domain.Account> accounts = new
                List<FisharooCore.Core.Domain.Account>();
            accounts = _accountRepository.GetAccountByEmail(Email);
            if(accounts.Count == 1)
            {
                _email.SendPasswordReminderEmail(accounts[0].Email,
                    accounts[0].Password, accounts[0].Username);
                _view.ShowRecoverPasswordPanel(false);
                _view.ShowMessage("An email was sent to your
                            account!");
            }
            else
            {
                _view.ShowRecoverPasswordPanel(true);
                _view.ShowMessage("We couldn't find the account you
                            requested.");
            }

        }
    }
}
```

This page asks the user to provide their email address. It then looks up the account with that email address. If it finds the account it then uses the `Email.SendPasswordReminderEmail()` method to send the user's decrypted password to their email account.

The `SendPasswordReminderEmail()` method looks like this.

```
//FisharooCore/Core/Impl/Email.cs
        public void SendPasswordReminderEmail(string To,
            string EncryptedPassword, string Username)
        {
            string Message = "Here is the password you requested: " +
                    Cryptography.Decrypt(EncryptedPassword, Username);
            SendEmail(To, "", "", "Password Reminder", Message);
        }
```

Edit account

To save a bit of space I am going to forgo showing you the design portion of this code. It is just a basic form with text boxes and the like, and has the same validation requirements as the registration form did. There are a couple of anomalies however in the presenter logic in that if users don't change their password, we wouldn't want to save an empty string as their password. And if they do change their email address, we want to resend the email validation email.

```
//FisharooWeb/Account/EditAccount.aspx
using System;
using System.Collections;
using System.Configuration;
using System.Data;
using System.Linq;
using System.Web;
using System.Web.Security;
using System.Web.UI;
using System.Web.UI.HtmlControls;
using System.Web.UI.WebControls;
using System.Web.UI.WebControls.WebParts;
using System.Xml.Linq;
using Fisharoo.FisharooWeb.Account.Interface;
using Fisharoo.FisharooWeb.Account.Presenter;
namespace Fisharoo.FisharooWeb.Account
{
    public partial class EditAccount : System.Web.UI.Page,
                    IEditAccount
```

```
        {
            private EditAccountPresenter _presenter;
            protected void Page_Load(object sender, EventArgs e)
            {
                _presenter = new EditAccountPresenter();
                _presenter.Init(this, IsPostBack);
            }
            protected void btnSave_Click(object sender, EventArgs e)
            {
                _presenter.UpdateAccount(txtOldPassword.
             Text,txtNewPassword.Text,lblUsername.Text, txtFirstName.Text,
                    txtLastName.Text, txtEmail.Text,
                        txtZipCode.Text,Convert.
                        ToDateTime(txtBirthDate.Text));
            }
            public void ShowMessage(string Message)
            {
                lblMessage.Text = Message;
            }
            public void
                        LoadCurrentInformation
                        (FisharooCore.Core.Domain.Account account)
            {
                txtBirthDate.Text =
            String.Format("{0:d}",account.BirthDate);
                txtEmail.Text = account.Email;
                txtFirstName.Text = account.FirstName;
                txtLastName.Text = account.LastName;
                txtZipCode.Text = account.Zip;
                lblUsername.Text = account.Username;
            }
        }
    }

    //FisharooWeb/Account/Interface/IEditAccount
    namespace Fisharoo.FisharooWeb.Account.Interface
    {
        public interface IEditAccount
        {
            void ShowMessage(string Message);
            void LoadCurrentInformation(FisharooCore.Core.Domain.Account
                    account);
        }
    }
```

```csharp
//FisharooWeb/Account/Presenter/EditAccountPresenter.cs
using System;
using System.Data;
using System.Configuration;
using System.Linq;
using System.Web;
using System.Web.Security;
using System.Web.UI;
using System.Web.UI.HtmlControls;
using System.Web.UI.WebControls;
using System.Web.UI.WebControls.WebParts;
using System.Xml.Linq;
using Fisharoo.FisharooCore.Core;
using Fisharoo.FisharooCore.Core.DataAccess;
using Fisharoo.FisharooCore.Core.Impl;
using Fisharoo.FisharooWeb.Account.Interface;
using StructureMap;
namespace Fisharoo.FisharooWeb.Account.Presenter
{
    public class EditAccountPresenter
    {
        private IEditAccount _view;
        private IUserSession _userSession;
        private IAccountService _accountService;
        private IAccountRepository _accountRepository;
        private FisharooCore.Core.Domain.Account account;
        private IRedirector _redirector;
        private IEmail _email;
        public EditAccountPresenter()
        {
            _userSession = ObjectFactory.GetInstance<IUserSession>();
            _accountRepository =
                ObjectFactory.GetInstance<IAccountRepository>();
            _redirector = ObjectFactory.GetInstance<IRedirector>();
            _accountService =
                ObjectFactory.GetInstance<IAccountService>();
            _email = ObjectFactory.GetInstance<IEmail>();
        }
        public void Init(IEditAccount View, bool IsPostBack)
        {
            _view = View;
            if (_userSession.CurrentUser != null)
                account = _userSession.CurrentUser;
            else
```

```
                _redirector.GoToAccountLoginPage();
            if(!IsPostBack)
                LoadCurrentUser();
        }
        private void LoadCurrentUser()
        {
    _view.LoadCurrentInformation(_userSession.CurrentUser);
        }
        public void UpdateAccount(string OldPassword, string
                NewPassword, string Username,
            string FirstName, string LastName, string Email,
            string ZipCode, DateTime BirthDate)
        {

            //verify that this user is the same as the logged in user
            if(Cryptography.Encrypt(OldPassword,Username) ==
                account.Password)
            {
                if (Email != _userSession.CurrentUser.Email)
                {
                    if (!_accountService.EmailInUse(Email))
                    {
                        account.Email = Email;
                        account.EmailVerified = false;
                        _email.SendEmailAddressVerificationEmail(
                                    account.Username, Email);
                    }
                    else
                    {
                        _view.ShowMessage("The email your entered is
                                    already in our system!");
                        return;
                    }
                }
                if(!string.IsNullOrEmpty(NewPassword))
                    account.Password =
                        Cryptography.Encrypt(NewPassword, Username);

                account.FirstName = FirstName;
                account.LastName = LastName;
                account.Zip = ZipCode;
                account.BirthDate = BirthDate;
                _accountRepository.SaveAccount(account);
                _view.ShowMessage("Your account has been updated!");
            }
            else
```

```
        {
            _view.ShowMessage("The password you entered doesn't
                                match your current password!
                                Please try again.");
        }
    }
  }
}
```

One thing to notice with the presenter is that when it is first initialized, it loads an account and passes that data to the view for initial display. Then once the user edits their data, there are several validation steps that occur. The most important is that of the password and the email.

If the password is not changed, we want to make sure that we do not store an empty value to the system!

For the email, if a user changes it, we want to make sure that we resend the verification email again and flag the account as not having a validated email address.

Beyond that we are simply updating the account object via the `AccountRepository.Save()` method.

Implementing security

Now that we have all of our plumbing in place, we are at a point that we can lock down our site. Up until now someone could go wherever they wanted to on the site and we would not be able to stop them at all!

SiteMap

The primary .NET widget that we will use to lock down our site is the ASP.NET sitemap. This is a wonderful tool that can be used not only for security but also to display breadcrumb trails, your primary navigation, and many other useful page/file oriented tasks.

A `sitemap` file is made up of several `siteMapNodes`. Each node contains things such as URL, title, description, and roles by default. You can also add your own custom attributes. In our site we will use attributes for identifying links that belong in the `topnav`, the `footer nav`, as well as allowing the `siteMap` to help us with each page's title. Our current `siteMap` looks like this:

```xml
<?xml version="1.0" encoding="utf-8" ?>
<siteMap xmlns="http://schemas.microsoft.com/AspNet/
                    SiteMap-File-1.0" >
    <siteMapNode url="default.aspx" title="Home"  description="Home
```

```
                              page" pageTitle="Welcome to Fisharoo.com!"
                              roles="PUBLIC">
    <!-- TOP NAV NODES -->
        <siteMapNode url="/account/default.aspx" title="My Account"
            description="" pageTitle="" roles="PUBLIC">
          <siteMapNode url="/account/EditAccount.aspx" title="Edit
             Account" description="" pageTitle="" roles="PUBLIC" />
          <siteMapNode url="/account/Login.aspx" title="Login"
              description="" pageTitle="" roles="PUBLIC" />
          <siteMapNode url="/account/RecoverPassword.aspx"
                    title="Recover Password" description="Recover Your
                    Password" pageTitle="Recover your password"
                    roles="PUBLIC" />
          <siteMapNode url="/account/Register.aspx" title="Register"
                 description="" pageTitle="" roles="PUBLIC" />
          <siteMapNode url="/account/VerifyEmail.aspx" title="Verify
                 Email" description="Verify your email address"
                 pageTitle="Email Verification" roles="PUBLIC" />
          <siteMapNode url="/account/AccessDenied.aspx" title="Access
                 Denied" description="Access Denied"
                 pageTitle="Access Denied" roles="PUBLIC" />
        </siteMapNode>
        <siteMapNode url="/profile/default.aspx" title="Profile"
                 description="" topnav="1" pageTitle=""
                 roles="PUBLIC"></siteMapNode>
        <siteMapNode url="/friends/default.aspx" title="Friends"
                 description="" topnav="1" pageTitle=""
                 roles="PUBLIC"></siteMapNode>
        <siteMapNode url="/mail/default.aspx" title="Mail"
                 description="" topnav="1" pageTitle=""
                 roles="PUBLIC"></siteMapNode>
        <siteMapNode url="/galleries/default.aspx" title="Galleries"
                 description="" topnav="1" pageTitle=""
                 roles="PUBLIC"></siteMapNode>
        <siteMapNode url="/groups/default.aspx" title="Groups"
                 description="" topnav="1" pageTitle=""
                 roles="PUBLIC"></siteMapNode>
        <siteMapNode url="/virtualtanks/default.aspx" title="Virtual
                       Tanks" description="" topnav="1" pageTitle=""
                       roles="PUBLIC"></siteMapNode>
        <siteMapNode url="/forum/default.aspx" title="Forum"
                       description="" topnav="1" pageTitle=""
                       roles="PUBLIC"></siteMapNode>
        <siteMapNode url="/blogs/default.aspx" title="Blogs"
                       description="" topnav="1" pageTitle=""
                       roles="PUBLIC"></siteMapNode>
    <!-- /TOP NAV NODES -->
```

```
<!-- FOOTER NODES -->
    <siteMapNode url="AboutUs.aspx" title="About Us"
                    · description="About Us" footernav="1"
                    pageTitle="" roles="PUBLIC"></siteMapNode>
    <siteMapNode url="Advertisers.aspx" title="Advertisers"
                    description="Click here to learn more about
                    advertising on our site" footernav="1"
                    pageTitle="" roles="PUBLIC"></siteMapNode>
    <siteMapNode url="Help.aspx" title="Help" description="Click
                    here to enter our help section" footernav="1"
                    pageTitle="" roles="PUBLIC"></siteMapNode>
    <siteMapNode url="Privacy.aspx" title="Privacy"
                    description="Click here to learn about our
                    privacy policy" footernav="1" pageTitle=""
                    roles="PUBLIC"></siteMapNode>
    <siteMapNode url="Terms.aspx" title="Terms" description="Click
                    here to learn about our terms and conditions"
                    footernav="1" pageTitle=""
                    roles="PUBLIC"></siteMapNode>
<!-- /FOOTER NODES-->
<!-- NONE NAVIGATION NODES -->
    <siteMapNode url="Search.aspx" title="Search"
                    description="Click here to perform a site
                    search" pageTitle=""
                    roles="PUBLIC"></siteMapNode>
    <siteMapNode url="Error.aspx" title="Error" description="An
                    error has occured" pageTitle=""
                    roles="PUBLIC"></siteMapNode>
<!-- /NONE NAVIGATION NODES -->
    </siteMapNode>
</siteMap>
```

SiteMap wrapper

As with all of the other controls and classes that .NET exposes to us, it is a good idea to wrap the `SiteMap` class. I did this by creating a `Navigation` class. It not only exposes all the properties that `SiteMap` does, but it also adds a bit more control to the way we interact with our nodes.

```
using System;
using System.Collections.Generic;
using System.Linq;
using System.Text;
using System.Web;
using Fisharoo.FisharooCore.Core.Domain;
using StructureMap;
```

```
namespace Fisharoo.FisharooCore.Core.Impl
{
    [Pluggable("Default")]
    public class Navigation : INavigation
    {
        private IUserSession _userSession;
        private IRedirector _redirector;
        private Account _account;
        public Navigation()
        {
            _userSession = ObjectFactory.GetInstance<IUserSession>();
            _redirector = ObjectFactory.GetInstance<IRedirector>();
            _account = _userSession.CurrentUser;
        }

        public List<SiteMapNode> AllNodes()
        {
            List<SiteMapNode> nodes = new List<SiteMapNode>();
            nodes.Add(SiteMap.RootNode);
            foreach (SiteMapNode node in SiteMap.RootNode.ChildNodes)
            {
                nodes.Add(node);
            }
            return nodes;
        }
        public List<SiteMapNode> PrimaryNodes()
        {
            List<SiteMapNode> primaryNodes = new List<SiteMapNode>();
            foreach (SiteMapNode node in AllNodes())
            {
                if (node["topnav"] != null &&
                CheckAccessForNode(node))
                    primaryNodes.Add(node);
            }
            return primaryNodes;
        }
        public List<SiteMapNode> FooterNodes()
        {
            List<SiteMapNode> footerNodes = new List<SiteMapNode>();
            foreach (SiteMapNode node in AllNodes())
            {
                if (node["footernav"] != null &&
                CheckAccessForNode(node))
                    footerNodes.Add(node);
```

```
        }
        return footerNodes;
    }
    private bool CheckAccessForNode(SiteMapNode node)
    {
        if (!node.Roles.Contains("PUBLIC"))
        {
            if (_account != null && _account.Permissions != null
                && _account.Permissions.Count > 0)
            {
                foreach (string role in node.Roles)
                {
                    if (!_account.HasPermission(role))
                        return false;
                }
                return true;
            }
            else
                return false;
        }
        return true;
    }
    public void CheckAccessForCurrentNode()
    {
        bool result = CheckAccessForNode(CurrentNode);
        if(result)
            return;
        else
            _redirector.GoToAccountAccessDenied();
    }
    public SiteMapNode RootNode
    {
        get { return SiteMap.RootNode; }
    }
    public SiteMapNode CurrentNode
    {
        get
        {
            return SiteMap.CurrentNode;
        }
    }
}
}
```

All nodes

By default the `SiteMap` class doesn't return all nodes so to speak. It provides you with a call to the `RootNode` and a call to its children. As you can see in our first method, we simply created an `AllNodes()` call that returns "all nodes".

```
public List<SiteMapNode> AllNodes()
{
    List<SiteMapNode> nodes = new List<SiteMapNode>();
    nodes.Add(SiteMap.RootNode);
    foreach (SiteMapNode node in SiteMap.RootNode.ChildNodes)
    {
        nodes.Add(node);
    }
    return nodes;
}
```

Navigation

Our site will have several navigation sections. Here we have:

- Top navigation
- Primary navigation
- Secondary navigation
- Left navigation
- Footer navigation

If we had to dig through all of the navigation collections, each time we needed them we may find it quite cumbersome. Instead we will add methods to the classes that produce the required sub-selection of nodes.

The `PrimaryNodes()` method is the first example of such a method. It produces a list of nodes that go in the primary navigation section by iterating through all the nodes returned by the `AllNodes()` method looking for each node with a custom `topnav` attribute. You will notice a special filter though in addition to this. With each `topnav` node that is found, a security check is performed to see if the current user should have access to this node. If not, the node is not displayed.

```
public List<SiteMapNode> PrimaryNodes()
{
    List<SiteMapNode> primaryNodes = new List<SiteMapNode>();
    foreach (SiteMapNode node in AllNodes())
    {
        if (node["topnav"] != null &&
            CheckAccessForNode(node))
```

```
                    primaryNodes.Add(node);
        }
        return primaryNodes;
    }
```

The `FooterNodes()` method is exactly the same as the `PrimaryNodes()` method with the exception that it looks for a `footernav` attribute. This method also checks to make sure that the user has access to a specified collection of nodes.

```
public List<SiteMapNode> FooterNodes()
{
    List<SiteMapNode> footerNodes = new List<SiteMapNode>();
    foreach (SiteMapNode node in AllNodes())
    {
        if (node["footernav"] != null &&
            CheckAccessForNode(node))
            footerNodes.Add(node);
    }
    return footerNodes;
}
```

Checking access

This brings us to the `CheckAccessToNode()` method, which we are using in our other methods. This method looks at the passed in node and checks its `Roles` collection. It first checks to see if the `PUBLIC` role is specified. If so, all remaining checks are not performed. We then move to see if there is an account present, that is, whether any user has logged in. If there is a user, we check their permissions property. If that exists, we check to see if there are any permissions in the permission list. We then iterate through each role specified in the node and check to make sure that the account has that permission. If the account doesn't contain any of the specified permissions we return false. If all the permissions are valid then we return true.

```
private bool CheckAccessForNode(SiteMapNode node)
{
    if (!node.Roles.Contains("PUBLIC"))
    {
        if (_account != null && _account.Permissions != null
            && _account.Permissions.Count > 0)
        {
            foreach (string role in node.Roles)
            {
                if (!_account.HasPermission(role))
                    return false;
            }
```

```
                    return true;
            }
            else
                    return false;
        }
        return true;
}
```

Security

Up until now we have discussed navigational aspects of this class. But seeing how security is rolled into this so deeply, it makes sense that we would also have something to check the current node for security reasons rather than just displaying links. This brings us to the `CheckAccessForCurrentNode()` method.

The `CheckAccessForCurrentNode()` method wraps the `CheckAccessForNode()` method and passes in the current `SiteMap` node. If there is sufficient access to the current node, no action is performed. However, if access to the current node is denied, then the user is automatically redirected to the access denied page by way of the `Redirector` class.

```
public void CheckAccessForCurrentNode()
{
    bool result = CheckAccessForNode(CurrentNode);
    if(result)
        return;
    else
        _redirector.GoToAccountAccessDenied();
}
```

Implementing navigation and security

With this wrapper in place we now have a way to easily restrict where our users go and what forms of navigation they see. All we have to do is make calls into this class to get a list of nodes for the appropriate navigation section. We also need to make a call into the `CheckAccessForCurrentNode()` method at some global point.

In our case these calls will be made from our master page as it controls both global access and navigational display. So the first thing we will do is add a call to the `CheckAccessForCurrentNode()` in the `Page_Load()` method of the `SiteMaster.Master` page.

```
protected void Page_Load(object sender, EventArgs e)
{
    _navigation.CheckAccessForCurrentNode();
    ...
```

For navigational purposes (not really covered too much to this point) we have a simple repeater that will iterate over SiteMapNodes. In the design view we have a repeater that looks like this:

```
<asp:Repeater ID="repPrimaryNav" OnItemDataBound="repPrimaryNav_
ItemDataBound" runat="server">
    <ItemTemplate>
        <asp:HyperLink ID="linkPrimaryNav" CssClass="PrimaryNavLink"
                       runat="server"></asp:HyperLink>
    </ItemTemplate>
</asp:Repeater>
```

Then for the Page_Load() method, we have the following binding code in the Master page's code behind:

```
repPrimaryNav.DataSource = _navigation.PrimaryNodes();
repPrimaryNav.DataBind();
```

If we only had this code, we wouldn't have any navigation. This is where the OnItemDataBound="repPrimaryNav_ItemDataBound" property comes in handy. It basically states that the repPrimaryNav_ItemDataBound() method will be our OnItemDataBound event handler.

This method will be responsible for displaying all the links. It also takes care of formatting the links to properly show which section you are in.

```
protected void repPrimaryNav_ItemDataBound(object sender,
RepeaterItemEventArgs e)
{
    HyperLink linkPrimaryNav = e.Item.FindControl("linkPrimaryNav")
                               as HyperLink;
    SiteMapNode node = (SiteMapNode) e.Item.DataItem;
    linkPrimaryNav.Text = node.Title;
    linkPrimaryNav.NavigateUrl = node.Url;
    if (node == _navigation.CurrentNode || node ==
                               _navigation.CurrentNode.ParentNode)
    {
        linkPrimaryNav.CssClass = "PrimaryNavLinkActive";
    }
}
```

Summary

In this chapter we implemented user registration. This allowed us to gather data about our users so that they could become a member of our community. In addition to gathering the data, we briefly covered the ways to store some of the more important information. We also created a CAPTCHA tool to reduce the amount of spam our community would have to deal with. We also provided some tools for the newly registered users so that they could remind themselves of their passwords and edit their account data. Once the registration tools were put in place, we then discussed and implemented an easy way to manage sitewide navigation and security.

With the account creation and management tools in place, we can now move on to other chapters. It was important to get this chapter under our belts as all the following chapters will use many of the features we created here.

4
User Profiles

While user accounts are a requirement for the system to work, user profiles are a must for your community to work. A user profile allows your users to share all sorts of details about themselves. It should be very flexible so that you can easily extend the capabilities of your users' profiles as your community matures and morphs over time.

In this chapter we will discuss the basics of setting up a user profile. This will include collecting various personal tidbits about your users, some contact information, and so on. We will also go over the concept of allowing your users to upload an **avatar** (an icon or image associated with a user's profile) as well as integrating with a third-party avatar service, **Gravatar**. Part of the uploading of a custom avatar will take us into some image manipulation so that all avatars are of equal size and shape on our site!

With this out of the way we can move on to putting the users' public profile together and discuss how that profile can be accessed with a custom homepage or fancy URL. Once we have collected some data about our users — for other users of our site to see — we will need to discuss giving our users control of their privacy settings and allowing them to lock down the display of that data.

The last part of this chapter will get into the creation of a news feed, which keeps track of what our users are doing. This will be a very important feature once the concept of Friends comes into play in the following chapter.

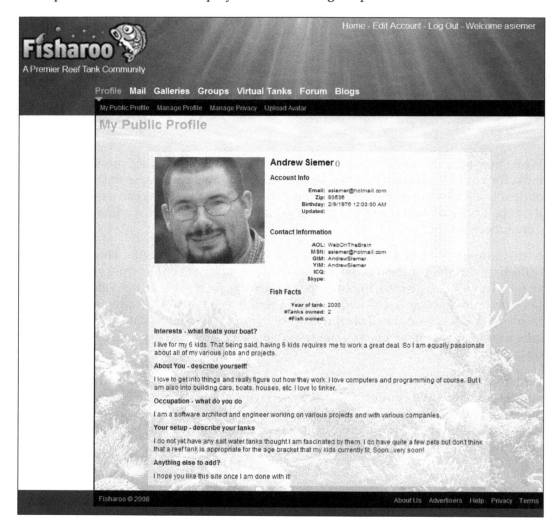

Problem

I am not going to discuss the profiles capability of .NET for the same reason that I chose not to write about the membership capabilities of .NET. This topic is widely covered in many books and on many of the top blog sites. I thought it might be more interesting to discuss a custom implementation of creating a profile and dynamic attributes so that a member's profile could be expanded with time. Also, this will get us a bit deeper into LINQ and how our framework works.

Another interesting topic that must be discussed absolutely while building profiles is avatars. An avatar is a small icon or image that is associated with each user's profile. This allows you to visually pick a profile out of the group with ease. Generally, an avatar is displayed next to just about everything a user does or interacts with. This could be their blog posts, forum posts, comments, and so on. It provides a sort of virtual face-to-face feeling. Here are some example avatars:

Of course, we could take a weak approach and not allow our users to create custom avatars—certain communities do this. We could just provide a gallery of canned avatars for a user to associate with their profile. But the biggest draw to any community site is its ability for the users to have as much free expression as possible. For this reason, we will discuss the other end of the spectrum when it comes to custom avatars.

We need a way for the users to upload their own pictures of just about any size (though we will have a file size constraint! No 10MB images to process please!). Knowing that an avatar is usually closer to the size of an icon rather than a poster, we will need to tackle resizing an image. Also, as we know that images can come in just about any shape, it would be really cool if we could figure out a UI that allows the user to select a specific section of the uploaded image and constrain that selection to a specific shape. We would prefer a square shape as it is the easiest to work with.

Now crop your avatar
Images come in all shapes and sizes so we have provided you with a tool that will allow you to select the section of your image that you would like to use for your avatar.

Perform Crop

In addition to custom avatars, there are many services available these days that provide centralized avatars. This allows a user to upload and manage their avatars in one place and have them automatically feed out to all the sites that they are a member of. We will take a look at how to use one of the largest and most popular services, Gravatar.

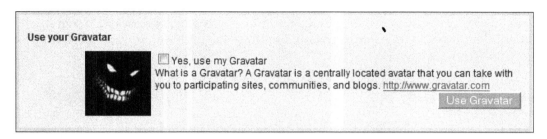

Once we have all the data collection and profile configuration utilities out of the way, we will tackle the issue of displaying that data to our community. A good feature to take on here is the concept of a fancy URL, which will allow our users to have their own personal homepage within our community. A sample page would look like this: www.fisharoo.com/andrewsiemer.

A very popular feature that Facebook has is the concept of a continuous feed about you, your friends, and activities in the community. This sort of feature has become so popular that MySpace has recently implemented a version. I think that this has to be one of my favorite features as it gives me something new to look at on a near daily basis. The more friends you are tracking (covered in Chapter 6), the more the entries you will have to follow. As these feeds or alerts (we will call ours The Filter) generally go on a user's private homepage, and as it is a major subsystem that many other features will dump into, we should address the underlying framework for this now rather than later.

Design

Let's take a look at what the design for these features would look like.

Profile

Our profiles will collect basic data about a user. Some items that we will collect are:

- Various IM (Instant Messaging) IDs
- The users' post/comments
- Some basic fish related information such as how many fish tanks they have and how many fishes they have

In addition to this we will allow our profiles to have dynamic attributes. While these could be dynamic from a user's point of view, we will currently restrict this feature to allow only an administrator of the site to add additional attributes. Some examples of dynamic attributes are "about you", "occupation", and "your (reef/aquarium) setup".

The image will look like this:

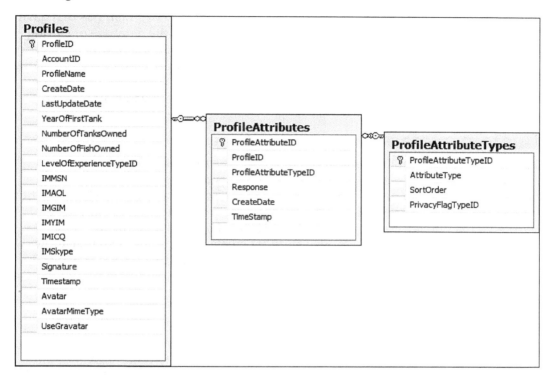

This structure basically allows a profile to have as many extended attributes as the site administrator wants to collect data for.

Manage profile

As we will have several bits of data to manage, we need to consider how best to present this to the user. Also, we don't want to create a bunch of different screens to manage this as it will become a nightmare for us. So I am thinking that we will use a simple step-by-step Wizard type interface so that we can break the data collection/management process into logical steps. This should not only be easier for the user to work with but also to give us a one stop development shop with regards to building this feature.

Avatar

There are many ways to manage images in a system. The top two methods that have been debated heavily over the years is storing the images in the database or storing them on the file system. For every day image galleries, I am all for storing them on the file system. However, something that is used as frequently as an avatar (given the diminutive size of an avatar) can be stored directly with the profiles in the database (look at the **Profiles** table in the previous image—**Avatar** and **AvatarMimeType**).

Custom avatars

Most of us would think that uploading an image or a file is simple. However, resizing an image in a way that it doesn't look all distorted is indeed a challenge. Moreover, we want to upsize and/or crop the image so that it is a perfect square. But we can't squish the user's image into a square. Also we can't just pick out a square portion of the uploaded picture at random! The avatar could end up having just the nose rather than the head. So we need to either create a UI (or find one) that allows the user to specify which section of the uploaded image to use.

Gravatar

`Gravatar.com` and other similar sites have another interesting idea. They allow you to store an avatar in one centralized location and reference it from other sites. This way, if you ever wanted to change your avatar, you could simply go to one location, make the change, and your avatar would be changed across all the sites that reference it. I felt this was something that we could easily implement—so why not include it? There is hardly a reason not to give your users additional flexibility.

Public profile

One of the major drivers for a community site is the voyeuristic nature of a majority of the human population. So to appease this drive, it is very important to present a public area for our users to express and share with the world. This will be a major launching pad for our other features in the following chapters. It is one of the primary places where friends will meet, new messages will be created, and so on.

Custom homepage

Most users of the Internet are used to seeing a URL that looks something like this: `http://www.domain.com/somepage.aspx?id=asduiw892lslcm&t=89889`. While computers can read this easily, it is absolutely meaningless to a human. So, as we already have a public profile page for each of our users, why not allow an easy way for curious folk to locate that page. More importantly why not provide an easy way for our users to share their public profile. Instead of the previous URL, we will make a URL that looks more like `http://www.fisharoo.com/YourUsername`.

Privacy

Once we have provided our users with all these tools to enter their personal data, it is very important that we provide them with a way to manage who sees that data. In this chapter, we will focus on creating the base system that we can later extend upon in the following chapters. In this chapter we will look at how to keep the user's data either public or private. The system that we will create should be flexible enough to allow us to protect a single piece of data, or an entire section of data. An example could be that we want to protect a user's social security data individually (we won't store socials though!) and protect all the users' IM accounts with one flag.

We will use the following image for our privacy settings:

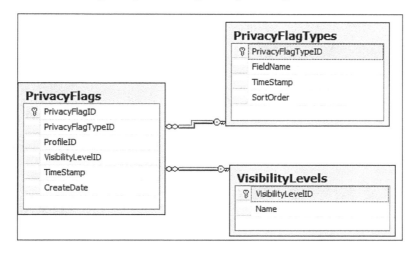

Here the flags are the actual user settings. The flag types are the specific data or areas of data to be protected. As this will be statically defined in the system, this data need not be directly manageable. The visibility level boils down to public, private, and friends-only. With this structure, the end user will be able to configure each flag type independently.

News feed

As I had mentioned earlier, the news feed section is one of my favorite features on any community. I think if this area is created correctly, it will have the most activity and possibly the most value for the users. It essentially allows a user to keep track of other users.

There are several ways in which we can execute this type of functionality. We could keep the data scattered about for all the various types of notifications that we want to track. Or we could centralize it and disconnect it from the relational model. I am opting to keep things simple (as usual). So in our case, when a notification is generated it will be stored in a simple structure that will allow us to be more efficient with regards to getting this data quickly to our users.

The image will look like this:

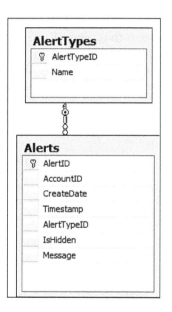

Alerts are generated by each user. All these alerts will show up in a user's homepage so that he/she can see what they are up to chronologically. Again, as we have not yet covered the concept of a Friend, now we can't build much that is friend-specific. But in the next chapter, we will see how with this system friends can subscribe to one another's news feed.

Solution

Now, let's take a look at how we can go about implementing these new features.

Implementing the database

We will start by implementing our database and work our way up from there.

The Profiles table

Before we can really put an interface together, we need to discuss how the data for a profile will be stored. Here is the profiles table:

Column Name	Data Type	Allow Nulls
▶🔑 ProfileID	int	☐
AccountID	int	☐
ProfileName	varchar(100)	☑
CreateDate	smalldatetime	☑
LastUpdateDate	smalldatetime	☑
YearOfFirstTank	int	☐
NumberOfTanksOwned	int	☐
NumberOfFishOwned	int	☐
LevelOfExperienceTyp...	int	☐
IMMSN	varchar(40)	☐
IMAOL	varchar(40)	☐
IMGIM	varchar(40)	☐
IMYIM	varchar(40)	☐
IMICQ	varchar(40)	☐
IMSkype	varchar(40)	☐
Signature	varchar(300)	☐
Timestamp	timestamp	☐
Avatar	varbinary(MAX)	☑
AvatarMimeType	varchar(10)	☑
UseGravatar	int	☐

So let's discuss some of the fields that are somewhat less than normal. In this case, I am referring to the **varbinary(MAX)** field for the **Avatar** storage. With the MAX size constraint (not much of a constraint!), a person could technically store a DVD in this field. This of course would be ridiculous, so we need to make sure that there are some constraints on the front end so that file storage size is kept to a minimum. As you will see later, this field is essentially a character array!

Level of Experience

Once we have our base profile container in place, we can create some of the surrounding tables. The easiest of which is the level of experience system. This will be used as other features of the site are built. Initially, a user can come in and set up his/her profile and claim a level of experience. Then as the user adds posts to the forum, creates new blog entries, or interacts with our community in any other way, we can adjust the user's level of experience dynamically.

	Column Name	Data Type	Allow Nulls
▶🔑	LevelOfExperienceTyp...	int	☐
	LevelOfExperience	varchar(50)	☐
	Timestamp	timestamp	☐
	SortOrder	tinyint	☐

The Attributes table

The next easiest portion of the profile system is the dynamic attributes system. Recall that this will allow the site administrator to easily extend the data that is collected for each user. There are two tables. The first one shows user entered attributes as follows:

	Column Name	Data Type	Allow Nulls
▶🔑	ProfileAttributeID	int	☐
	ProfileID	int	☐
	ProfileAttributeTypeID	int	☐
	Response	varchar(2000)	☐
	CreateDate	smalldatetime	☐
	TimeStamp	timestamp	☐

And the next one shows attribute types:

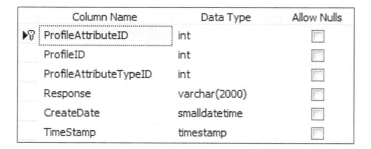

	Column Name	Data Type	Allow Nulls
▶🔑	ProfileAttributeTypeID	int	☐
	AttributeType	varchar(50)	☐
	SortOrder	int	☐
	PrivacyFlagTypeID	int	☐

The Privacy table

Now we can discuss the privacy system. This is simply a one-to-many relationship system with some configuration/lookup tables on the child side of the relationship. We have `PrivacyFlags` for storing the user created values.

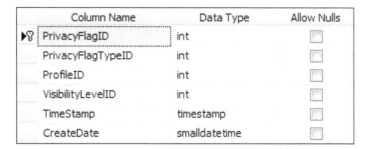

	Column Name	Data Type	Allow Nulls
▶🔑	PrivacyFlagID	int	☐
	PrivacyFlagTypeID	int	☐
	ProfileID	int	☐
	VisibilityLevelID	int	☐
	TimeStamp	timestamp	☐
	CreateDate	smalldatetime	☐

We then have `PrivacyFlagTypes` to define what the flag is protecting.

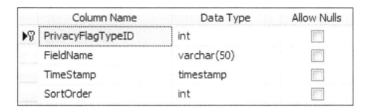

	Column Name	Data Type	Allow Nulls
▶🔑	PrivacyFlagTypeID	int	☐
	FieldName	varchar(50)	☐
	TimeStamp	timestamp	☐
	SortOrder	int	☐

And finally, we have the `VisibilityLevels`, which defines who can see the protected data.

	Column Name	Data Type	Allow Nulls
▶🔑	VisibilityLevelID	int	☐
	Name	varchar(50)	☐

The Alerts table

Now, we are on to the tables that will support our news feed or "Filter" concept on the profile page. This includes the `Alerts` table.

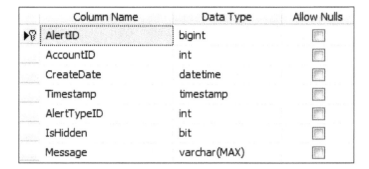

And the `AlertTypes` table.

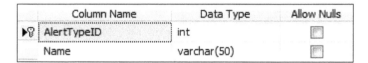

An interesting field to discuss here is the **IsHidden** field. We will use this later so that a user can hide an alert from his/her news feed. We can also use it so that the user can hide a whole set of alerts based on its alert type.

Creating the relationships

Once all the tables are completed, we can create all the relationships.

For this set of tables, we have relationships between the following tables:

- `Profiles` and `LevelOfExperienceTypes`
- `Profiles` and `ProfileAttributes`
- `Profiles` and `PrivacyFlags`
- `Profiles` and `Accounts`
- `ProfileAttributes` and `ProfileAttributeTypes`
- `PrivacyFlags` and `PrivacyFlagTypes`
- `PrivacyFlags` and `VisibilityLevels`
- `Accounts` and `Alerts`
- `Alerts` and `AlertTypes`

Setting up the data access layer

Unlike in the last chapter, our data access layer will be much less involved. All the ground work has already been completed. So from now on, when we speak about setting up the data access layer, all we are really speaking about is opening up the `Fisharoo.dbml` file and dragging our new tables on to the design surface.

So let's do that now through the following steps:

- Open the `Fisharoo.dbml` file.
- Open up your **Server Explorer** window.
- Expand your Fisharoo connect.
- Expand your tables. If you don't see your new tables, try hitting the **Refresh** icon or right-click on tables and click **Refresh**.
- Then drag your new tables onto the design surface.

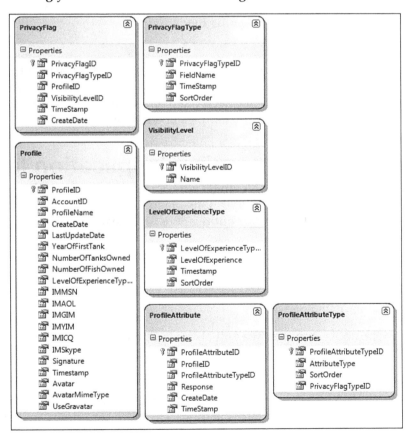

Keep in mind that we are not letting LINQ to track our relationships. So go ahead and delete them from the design surface. Your design surface should have all the items as seen in the previous screenshot (though perhaps in a different arrangement!).

Hit **Save** and you should now have a longer list of domain objects to play with!

Building repositories

With the addition of new tables will come the addition of new repositories to get to the data stored in the tables. We will be creating the following repositories to support our profile needs.

- ProfileRepository
- ProfileAttributeRepository
- PrivacyRepository
- LevelOfExperienceTypeRepository
- AlertRepository

Each of our repositories will have a method for selecting on the basis of the ID, selecting on the basis of the parent ID, for save and delete. Once you have seen one repository, you have pretty much seen them all. Review previous chapters, appendices, or the included code for examples of a repository.

Implementing the services/application layer

Once all the repositories are built for single-serving purposes, we can begin to create the services layer. Again, this layer is responsible for assembling aggregates and performing complex actions with our entities. We will create the following services:

- ProfileService
- PrivacyService
- AlertService
- ProfileAttributeService

In addition to the above services, we will also need to modify a couple of services.

ProfileService

Our profile entity is fairly simple now. But as we continue to build new features, our profile entity will continue to become more and more complex. Currently, a profile only has a list of its extended attributes. Down the road, we will eventually be adding many other lists of children to it.

Let's extend our profile object so that it is aware of its attribute children. Navigate to your domain folder and create a new partial `Profile` class. In this class, let's add a property for the list of ProfileAttributes.

```
public List<ProfileAttribute> Attributes { get; set;}
```

While we are here, let's also add a property to hold the `LevelOfExperienceType` for this profile.

```
public LevelOfExperienceType LevelOfExperienceType { get; set; }
```

Now we can look at building our `ProfileService`. Create a new class in the `Core.Impl` directory called `ProfileService`. This service will be responsible for assembling a profile by an `AccountID` and disassembling a profile to save it. Let's start with the assembly process:

```
public Profile LoadProfileByAccountID(Int32 AccountID)
{
    Profile profile = _profileRepository.GetProfileByAccountID(Accoun
tID);
    List<ProfileAttribute> attributes = new List<ProfileAttribute>();
    LevelOfExperienceType levelOfExperienceType;
    if (profile != null && profile.ProfileID > 0)
    {
        attributes = _profileAttributeService.
                        GetProfileAttributesByProfileID
                        (profile.ProfileID);
        levelOfExperienceType =
                            _levelOfExperienceTypeRepository.
                            GetLevelOfExperienceTypeByID
                            (profile.LevelOfExperienceTypeID);

        profile.Attributes = attributes;
        profile.LevelOfExperienceType = levelOfExperienceType;
    }
    return profile;
}
```

As you can see, this method is responsible for getting a profile and all of its children objects by an `AccountID`. It starts by attempting to retrieve the profile. If the profile is not null, it then attempts to get a list of profile attributes and the `LevelOfExperienceType` for that profile. The method then adds those retrieved values to the profile and returns the profile.

A service is solely responsible for making complex tasks easy to work with and re-usable as you can see in the LoadProfileByAccountID method we have just seen:

Now let's look at what we need to do to save a profile with an equally complex structure:

```
public void SaveProfile(Profile profile)
{
    Int32 profileID;
    profileID = _profileRepository.SaveProfile(profile);
    foreach (ProfileAttribute attribute in profile.Attributes)
    {
        attribute.ProfileID = profileID;
        _profileAttributeRepository.SaveProfileAttribute(attribute);
    }
    _userSession.CurrentUser.Profile =
                        LoadProfileByAccountID
                        (_userSession.CurrentUser.AccountID);
}
```

With this method, we take in a profile. We quickly toss the profile to the profile repository, which knows how to deal with that simple entity. We then strip out each attached profile attribute and toss it to the profile attribute repository and save it. As we store the LevelOfExperienceTypeID with the profile, we don't have to worry about stripping the LevelOfExperienceType out of the profile object to save it!

Account service

Now that we have our ProfileService created, let's extend our AccountService to take advantage of our new features.

Open the AccountService.cs file. Navigate down to the GetAccountByID method. Right after the loading of an Account object, add the following code:

```
Account account = _accountRepository.GetAccountByID(AccountID);
Profile profile = _profileService.LoadProfileByAccountID(AccountID);
if(profile != null)
{
    account.Profile = profile;
}
List<Permission> permissions =
                        _permissionRepository.
                        GetPermissionsByAccountID(AccountID);
                        foreach (Permission permission
                                    in permissions)
{
    account.AddPermission(permission);
}
```

This method now returns an `Account` object with its fully hydrated Profile attached to it.

Now, let's extend our `Login` method in the same `AccountService.cs` file. When the user attempts to login, we get their account with the method that we just extended (`GetAccountByID`). This means that we now have their profile as well! We can now make a decision as to whether we have a user with a fully created profile or not and redirect them accordingly. Let's update the `AccountService.cs` `Login()` method with the following code:

```
if (account.EmailVerified)
{
    _userSession.LoggedIn = true;
    _userSession.Username = Username;
    _userSession.CurrentUser = GetAccountByID(account.AccountID);
    if(_userSession.CurrentUser.Profile != null &&
      _userSession.CurrentUser.Profile.ProfileID > 0)
        _redirector.GoToProfilesDefault();
    else
        _redirector.GoToProfilesManageProfile();
}
```

Of course, this means that we need to add these new methods to our `Redirector` class! Here is the code:

```
public void GoToProfilesProfile()
{
    Redirect("~/Profiles/Profile.aspx");
}
public void GoToProfilesDefault()
{
    Redirect("~/Profiles/Default.aspx");
}
```

Privacy service

The privacy service is currently solely responsible for determining if a piece of data or a section that displays multiple types of data can be displayed or not. It has a method named `ShouldShow()` that returns a boolean value.

```
public bool ShouldShow(Int32 PrivacyFlagTypeID,
    Account AccountBeingViewed,
    Account Account,
    List<PrivacyFlag> Flags)
{
```

```
        bool result;
        //CHAPTER 5 - come back to this when we start friends
        bool isFriend = false;
        //flag marked as private test
        if(Flags.Where(f => f.PrivacyFlagTypeID == PrivacyFlagTypeID &&
    f.VisibilityLevelID == (int)VisibilityLevel.VisibilityLevels.Private).
    FirstOrDefault() != null)
            result = false;
        //flag marked as friends only test
        else if (Flags.Where(f => f.PrivacyFlagTypeID ==
                        PrivacyFlagTypeID && f.VisibilityLevelID ==
                        (int)VisibilityLevel.VisibilityLevels
                        Friends).
            FirstOrDefault() != null && isFriend)
        result = true;
        else if (Flags.Where(f => f.PrivacyFlagTypeID ==
                        PrivacyFlagTypeID && f.VisibilityLevelID ==
                        (int)VisibilityLevel.VisibilityLevels.Public)
            .FirstOrDefault() != null)
            result = true;
        else
            result = false;
        return result;
    }
```

Note that we are using enum rather than record numbers to test against. In order to use these enum values represented by the VisibilityLevel.VisibilityLevels, we will have to create a new partial VisibilityLevel class. Navigate to Core. Domain and create a new class file named VisibilityLevel. In there, enter the following code:

```
public enum VisibilityLevels
{
    Private = 1,
    Friends = 2,
    Public = 3
}
```

On to the ShouldShow method! This method may look complex but is really just checking many different relationships. This method takes into mind the account that is being viewed, the account doing the viewing, the PrivacyFlagType that is being viewed, and a list of PrivacyFlags for the account being viewed.

The method then checks to see if the data is flagged as private, in which case no one but the owner can see it. It then checks to see if the account being viewed and the account doing the viewing are friends, and whether or not the data is marked viewable by friends. As we have not yet implemented Friends, I left a note so that we can come back and rework this section when we get to this concept in Chapter 6.

```
//CHAPTER 5 - come back to this when we start friends
```

And finally, we check to see if the data is marked as public in which case everyone can view it.

Alert service

The AlertService boils down to a wrapper for saving alerts into the system and getting them back out again. Rather than having the client code format a new alert message, we will add new custom alert wrappers such as AddAccountModifiedAlert(). This will not only give us a place to manage how alerts are formatted and stored in our system, but it will also give us a place to modify when we want to extend the system to handle new concepts such as the ability for Friends to get subscribed to your alerts.

```
//Core/Impl/AlertService.cs
private void Init()
{
    account = _userSession.CurrentUser;
    alert = new Alert();
    alert.AccountID = account.AccountID;
    alert.CreateDate = DateTime.Now;
}
...
public void AddAccountModifiedAlert()
{
    Init();
    alertMessage = "<div class=\"AlertHeader\">" +
    GetProfileUrl(account.Username) +
                " modified their account.</div>";
    alert.Message = alertMessage;
    alert.AlertTypeID = (int) AlertType.AlertTypes.AccountModified;
    SaveAlert(alert);
}
...
private void SaveAlert(Alert alert)
{
    _alertRepository.SaveAlert(alert);
}
```

Profile Attribute Service

This service is responsible for assembling a `ProfileAttribute` with its corresponding `ProfileAttributeType` based on the `ProfileAttributeTypeID` that is stored with the `ProfileAttribute`. This is pretty straightforward to implement as it simply makes a call into the `ProfileAttributeRepository` to get a list of `ProfileAttributes` by the specified `ProfileID`. It then iterates through each `ProfileAttribute` and determines its `ProfileAttributeType` via another call into the `ProfileAttributeRepository`.

Keep in mind that this multitrip approach is not the best way to do things with regards to performance. All these round trips could end up being quite costly. However, I have plans to implement a cache layer in the last chapter of this book that you can wrap around all the repositories. Once this is completed, we will be fetching frequently used items out of memory in which case all the round trips won't hurt us.

```
public List<ProfileAttribute> GetProfileAttributesByProfileID(Int32
ProfileID)
{
    List<ProfileAttribute> attributes =
                                profileAttributeRepository.
                                GetProfileAttributesByProfileID
                                (ProfileID);
    foreach (ProfileAttribute attribute in attributes)
    {
        attribute.ProfileAttributeType =
                                profileAttributeRepository.
                                GetProfileAttributeTypeByID
                                (attribute.ProfileAttributeTypeID);
    }
    return attributes;
}
```

Implementing the presentation layer

Now that the entire backend is created and ready to go, let's move on to discussing how we will make the presentation work for us. While the privacy features could just as easily be implemented after everything else, I think it will be easiest if we get it ready first. Then as we build the other areas out, we can sew in our privacy checking where it is needed.

Privacy

Now, let's implement the privacy feature.

Manage privacy

As with all the other types of data we will be collecting from our users, we need to provide a way for our users to manage their privacy—which is not really about data entry though. In this case, we will be providing a way for our user to check who can see a certain section of their data, and who has access to their entire data. We will create a page that is dynamically built based on the `PrivacyFlagTypes` that are defined in the database.

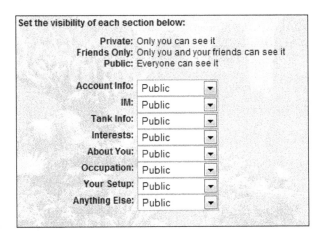

As the view always gets us started, let's take a look at the code there first. As a good chunk of this page is built on the fly, the mark-up for this page is relatively simple. It consists of some instructions explaining what each visibility type is, and a placeholder for our dynamic form elements.

```
//Profiles/ManagePrivacy.aspx
<%@ Page Language="C#" MasterPageFile="~/SiteMaster.Master"
AutoEventWireup="true" CodeBehind="ManagePrivacy.aspx.cs"
Inherits="Fisharoo.FisharooWeb.Profiles.ManagePrivacy" %>
<asp:Content ContentPlaceHolderID="Content" runat="server">
    <div class="divContainer">
        <div class="divContainerTitle">Set the visibility of each
                   section below:</div>
        <div class="divContainerRow">
            <div class="divContainerCellHeader">Private:</div>
            <div class="divContainerCell">Only you can see it</div>
        </div>
        <div class="divContainerRow">
```

```
        <div class="divContainerCellHeader">Friends Only:</div>
        <div class="divContainerCell">Only you and your friends
                can see it</div>
    </div>
    <div class="divContainerRow">
        <div class="divContainerCellHeader">Public:</div>
        <div class="divContainerCell">Everyone can see it</div>
    </div>
    <div class="divContainerRow"> </div>
    <div class="divContainerRow">
        <asp:PlaceHolder ID="phPrivacyFlagTypes"
                    runat="server"></asp:PlaceHolder>
    </div>
    <div class="divContainerFooter">
        <asp:Label ID="lblMessage" runat="server"
            ForeColor="Red"></asp:Label>
        <asp:Button ID="btnSave" runat="server" Text="Save
          Privacy Settings" OnClick="btnSave_Click" />
    </div>
</div>
</asp:Content>
```

This then brings us to our code behind. Of course, it inherits from an interface so that we can pass a reference from this page to our ManagePrivacyPresenter class. As with most Model View Presenter (MVP) pages, we have to new up our presenter file. To get started we pass a reference of this page to the presenter. The thing that is a bit different here is that we are doing this within an overridden OnInit() method rather than in the Page_Load() method. This is done so that our dynamically rendered controls will exist in ViewState. The Page_Load() method occurs after ViewState is already established. This means that if our dynamic controls were added in Page_Load(). we would not have access to their toggled values after the first postback.

```
//Profiles/ManagePrivacy.aspx.cs
public partial class ManagePrivacy : System.Web.UI.Page,
IManagePrivacy
    {
        private ManagePrivacyPresenter _presenter;
        protected override void OnInit(EventArgs e)
        {
            base.OnInit(e);
            _presenter = new ManagePrivacyPresenter();
            _presenter.Init(this);

        }
```

```
public void ShowPrivacyTypes(List<PrivacyFlagType>
                             PrivacyFlagTypes,
                             List<VisibilityLevel>
                             VisibilityLevels,
                             List<PrivacyFlag> PrivacyFlags)
{
    foreach (PrivacyFlagType type in PrivacyFlagTypes)
    {
        //Add the field name to the display
        phPrivacyFlagTypes.Controls.Add(new
                            LiteralControl("<div class=\
                            "divContainerRow\">"));
                            //start container
        phPrivacyFlagTypes.Controls.Add(new
                            LiteralControl("<div class=\
                            "divContainerCellHeader\">"));
                            //start cell header
        phPrivacyFlagTypes.Controls.Add(new
                        LiteralControl(type.
                                    FieldName + ":"));
        phPrivacyFlagTypes.Controls.Add(new
                            LiteralControl("</div>"));
                            //end cell header
        phPrivacyFlagTypes.Controls.Add(new
                        LiteralControl("<div class=\
                            "divContainerCell\">"));
                            //start cell
        //Create the visibility drop down
        DropDownList ddlVisibility = new DropDownList();
        ddlVisibility.ID = "ddlVisibility" +
                        type.PrivacyFlagTypeID.ToString();
        foreach (VisibilityLevel level in VisibilityLevels)
        {
            ListItem li = new
                        ListItem(level.Name,level.
                        VisibilityLevelID.ToString());
            if(!IsPostBack)
                li.Selected =
                        _presenter.IsFlagSelected
                        (type.PrivacyFlagTypeID,
                        level.VisibilityLevelID,
                        PrivacyFlags);
            ddlVisibility.Items.Add(li);
        }
        phPrivacyFlagTypes.Controls.Add(ddlVisibility);
        phPrivacyFlagTypes.Controls.Add(new
                            LiteralControl("</div>"));
```

```
                                            //end cell
            phPrivacyFlagTypes.Controls.Add(new
                                LiteralControl("</div>"));
                                            //end container
        }
    }
    protected void btnSave_Click(object sender, EventArgs e)
    {
        lblMessage.Text = "";
        foreach (PrivacyFlagType type in
            _presenter.GetPrivacyFlagTypes())
        {
            DropDownList ddlVisibility =
                phPrivacyFlagTypes.FindControl("ddlVisibility" +
                                    type.PrivacyFlagTypeID.
                                ToString())as DropDownList;
            if(ddlVisibility != null)
                _presenter.SavePrivacyFlag(type.PrivacyFlagTypeID,
                    Convert.ToInt32(ddlVisibility.SelectedValue));
        }
        lblMessage.Text = "Your privacy settings were saved
                            successfully!";
    }
    public void ShowMessage(string Message)
    {
        lblMessage.Text += Message;
    }
}
```

The thing to note here is that as with all presenter controlled pages, the view calls an Init() method, which is a method in the presenter responsible for loading the page. The presenter calls into the ShowPrivacyTypes() method in the view passing in what is needed to dynamically build the UI. The ShowPrivacyTypes() method then iterates through all the values of the passed in lists to add drop-downs to the place holder in the .aspx page. While loading the UI, it also attempts to locate the current value for each menu to load.

We then have the btnSave_Click() event handler btnSave_Click(). This method is responsible for extracting the current selections and passing those values upstream to the presenter to persist the data to the database.

Next, we have a ShowMessage() method, which allows the presenter to pass messages back to the user of this page.

The presenter, `ManagePrivacyPresenter`, provides us with various methods to load and handle events from the `ManagePrivacy` page. Here is the code:

```
public class ManagePrivacyPresenter
    {
        private IPrivacyRepository _privacyRepository;
        private IProfileService _profileService;
        private Profile profile;
        private IUserSession _userSession;
        private Account account;
        private List<PrivacyFlagType> privacyFlagTypes;
        private List<VisibilityLevel> visibilityLevels;
        private List<PrivacyFlag> privacyFlags;
        private IManagePrivacy _view;
        public ManagePrivacyPresenter()
        {
            _privacyRepository =
                    ObjectFactory.GetInstance<IPrivacyRepository>();
            _profileService =
                    ObjectFactory.GetInstance<IProfileService>();
            _userSession = ObjectFactory.GetInstance<IUserSession>();
            account = _userSession.CurrentUser;
            profile =
            _profileService.LoadProfileByAccountID(account.AccountID);
        }
        public void Init(IManagePrivacy View)
        {
            _view = View;
            LoadPrivacyTypes();
        }
        private void LoadPrivacyTypes()
        {
            privacyFlagTypes =
                    _privacyRepository.GetPrivacyFlagTypes();
            visibilityLevels =
                    _privacyRepository.GetVisibilityLevels();
            privacyFlags =
                    _privacyRepository.GetPrivacyFlagsByProfileID
                    (profile.ProfileID);
            _view.ShowPrivacyTypes(privacyFlagTypes, visibilityLevels,
                                                     privacyFlags);
        }
        public List<PrivacyFlagType> GetPrivacyFlagTypes()
        {
            return privacyFlagTypes;
```

```
        }
        public void SavePrivacyFlag(Int32 PrivacyFlagTypeID, Int32
                                   VisibilityLevelID)
        {
            foreach (PrivacyFlag flag in privacyFlags)
            {
                if (flag.PrivacyFlagTypeID == PrivacyFlagTypeID)
                {
                    flag.VisibilityLevelID = VisibilityLevelID;
                    _privacyRepository.SavePrivacyFlag(flag);
                    return;
                }
            }
            //not in collection?  Add a new one
            PrivacyFlag newFlag = new PrivacyFlag();
            newFlag.PrivacyFlagTypeID = PrivacyFlagTypeID;
            newFlag.VisibilityLevelID = VisibilityLevelID;
            newFlag.ProfileID = profile.ProfileID;
            newFlag.CreateDate = DateTime.Now;
            privacyFlags.Add(newFlag);
            _privacyRepository.SavePrivacyFlag(newFlag);
        }
        public bool IsFlagSelected(Int32 PrivacyFlagTypeID, Int32
                                   VisibilityLevelID, List
                                   <PrivacyFlag> PrivacyFlags)
        {
            List<PrivacyFlag> result = PrivacyFlags.Where(pf =>
                                       pf.PrivacyFlagTypeID ==
                                       PrivacyFlagTypeID &&
                                       pf.VisibilityLevelID ==
                                       VisibilityLevelID).ToList();
            if (result.Count > 0)
            {
                return true;
            }
            return false;
        }
    }
```

The constructor for this class asks `StructureMap` to load up all the repositories and services that are needed for this page to function. In addition to the toolsets, we also create an account and profile to interact with during the life of the presenter.

We then have the `Init()` method, which simply captures the view reference. It then calls the `LoadPrivacyTypes()` to initialize the calling page's UI. This method gets a list of privacy flag types, visibility levels, and the current privacy flags for the current user. The `ShowPrivacyTypes()` is then called in the view to display the UI.

The `GetPrivacyFlagTypes()` method is called from the view when saving the data so that we can iterate over the UI in the same way that we built it. We use a list of `PrivacyFlagTypes` to build the UI so it is only fitting that we also use it to destruct the UI!

This then brings us to the `SavePrivacyFlag()` method, which is responsible for interacting with the save button click event in the view. This method simply iterates over the passed in `PrivacyFlags` and saves them to the database.

The `IsFlagSelected()` method is used by the view to determine which item in each privacy type list was selected previously.

With all this done, we are now free to call into the `PrivacyService` class to see if an area should be shown or not. Although we have privacy data to work with, determining if we should show something or shouldn't, won't currently do us any good as there is no way to add profile data at this time! Let's add a profile management page.

Manage profile

As I know that this area has a big chance of growing and expanding as the site grows, I have decided to build this page using a series of wizard steps. The code for the UI is not difficult by any means, but it is longer than I want to show here in the text! So I will show you the steps.

Here, we collect some attributes about the user's fish tank as shown in the screenshot:

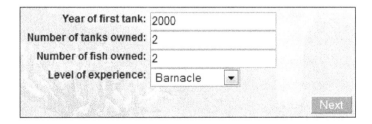

Then, we gather the user's signature (which we can use for any postings to the forum or other features).

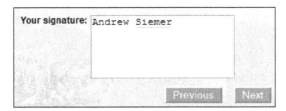

Next we collect all of the user's methods to communicate with other users in the site. We focus on collecting their Instant Messenging client IDs here.

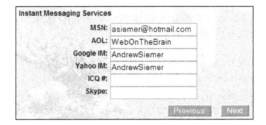

Then, we have some attributes about the user that we can display on their profile page.

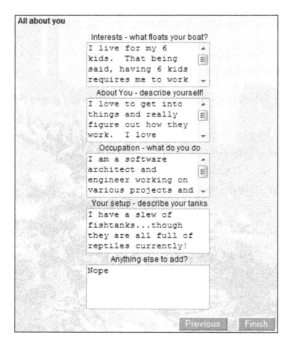

The only steps that are a bit different from the norm are the first and the last steps. The first step's **level of experience** menu and all the inputs in the last step are dynamically generated. In order to do this, we have to load them in the `OnInit()` method rather than in the `Page_Load()` method.

```
//Profiles/ManageProfile.aspx.cs
protected override void OnInit(EventArgs e)
{
    _presenter = new ManageProfilePresenter();
    _presenter.Init(this,IsPostBack);
}
```

This calls into the presenter, which initiates the UI with a couple of previously discussed repository methods.

```
//Profiles/Presenter/ManageProfilePresenter.cs
public void Init(IManageProfile view, bool IsPostback)
{
    _view = view;

    _view.LoadLevelOfExperienceTypes(_levelOfExperienceTypeRepository.Get
                                AllLevelOfExperienceTypes());
        _view.LoadProfileAttributeTypes(_profileAttributeRepository.
    GetProfil
                                eAttributeTypes());
}
```

The presenter then feeds the data back to the UI to dynamically create the required controls, appropriately format them, and finally display the output. As this was done via the `OnInit()` method, all these controls will exist in ViewState and be made accessible as normal.

```
//Profiles/ManageProfile.aspx.cs
public void LoadLevelOfExperienceTypes(List<LevelOfExperienceType>
                                    types)
{
    foreach (LevelOfExperienceType type in types)
    {
        ListItem li = new
                    ListItem(type.LevelOfExperience,type.
                            LevelOfExperienceTypeID.ToString());
        ddlLevelOfExperience.Items.Add(li);
    }
}
...
public void LoadProfileAttributeTypes(List<ProfileAttributeType>
                                    types)
```

```
{
    foreach (ProfileAttributeType type in types)
    {
        Label lbl = new Label();
        lbl.ID = "lblAttribute" +
                            type.ProfileAttributeTypeID.ToString();
        lbl.Text = type.AttributeType;
        Label lblAttributeTypeID = new Label();
        lblAttributeTypeID.ID = "lblAttributeTypeID" +
                            type.ProfileAttributeTypeID.ToString();
        lblAttributeTypeID.Text =
                            type.ProfileAttributeTypeID.ToString();
        lblAttributeTypeID.Visible = false;
        Label lblProfileAttributeID = new Label();
        lblProfileAttributeID.ID = "lblProfileAttributeID" +
                            type.ProfileAttributeTypeID.ToString();
        lblProfileAttributeID.Visible = false;
        Label lblProfileAttributeTimestamp = new Label();
        lblProfileAttributeTimestamp.ID =
                            "lblProfileAttributeTimestamp" +
                            type.ProfileAttributeTypeID.ToString();
        lblProfileAttributeTimestamp.Visible = false;
        TextBox tb = new TextBox();
        tb.ID = "txtProfileAttribute" +
                    type.ProfileAttributeTypeID.ToString();
        tb.TextMode = TextBoxMode.MultiLine;
        tb.Columns = 20;
        tb.Rows = 3;
        CustomValidator cv = new CustomValidator();
        cv.ControlToValidate = "txtProfileAttribute" +
                            type.ProfileAttributeTypeID.ToString();
        cv.ClientValidationFunction = "MaxLength2000";
        cv.ErrorMessage = "This field can only be 2000 characters
                            long!";
        cv.Text = "*";
        cv.ForeColor = System.Drawing.Color.Red;
        phAttributes.Controls.Add(lblAttributeTypeID);
        phAttributes.Controls.Add(lblProfileAttributeID);
        phAttributes.Controls.Add(lblProfileAttributeTimestamp);
        phAttributes.Controls.Add(lbl);
        phAttributes.Controls.Add(new LiteralControl("<BR>"));
        phAttributes.Controls.Add(tb);
        phAttributes.Controls.Add(cv);
        phAttributes.Controls.Add(new LiteralControl("<BR>"));
    }
}
```

Once the UI is created, the rest is a simple matter of plumbing and UI upkeep. In the Page_Load() method, we get the active profile if there is one and populate the UI with the profile data. Each time someone clicks the **Next** button, we clear the error message label. And when the **Finish** button is clicked, we extract the data from the UI and pass it to the presenter to be saved to the database.

Avatar

Now let's look at creating the user's Avatar, which will be displayed next to all his/her interactions with the site.

Upload avatar

Pretty much all the work for this feature occurs in the presenter. The UI presents a file upload box with a standard browse button and an additional button to submit the selected file. When the submit button is clicked, the view passes the PostedFile to the UploadFile() method of the presenter.

```
//Profiles/Presenter/UploadAvatarPresenter.cs
public void UploadFile(HttpPostedFile File)
{
    string extension = Path.GetExtension(File.FileName).ToLower();
    string mimetype;
    byte[] uploadedImage = new byte[File.InputStream.Length];
    switch (extension)
    {
        case ".png":
        case ".jpg":
        case ".gif":
            mimetype = File.ContentType;
            break;
        default:
            _view.ShowMessage("We only accept .png, .jpg, and
                              .gif!");
            return;
            break;
    }
    if (File.ContentLength / 1000 < 1000)
    {
        File.InputStream.Read(uploadedImage, 0,
                              uploadedImage.Length);
        profile.Avatar = uploadedImage;
        profile.AvatarMimeType = mimetype;
        profile.UseGravatar = 0;
        _profileRepository.SaveProfile(profile);
```

```
            _view.ShowCropPanel();
    }
    else
    {
        _view.ShowMessage("The file you uploaded is larger than the
                        1mb limit.  Please reduce the size
                        of your file and try again.");
    }
}
```

This method is responsible for receiving the file and performing some basic checks on the file. We first get the extension of the file being uploaded and check to make sure that the file that was uploaded is an image that we support. If not, we show a message stating the issue.

Once we make it past that check, we check to make sure that the file size is not too large. If the file is in an acceptable size, we read the file into the uploadedImage byte array. We then pass the byte array into the current profile's Avatar property along with its mimetype (we also set the UseGravatar flag to 0, which we will discuss shortly). Finally, we save this data to the user's profile and update the display to show the cropping UI. Alternatively, if the file size was too large, we show an error message.

Image manipulation

To start with, the entire UI for this image cropping tool is located here: http://www. defusion.org.uk/code/javascript-image-cropper-ui-using-prototype- scriptaculous/. This is an open source JavaScript tool that provides us with all the fancy interface options that can be dragged and resized. It uses prototype (http://www.prototypejs.org/), scriptaculous (http://script.aculo.us/), and some fancy foot work from Dave Spurr. To implement this script, download the source from the defusion site above (leave a donation if you like it!) and include the references to the prototype, scriptaculous, and cropper files.

```
<script type="text/javascript" src="/js/cropper/lib/prototype.js"
        language="javascript"></script>
<script type="text/javascript"
                src="/js/cropper/lib/scriptaculous.js?
                load=builder,dragdrop" language="javascript"></script>
<script type="text/javascript" src="/js/cropper/cropper.js"
        language="javascript"></script>
```

Once you have the JavaScript side plugged in, we need to add some items to our ASPX page to get this widget factory working. To start with, we need to add an image control that will load the image that we want to operate on.

```
<asp:Image ImageUrl="~/images/ProfileAvatar/ProfileImage.aspx"
id="imgCropImage" runat="server"/>
```

 Note that this Image control has an `ImageUrl` reference to a page rather than an image. The `images/ProfileAvatar/ProfileImage.aspx` page displays a user's avatar depending on the current configuration of his/her profile. If it doesn't have an avatar, it shows a default avatar. If it is decided to use the Gravatar service instead (discussed shortly) it shows the avatar stored on Gravatar. On the other hand, if the profile has an avatar, it is displayed.

This is optional, but the cropper script provides us with a preview of what we are doing. To implement this, we need to have a location for the preview to output in the form of a `div` tag.

```
<div id="previewWrap"></div>
```

We then need to add a JavaScript function that hooks up the cropper scripts to our UI. This script sets some of the basic properties such as what the image's ID is, where to stash the output for the preview, the minimum height and width, a fixed ratio (forcing the cropper to be a square in our case), and what to do when the cropping is complete.

```
<script type="text/javascript" language="javascript">
    Event.observe( window, 'load', function() {
        new Cropper.ImgWithPreview(
            'ct100_Content_imgCropImage',
            {
                previewWrap: 'previewWrap',
                minWidth: 100,
                minHeight: 100,
                ratioDim: {x: 100,y: 100},
                displayOnInit: true,
                onEndCrop: onEndCrop
            }
        );
    } );
</script>
```

We want the cropper to store some of the data that is captured in some hidden fields so that we can work with it on the server side. To do that, we will add some `HiddenField` controls to the inside of the crop panel.

```
<asp:HiddenField ID="hidX1" runat="server" />
<asp:HiddenField ID="hidY1" runat="server" />
<asp:HiddenField ID="hidX2" runat="server" />
<asp:HiddenField ID="hidY2" runat="server" />
<asp:HiddenField ID="hidWidth" runat="server" />
<asp:HiddenField ID="hidHeight" runat="server" />
```

We then need to add a function that handles the `onEndCrop` event that is fired off by the cropper. This will actually handle storing the data into the `HiddenField` controls.

```
<script type="text/javascript">
function onEndCrop( coords, dimensions )
{
    $( 'ctl00_Content_hidX1' ).value = coords.x1;
    $( 'ctl00_Content_hidY1' ).value = coords.y1;
    $( 'ctl00_Content_hidX2' ).value = coords.x2;
    $( 'ctl00_Content_hidY2' ).value = coords.y2;
    $( 'ctl00_Content_hidWidth' ).value = dimensions.width;
    $( 'ctl00_Content_hidHeight' ).value = dimensions.height;
}
</script>
```

Now, once a user has selected the area of the image that he/she would like to use for the avatar and submits that selection to the server, we have what we need to perform an image crop. The presenter's `CropFile()` method will handle this task.

```
//Profiles/Presenter/UploadAvatarPresenter.cs
public void CropFile(Int32 X, Int32 Y, Int32 Width, Int32 Height)
{
    byte[] imageBytes = profile.Avatar.ToArray();
    using (MemoryStream ms = new MemoryStream(imageBytes, 0,
                                         imageBytes.Length))
    {
        ms.Write(imageBytes, 0, imageBytes.Length);
        System.Drawing.Image img =
            System.Drawing.Image.FromStream(ms, true);
        Bitmap bmpCropped = new Bitmap(200, 200);
        Graphics g = Graphics.FromImage(bmpCropped);
        Rectangle rectDestination = new Rectangle(0, 0,
                            bmpCropped.Width, bmpCropped.Height);
        Rectangle rectCropArea = new Rectangle(X,Y,Width,Height);
```

```
        g.DrawImage(img, rectDestination, rectCropArea,
                    GraphicsUnit.Pixel);
        g.Dispose();
        MemoryStream stream = new MemoryStream();
        bmpCropped.Save(stream,
                    System.Drawing.Imaging.ImageFormat.Jpeg);
        Byte[] bytes = stream.ToArray();
        profile.Avatar = bytes;
        _profileRepository.SaveProfile(profile);
    }
    _view.ShowApprovePanel();
}
```

This method expects the X and Y coordinates of where the crop is to start as well as the width and height of the crop. This gives us the location of the square that we plan to extract from our uploaded image.

We then load the image that is currently stored in the profile into the `imageBytes` byte array. Once we have the data stored in the array, we load it into memory. Note that we perform this task inside a `using` statement. This ensures that all the resources are released once we are complete with our operation.

We then load the memory stream into an Image. Now, we create a new `Bitmap` object, `bmpCropped` with the size of the avatar that we wish to achieve. This will store our completed avatar. We then create a `Graphics` object, `g`, which will actually carry out the cropping on the `bmpCropped` `Bitmap`.

Now we are ready to actually perform the surgery on our image! We will start by creating two rectangles—one rectangle to hold our final image, and the other to hold the image to be cropped from our original image. We then call the `DrawImage()` method on our `Graphics` object and pass in our `Image`, the destination coordinates, the crop coordinates, and the unit of measure—pixels in this case. This results in the `bmpCropped` image having the appropriately cropped portion of our originally uploaded image.

Now, we pass that new image back into memory. We then convert it into a byte array, and finally save it back to our profile.

Gravatar

As we have discussed earlier, Gravatar is a service that allows you to store your avatars in a central place. It allows you to associate an avatar to your email address so that other sites (like ours) can reference it later. This is great for a user who has profiles scattered all over the Internet!

In order for our users to use the Gravatar service, all they have to do is check the box on the initial page of the upload avatar screen. When they hit **submit**, we set the UseGravatar property of their Profile to 1. Then whenever we call the ProfileImage.aspx page to display the avatar, we must use the Gravatar instead of the locally stored avatar.

In order to make a call into the Gravatar service, we have to create a URL with a properly formatted email address in the form of a hexadecimal MD5 hash. I created a method in our Cryptography class to perform this conversion for us.

```
public static string CreateMD5Hash(string StringToHash)
{
    MD5 md5Hasher = MD5.Create();
    byte[] data =
      md5Hasher.ComputeHash(Encoding.Default.GetBytes(StringToHash));
    StringBuilder sBuilder = new StringBuilder();
    for (int i = 0; i < data.Length; i++)
    {
        sBuilder.Append(data[i].ToString("x2"));
    }
    return sBuilder.ToString();
}
```

I then created a simple extension method that handles the conversion for us in a more simplified manner than calling into the Cryptography suite directly.

```
public static string ToMD5Hash(this string s)
{
    return Cryptography.CreateMD5Hash(s);
}
```

Now we have enough background to see the method in the ProfileImage.aspx.cs file that loads the Gravatar.

```
public string GetGravatarURL()
{
    defaultAvatar = Server.UrlPathEncode(_webContext.RootUrl +
                                "/images/ProfileAvatar/Male.jpg");
    gravatarURL = "http://www.gravatar.com/avatar.php?";
    gravatarURL += "gravatar_id=" + account.Email.ToMD5Hash();
    gravatarURL += "&rating=r";
    gravatarURL += "&size=80";
    gravatarURL += "&default=" + defaultAvatar;
    return gravatarURL;
}
```

The properties that we discussed are fairly easy to figure out. However, you can get a full listing of how to work with the Gravatar service here: `http://site.gravatar.com/site/implement#section_1_1`

Public profile

Now that we have:

- Privacy figured out
- Have provided a way for our users to manage their profile data
- Allowed them to upload and appropriately format their avatar

We need to provide our users with a page that displays all their data.

For the most part this is simply another "plumbing page", meaning that we are just displaying data here. Nothing overly complex! So I will skip most of the leg work and get right to the nitty gritty, which is how our privacy stuff is handled.

In the ASPX page, I have stored everything within panels such as this:

```
<asp:Panel ID="pnlPrivacyAccountInfo" runat="server">
    <div class="divContainerTitle">Account Info</div>
    <div class="divInnerRowHeader">Email:</div>
    <div class="divInnerRowCell"><asp:Literal ID="litEmail"
runat="server"></asp:Literal> </div>
    <div class="divInnerRowHeader">Zip:</div>
    <div class="divInnerRowCell"><asp:Literal ID="litZip"
runat="server"></asp:Literal> </div>
    <div class="divInnerRowHeader">Birthday:</div>
    <div class="divInnerRowCell"><asp:Literal ID="litBirthDate"
runat="server"></asp:Literal> </div>
    <div class="divInnerRowHeader">Updated:</div>
    <div class="divInnerRowCell"><asp:Literal ID="litLastUpdateDate"
runat="server"></asp:Literal> </div><br />
</asp:Panel>
```

This allows me to easily lock down an area of data where I need to. In the presenter for this page, I have a `TogglePrivacy()` method.

```
private void TogglePrivacy()
{
    _view.pnlPrivacyIMVisible(_privacyService.ShouldShow((int)Pri
vacyFlagType.PrivacyFlagTypes.IM,_accountBeingViewed, _account, _
privacyFlags));
    _view.pnlPrivacyAccountInfoVisible(_privacyService.ShouldShow((int
)PrivacyFlagType.PrivacyFlagTypes.AccountInfo,_accountBeingViewed,
```

```
_account, _privacyFlags));
    _view.pnlPrivacyTankInfoVisible(_privacyService.ShouldShow((int)Pr
ivacyFlagType.PrivacyFlagTypes.TankInfo,_accountBeingViewed, _account,
_privacyFlags));
}
```

This method makes a call to the `PrivacyService.ShouldShow()` method, which returns a Boolean value of whether or not the item should be displayed. This Boolean value is directly set to the `Panel.Visible` property in the view that effectively shows or hides the data in question.

Custom homepage

When I say "custom homepage", I am really referring to the public profile page in an easy to get to manner. This is really a fancy URL, something like `http://www.fisharoo.com/asiemer`. We could even take it as far as `http://asiemer.fisharoo.com` or something along those lines! We will stick with the first example in our case.

To implement this, we need to do a couple of quick and easy steps. First, we need to create a new `HttpModule`. HTTP modules are executed in the ASP.NET pipeline prior to HTTP handlers. They have full control over the request and can modify it in any way that they see fit. Once all the modules in the pipeline have had their chance to interact with the request, the HTTP handlers in the pipeline get their chance to interact with the request. The HTTP handlers then pass the result back through the HTTP modules. It looks something like this:

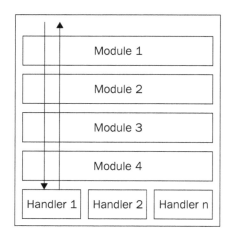

What we want to do is allow the users to specify their username as a directory on our site. So we will create a module that will check to see if the specified file exists. If it doesn't, we will add an additional check to see if the specified directory is actually a username. If we find that the directory is a username, then we will redirect the user's request to the `Profile.aspx` page and load the specified profile.

```
public class UrlRewrite : IHttpModule
{
    private IAccountRepository _accountRepository;
    public UrlRewrite()
    {
        _accountRepository =
                ObjectFactory.GetInstance<IAccountRepository>();
    }
    public void Init(HttpApplication application)
    {
        //let's register our event handler
        application.PostResolveRequestCache +=
            (new EventHandler(this.Application_OnAfterProcess));
    }
    public void Dispose()
    {

    }
    private void Application_OnAfterProcess(object source,
                                        EventArgs e)
    {
        HttpApplication application = (HttpApplication)source;
        HttpContext context = application.Context;
        string[] extensionsToExclude = { ".axd", ".jpg", ".gif",
                            ".png", ".xml", ".config", ".css", "
                            .js", ".aspx", ".htm", ".html" };
        foreach (string s in extensionsToExclude)
        {
            if
              (application.Request.PhysicalPath.ToLower().Contains(s))
                return;
        }
        if (!File.Exists(application.Request.PhysicalPath))
        {
            string username = application.Request.Path.Replace("/",
                                                    "");
            Account account =
                    _accountRepository.GetAccountByUsername(username);
            if (account != null)
```

```
                 {
                    string UserURL = "~/Profiles/profile.aspx?AccountID="
                                   + account.AccountID.ToString();
                    context.Response.Redirect(UserURL);            }
                else
                {
                    context.Response.Redirect("~/PageNotFound.aspx");
                }
            }
        }
    }
```

First, notice that this class inherits the IHttpModule interface. This ensures that the code that we plan to plug into the ASP.NET pipeline conforms to what is expected by that pipeline. This interface expects us to have the Init() and Dispose() methods.

Then in the constructor we load our AccountRepository. We do this to perform our username lookup with the extracted entry.

We then get to our Init() method, which hooks up our Application_ OnAfterProcess() event handler to the HttpApplication. PostResolveRequestCache event. This allows our module to handle the events and interact with the pipeline.

In the Application_OnAfterProcess() method, we load up instances of the HttpApplication and HttpContext objects so that we can work with the current request. Next, we have a string array that holds all the extensions of all the file types that we don't want to process. This is important as there are some types of files that can't be processed by our file system checking (such as .axd) and some files that we don't want to process simply because of the resources that are used by this method.

Once we have made it past our checks and balances, we can finally check the file system to see if the resource exists. If it doesn't, then we can extract the path of the file requested, which essentially gives us the requested username. We then attempt to load an Account object with that username. If the Account is null, we send the requester to the PageNotFound.aspx page. If an Account was found, we then redirect the requester to the Profile.aspx page where we load the appropriate profile.

One last step before any of this will work! We need to plug our custom module into the web.config file so that it is actually loaded into the pipeline when the application is launched. Add the following entry to the web.config file in the <httpModules> section:

```
<add type="Fisharoo.FisharooWeb.Handlers.UrlRewrite, Fisharoo.
FisharooWeb" name="UrlRewrite" />
```

News feed

The last concept that we will cover in our discussion about building profiles is news feed. A news feed allows us to see what we have been doing with our account, friends, our photos, and any other changes in the system. More importantly, it will allow us to see what our friends have been doing with all their data such as when they add a new photo.

This system will be built on the alerts system that we have already discussed. Any time we want to add a new alert to the system based on an action performed by our user or the system, we simply make a call into the AlertService and select the appropriate method such as AddNewAvatarAlert(). Once the site is peppered with the addition of alerts to the system, we will have a fairly active news feed to follow. Now, we just need a place to read this feed!

Knowing that this news feed will easily be one of the most active pages on our site, we should put it on the users' homepage so that they can see it as soon as they log in.

To implement this, all we need is a repeater on the homepage, which we can hook up to a list of alerts for the current user.

```
<asp:Repeater ID="repFilter" runat="server">
    <ItemTemplate>
        <asp:Label ID="lblMessage" runat="server" Text='<%#
                ((Alert)Container.DataItem).Message  %>'></asp:Label>
    </ItemTemplate>
    <SeparatorTemplate>
        <div class="AlertSeparator"></div>
    </SeparatorTemplate>
</asp:Repeater>
```

Then from the presenter, we need to pass the view, the appropriate data to bind to.

```
private void ShowDisplay()
{
_view.ShowAlerts(_alertService.GetAlertsByAccountID(_userSession.Curr
                entUser.AccountID));
}
```

Once we get into the concept of *Friends,* this page will be much more active as users can see their alerts as well as their friends!

Summary

We have covered a lot of ground in this chapter. We have discussed the concept of a profile and a way for our users to manage their data. We have also built a way for our users to manage their privacy regarding their profile data. We have also created tools for our users to manage a custom avatar as well as a way to hook up to their centrally stored Gravatar. With all of these features out of the way, we have created a public profile for our users. And finally, we also created a default landing page for users where they can see their alerts.

5
Friends

The subject of this chapter is the key to the success of any community. Your friend features will be the main reason for people to interact with your community. It is also the biggest drive for your users to advertise for you. "Hey Peter, come and check this out. I love it, so will you!" — a friend in a community site, like in life, is someone who you have something in common with, enjoy the company of, or turn to when you have something to discuss. A circle of friends can be thought of as a sub-community within a community.

This chapter will show you how to take advantage of people's nature to congregate around things that they enjoy, find useful, or that intrigue them. We will start this chapter by extending the framework to allow for relationships to be built between our users. We will then add some features that allow our users to locate all of their existing friends, as well as make new friends. Then we will have a discussion about providing real time status updates in the form of a micro blog to feed the voyeuristic nature of our friends. Once we have these aspects in place, we will update our alerts system so that all of our friends can stay in touch with everything we are doing.

Problem

There are many aspects to building relationships in any community—real or virtual. First and foremost is initiating contact with the people whom you will eventually call your friends. The easiest way to locate someone who you might want to call a friend is to directly invite the people whom you already know as a friend. We will do this in a few ways.

- First, we will provide a way for our users to search the site for friends who are also members.

- Second, we will create a form that allows you to enter your friends' email IDs and invite them directly.

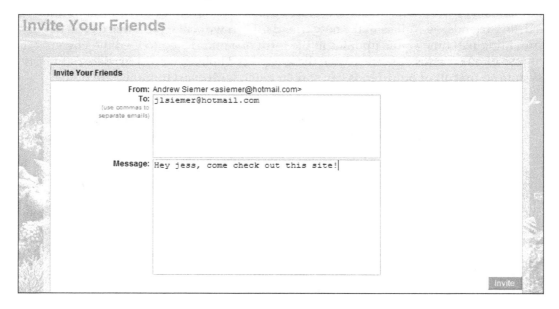

- Third, we will create a form that allows you to import all of your contacts from Outlook.

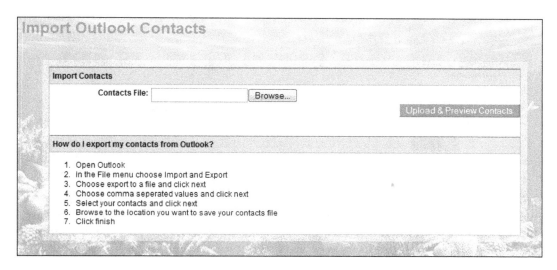

All of these methods of inviting a friend into the system would of course generate an email invite (and eventually a system based message—see next chapter). The user would have the ability to then follow the link into the system and either sign up or log in to accept the request.

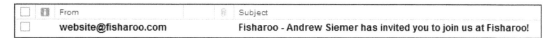

The preceding screenshot shows a sample email that the user would receive in their inbox.

And following is the message that would be seen:

Once the user has clicked on the link in their email, he/she will be taken to a page displaying the request.

Once we have a way for our users to attach friends to their profile, we need to start integrating the concept of friends into the fabric of our site. We will need a way for our users to view all of their friends. We will also need a way for our users to remove the relationships (for those users who are no longer friends!).

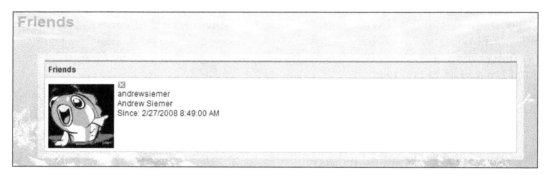

Then we will need to add friends to our user's public profile.

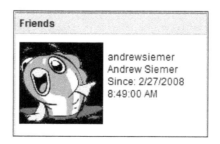

While this is a good first pass at integrating the concept of friends into our site, there are a couple more steps for true integration. We need to add friend request and friend confirm alerts. We also need to modify the alert system so that when users modify their profile, change their avatar, or any other alert that is triggered by users of our system, all of their friends are notified on **The Filter**.

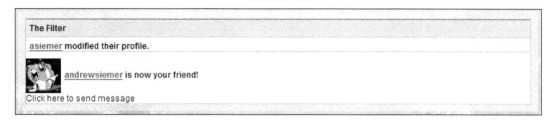

Once this is done we have one final topic to cover — which sort of fits in the realm of friends — the concept of **Status Updates**. This is a form of a micro blog. It allows users to post something about:

- What they are currently doing
- Where they are or
- What they are thinking about

This is then added to their profile and sent out to their friends' filters.

The box in the preceding screenshot is where the user can enter his/her **Status Updates**.

Each of these updates will also be shown on the updates view and in their filter views.

Status Updates
3/10/2008 12:26:00 AM - going to bed now...tired
3/9/2008 6:54:00 PM - hello world

This really helps to keep **The Filter** busy and helps people feel involved with their friends.

 Twitter.com is this concept to the max. Their whole site is centered around the concept of the micro blog. I have seen cases where someone will post to Twitter—"I am going to such and such bar. If you are in the area, meet me for a drink!" As you can hook your cell phone up to their site, people get immediate notification regarding the post. This is the ultimate form of community, in my mind, in that if you have hundreds of friends someone is bound to be in your area. Very cool!!

Design

Now let's talk about the design of these features.

Friends

This chapter is an attempt to throw light on the infrastructure needs and more heavily focused on the UI side for creating and managing relationships. That being said, there is always some form of groundwork that has to be in place prior to adding new features.

In this case we need to add the concept of a friend prior to having the ability to create friendships. This concept is a relatively simple one as it is really only defining a relationship between two accounts. We have the account that requested the relationship and the account that accepted the relationship.

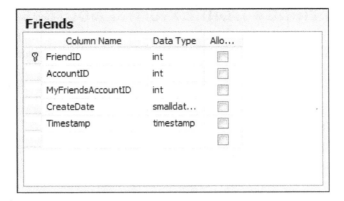

This allows an account to be linked to as many other accounts as they wish.

Finding Friends

Like in life, it is very difficult to create friends without first locating and meeting people. For that reason the various ways to locate and invite someone to be your friend is our first topic.

Searching for a Friend

The easiest way to locate friends who might be interested in the same site that you are is to search through the existing user base. For that reason we will need to create a simple keyword search box that is accessible from any page on the site. This search feature should take a look at several fields of data pertaining to an account and return all possible users. From the search results page we should be able to initiate a friend request.

Inviting a Friend

The next best thing to locating friends who are already members of the site is to invite people who you know out of the site. The quickest way to implement this is to allow a user to manually enter an email address or many email addresses, type a message, and then submit. This would be implemented with a simple form that generates a quick email to the recipient list. In the body of the email will be a link that allows the recipients to come in to our site.

Importing Friends from External Sources

An obvious extension of the last topic is to somehow automate the importing process of contacts from an email management tool. We will create a toolset that allows the user to export their contacts from Outlook and import them via a web form. The user should then be able to select the contacts that they want to invite.

Sending an Invitation

With all the three of the above methods we will end up sending out an invitation email. We could simply send out an email with a link to the site. However, we need to maintain:

- Who has been invited
- Who initiated the invitation and
- When this occurred

Then in the email, rather than just invite people in, we want to assign the user a key so that we can easily identify them on their way in. We will use a system generated **GUID** to do this. In the case of inviting an existing user, we will allow him/her to log in to acknowledge the new friendship. In the case of a non-member user who was invited, we will allow him/her to create a new account. In both cases we will populate the invitation with the invited user's **Account ID** so that we have some history about the relationship.

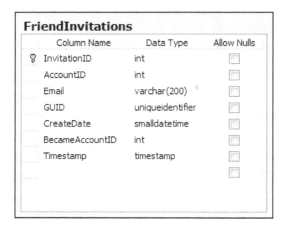

Adding Friend Alerts to The Filter

Once we have the framework in place for inviting and accepting friendship requests, we need to extend our existing system with alerts. These alerts should show up on existing user's Filters to show that they sent an invitation. We should also have alerts showing that a user has been invited. Once a user has accepted a friendship we should also have an alert.

Interacting With Your Friends

Now let's discuss some of the features that we need to interact with our friends.

Viewing Your Friends

Friends are only good if a user can interact with them. The first stop along this train of thought is to provide a page that allows a user to see all the friends he/she has. This is a jumping off point for a user to view the profile of friends. Also, as the concept of a user's profile grows, more data can be shown about each friend in an at-a-glance format.

In addition to an all **Friends** page, we can add friends' views to a user's public profile so that other users can see the relationships.

Managing your friends

Now that we can see into all the relationships we can finally provide the users with the ability to remove a relationship. In our initial pass this will be a permanent deletion of the relationship.

Following Your Friends

Now, we can extend the alert system so that when alerts are generated for a common user, such as updating their profile information, uploading a new photo, or any other user specific task, all the user's friends are automatically notified via their Filter.

Providing Status Updates to Your Friends

Somewhat related to friend-oriented relationships and **The Filter** is the concept of micro blogs. We need to add a way for a user to send a quick blurb about what they are doing, what they are thinking, and so on. This would also show up on the Filters of all the user's friends. This feature creates a lot of dynamic content on an end user's homepage, which keeps things interesting.

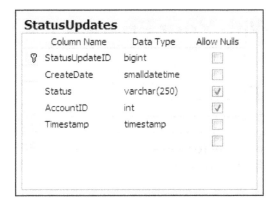

Solution

Now let's look at our solution.

Implementing the Database

Let's look at the tables that are needed to support these new features.

The Friends Table

As the concept of friends is our base discussion for this chapter, we will immediately dive in and start creating the tables around this subject. As you have seen previously this is very straightforward table structure that simply links one account to the other.

	Column Name	Data Type	Allow Nulls
▶🔑	FriendID	int	☐
	AccountID	int	☐
	MyFriendsAccountID	int	☐
	CreateDate	smalldatetime	☐
	Timestamp	timestamp	☐

All these fields should be totally understandable. Here's the SQL:

```
CREATE TABLE [dbo].[Friends](
    [FriendID] [int] IDENTITY(1,1) NOT NULL,
    [AccountID] [int] NOT NULL,
    [MyFriendsAccountID] [int] NOT NULL,
    [CreateDate] [smalldatetime] NOT NULL CONSTRAINT
                [DF_Friends_CreateDate] DEFAULT (getdate()),
    [Timestamp] [timestamp] NOT NULL,
 CONSTRAINT [PK_Friends] PRIMARY KEY CLUSTERED
(
    [FriendID] ASC
)WITH (PAD_INDEX  = OFF, STATISTICS_NORECOMPUTE  = OFF,
      IGNORE_DUP_KEY = OFF, ALLOW_ROW_LOCKS  = ON, ALLOW_PAGE_LOCKS
      = ON) ON [PRIMARY]
) ON [PRIMARY]
```

Friend Invitations

This table is responsible for keeping track of who has been invited to the site, by whom, and when. It also holds the key (**GUID**) that is sent to the friends so that they can get back into the system under the appropriate invitation. Once a friend has accepted the relationship, their **AccountID** is stored here too, so that we can see how relationships were created in the past.

	Column Name	Data Type	Allow Nulls
▶🔑	InvitationID	int	☐
	AccountID	int	☐
	Email	varchar(200)	☐
	GUID	uniqueidentifier	☐
	CreateDate	smalldatetime	☐
	BecameAccountID	int	☐
	Timestamp	timestamp	☐

Here is that SQL:

```
CREATE TABLE [dbo].[FriendInvitations](
    [InvitationID] [int] IDENTITY(1,1) NOT NULL,
    [AccountID] [int] NOT NULL,
    [Email] [varchar](200) NOT NULL,
    [GUID] [uniqueidentifier] NOT NULL,
    [CreateDate] [smalldatetime] NOT NULL CONSTRAINT
                [DF_Invitations_CreateDate] DEFAULT (getdate()),
```

```
    [BecameAccountID] [int] NOT NULL CONSTRAINT
              [DF_FriendInvitations_BecameAccountID]  DEFAULT ((0)),
    [Timestamp] [timestamp] NOT NULL,
 CONSTRAINT [PK_Invitations] PRIMARY KEY CLUSTERED
(
    [InvitationID] ASC
)WITH (PAD_INDEX  = OFF, STATISTICS_NORECOMPUTE  = OFF,
       IGNORE_DUP_KEY = OFF, ALLOW_ROW_LOCKS  = ON, ALLOW_PAGE_LOCKS
     = ON) ON [PRIMARY]
) ON [PRIMARY]
```

Status Updates

Status Updates allow a user to tell their friends what they are doing at that time. This is a micro blog so to speak.

 A **micro blog** allows a user to write small blurbs about anything. Examples of this are Twitter and Yammer. For more information take a look here: http://en.wikipedia.org/wiki/Micro-blogging.

The table needed for this is also simple. It tracks who said what, what was said, and when.

Column Name	Data Type	Allow Nulls
▶🔑 StatusUpdateID	bigint	☐
CreateDate	smalldatetime	☐
Status	varchar(250)	☑
AccountID	int	☑
Timestamp	timestamp	☐

Here is that SQL code for that table:

```
CREATE TABLE [dbo].[StatusUpdates](
[StatusUpdateID] [bigint] IDENTITY(1,1) NOT NULL,
    [CreateDate] [smalldatetime] NOT NULL CONSTRAINT
                 [DF_StatusUpdates_CreateDate]  DEFAULT (getdate()),
    [Status] [varchar](250) NULL,
    [AccountID] [int] NULL,
    [Timestamp] [timestamp] NOT NULL,
 CONSTRAINT [PK_StatusUpdates] PRIMARY KEY CLUSTERED
(
    [StatusUpdateID] ASC
)WITH (PAD_INDEX  = OFF, STATISTICS_NORECOMPUTE  = OFF,
```

```
        IGNORE_DUP_KEY = OFF, ALLOW_ROW_LOCKS  = ON, ALLOW_PAGE_LOCKS
        = ON) ON [PRIMARY]
) ON [PRIMARY]
```

Creating the Relationships

Here are the relationships that we need for the tables we just discussed:

- Friends and Accounts via the owning account
- Friends and Accounts via the friends account
- FriendInvitations and Accounts
- StatusUpdates and Accounts

Friends Constraints

```
ALTER TABLE [dbo].[Friends]  WITH CHECK ADD  CONSTRAINT [FK_Friends_
Accounts] FOREIGN KEY([AccountID])
REFERENCES [dbo].[Accounts] ([AccountID])
GO
ALTER TABLE [dbo].[Friends] CHECK CONSTRAINT [FK_Friends_Accounts]
GO
ALTER TABLE [dbo].[Friends]  WITH CHECK ADD  CONSTRAINT [FK_Friends_
Accounts1] FOREIGN KEY([MyFriendsAccountID])
REFERENCES [dbo].[Accounts] ([AccountID])
GO
ALTER TABLE [dbo].[Friends] CHECK CONSTRAINT [FK_Friends_Accounts1]
```

FriendInvitations constraints

```
ALTER TABLE [dbo].[FriendInvitations]  WITH CHECK ADD  CONSTRAINT [FK_
FriendInvitations_Accounts] FOREIGN KEY([AccountID])
REFERENCES [dbo].[Accounts] ([AccountID])
GO
ALTER TABLE [dbo].[FriendInvitations] CHECK CONSTRAINT [FK_
FriendInvitations_Accounts]
```

StatusUpdates constraints

```
ALTER TABLE [dbo].[StatusUpdates]  WITH CHECK ADD  CONSTRAINT [FK_
StatusUpdates_Accounts] FOREIGN KEY([AccountID])
REFERENCES [dbo].[Accounts] ([AccountID])
GO
ALTER TABLE [dbo].[StatusUpdates] CHECK CONSTRAINT [FK_StatusUpdates_
Accounts]
```

Setting Up the Data Access Layer

Let's extend the data access layer now to handle these new tables. Open your `Fisharoo.dbml` file and drag in these three new tables.

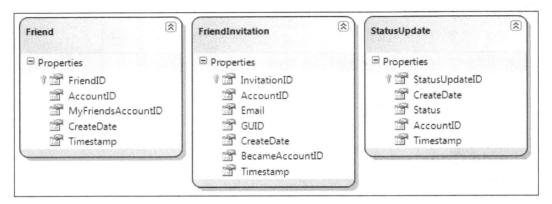

Recall from the past chapters that we are not allowing LINQ to manage these relationships for us. So go ahead and remove the relationships from the surrounding tables. Once you hit **Save** we should have three new classes to work with!

Building Repositories

As always, with these new tables will come new repositories. The following repositories will be created:

- `FriendRepository`
- `FriendInvitationRepository`
- `StatusUpdateRepository`

In addition to the creation of the above repositories, we will also need to modify the `AccountRepository`.

FriendRepository

Most of our repositories will always follow the same design. They provide a way to get at one record, many records by a parent ID, save a record, and delete a record.

This repository differs slightly from the norm when it is time to retrieve a list of friends in that it has two sides of the relationship to look at—on one side where it is the owning Account of the Friend relationship, and on the other side where the relationship is owned by another account. Here is that method:

```
public List<Friend> GetFriendsByAccountID(Int32 AccountID)
{
    List<Friend> result = new List<Friend>();
    using(FisharooDataContext dc = conn.GetContext())
    {
        //Get my friends direct relationship
        IEnumerable<Friend> friends = (from f in dc.Friends
                                       where f.AccountID == AccountID
                                       &&
                                       f.MyFriendsAccountID AccountID
                                       select f).Distinct();
        result = friends.ToList();
        //Getmy friends indirect relationship
        var friends2 = (from f in dc.Friends
                        where f.MyFriendsAccountID == AccountID &&
                        f.AccountID != AccountID
                        select new
                        {
                            FriendID = f.FriendID,
                            AccountID = f.MyFriendsAccountID,
                            MyFriendsAccountID = f.AccountID,
                            CreateDate = f.CreateDate,
                            Timestamp = f.Timestamp
                        }).Distinct();
        foreach (object o in friends2)
        {
            Friend friend = o as Friend;
            if(friend != null)
                result.Add(friend);
        }
    }
    return result;
}
```

This method queries for all friends that are owned by this account. It then queries for the reverse relationship where this account is owned by another account. Then it adds the second query to the first and returns that result.

Here is the method that gets the Accounts of our Friends.

```
public List<Account> GetFriendsAccountsByAccountID(Int32 AccountID)
{
    List<Friend> friends = GetFriendsByAccountID(AccountID);
    List<int> accountIDs = new List<int>();
    foreach (Friend friend in friends)
```

```
    {
        accountIDs.Add(friend.MyFriendsAccountID);
    }
    List<Account> result = new List<Account>();
    using(FisharooDataContext dc = conn.GetContext())
    {
        IEnumerable<Account> accounts = from a in dc.Accounts
                                        where
                                        accountIDs.Contains(a.AccountID)
                                        select a;
        result = accounts.ToList();
    }
    return result;
}
```

This method first gathers all the friends (via the first method we discussed) and then queries for all the related accounts. It then returns the result.

FriendInvitationRepository

Like the other repositories this one has the standard methods. In addition to those we also need to be able to retrieve an invitation by **GUID** or the invitation key that was sent to the friend.

```
public FriendInvitation GetFriendInvitationByGUID(Guid guid)
{
    FriendInvitation friendInvitation;
    using(FisharooDataContext dc = conn.GetContext())
    {
        friendInvitation = dc.FriendInvitations.Where(fi => fi.GUID
                                        == guid).FirstOrDefault();
    }
    return friendInvitation;
}
```

This is a very straightforward query matching the **GUID** values.

In addition to the above method we will also need a way for invitations to be cleaned up. For this reason we will also have a method named CleanUpFriendInvitations().

```
//removes multiple requests by the same account to the same email
account
public void CleanUpFriendInvitationsForThisEmail(FriendInvitation
                                        friendInvitation)
{
```

```
using (FisharooDataContext dc = conn.GetContext())
{
    IEnumerable<FriendInvitation> friendInvitations = from fi in
                    dc.FriendInvitations
                    where fi.Email ==
                    friendInvitation.Email &&

                    fi.BecameAccountID == 0 &&

                    fi.AccountID == friendInvitation.AccountID
                    select fi;
    foreach (FriendInvitation invitation in friendInvitations)
    {
        dc.FriendInvitations.DeleteOnSubmit(invitation);
    }
    dc.SubmitChanges();
}
}
```

This method is responsible for clearing out any invitations in the system that are sent from account A to account B and have not been activated (account B never did anything with the invite). Rather than checking if the invitation already exists when it is created, we will allow them to be created time and again (checking each invite during the import process of 500 contacts could really slow things down!). When account B finally accepts one of the invitations all of the others will be cleared. Also, in case account B never does anything with the invites, we will need a database process that periodically cleans out old invitations.

StatusUpdateRepository

Other than the norm, this repository has a method that gets `topN` `StatusUpdates` for use on the profile page.

```
public List<StatusUpdate> GetTopNStatusUpdatesByAccountID(Int32
AccountID, Int32 Number)
{
    List<StatusUpdate> result = new List<StatusUpdate>();
    using (FisharooDataContext dc = conn.GetContext())
    {
        IEnumerable<StatusUpdate> statusUpdates = (from su in
                        dc.StatusUpdates
                        where su.AccountID ==
                        AccountID
                        orderby su.CreateDate descending
                        select
                        su).Take(Number);
```

```
            result = statusUpdates.ToList();
        }
        return result;
    }
```

This is done with a standard query with the addition of the `Take()` method, which translates into a `TOP` statement in the resulting SQL.

AccountRepository

With the addition of our search capabilities we will require a new method in our `AccountRepository`. This method will be the key for searching accounts.

```
public List<Account> SearchAccounts(string SearchText)
{
    List<Account> result = new List<Account>();
    using (FisharooDataContext dc = conn.GetContext())
    {
        IEnumerable<Account> accounts = from a in dc.Accounts
                where(a.FirstName + " " +
                        a.LastName).Contains(SearchText) ||
                    a.Email.Contains(SearchText) ||
                    a.Username.Contains(SearchText)
                select a;
        result = accounts.ToList();
    }
    return result;
}
```

This method currently searches through a user's first name, last name, email address, and username. This could of course be extended to their profile data and many other data points (all in good time!).

Implementing the Services/Application Layer

Now that we have the repositories in place we can begin to create the services that sit on top of those repositories. We will be creating the following services:

*   `FriendService`

In addition to that we will also be extending these services:

*   `AlertService`
*   `PrivacyService`

FriendService

The `FriendService` currently has a couple of duties. We will need it to tell us whether or not a user is a `Friend` or not so that we can extend the `PrivacyService` to consider friends (recall that we currently only understand public and private settings!). In addition to that we need our `FriendService` to be able to handle creating `Friends` from a `FriendInvitation`.

```
public bool IsFriend(Account account, Account accountBeingViewed)
{
    if(account == null)
        return false;
    if(accountBeingViewed == null)
        return false;
    if(account.AccountID == accountBeingViewed.AccountID)
        return true;
    else
    {
        Friend friend =
                _friendRepository.GetFriendsByAccountID
                (accountBeingViewed.AccountID).
                Where(f => f.MyFriendsAccountID ==
                account.AccountID).FirstOrDefault();
        if(friend != null)
            return true;
    }
    return false;
}
```

This method needs to know who is making the request as well as who it is making the request about. It then verifies that both accounts are not null so that we can use them down the road and returns `false` if either of them are null. We then check to see if the user that is doing the viewing is the same user as is being viewed. If so we can safely return `true`. Then comes the fun part—currently we are using the `GetFriendsByAccountID` method found in the `FriendRepository`. We iterate through that list to see if our friend is there in the list or not. If we locate it, we return `true`. Otherwise the whole method has failed to locate a result and returns `false`.

Keep in mind that this way of doing things could quickly become a major performance issue. If you are checking security around several data points frequently in the same page, this is a large query and moves a lot of data around. If someone had 500 friends this would not be acceptable. As our goal is for people to have lots of friends, we generally would not want to follow this way. Your best bet then is to create a LINQ query in the FriendsRepository to handle this logic directly only returning true or false. However, I know that I am going to be caching the results of this query (and many others) down the road, so I am less likely to feel the pain from this query and am thereby keeping my repository free of an additional method.

Now comes our CreateFriendFromFriendInvitation method, which as the name suggests (drum role please) creates a friend from a friend invitation! I love names that are human readable without any other prompts.

```
public void CreateFriendFromFriendInvitation(Guid InvitationKey,
Account InvitationTo)
{
    //update friend invitation request
    FriendInvitation friendInvitation =
                    _friendInvitationRepository.
                    GetFriendInvitationByGUID(InvitationKey);
    friendInvitation.BecameAccountID = InvitationTo.AccountID;
    _friendInvitationRepository.SaveFriendInvitation(
                                    friendInvitation);
    _friendInvitationRepository.CleanUpFriendInvitationsForThisEmail(
                                            friendInvitation);
    //create friendship
    Friend friend = new Friend();
    friend.AccountID = friendInvitation.AccountID;
    friend.MyFriendsAccountID = InvitationTo.AccountID;
    _friendRepository.SaveFriend(friend);
    Account InvitationFrom =
                        _accountRepository.GetAccountByID
                        (friendInvitation.AccountID);
    _alertService.AddFriendAddedAlert(InvitationFrom, InvitationTo);
    //CHAPTER 6
    //TODO: MESSAGING - Add message to inbox regarding new
                    friendship!
}
```

This method expects the `InvitationKey` (in the form of a system generated GUID) and the Account that is wishing to create the relationship. It then gets the `FriendInvitation` and updates the `BecameAccountID` property of the new friend. We then make a call to flush any other friend invites between these two users. Once we have everything cleaned up we add a new alert to the system (covered shortly) letting the account that initiated this invitation know that the invitation was accepted.

Notice that we will also need to add something here to send a message via the messaging system (covered in the next chapter!).

AlertService

The alert service is essentially a wrapper to post an alert to the user's profile on **The Filter**. All the plumbing for this was covered in a previous chapter. So the additional methods that we have added are very similar to what was done previously. I will post these methods here so you can see them—but I don't think they really require too much explanation.

```
public void AddStatusUpdateAlert(StatusUpdate statusUpdate)
{
    alert = new Alert();
    alert.CreateDate = DateTime.Now;
    alert.AccountID = _userSession.CurrentUser.AccountID;
    alert.AlertTypeID = (int)AlertType.AlertTypes.StatusUpdate;
    alertMessage = "<div class=\"AlertHeader\">" +
                GetProfileImage(_userSession.CurrentUser.AccountID)
              + GetProfileUrl(_userSession.CurrentUser.Username) + "
          " + statusUpdate.Status + "</div>";
    alert.Message = alertMessage;
    SaveAlert(alert);
    SendAlertToFriends(alert);
}
public void AddFriendRequestAlert(Account FriendRequestFrom, Account
                FriendRequestTo, Guid requestGuid, string Message)
{
    alert = new Alert();
    alert.CreateDate = DateTime.Now;
    alert.AccountID = FriendRequestTo.AccountID;
    alertMessage = "<div class=\"AlertHeader\">" +
                GetProfileImage(FriendRequestFrom.AccountID) +
                GetProfileUrl(FriendRequestFrom.Username)
                + " would like to be
                                        friends!</div>";
    alertMessage += "<div class=\"AlertRow\">";
```

```
        alertMessage += FriendRequestFrom.FirstName + " " +
                        FriendRequestFrom.LastName +
                        " would like to be friends with you!  Click this
                        link to add this user as a friend: ";
        alertMessage += "<a href=\"" + _configuration.RootURL +
        "Friends/ConfirmFriendshipRequest.aspx?InvitationKey=" +
                requestGuid.ToString() + "\">" + _configuration.RootURL +
        "Friends/ConfirmFriendshipRequest.aspx?InvitationKey=" +
                requestGuid.ToString() + "</a><HR>" + Message + "</div>";
        alert.Message = alertMessage;
        alert.AlertTypeID = (int) AlertType.AlertTypes.FriendRequest;
        SaveAlert(alert);
}
public void AddFriendAddedAlert(Account FriendRequestFrom, Account
FriendRequestTo)
{
    alert = new Alert();
    alert.CreateDate = DateTime.Now;
    alert.AccountID = FriendRequestFrom.AccountID;
    alertMessage = "<div class=\"AlertHeader\">" +
                    GetProfileImage(FriendRequestTo.AccountID) +
                    GetProfileUrl(FriendRequestTo.Username) + " is now
                    your friend!</div>";
    alertMessage += "<div class=\"AlertRow\">" +
            GetSendMessageUrl(FriendRequestTo.AccountID) + "</div>";
    alert.Message = alertMessage;
    alert.AlertTypeID = (int)AlertType.AlertTypes.FriendAdded;
    SaveAlert(alert);
    alert = new Alert();
    alert.CreateDate = DateTime.Now;
    alert.AccountID = FriendRequestTo.AccountID;
    alertMessage = "<div class=\"AlertHeader\">" +
                    GetProfileImage(FriendRequestFrom.AccountID) +
                    GetProfileUrl(FriendRequestFrom.Username) + " is
                    now your friend!</div>";
    alertMessage += "<div class=\"AlertRow\">" +
            GetSendMessageUrl(FriendRequestFrom.AccountID) + "</div>";
    alert.Message = alertMessage;
    alert.AlertTypeID = (int)AlertType.AlertTypes.FriendAdded;
    SaveAlert(alert);
    alert = new Alert();
    alert.CreateDate = DateTime.Now;
    alert.AlertTypeID = (int) AlertType.AlertTypes.FriendAdded;
    alertMessage = "<div class=\"AlertHeader\">" + GetProfileUrl(Frien
dRequestFrom.Username) + " and " +
```

```
                    GetProfileUrl(FriendRequestTo.Username) + " are
                    now friends!</div>";
    alert.Message = alertMessage;
    alert.AccountID = FriendRequestFrom.AccountID;
    SendAlertToFriends(alert);
    alert.AccountID = FriendRequestTo.AccountID;
    SendAlertToFriends(alert);
}
```

PrivacyService

Now that we have a method to check if two people are friends or not we can finally
extend our PrivacyService to account for friends. Remember that up to this point
we are only interrogating whether something is marked as private or public. Friends
is marked false by default!

```
public bool ShouldShow(Int32 PrivacyFlagTypeID,
    Account AccountBeingViewed,
    Account Account,
    List<PrivacyFlag> Flags)
{

    bool result;

    bool isFriend = _friendService.IsFriend(
                Account,AccountBeingViewed);
    //flag marked as private test
    if(Flags.Where(f => f.PrivacyFlagTypeID == PrivacyFlagTypeID &&
                    f.VisibilityLevelID ==
                    (int)VisibilityLevel.VisibilityLevels.Private)
                    .FirstOrDefault() != null)
        result = false;
    //flag marked as friends only test
    else if (Flags.Where(f => f.PrivacyFlagTypeID ==
                    PrivacyFlagTypeID && f.VisibilityLevelID ==
                    (int)VisibilityLevel.VisibilityLevels.Friends)
                    .FirstOrDefault() != null && isFriend)
        result = true;
    else if (Flags.Where(f => f.PrivacyFlagTypeID ==
                    PrivacyFlagTypeID && f.VisibilityLevelID ==
                    (int)VisibilityLevel.VisibilityLevels.Public)
                    .FirstOrDefault() != null)
        result = true;
    else
        result = false;
    return result;
}
```

All we did here is point the `isFriend` variable at the result of the new `IsFriend()` method in the `FriendService`. Everything else was handled previously!

Implementing the Presentation Layer

Now that we have the base framework in place we can start to discuss what it will take to put it all together. Like I said earlier, this chapter is less about framework and more about the UI that utilizes the new and existing framework!

Searching for Friends

Let's see what it takes to implement a search for friends.

SiteMaster

Let's begin with searching for friends. We haven't covered too much regarding the actual UI and nothing regarding the master page of this site. I don't want this to be about design! So I will simply say that we have added a text box and a button to the master page to take in a search phrase.

When the button is clicked this method in the `MasterPage` code behind is fired.

```
protected void ibSearch_Click(object sender, EventArgs e)
{
    _redirector.GoToSearch(txtSearch.Text);
}
```

As you can see it simply calls the `Redirector` class and routes the user to the `Search.aspx` page passing in the value of `txtSearch` (as a query string parameter in this case).

```
public void GoToSearch(string SearchText)
{
    Redirect("~/Search.aspx?s=" + SearchText);
}
```

Search

The `Search.aspx` page has no interface. It expects a value to be passed in from the previously discussed text box in the master page. With this text phrase we hit our `AccountRepository` and perform a search using the `Contains()` operator. The returned list of `Accounts` is then displayed on the page.

For the most part, this page is all about MVP plumbing. If we weren't using MVP it would all be very straightforward. I am going to assume that you are up to speed with MVP from this point on and stick to the fun stuff from here on. Here is the repeater that displays all our data.

```
<%@ Register Src="~/UserControls/ProfileDisplay.ascx"
TagPrefix="Fisharoo" TagName="ProfileDisplay" %>
...
<asp:Repeater ID="repAccounts" runat="server"
                OnItemDataBound="repAccounts_ItemDataBound">
    <ItemTemplate>
        <Fisharoo:ProfileDisplay ShowDeleteButton="false"
                    ID="pdProfileDisplay" runat="server">
                    </Fisharoo:ProfileDisplay>
    </ItemTemplate>
</asp:Repeater>
```

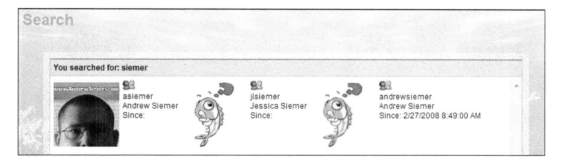

The fun stuff in this case comes in the form of the ProfileDisplay user control that was created so that we have an easy way to display profile data in various places with one chunk of reusable code that will allow us to make global changes.

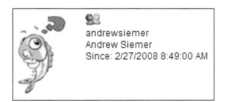

If you have not used user controls before I will quickly explain how they work. Basically, a user control is like a small self-contained page that you can then insert into your page (or master page). It has its own UI and it has its own code behind (so make sure it also gets its own MVP plumbing!). Also, like a page, it is at the end of the day a simple object, which means that it can have properties, methods, and everything else that you might think to use.

Once you have defined a user control you can use it in a few ways. You can programmatically load it using the `LoadControl()` method and then use it like you would use any other object in a page environment. Or like we did here, you can add a page declaration that registers the control for use in that page. You will notice that we specified where the source for this control lives. Then we gave it a tag prefix and a tag name (similar to using `asp:Control`). From that point onwards we can refer to our control in the same way that we can declare a `TextBox`!

You should see that we have `<Fisharoo:ProfileDisplay ... />`. You will also notice that our tag has custom properties that are set in the tag definition. In this case you see `ShowDeleteButton="false"`.

Here is the user control code in order of display, code behind, and the presenter (omitting the interface of the view as usual).

```
//UserControls/ProfileDisplay.ascx
<%@ Import namespace="Fisharoo.FisharooCore.Core.Domain"%>
<%@ Control Language="C#" AutoEventWireup="true"
        CodeBehind="ProfileDisplay.ascx.cs" Inherits="Fisharoo.
FisharooWeb.UserControls.ProfileDisplay" %>
<div style="float:left;">
    <div style="height:130px;float:left;">
        <a href="/Profiles/Profile.aspx?AccountID=<asp:Literal
            id='litAccountID' runat='server'></asp:Literal>">
        <asp:Image style="padding:5px;width:100px;height:100px;"
            ImageAlign="Left" Width="100"
                Height="100" ID="imgAvatar"
                ImageUrl="~/images/ProfileAvatar/ProfileImage.aspx"
                    runat="server" /></a>
        <asp:ImageButton ImageAlign="AbsMiddle" ID="ibInviteFriend"
                runat="server" Text="Become Friends"
        OnClick="lbInviteFriend_Click"
        ImageUrl="~/images/icon_friends.gif"></asp:ImageButton>
        <asp:ImageButton ImageAlign="AbsMiddle" ID="ibDelete"
                        runat="server" OnClick="ibDelete_Click"
                        ImageUrl="~/images/icon_close.gif" /><br />
        <asp:Label ID="lblUsername" runat="server"></asp:Label><br />
        <asp:Label ID="lblFirstName" runat="server"></asp:Label>
        <asp:Label ID="lblLastName" runat="server"></asp:Label><br />
        Since: <asp:Label ID="lblCreateDate"
                    runat="server"></asp:Label><br />
        <asp:Label ID="lblFriendID" runat="server"
            Visible="false"></asp:Label>
    </div>
</div>
//UserControls/ProfileDisplay.ascx.cs
```

```
using System;
using System.Collections;
using System.Configuration;
using System.Data;
using System.Linq;
using System.Web;
using System.Web.Security;
using System.Web.UI;
using System.Web.UI.HtmlControls;
using System.Web.UI.WebControls;
using System.Web.UI.WebControls.WebParts;
using System.Xml.Linq;
using Fisharoo.FisharooCore.Core.Domain;
using Fisharoo.FisharooWeb.UserControls.Interfaces;
using Fisharoo.FisharooWeb.UserControls.Presenters;
namespace Fisharoo.FisharooWeb.UserControls
{
    public partial class ProfileDisplay : System.Web.UI.UserControl,
                                          IProfileDisplay
    {
        private ProfileDisplayPresenter _presenter;
        protected Account _account;
        protected void Page_Load(object sender, EventArgs e)
        {
            _presenter = new ProfileDisplayPresenter();
            _presenter.Init(this);
            ibDelete.Attributes.Add("onclick","javascript:return
                        confirm('Are you sure you want
                                to delete this friend?')");
        }

        public bool ShowDeleteButton
        {
            set
            {
                ibDelete.Visible = value;
            }
        }

        public bool ShowFriendRequestButton
        {
            set
            {
                ibInviteFriend.Visible = value;
            }
```

```
        }

        public void LoadDisplay(Account account)
        {
            _account = account;
            ibInviteFriend.Attributes.Add("FriendsID",
                    _account.AccountID.ToString());
            ibDelete.Attributes.Add("FriendsID",
                            _account.AccountID.ToString());
            litAccountID.Text = account.AccountID.ToString();
            lblLastName.Text = account.LastName;
            lblFirstName.Text = account.FirstName;
            lblCreateDate.Text = account.CreateDate.ToString();
            imgAvatar.ImageUrl += "?AccountID=" +
                            account.AccountID.ToString();
            lblUsername.Text = account.Username;
            lblFriendID.Text = account.AccountID.ToString();
        }

        protected void lbInviteFriend_Click(object sender,
                                            EventArgs e)
        {
            _presenter = new ProfileDisplayPresenter();
            _presenter.Init(this);
            _presenter.SendFriendRequest(Convert.ToInt32(
                            lblFriendID.Text));
        }

        protected void ibDelete_Click(object sender, EventArgs e)
        {
            _presenter = new ProfileDisplayPresenter();
            _presenter.Init(this);
            _presenter.DeleteFriend(Convert.ToInt32(
                            lblFriendID.Text));
        }
    }
}
//UserControls/Presenter/ProfileDisplayPresenter.cs
using System;
using System.Data;
using System.Configuration;
using System.Linq;
using System.Web;
using System.Web.Security;
using System.Web.UI;
using System.Web.UI.HtmlControls;
```

```
using System.Web.UI.WebControls;
using System.Web.UI.WebControls.WebParts;
using System.Xml.Linq;
using Fisharoo.FisharooCore.Core;
using Fisharoo.FisharooCore.Core.DataAccess;
using Fisharoo.FisharooWeb.UserControls.Interfaces;
using StructureMap;
namespace Fisharoo.FisharooWeb.UserControls.Presenters
{
    public class ProfileDisplayPresenter
    {
        private IProfileDisplay _view;
        private IRedirector _redirector;
        private IFriendRepository _friendRepository;
        private IUserSession _userSession;
        public ProfileDisplayPresenter()
        {
            _redirector = ObjectFactory.GetInstance<IRedirector>();
            _friendRepository =
                    ObjectFactory.GetInstance<IFriendRepository>();
            _userSession = ObjectFactory.GetInstance<IUserSession>();
        }
        public void Init(IProfileDisplay view)
        {
            _view = view;
        }
        public void SendFriendRequest(Int32 AccountIdToInvite)
        {
            _redirector.GoToFriendsInviteFriends(AccountIdToInvite);
        }
        public void DeleteFriend(Int32 FriendID)
        {
            if (_userSession.CurrentUser != null)
            {
                _friendRepository.DeleteFriendByID(
                    _userSession.CurrentUser.AccountID, FriendID);
                HttpContext.Current.Response.Redirect(HttpContext.
                                        Current.Request.RawUrl);
            }
        }
    }
}
```

All this logic and display is very standard. You have the MVP plumbing, which makes up most of it. Outside of that you will notice that the `ProfileDisplay` control has a `LoadDisplay()` method responsible for loading the UI for that control. In the `Search` page this is done in the `repAccounts_ItemDataBound()` method.

```
protected void repAccounts_ItemDataBound(object sender,
                                         RepeaterItemEventArgs e)
{
    if(e.Item.ItemType == ListItemType.Item || e.Item.ItemType ==
                     ListItemType.AlternatingItem)
    {
        ProfileDisplay pd = e.Item.FindControl("pdProfileDisplay") as
                         ProfileDisplay;
        pd.LoadDisplay((Account)e.Item.DataItem);
        if(_webContext.CurrentUser == null)
            pd.ShowFriendRequestButton = false;
    }
}
```

The `ProfileDisplay` control also has a couple of properties—one to show/hide the delete friend button and the other to show/hide the invite friend button. These buttons are not appropriate for every page that the control is used in. In the search results page we want to hide the **Delete** button as the results are not necessarily friends. We would want to be able to invite them in that view. However, in a list of our friends the **Invite** button (to invite a friend) would no longer be appropriate as each of these users would already be a friend. The **Delete** button in this case would now be more appropriate.

Clicking on the **Invite** button makes a call to the `Redirector` class and routes the user to the `InviteFriends` page.

```
//UserControls/ProfileDisplay.ascx.cs
public void SendFriendRequest(Int32 AccountIdToInvite)
{
    _redirector.GoToFriendsInviteFriends(AccountIdToInvite);
}

//Core/Impl/Redirector.cs
public void GoToFriendsInviteFriends(Int32 AccoundIdToInvite)
{
    Redirect("~/Friends/InviteFriends.aspx?AccountIdToInvite=" +
            AccoundIdToInvite.ToString());
}
```

Invite Your Friends

This page allows us to manually enter email addresses of friends that we want to invite. It is a standard **From, To, Message** format where the system specifies the sender (you), you specify who to send to and the message that you want to send.

```
//Friends/InviteFriends.aspx
<%@ Page Language="C#" MasterPageFile="~/SiteMaster.Master"
    AutoEventWireup="true" CodeBehind="InviteFriends.aspx.cs"
    Inherits="Fisharoo.FisharooWeb.Friends.InviteFriends" %>
<asp:Content ContentPlaceHolderID="Content" runat="server">
    <div class="divContainer">
        <div class="divContainerBox">
            <div class="divContainerTitle">Invite Your Friends</div>
            <asp:Panel ID="pnlInvite" runat="server">
                <div class="divContainerRow">
                    <div class="divContainerCellHeader">From:</div>
                    <div class="divContainerCell"><asp:Label
                        ID="lblFrom" runat="server"></asp:Label></div>
                </div>
                <div class="divContainerRow">
                    <div class="divContainerCellHeader">To:<br /><div
                        class="divContainerHelpText">(use commas
                        to<BR />separate emails)</div></div>
                    <div class="divContainerCell"><asp:TextBox
                            ID="txtTo" runat="server"
                        TextMode="MultiLine" Columns="40"
                            Rows="5"></asp:TextBox></div>
                </div>
                <div class="divContainerRow">
                    <div
                        class="divContainerCellHeader">Message:</div>
                    <div class="divContainerCell"><asp:TextBox
                            ID="txtMessage" runat="server"
                        TextMode="MultiLine" Columns="40"
                            Rows="10"></asp:TextBox></div>
                </div>
                <div class="divContainerFooter">
                    <asp:Button ID="btnInvite" runat="server"
                            Text="Invite" OnClick="btnInvite_Click" />
                </div>
            </asp:Panel>
            <div class="divContainerRow">
                <div class="divContainerCell"><br /><asp:Label
                        ID="lblMessage" runat="server">
                    </asp:Label><br /><br /></div>
```

```
            </div>
         </div>
      </div>
   </asp:Content>
```

Running the code will display the following:

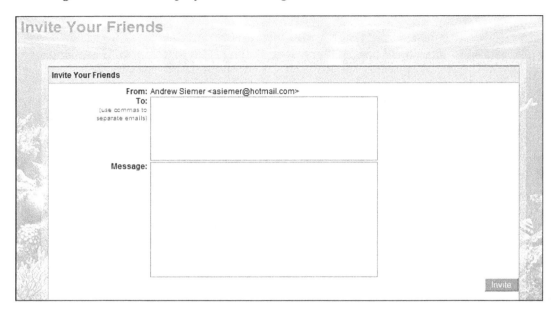

This is a simple page so the majority of the code for it is MVP plumbing. The most important part to notice here is that when the **Invite** button is clicked the presenter is notified to send the invitation.

```
//Friends/InviteFriends.aspx.cs
using System;
using System.Collections;
using System.Configuration;
using System.Data;
using System.Linq;
using System.Web;
using System.Web.Security;
using System.Web.UI;
using System.Web.UI.HtmlControls;
using System.Web.UI.WebControls;
using System.Web.UI.WebControls.WebParts;
using System.Xml.Linq;
using Fisharoo.FisharooWeb.Friends.Interface;
```

```
using Fisharoo.FisharooWeb.Friends.Presenter;
namespace Fisharoo.FisharooWeb.Friends
{
    public partial class InviteFriends : System.Web.UI.Page,
                                         IInviteFriends
    {
        private InviteFriendsPresenter _presenter;
        protected void Page_Load(object sender, EventArgs e)
        {
            _presenter = new InviteFriendsPresenter();
            _presenter.Init(this);
        }

        protected  void btnInvite_Click(object sender, EventArgs e)
        {
            _presenter.SendInvitation(txtTo.Text,txtMessage.Text);
        }

        public void DisplayToData(string To)
        {
            lblFrom.Text = To;
        }

        public void TogglePnlInvite(bool IsVisible)
        {
            pnlInvite.Visible = IsVisible;
        }

        public void ShowMessage(string Message)
        {
            lblMessage.Text = Message;
        }

        public void ResetUI()
        {
            txtMessage.Text = "";
            txtTo.Text = "";
        }
    }
}
```

Once this call is made we leap across to the presenter (more plumbing!).

```
//Friends/Presenter/InviteFriendsPresenter.cs
using System;
using System.Data;
using System.Configuration;
```

```
using System.Linq;
using System.Web;
using System.Web.Security;
using System.Web.UI;
using System.Web.UI.HtmlControls;
using System.Web.UI.WebControls;
using System.Web.UI.WebControls.WebParts;
using System.Xml.Linq;
using Fisharoo.FisharooCore.Core;
using Fisharoo.FisharooCore.Core.DataAccess;
using Fisharoo.FisharooCore.Core.Domain;
using Fisharoo.FisharooWeb.Friends.Interface;
using StructureMap;
namespace Fisharoo.FisharooWeb.Friends.Presenter
{
    public class InviteFriendsPresenter
    {
        private IInviteFriends _view;
        private IUserSession _userSession;
        private IEmail _email;
        private IFriendInvitationRepository
            _friendInvitationRepository;
        private IAccountRepository _accountRepository;
        private IWebContext _webContext;
        private Account _account;
        private Account _accountToInvite;

        public void Init(IInviteFriends view)
        {
            _view = view;
            _userSession = ObjectFactory.GetInstance<IUserSession>();
            _email = ObjectFactory.GetInstance<IEmail>();
            _friendInvitationRepository =
                                ObjectFactory.GetInstance<
                                IFriendInvitationRepository>();
            _accountRepository =
                    ObjectFactory.GetInstance<IAccountRepository>();
            _webContext = ObjectFactory.GetInstance<IWebContext>();
            _account = _userSession.CurrentUser;
            if (_account != null)
            {
                _view.DisplayToData(_account.FirstName + " " +
                                _account.LastName + " &lt;" +
                                _account.Email + "&gt;");
                if (_webContext.AccoundIdToInvite > 0)
```

```
                {
                    _accountToInvite =
                                _accountRepository.GetAccountByID
                                (_webContext.AccoundIdToInvite);
                    if (_accountToInvite != null)
                    {
                        SendInvitation(_accountToInvite.Email,
                                _account.FirstName + " " +
                                _account.LastName + " would like
                                to be your friend!");
                        _view.ShowMessage(_accountToInvite.Username +
                                " has been sent a friend request!");
                        _view.TogglePnlInvite(false);
                    }
                }
            }
        }

        public void SendInvitation(string ToEmailArray, string
                                Message)
        {
            string resultMessage = "Invitations sent to the following
                                recipients:<BR>";
            resultMessage +=
                    _email.SendInvitations
                    (_userSession.CurrentUser,ToEmailArray, Message);
            _view.ShowMessage(resultMessage);
            _view.ResetUI();
        }
    }
}
```

The interesting thing here is the SendInvitation() method, which takes in a comma delimited array of emails and the message to be sent in the invitation. It then makes a call to the Email.SendInvitations() method.

```
//Core/Impl/Email.cs
public string SendInvitations(Account sender, string ToEmailArray,
                        string Message)
{
    string resultMessage = Message;
    foreach (string s in ToEmailArray.Split(','))
    {
        FriendInvitation friendInvitation = new FriendInvitation();
        friendInvitation.AccountID = sender.AccountID;
        friendInvitation.Email = s;
```

```
friendInvitation.GUID = Guid.NewGuid();
friendInvitation.BecameAccountID = 0;
_friendInvitationRepository.SaveFriendInvitation(
                            friendInvitation);
//add alert to existing users alerts
Account account = _accountRepository.GetAccountByEmail(s);
if(account != null)
{
    _alertService.AddFriendRequestAlert(_userSession.
        CurrentUser, account, friendInvitation.GUID, Message);
}
//CHAPTER 6
//TODO: MESSAGING - if this email is already in our system
                    add a message through messaging system
//if(email in system)
//{
//      add message to messaging system
//}
//else
//{
//      send email
SendFriendInvitation(s, sender.FirstName, sender.LastName,
                    friendInvitation.GUID.ToString(), Message);
//}
resultMessage += "● " + s + "<BR>";
    }
    return resultMessage;
}
```

This method is responsible for parsing out all the emails, creating a new `FriendInvitation`, and sending the request via email to the person who was invited. It then adds an alert to the invited user if they have an `Account`. And finally we have to add a notification to the messaging system once it is built.

Outlook CSV Importer

The **Import Contacts** page is responsible for allowing our users to upload an exported contacts file from MS Outlook into our system. Once they have imported their contacts the user is allowed to select which email addresses are actually invited into our system.

Importing Contacts

As this page is made up of a couple of views, let's begin with the initial view.

```
//Friends/OutlookCsvImporter.aspx
<asp:Panel ID="pnlUpload" runat="server">
    <div class="divContainerTitle">Import Contacts</div>
    <div class="divContainerRow">
        <div class="divContainerCellHeader">Contacts File:</div>
        <div class="divContainerCell"><asp:FileUpload ID="fuContacts"
            runat="server" /></div>
    </div>
    <div class="divContainerRow">
        <div class="divContainerFooter"><asp:Button ID="btnUpload"
            Text="Upload & Preview Contacts" runat=
                        "server" OnClick="btnUpload_Click" /></div>
    </div>
    <br /><br />
    <div class="divContainerRow">
        <div class="divContainerTitle">How do I export my contacts
                                from Outlook?</div>
        <div class="divContainerCell">
            <ol>
                <li>
                    Open Outlook
                </li>
                <li>
                    In the File menu choose Import and Export
                </li>
                <li>
                    Choose export to a file and click next
                </li>
                <li>
                    Choose comma seperated values and click next
                </li>
                <li>
                    Select your contacts and click next
                </li>
                <li>
                    Browse to the location you want to save your
                    contacts file
                </li>
                <li>
                    Click finish
                </li>
```

```
            </ol>
          </div>
        </div>
      </asp:Panel>
```

As you can see from the code we are working in panels here. This panel is responsible for allowing a user to upload their **Contacts CSV File**. It also gives some directions to the user as to how to go about exporting contacts from Outlook.

This view has a file upload box that allows the user to browse for their CSV file, and a button to tell us when they are ready for the upload.

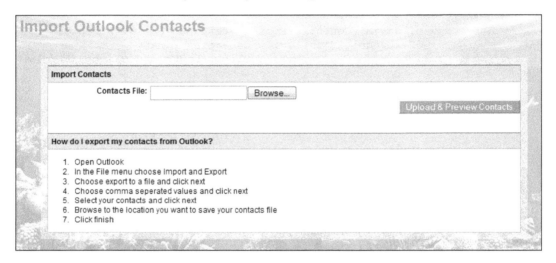

There is a method in our presenter that handles the button click from the view.

```
//Friends/Presenter/OutlookCsvImporterPresenter.cs
public void ParseEmails(HttpPostedFile file)
{
    using (Stream s = file.InputStream)
    {
        StreamReader sr = new StreamReader(s);
        string contacts = sr.ReadToEnd();
        _view.ShowParsedEmail(_email.ParseEmailsFromText(contacts));
    }
}
```

This method is responsible for handling the upload process of the `HttpPostedFile`. It puts the file reference into a `StreamReader` and then reads the stream into a string variable named `contacts`. Once we have the entire list of contacts we can then call into our `Email` class and parse all the emails out.

```
//Core/Impl/Email.cs
public List<string> ParseEmailsFromText(string text)
{
    List<string> emails = new List<string>();
    string strRegex = @"\w+([-+.]\w+)*@\w+([-.]\w+)*\.\w+([-.]\w+)*";
    Regex re = new Regex(strRegex, RegexOptions.Multiline);
    foreach (Match m in re.Matches(text))
    {
        string email = m.ToString();
        if(!emails.Contains(email))
            emails.Add(email);
    }
    return emails;
}
```

This method expects a string that contains some email addresses that we want to parse. It then parses the emails using a regular expression (which we won't go into details about!). We then iterate through all the matches in the Regex and add the found email addresses to our list provided they aren't already present. Once we have found all the email addresses, we will return the list of unique email addresses.

The presenter then passes that list of parsed emails to the view.

Selecting Contacts

Once we have handled the upload process and parsed out the emails, we then need to display all the emails to the user so that they can select which ones they want to invite.

Now you could do several sneaky things here. Technically the user has uploaded all of their email addresses to you. You have them. You could store them. You could invite every single address regardless of what the user wants. And while this might benefit your community over the short run, your users would eventually find out about your sneaky practice and your community would start to dwindle. Don't take advantage of your user's trust!

The code for this display looks like this:

```
//Friends/OutlookCsvImporter.aspx
<asp:Panel visible="false" ID="pnlEmails" runat="server">
    <div class="divContainerTitle">Select Contacts</div>
    <div class="divContainerFooter"><asp:Button
            ID="btnInviteContacts1" runat="server"
            OnClick="btnInviteContacts_Click"
            Text="Invite Selected Contacts"
    /></div>
```

```
<div class="divContainerCell" style="text-align:left;">
    <asp:CheckBoxList ID="cblEmails"  RepeatColumns="2"
                runat="server"></asp:CheckBoxList>
</div>
<div class="divContainerFooter"><asp:Button
        ID="btnInviteContacts2" runat="server"
    OnClick="btnInviteContacts_Click"
        Text="Invite Selected Contacts" /></div>
</asp:Panel>
```

Notice that we have a checkbox list in our panel. This checkbox list is bound to the returned list of email addresses.

```
public void ShowParsedEmail(List<string> Emails)
{
    pnlUpload.Visible = false;
    pnlResult.Visible = false;
    pnlEmails.Visible = true;
    cblEmails.DataSource = Emails;
    cblEmails.DataBind();
}
```

The output so far looks like this:

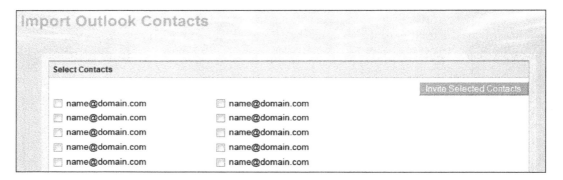

Now the user has a list of all the email addresses that they uploaded, which they can then go through selecting the ones that they want to invite into our system. Once they are through selecting the emails that they want to invite, they can click on the **Invite** button.

We then iterate through all the items in the checkbox list to locate the selected items.

```
protected void btnInviteContacts_Click(object sender, EventArgs e)
{
    string emails = "";
    foreach (ListItem li in cblEmails.Items)
    {
        if(li != null && li.Selected)
            emails += li.Text + ",";
    }
    emails = emails.Substring(0, emails.Length - 1);
    _presenter.InviteContacts(emails);
}
```

Once we have gathered all the selected emails we pass them to the presenter to run the invitation process.

```
public void InviteContacts(string ToEmailArray)
{
    string result = _email.SendInvitations(_userSession.CurrentUser,
                                           ToEmailArray, "");
    _view.ShowInvitationResult(result);
}
```

The presenter promptly passes the selected items to the Email class to handle the invitations. This is the same method that we used in the last section to invite users.

```
//Core/Impl/Email.cs
public string SendInvitations(Account sender, string ToEmailArray,
                             string Message)
{
    ...
}
```

We then output the result of the emails that we invited into the third display.

```
<asp:Panel ID="pnlResult" runat="server" Visible="false">
    <div class="divContainerTitle">Invitations Sent!</div>
    <div class="divContainerCell">
        Invitations were sent to the following emails:<br />
        <asp:Label ID="lblMessage" runat="server"></asp:Label>
    </div>
</asp:Panel>
```

Confirm Friendship

Having covered all these ways to invite someone into our site, we now need to look at what the invited user sees in the invitation. Let's start with what they would see in their inbox.

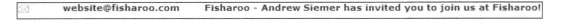

The user gets an email in their inbox telling them that so and so has invited them to come to Fisharoo.

Once they open that email they can see the request again as well as the link that they can follow to the site to take advantage of the invitation.

As you can see this link brings them to `server/Friends/ ConfirmFriendshipRequest.aspx` with a GUID for an invitation key. There are two screens that the user might see after this point.

The first screen is for the users who are already members. It asks them to log in again to confirm the friendship.

The other screen is for the users who aren't members, or the users who aren't logged in.

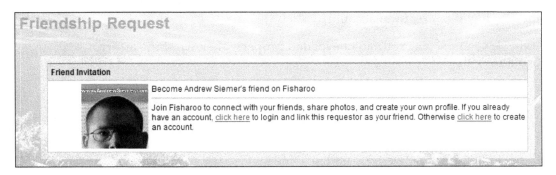

The only real logic in the ConfirmFriendshipRequest.aspx page is to check the GUID that is passed in to make sure that it is valid. This happens in the presenter of this page.

```
public void Init(IConfirmFriendshipRequest view)
{
    _view = view;
    if (!string.IsNullOrEmpty(_webContext.FriendshipRequest))
    {
        FriendInvitation friendInvitation =
            _friendInvitationRepository.GetFriendInvitationByGUID(new
                            Guid(_webContext.FriendshipRequest));
        if(friendInvitation != null)
        {
            if (_webContext.CurrentUser != null)
                LoginClick();

            Account account =
                    _accountRepository.GetAccountByID
                    (friendInvitation.AccountID);
            _view.ShowConfirmPanel(true);
            _view.LoadDisplay(_webContext.FriendshipRequest,
                    account.AccountID, account.FirstName,
                    account.LastName, _configuration.SiteName );
        }
        else
        {
            _view.ShowConfirmPanel(false);
            _view.ShowMessage("There was an error validating your
                            invitation.");
        }
    }
}
```

Either we can load a `friendInvitation` from the GUID or not. If we can, then we check to see if the user is already a member of the system and logged in. If they are logged in we automatically redirect them to the login screen. Otherwise we prompt them to log in or create an account.

If the `friendInvitaiton` can't be loaded properly then we show an error explaining that.

Where the real magic occurs for the invitation process is in the login and registration pages.

Login

In the login presenter we have added some logic to the `Init` method to recognize if we have a friendship request or not.

```
//Accounts/Presenter/LoginPresenter.cs
public void Init(ILogin view)
{
    _view = view;
    _accountService = ObjectFactory.GetInstance<IAccountService>();
    _redirector = ObjectFactory.GetInstance<IRedirector>();
    _webContext = ObjectFactory.GetInstance<IWebContext>();
    if(!string.IsNullOrEmpty(_webContext.FriendshipRequest))
        _view.DisplayMessage("Login to add this friend!");
}
```

This logic lets the user know that by logging in they will be accepting the friend request.

Then in the `AccountService.cs` file we have added some additional logic. If the login is a success and there is a friend request, we confirm the request and make these two users friends, via the `FriendService` we discussed earlier.

```
//Core/Impl/AccountService.cs
public string Login(string Username, string Password)
{
        . . .
            if (account.EmailVerified)
            {
                _userSession.LoggedIn = true;
                _userSession.Username = Username;
                _userSession.CurrentUser =
                            GetAccountByID(account.AccountID);
                if(!string.IsNullOrEmpty(_webContext.
                            FriendshipRequest))
```

```
        {
                _friendService.CreateFriendFromFriendInvitation(
                new Guid(_webContext.FriendshipRequest),
                _userSession.CurrentUser);
        }
            ...

    }
```

Registration

If the invited friend is not already a user of the site, then we allow them to walk through the registration site as normal. Once the registration is complete, we not only register them but we also create the friendship.

```
//Accounts/Presenter/RegisterPresenter.cs
public void Register(string Username, string Password,
                string FirstName, string LastName, string Email,
                string Zip, DateTime BirthDate, string Captcha,
                bool AgreesWithTerms, Int32 TermID)
{
    ...

                //if this registration came via a friend request...
                if(friendInvitation != null)
                {
                        _friendService.CreateFriendFromFriendInvitation(ne
    w Guid(_webContext.FriendshipRequest),newAccount);
                }
    ...

}
```

Show Friends

Now that we have everything we need to invite and accept a friend, we need the ability to see our friends. For this we will add to our Friends section landing page (Default.aspx) a list of all our friends. This will actually be quite easy as we will use our ProfileDisplay user control that we created earlier for our Search page.

This page will simply consist of a repeater with our ProfileDisplay control. We set the ShowFriendRequestButton to false as these are already our friends.

```
<asp:Repeater ID="repFriends" runat="server"
                OnItemDataBound="repFriends_ItemDataBound">
    <ItemTemplate>
        <div class="divContainerRow" style="height:110px;">
            <div class="divContainerCell">
```

```
              <Fisharoo:ProfileDisplay
                    ShowFriendRequestButton="false"
               ID="pdProfileDisplay" runat="server" />
          </div>
        </div>
      </ItemTemplate>
    </asp:Repeater>
```

Our presenter then loads the display with all the current user's friends by calling into the `FriendRepository.GetFriendsAccountsByAccountID()` method and passing that collection down to the view.

```
public void LoadDisplay()
{
    _view.LoadDisplay(_friendRepository.GetFriendsAccountsByAccountID
                    (_userSession.CurrentUser.AccountID));
}
```

The view then hooks up the repeater's data source. On each `ItemDataBound` of the repeater we spin up the `ProfileDisplay` user control

```
protected void repFriends_ItemDataBound(object sender,
                                        RepeaterItemEventArgs e)
{
    if(e.Item.ItemType == ListItemType.Item || e.Item.ItemType ==
       ListItemType.AlternatingItem)
    {
        ProfileDisplay pdProfileDisplay =
            e.Item.FindControl("pdProfileDisplay") as ProfileDisplay;
            pdProfileDisplay.LoadDisplay(((Account)e.Item.DataItem));
    }
}
```

We then end up with this output:

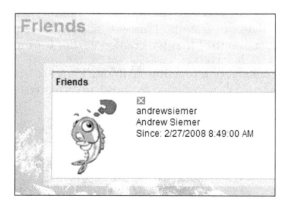

I have not done it yet, but down the road we are most likely to have some form of pagination implemented here too!

Friends on Profile

After having a page that shows all of our friends, it should be easy to update our public profile to show a handful of friends. To do this we will open the `Profile.aspx` page and add to it a bit.

We are simply going to add the same sort of repeater to the profile page as we did in the case of the `Friends/Default.aspx` page.

```
<asp:Repeater ID="repFriends" runat="server"
                    OnItemDataBound="repFriends_ItemDataBound">
    <ItemTemplate>
        <Fisharoo:ProfileDisplay ShowFriendRequestButton="false"
                ShowDeleteButton="false" ID="pdProfileDisplay"
                                runat="server" />
    </ItemTemplate>
</asp:Repeater>
```

Then in our `ProfilePresenter.cs` file we have added a line that loads that repeater.

```
public void Init(IProfile View)
{
    _view = View;
    _view.SetAvatar(_accountBeingViewed.AccountID);
    _view.DisplayInfo(_accountBeingViewed);
    _view.LoadFriends(_friendRepository.GetFriendsAccountsByAccountID(_
    accountBeingViewed.AccountID));
    _view.LoadStatusUpdates(_statusUpdateRepository.
GetTopNStatusUpdatesB
                        yAccountID(_accountBeingViewed.AccountID,5));
    TogglePrivacy();
}
```

And in the `Profile.aspx.cs` file we have added an event handler for `repFriends_ItemDataBound()` that takes care of loading each `ProfileDisplay` control.

```
protected void repFriends_ItemDataBound(object sender,
                                RepeaterItemEventArgs e)
{
    if(e.Item.ItemType == ListItemType.Item || e.Item.ItemType ==
                        ListItemType.AlternatingItem)
    {
        ProfileDisplay pdProfileDisplay =
            e.Item.FindControl("pdProfileDisplay") as ProfileDisplay;
        pdProfileDisplay.LoadDisplay(((Account)e.Item.DataItem));
    }
}
```

Status Updates

Status updates (our micro blog) are very simple to implement at this point. We will need to open the master page and add a small section to take in and display a top listing of these updates.

In our master page we will add a panel to our global display. It will be responsible for taking in new updates as well as displaying the most recent updates.

```
//SiteMaster.master
<asp:Panel ID="pnlStatusUpdate" runat="server">
    <div class="divContainer">
        <div class="divContainerBox">
            <div class="divContainerTitle">Status Updates</div>
            <div class="divContainerCell">
                <asp:TextBox Width="85" style="font-size:9px;
                    padding-left:0px;padding-right:0px;"
                    id="txtStatusUpdate" runat="server"></asp:TextBox>
                <asp:Button style="font-size:9px;
                    padding-left:0px;padding-right:0px;"
                    ID="btnAddStatus" runat="server" Text=
                    "Add" OnClick="btnAddStatus_Click" /><br />
                <asp:Repeater runat="server" ID="repStatus">
                    <ItemTemplate>
                        <asp:Label ID="Label1" Text='
                            <%# ((StatusUpdate)Container.DataItem).
                            CreateDate.ToString() %>'
                     runat="server" style="font-size:9px;"></asp:Label> -
                        <asp:Label ID="Label2" Text='
                            <%# ((StatusUpdate)Container.DataItem).
                            Status %>' runat="server"
                            style="font-size:9px;"></asp:Label>
                    </ItemTemplate>
                    <SeparatorTemplate>
                        <div class="divContainerSeparator"></div>
                    </SeparatorTemplate>
                </asp:Repeater><br />
                <asp:Button ID="btnShowAllStatusUpdates"
                        runat="server" Text="View All" OnClick=
                        "btnShowAllStatusUpdates_Click" />
            </div>
        </div></div>
</asp:Panel>
```

Once the display is in place, we need to add a method to capture our button clicks so that we can add new updates.

```
//SiteMaster.master.cs
protected void btnAddStatus_Click(object sender, EventArgs e)
{
    StatusUpdate su = new StatusUpdate();
    su.CreateDate = DateTime.Now;
    su.AccountID = _userSession.CurrentUser.AccountID;
    su.Status = txtStatusUpdate.Text;
    _statusRepository.SaveStatusUpdate(su);
    _alertService.AddStatusUpdateAlert(su);
    _redirector.GoToHomePage();
}
```

This method spins up a new StatusUpdate and adds it to the StatusUpdateRepository. While we are here we need to add another method to handle the button click to show all status updates.

```
//SiteMaster.master.cs
protected void btnShowAllStatusUpdates_Click(object sender,
                                             EventArgs e)
{
    _redirector.GoToProfilesStatusUpdates();
}
```

As you can see, this method simply redirects via the Redirector class to the Profiles/StatusUpdates.aspx page.

This then takes us to displaying our top StatusUpdates in the master page. To do this we need to add the method that gets the top N StatusUpdates.

```
//SiteMaster.master.cs
protected void LoadStatus()
{
    repStatus.DataSource =
        _statusRepository.GetTopNStatusUpdatesByAccountID(_
                    userSession.CurrentUser.AccountID, 5);
    repStatus.DataBind();
}
```

With this in place we need to update the `Page_Load()` method of the master page so that the status updates are loaded when there is a user logs into the site.

```
//SiteMaster.master.cs
protected void Page_Load(object sender, EventArgs e)
{
    ...
    if (_userSession.CurrentUser != null)
    {
        LoadStatus();
        pnlStatusUpdate.Visible = true;
    }
    else
        pnlStatusUpdate.Visible = false;
}
```

Now that we have a way to capture new status updates as well as a way to display the most recent updates, we need to provide a way for our user to see all of their updates. We will do this with a page dedicated to showing this data.

```
//Friends/StatusUpdates.aspx
<asp:Repeater ID="repStatusUpdates" runat="server">
    <ItemTemplate>
        <%# ((StatusUpdate)Container.DataItem).CreateDate.ToString()
        %> -
        <%# ((StatusUpdate)Container.DataItem).Status %>
    </ItemTemplate>
    <SeparatorTemplate>
        <div class="divContainerSeparator"></div>
    </SeparatorTemplate>
</asp:Repeater>
```

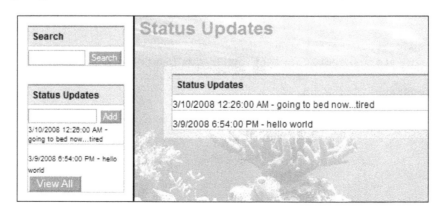

This page of course has the same plumbing issues as do the others. But it basically boils down to calling into the `StatusUpdateRepository` and get all `StatusUpdates` for a given Account. The only difference between this and showing the TopN `StatusUpdates`, as we did on the master page, is that we will show all the updates here.

This is another page that will eventually benefit from having pagination implemented.

Summary

This chapter was certainly less about building the framework and more about reworking some existing items so that they could be more friends-oriented. We have provided various methods to locate and invite friends to join us. We also extended some systems so that our friends could stay in touch with us and what we are doing on the site in the form of alerts and status updates. We now have a site that allows us to connect with and interact with others. This is the first among the many chapters that has really helped us put the community feeling into our community.

6
Messaging

Given that our site's focus is to gather people together so that they can interact with each other, we need a way for them to interact. The primary way for people to interact with one another is through direct communication. We will build a system to perform this communication in a way that is similar to sending an email from a standard email client such as Outlook or Hotmail.

We will provide a way for our users to create and send messages via the Xinha WYSIWYG editor.

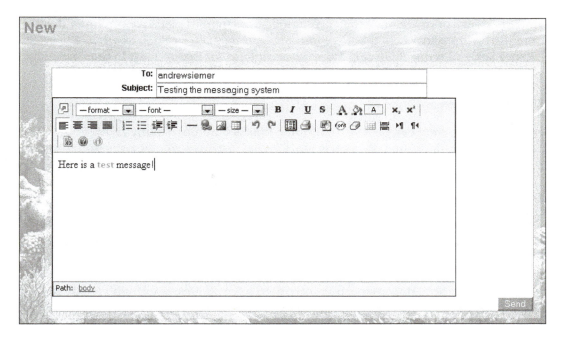

Once a user can create and send messages, we will then create a way for other users to receive and read those messages.

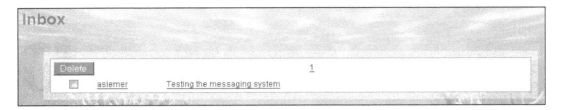

The emails will queue up in their inbox, and from there they will be able to read their messages.

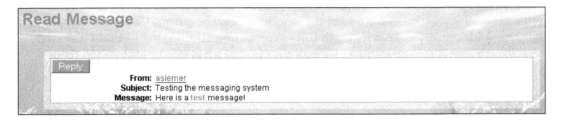

And of course, once we have this messaging subsystem in place we can hook our other features up in a way that they too can send messages — such as when a user accepts a friend request we can show the acceptance of that request in their Inbox.

Problem

A messaging system can be a very complex topic as there are many facets to be covered. The basic system, though, should be able to manage messages, senders and recipients, folders to contain the messages, and email notifications. In our case, we are going to try and keep things simple where it makes sense to do so. But in one area, we will do things in a more complicated approach simply because it will result in less wear and tear on the overall system.

Rather than follow a standard email messaging system where each person gets a physical copy of a message, we are going to build our system in the same way that the MS Exchange server works. We are going to make one copy of a message and subscribe users to that message. So rather than have 50 messages for 50 recipients, we will have one message and 50 recipient subscriptions.

The next complexity (although not that complex) lies in building a WYSIWYG (what you see is what you get) messaging editor. For this feature, there are many open source WYSIWYG editors; we will use one of those to save us a bit of time. We will be using the most popular editor—XINHA. This editor can be downloaded for free here at `http://xinha.webfactional.com/`. You may have seen this editor already. It is widely used across many popular community sites.

Design

Let's take a look at the design of these features.

Messages

Messages are the core of any messaging system. Generally, a message would contain details on the sender of the message, receiver of the message, and other metadata about the message, subject, and body. In our case, the message will be more simplistic. Our messages will contain the sender, subject, body, and the data sent. It will also contain details of the type of message (message, friend request, and so on).

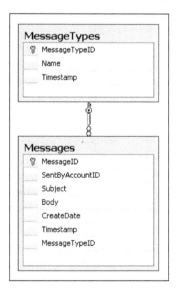

We will need to create a page that allows a user to compose a new message. This interface should also allow a user to add his/her friends easily rather than force them to remember everyone. Also, this interface should allow a user to quickly snap together some HTML without ever having to look at HTML. This can be accomplished with a WYSIWYG editor.

Recipients

As we have already discussed that we are going to move some of the complexity away from the message, following a subscription model instead, you will find that most of the complexity of this system lies around the recipient concepts.

In this case, the recipient subscription is what will be contained in a folder and will have a read status. With this design, we can remove some of the burden from our database. The overhead of doing this of course means that we now need to manage our data more smartly as it is kept in many pieces.

A more simple design that would result in more copies of data to be managed would be to create one message for each recipient. This is easier as each message can easily be deleted and moved around without having to worry about the copies of that message of the other recipients. Having said that, if the message is quite large, and more importantly if we were to allow file attachments, most of the copy would be identical for each recipient. This would quickly bloat your database!

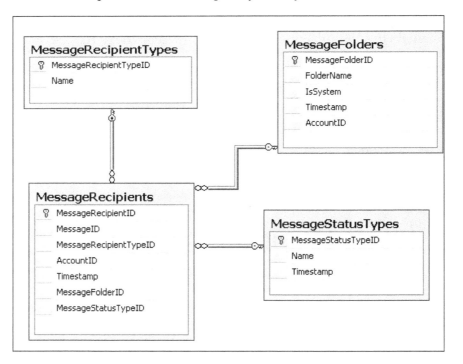

Solution

Now let's take a look at our solution.

Implementing the database

First let's take a look at what tables are needed:

Messages

A message will primarily be made up of the subject and its body. In addition to that we will need to know what type of message we are sending so that we can do some more fancy things in the UI down the road. In addition to this, we are going to maintain who owns the message or created the message at this level.

Column Name	Data Type	Allow Nulls
▶🔑 MessageID	bigint	☐
SentByAccountID	int	☐
Subject	varchar(250)	☐
Body	varchar(MAX)	☐
CreateDate	smalldatetime	☐
Timestamp	timestamp	☐
MessageTypeID	int	☐

There aren't really any major complexities to note here other than the fact that the **Body** is made up of a **varchar(MAX)** data type. If you feel this is too large for your system, feel free to make it anything you are comfortable with. Note that we have a **Timestamp** with this table, as with other chapters. This allows LINQ to do its magic with regards to our data layer.

MessageTypes

Message Types allows us to assign a type to our messages. This is purely a lookup table that will allow us to know what the types are during queries. We will keep a list of enums in the code to make the lookups easier from that end.

Column Name	Data Type	Allow Nulls
▶🔑 MessageTypeID	int	☐
Name	varchar(150)	☐
Timestamp	timestamp	☐

MessageRecipients

A message recipient is simply the receiving party to the message. But as we try to minimize the data that we manage in our system, the message recipient is also a very important part of the message. In our case, it is the receiving party as well as all the things that the receiving party does with their subscription of that message. We will use this subscription to denote which folder the receiver is keeping the message in, and whether the receiver has read the message or not. Also, if the receiver chooses to delete the message, he/she can just delete the subscription to a message (unless they are the last subscription, in which case we will delete the message as well).

The SQL for this subscription is actually quite straightforward. It tracks a relationship to the message, a relationship to the receiver, which folder the subscription is currently in, and the status of the message for this receiver.

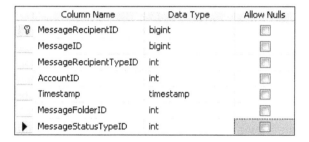

	Column Name	Data Type	Allow Nulls
🔑	MessageRecipientID	bigint	☐
	MessageID	bigint	☐
	MessageRecipientTypeID	int	☐
	AccountID	int	☐
	Timestamp	timestamp	☐
	MessageFolderID	int	☐
▶	MessageStatusTypeID	int	☐

MessageRecipientTypes

The message recipient type allows us to track the receiver of this message addressed in the **TO**, **CC**, or **BCC** fields. Initially, our interface will only have a **TO** field. I figure that we should add this bit of metadata though just in case we want to expand our capabilities down the road! This is another example of a lookup table that we might need to use in the SQL queries. In our case, we will have an enum defined that maintains this lookup for us on the code side.

	Column Name	Data Type	Allow Nulls
▶🔑	MessageRecipientTypeID	int	☐
	Name	varchar(100)	☐

MessageStatusTypes

MessageStatusTypes allows us to track what a recipient is doing with his/her copy of the message, whether they have read the message, replied to the message, and so on. This is primarily so that we can change the UI to reflect its status to the recipient. However, we could also create a dashboard down the road for the senders of the messages to know whether their message was read or not and by whom (think of all the big brother things one could do...but probably should not do!).

Column Name	Data Type	Allow Nulls
MessageStatusTypeID	int	☐
Name	varchar(100)	☐
Timestamp	timestamp	☐

MessageFolders

MessageFolders in our first round of implementation will simply hold copies of new messages in the Inbox and copies of sent messages in the Sent folder. We will also have a trash folder and a spam folder. That said, I always wanted to build a system with the future in mind if it doesn't require a lot of extra work, and so we have also baked in the concept of a user being able to create and manage his/her own folders.

Therefore, rather than just see the MessageFolders table as another lookup table, you will see that there is an **IsSystem** flag to denote which folders are to be seen system-wide. And you will see an **AccountID** column for custom folders so that we know who owns which folders.

Column Name	Data Type	Allow Nulls
MessageFolderID	int	☐
FolderName	varchar(100)	☐
IsSystem	bit	☐
Timestamp	timestamp	☐
AccountID	int	☐

Creating the relationships

Once all the tables are created, we can create the relationships.

For this set of tables, we have relationships between the following tables:

- Messages and MessageRecipients
- Messages and Accounts
- Messages and MessageTypes
- MessageRecipients and MessageRecipientTypes
- MessageRecipients and MessageFolders
- MessageRecipients and MessageStatusTypes

Setting up the data access layer

The data access layer in this case is very straightforward. Open up your `Fisharoo.dbml` file and drag all of your new messaging oriented tables.

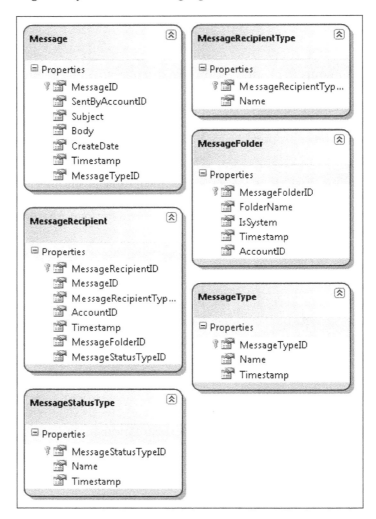

Remember that we are not letting LINQ track our relationships at this point (to avoid built in concurrency management issues). So be sure to remove all the relationships that pop up as you drag your tables on to the design surface. Once you save this, you should now have a list of new domain objects in your arsenal.

Building repositories

With these new tables come some additional repositories. We will create the following repositories.

- `MessageRepository`
- `MessageRecipientRepository`
- `MessageFolderRepository`

As we have gone over the creation of repositories in the previous chapters, we will not cover all the details again. We will create a method for selecting a single entity by ID, a group of entities by their parents, saving entities, and deleting entities.

Having said that, there are a couple of methods that have something special in the set of repositories. As we are using message subscriptions, we don't necessarily want to delete recipients haphazardly. We may want to delete a recipient, and if that recipient is the last recipient with a subscription to a message, we may also want to delete the message. On the other end of the spectrum, if we do delete a message, we may also want to remove all the recipient subscriptions.

In addition to these different ways of deleting data, we will also run into a scenario where selecting a single entity from our repositories won't be quite good enough. So in this case, we have created an aggregate class that will allow us to select several entities out at once for use in our inbox scenarios.

MessageRepository

When we think of a standard inbox, we know that we need to see the messages that we have, who sent them, when they were sent, and at least the subject of their message. In this case, we have discussed two different entities here. When we think about the fact that we also need to know who they were sent to, we have added a third entity. While we could run three separate queries for this data, it would be better for us to run one query (as we would have done in the old days) and return the data that we need in one shot.

Having said that, we know that LINQ can only return one entity or a list of single entities. What do we do? In this case, we need to create an aggregate. This is a class that contains other entities. We will therefore create a `MessageWithRecipient` class that will contain the sender's account info, the message, and the recipient. This should provide us with enough data to represent messages in our inbox view later.

Before we write any queries, we first need to create the aggregate.

```
//Core/Domain/MessageWithRecipient.cs
namespace Fisharoo.FisharooCore.Core.Domain
{
```

```
public class MessageWithRecipient
{
    public Account Sender { get; set; }
    public Message Message { get; set; }
    public MessageRecipient MessageRecipient{ get; set; }
}
}
```

With this aggregate in place we can now turn our attention to the repository that will get all this data for us.

```
//Core/DataAccess/Impl/MessageRepository.cs
public List<MessageWithRecipient> GetMessagesByAccountID(Int32
        AccountID, Int32 PageNumber, MessageFolders Folder)
{
    List<MessageWithRecipient> result = new
        List<MessageWithRecipient>();
    using(FisharooDataContext dc = conn.GetContext())
    {
        IEnumerable<MessageWithRecipient> messages =
        (from r in dc.MessageRecipients
        join m in dc.Messages on r.MessageID equals
                m.MessageID
        join a in dc.Accounts on m.SentByAccountID equals
                a.AccountID
        where r.AccountID == AccountID && r.MessageFolderID ==
                (int)Folder
        orderby m.CreateDate descending
        select new MessageWithRecipient()
        {
                Sender = a,
                Message = m,
                MessageRecipient = r
        }).Skip((PageNumber - 1)*10).Take(10);
        result = messages.ToList();
    }
    return result;
}
```

This is a fun method! This method involves selecting a list of our MessageWithRecipient aggregate objects. The LINQ query is joining all the tables that we need and selecting a new instance of the MessageWithRecipient aggregate, which is then populated with the three classes that we need in the aggregate. Additionally, we have introduced some paging logic with the .Skip and .Take methods to produce a subset of the MessageWithRecipient objects.

In addition to the selection method above, we also need to discuss the delete method for this repository. As we have data holding a subscription to our message data, it is important that we first remove all the subscriptions prior to removing the message itself.

```
//Core/DataAccess/Impl/MessageRepository.cs
public void DeleteMessage(Message message)
{
    using(FisharooDataContext dc = conn.GetContext())
    {
        IEnumerable<MessageRecipient> recipients =
        dc.MessageRecipients.Where(mr => mr.MessageID ==
        message.MessageID);
        foreach(MessageRecipient mr in recipients)
        {
            dc.MessageRecipients.DeleteOnSubmit(mr);
        }
        dc.SubmitChanges();
        dc.Messages.DeleteOnSubmit(message);
        dc.SubmitChanges();
    }
}
```

This is easily accomplished by opening a new instance of the data context. We then get a list of recipients for this message. Once we have the list, we iterate over each recipient adding it to the context for deletion. Finally, we call SubmitChanges() to delete all the subscriptions effectively. We then delete the message as we normally would!

MessageRecipientRepository

The message recipient repository is considerably easier. It simply has an altered delete statement to adjust for the fact that if we delete the last subscription to a message, it will amount to deleting the message.

```
//Core/DataAccess/Impl/MessageRecipientRepository.cs
public void DeleteMessageRecipient(MessageRecipient messageRecipient)
{
    using(FisharooDataContext dc = conn.GetContext())
    {
        dc.MessageRecipients.Attach(messageRecipient,true);
        dc.MessageRecipients.DeleteOnSubmit(messageRecipient);
        dc.SubmitChanges();
        //if the last recipient was deleted
        //...also delete the message
        int RemainingRecipientCount =
```

```
                dc.MessageRecipients.Where(mr => mr.MessageID ==
                messageRecipient.MessageID).Count();
          if (RemainingRecipientCount == 0)
          {
                dc.Messages.DeleteOnSubmit(
                    dc.Messages.Where(m => m.MessageID ==
                    messageRecipient.MessageID).FirstOrDefault());
                dc.SubmitChanges();
          }
      }
}
```

In this method, we delete the recipient in question. We then get a count of the remaining recipients for the message , which has the last recipient removed. If that count is zero, then there are no more recipients remaining for that message. In that case we perform a delete on that message and remove it from the system as well.

Implementing the services/application layer

Once all the repositories are built for single serving, we can begin to create the services layer. Again, this layer is responsible for assembling aggregates and performing complex actions with our entities. We will create only one service for this chapter. We will also extend a couple of services.

- MessageService
- Email
- AlertService
- FriendService

MessageService

The MessageService will help us in one way—sending messages. Keep in mind that to send a message, we will need to create a Message, then create a MessageRecipient for the sender's copy, and then create one-to-many MessageRecipients for the receivers of the message. While this is not a complex task really, it is a very appropriate series of tasks for a service object!

```
//Core/Impl/MessageService.cs
public void SendMessage(string Body, string Subject, string[] To)
{
    Message m = new Message();
    m.Body = Body;
    m.Subject = Subject;
    m.CreateDate = DateTime.Now;
```

```
m.MessageTypeID = (int)MessageTypes.Message;
m.SentByAccountID = _userSession.CurrentUser.AccountID;
Int64 messageID = _messageRepository.SaveMessage(m);
//create a copy in the sent items folder for this user
MessageRecipient sendermr = new MessageRecipient();
sendermr.AccountID = _userSession.CurrentUser.AccountID;
sendermr.MessageFolderID = (int) MessageFolders.Sent;
sendermr.MessageRecipientTypeID = (int) MessageRecipientTypes.TO;
sendermr.MessageID = messageID;
sendermr.MessageStatusTypeID = (int)MessageStatusTypes.Unread;
_messageRecipientRepository.SaveMessageRecipient(sendermr);
//send to people in the To field
foreach (string s in To)
{
    Account toAccount = null;
    if (s.Contains("@"))
        toAccount = _accountRepository.GetAccountByEmail(s);
    else
        toAccount = _accountRepository.GetAccountByUsername(s);
    if(toAccount != null)
    {
        MessageRecipient mr = new MessageRecipient();
        mr.AccountID = toAccount.AccountID;
        mr.MessageFolderID = (int)MessageFolders.Inbox;
        mr.MessageID = messageID;
        mr.MessageRecipientTypeID = (int)
                            MessageRecipientTypes.TO;
        _messageRecipientRepository.SaveMessageRecipient(mr);
        _email.SendNewMessageNotification(_userSession.
                        CurrentUser,toAccount.Email);
    }
}
}
```

This should be very straightforward to follow. The first thing we do is to spin
up a new instance of the Message that we are sending. We then save it via the
MessageRepository and get back the new MessageID to work with down the line.

The next task is to make sure that we paste a copy of the message in the sender's
Sent Items folder. We do this by creating a MessageRecipient object and tying it
to the sender's account. You will notice that we have assigned it to the Sent Items
folder using an enum named MessageFolders, which has IDs that map to the
MessageFolders lookup table. This enum is stored next to a new domain object
named MessageFolder and looks like this:

```
//Core/Domain/MessageFolder.cs
namespace Fisharoo.FisharooCore.Core.Domain
{
    public enum MessageFolders
    {
        Inbox = 1,
        Sent = 2,
        Trash = 3,
        Spam = 4
    }
    public partial class MessageFolder
    {
    }
}
```

The next item in the `MessageService` is assigning the `MessageRecipientTypeID` to the sender's copy. The `MessageRecipientType` is to let the display know whether to show the `MessageRecipient` as a TO, CC, or BCC recipient. This is another enum value that maps back to a lookup table in the database and looks like this:

```
//Core/Domain/MessageRecipientType.cs
namespace Fisharoo.FisharooCore.Core.Domain
{
    public enum MessageRecipientTypes
    {
        TO = 1,
        CC = 2,
        BCC = 3
    }
    public partial class MessageRecipientType
    {
    }
}
```

We then move into a `foreach` loop in the `MessageService`, which is responsible for determining whether we are looking up a recipient via an email address or a username. It does this by testing the **To** value of the `MessageRecipients` to see if it has an ampersand or not, which would correspond to an email address.

Depending on whether the TO value is an email address or a username, we get a copy of an `Account` object. Once we have a valid `Account` object to work with, we move on to creating a new `MessageRecipient` for that `Account`. You should note that in this implementation of the `MessageRecipient`, we are placing the `Message` subscription into the `Inbox` instead of the `Sent Items` folder. This `MessageRecipient` is also of `MessageRecipientType` TO.

Email

Once the `MessageRecipient` is successfully created and persisted to the database, we then move on to sending an email notification to the `MessageRecipient`. The most important thing to note about the additional method of `SendNewMessageNotification()` is that we are sending a notification—not the whole message!

 I mention this because I feel it is important to note that one of the quickest ways to get your sites' IP addresses banned is to be determined to be a sender of spam. Since you are entirely responsible for the content that go out in your messages, you can't directly control what your users type in a message. So don't risk your reputation by sending the entire contents of their messages!

```
public void SendNewMessageNotification(Account sender, string ToEmail)
{
    foreach (string s in ToEmail.Split(new char[] {',',';'}))
    {
        string message = sender.FirstName + " " + sender.LastName +
        " has sent you a message on " + _configuration.SiteName + "!
         Please log in at " + _configuration.SiteName +
        " to view the message.<HR>";
        SendEmail(s, "", "", sender.FirstName + " " + sender.LastName
                +
            " has sent you a message on " +
            _configuration.SiteName + "!", message);
    }
}
```

This method breaks down all the `TO` recipients and creates a new email notification using our existing subsystem telling the recipients that they have a new message waiting for them in their `Inbox`.

AlertService

We created a placeholder in one of the previous chapters in our `AlertService` to allow us to insert a URL in our alerts that would allow the receiver of an alert to easily click into sending a message to the sender of that alert. At the time we created this, it was purely a placeholder as we didn't have any tools to send from. We will now create these tools, so that we can fill this placeholder out.

```
//TODO: MESSAGING - point to send message URL
private string GetSendMessageUrl(Int32 AccountID)
{
 return "<a href=\"[rootUrl]/mail/newmessage.aspx?AccountID=" +
    AccountID.ToString() + "\">Click here to send message</a>";
}
```

This method is simply responsible for creating a link to the new message page passing in the user you want to send a message to. This method is already called from several of our existing `AlertService` methods.

FriendService

We now need to extend our `FriendService`.
`CreateFriendFromFriendInvitation()` method. Remember that this method is responsible for creating a friend from an accepted invitation. We now want to add some logic to this that when a friend request is accepted, we send a new Message to the creator of that friend request letting them know that their request was accepted.

```
public void CreateFriendFromFriendInvitation(Guid InvitationKey,
Account InvitationTo)
{
    . . .
//CHAPTER 6
//add a message to the inbox regarding the new friendship!
Message m = new Message();
m.Subject = "You and " + InvitationTo.Username + " are now
            friends!";
m.Body = "You and <a href=\"" + _webContext.RootUrl +
InvitationTo.Username + "\">" + InvitationTo.Username + "</a> are
  now friends!";
m.CreateDate = DateTime.Now;
m.MessageTypeID = (int)MessageTypes.FriendConfirm;
m.SentByAccountID = InvitationFrom.AccountID;
Int64 messageID = _messageRepository.SaveMessage(m);
MessageRecipient mr = new MessageRecipient();
mr.AccountID = InvitationTo.AccountID;
mr.MessageFolderID = (int)MessageFolders.Inbox;
mr.MessageID = messageID;
mr.MessageRecipientTypeID = (int) MessageRecipientTypes.TO;
mr.MessageStatusTypeID = (int) MessageStatusTypes.Unread;
_messageRecipientRepository.SaveMessageRecipient(mr);
}
```

This additional code is going through the motions of creating a new message and a recipient for that message. In this case though, we are giving this message the `MessageTypeID` of `MessageTypes.FriendConfirm` (or a friend confirmation). Other than that, this code is straightforward.

Implementing the presentation layer

Now that our framework has been updated to handle the new concept of messaging, let's start creating some UI features so that we can use our new tools. We are going to need at least three pages to really utilize our messaging features. We will need a way to create and send a new message, a way to receive and view the messages, and a way to read an individual message. In addition to the creation of a message, we will need a way to easily choose from our list of friends, the recipients of our new messages. Also, while viewing our list of messages, we will need a way of drilling into different folders of messages. Let's get started!

New message

The UI for the new message page is relatively trivial. It consists of a **To** field, a **Subject** field, a message field, and a button to signify that we are ready to send the message. Where things are significantly different is in the use of the Xinha WYSIWYG editor! This is a JavaScript library that allows you to transform a multiline text box into a full-featured editor.

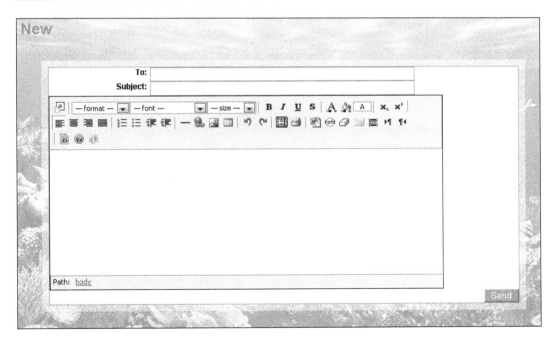

To get started with the integration of Xinha, we will first need to get the latest code base. This can be acquired from the code base of this book or by going to `http://xinha.webfactional.com/wiki/DownloadsPage`. Install this code base into a new Xinha directory off the root of the site.

Then open the `SiteMaster.Master` page. Directly after the body add the following JavaScript.

```
<script type="text/javascript">
    xinha_editors = null;
    xinha_editors = xinha_editors ? xinha_editors : [];
</script>
```

This code is not part of the standard install process. What it does is allow us to spin up multiple instances of the editor all throughout a single page. You will see this later.

Then further down in our master page, just before the ending body tag, we will insert another huge blob of JavaScript. This is a very large blob that could just as easily be inserted into an external `.js` file. I am not going to show it here. Please open the existing master page from this chapter to see it.

You will see that this blog is responsible for setting the vast amount of configuration options that Xinha exposes. This code is heavily commented and so should be understandable. Also, the configuration of this package is covered extensively on the net!

The only thing, but definitely the special one, I added to in this configuration is the very first line that sets the base URL of the site. In this case, I changed it to use a call into the `WebContext.RootUrl` property.

```
...
_editor_url = "<%= _webContext.RootUrl %>Xinha/";
...
```

This brings us back to our `NewMessage.aspx` page. Now that we have Xinha installed, we can add a line below our page UI that effectively ties our multiline text box control to the Xinha library. This is done with a snippet of JavaScript.

```
<script type="text/javascript">
    xinha_editors[xinha_editors.length] = 'ctl00_Content_txtMessage';
</script>
```

Note that this is using the same `xinha_editors` variable that we defined initially in the Master page! What we have done here is to insert this new control into an array of Xinha editors. Note that we are using the full `ClientID` of the text box that we want associated as an editor.

- To send a message
- To preload a recipient of a message (if linked to from an `Alert`) and
- To send a reply to a message

This is really the same thing with the exception that to send a reply to a message, we would first have to load that reply. We will get to that down the road!

To send a message, we have to bubble up the button click event through our code behind and into our presenter. As I have covered this concept extensively, I will not cover it here. So, in the presenter, we have added a method called `SendMessage()`, which takes in the **Subject**, Message, and an array of **To** entries.

```
public void SendMessage(string Subject, string Message, string[] To)
{
    _messageService.SendMessage(Message,Subject,To);
}
```

This method then calls into the `MessageService.SendMessage()` method and sends the message.

The preloading of a recipient is handled in the `Init()` method of the presenter. It checks to see if we have an `AccountID` in the QueryString (via our `WebContext` wrapper). If so, it gets the `Accounts Username` property and adds that to the **To** field in the UI.

Loading a reply message into the UI is very similar to loading a username. The `Init()` method checks the `WebContext` to see if we have a `MessageID` in the QueryString and loads the previous Message details into the UI.

```
//Mail/Presenter/NewMessagePresenter.cs
public void Init(INewMessage view)
{
    _view = view;
    if(_webContext.MessageID != 0)
        _view.LoadReply(_messageRepository.GetMessageByMessageID(_
          webContext.MessageID,_userSession.CurrentUser.AccountID));
    if(_webContext.AccountID != 0)
        _view.LoadTo(_accountRepository.GetAccountByID(
                    _webContext.AccountID).Username);
}
```

Friends control

The other important feature that we have as part of the NewMessage.aspx page is the ability to easily select a friend from a list of friends as the recipient of a message—similar to the idea of a contacts book. To achieve this, we will create a user control that lists our friends.

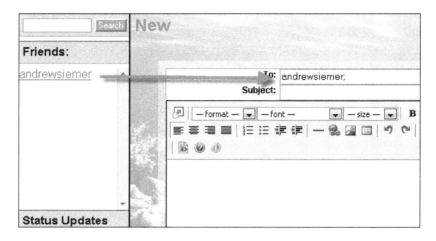

The UI for this control is just a simple Repeater object that outputs a friend's username. So let's take a look at what populates the UI. In the Init() method in the FriendPresenter.cs file, we have a call into the FriendRepository. GetFriendsAccountsByAccountID() method, which loads all the users' friends. This is bound to the repeater control in the UI.

```
//Mail/UserControls/Presenter/FriendsPresenter.cs
public void Init(IFriends view)
{
    _view = view;
    _view.LoadFriends(_friendRepository.
GetFriendsAccountsByAccountID(_us
                erSession.CurrentUser.AccountID));
}
```

In the code behind for our friend control, we insert a snippet of JavaScript to allow us to click on a friend and carry his/her username into our **To** field in our NewMessage UI.

```
//Mail/UserControls/Friends.aspx.cs
public void repFriends_ItemDataBound(object sender,
                                   RepeaterItemEventArgs e)
{
    if(e.Item.ItemType == ListItemType.Item || e.Item.ItemType ==
                      ListItemType.AlternatingItem)
    {
        HyperLink linkFriend = e.Item.FindControl("linkFriend") as
                          HyperLink;
        linkFriend.Attributes.Add("OnClick",
                              "javascript:document.forms[0].
                              ct100_Content_txtTo.value += '" +
                      ((Account)e.Item.DataItem).Username + ";';");
    }
}
```

Note that we are adding an attribute for the `OnClick` event of our link that will call a JavaScript to move the username to our **To** field with a semicolon delimiter.

This gives us a list of friends, but how do we tie that back into our UI? Open the `NewMessage.aspx` page. We will need to register the new control in the page and then add a reference to it in the page.

Just below the Page directive add the following code:

```
<%@ Register Src="~/Mail/UserControls/Friends.ascx"
             TagPrefix="Fisharoo" TagName="Friends" %>
```

Then add a new Content section to our page where the friends control will live:

```
<asp:Content ContentPlaceHolderID="LeftNavTop" runat="server">
    <Fisharoo:Friends ID="friends1" runat="server" />
</asp:Content>
```

This inserts the friends control into the top of our left nav!

Default (or Inbox)

Now that we can successfully send a message, we need a way to receive those messages. This is done in folder view of our messages. This is really just a page that shows a list of messages, who sent them, and when. We can either click on the sender to go to their profile page, or can click on the message to view it. We can also navigate through pages of messages with a list of page navigation links. And we will have the ability to delete one or many selected messages. Additionally, we will create a `Folders` control that will allow us to navigate through our various folders to see the messages in those containers.

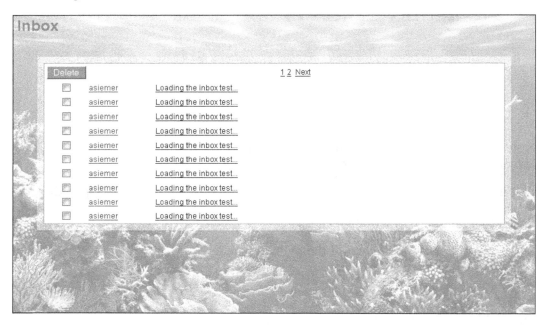

The UI for this page is very simple. It is just a repeater that iterates through the `MessageWithRecipient` collection that is passed to it. So let's take a look at the presenter, which actually populates our list of messages. As always this is accomplished in the `Init()` method of the presenter.

```
public void Init(IDefault view)
{
    _view = view;
    if (_userSession.CurrentUser != null)
    {
        _view.LoadMessages(_messageRepository.GetMessagesByAccountID(
                _userSession.CurrentUser.AccountID,
                _webContext.Page,
                (MessageFolders) _webContext.FolderID));
```

```
        _view.DisplayPageNavigation(
            _messageRepository.GetPageCount((MessageFolders)
            _webContext.FolderID,
            _userSession.CurrentUser.AccountID),
            (MessageFolders) _webContext.FolderID, _webContext.Page);
    }
}
```

We first check to see that the user of the page is actually logged in. We then make a call into the `MessageRepository` to get a list of messages by the user's `AccountID`. We also make a call into `MessageRepository` to get a page count (the number of pages of messages that we have to navigate through).

Loading messages into the UI is simply a matter of binding the `DataSource` to the repeater.

```
public void LoadMessages(List<MessageWithRecipient> Messages)
{
    repMessages.DataSource = Messages;
    repMessages.DataBind();
}
```

As this requires no explanation, let's jump right into how we go about building our page navigation. Recall that in the `Init()` of our presenter we had a call into the view of `DisplayPageNavigation()`, which received the `PageCount` of the folder we were working with, and the current page we were viewing. Here is that method:

```
public void DisplayPageNavigation(Int32 PageCount, MessageFolders
folder, Int32 CurrentPage)
{
    if(PageCount == CurrentPage)
        linkNext.Visible = false;
    if (CurrentPage == 1)
        linkPrevious.Visible = false;
    linkNext.NavigateUrl = "~/mail/default.aspx?folder=" + ((int)
                    folder).ToString() + "&page=" +
                    (CurrentPage + 1).ToString();
    linkPrevious.NavigateUrl = "~/mail/default.aspx?folder=" + ((int)
                    folder).ToString() + "&page=" +
                    (CurrentPage - 1).ToString();
    for(int i = 1; i<=PageCount;i++)
    {
        HyperLink link = new HyperLink();
        link.Text = i.ToString();
        link.NavigateUrl = "~/mail/default.aspx?folder=" +
                ((int)folder).ToString() + "&page=" + i.ToString();
        phPages.Controls.Add(link);
        phPages.Controls.Add(new LiteralControl(" "));
    }
}
```

This chunk of code interacts with three controls in our UI—two hyperlinks, one that displays **Previous** and one displaying **Next**, and a `PlaceHolder` control that will hold the individual page numbers of all the pages for this data set.

This method initially determines if we should show the **Next** or **Previous** links based on our current page and our total page count. We then hook up the navigation property of each of those links to take us to the next page or the previous page of data. After that we use a `for` loop to iterate through all the possible pages, from 1 to `PageCount`, making a new hyperlink for each iteration that contains the location of that page.

The other feature of this page is the ability to delete messages—as many or as few as we like. This is primarily achieved with a helper function in the code behind of the view that extracts all the messages that are selected, which can be called from within the presenter. This allows the presenter to remain in control!

```
public List<Int32> ExtractSelectedMessages()
{
    List<Int32> result = new List<Int32>();
    foreach (RepeaterItem item in repMessages.Items)
    {
        if(item.ItemType == ListItemType.Item || item.ItemType ==
            ListItemType.AlternatingItem)
        {
            CheckBox chkMessage = item.FindControl("chkMessage") as
                                    CheckBox;
            Int32 messageID =
                Convert.ToInt32(chkMessage.Attributes["MessageID"]);
            if(chkMessage.Checked)
                result.Add(messageID);
        }
    }
    return result;
}
```

This method iterates through all the check boxes to see if they are selected or not. If they are, then it extracts the `MessageID` from an attribute that was created when we loaded the display. A collection of `MessageID`s is then returned to the caller.

This then brings us to the `Delete` method in the presenter. It is called from a button click event that is bubbled up to the presenter, which then calls into the view to get a list of selected `MessageID`s. Then using the `MessageRepository` we get a copy of that message. With the copy, we then call into the `MessageRecipientRepository`. `DeleteMessageRecipient()` method and delete each selected `MessageRecipient`.

Folders

I hate to sound like a broken record but I find myself saying that this UI is also simple. Well...it is! This UI is also made up of a `Repeater` that displays the bound data. In this case, we are displaying folders as hyperlinks, which then link to the same `Default.aspx` page, but additionally pass in the folder that we are interested in viewing.

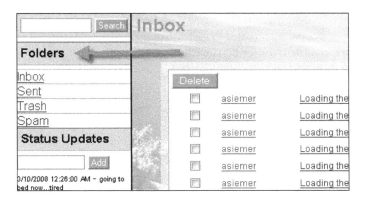

I am going to jump right in to the presenter so that we can see the `DataSource` for our data.

```
public void Init(IFolders view)
{
    _view = view;
    _view.LoadFolders(_messageFolderRepository.
GetMessageFoldersByAccountID(_userSession.CurrentUser.AccountID));
}
```

In this case, we are calling into the `MessageFolderRepository` to get a list of folders for this user. We bind that directly to the UI through our view. The view then iterates through the data in our repeater. In our `ItemDataBound` method — in the code behind of the view — we update each hyperlink in the UI.

```
protected void repFolders_ItemDataBound(object sender,
RepeaterItemEventArgs e)
{
    if (e.Item.ItemType == ListItemType.Item || e.Item.ItemType ==
        ListItemType.AlternatingItem)
    {
        HyperLink linkFolder = e.Item.FindControl("linkFolder") as
                               HyperLink;
        linkFolder.Text =
        ((MessageFolder)e.Item.DataItem).FolderName;
```

```
        linkFolder.NavigateUrl = "~/Mail/Default.aspx?folder=" +
        ((MessageFolder) e.Item.DataItem).MessageFolderID.ToString();
        linkFolder.Attributes.Add("FolderID",
        ((MessageFolder)e.Item.DataItem).
        MessageFolderID.ToString());
    }
}
```

This creates a list of folders for us in a control. But how do we get it into our UI? To do this, we have to go back to our `Default.aspx` page. This will be done exactly the same way we did for our friends control in our new message page. Open the default page so that we can add the `Folders` control.

```
<%@ Register Src="~/Mail/UserControls/Folders.ascx"
        TagPrefix="Fisharoo" TagName="Folders" %>
<asp:Content ContentPlaceHolderID="LeftNavTop" runat="server">
    <Fisharoo:Folders id="Folders1"
            runat="server"></Fisharoo:Folders>
</asp:Content>
```

Read message

Reading a message is not that difficult at all. We are just loading a message into a static UI based on the `MessageID` that is passed into the page. Let's first discuss the UI (which could easily be made more complex down the road!). This UI will consist of a **From** Label, a **Subject** Label, a **Message** Label, and a **Reply** button.

Here is the message view:

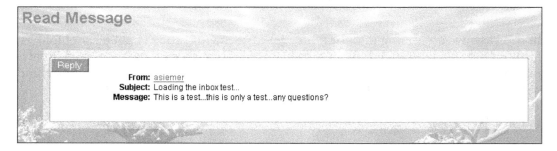

And here is what will be seen when replying to the message:

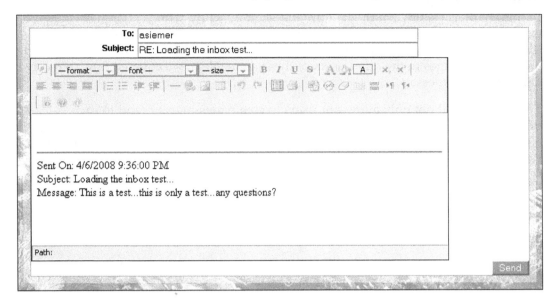

As usual, as all the leg work is done in the presenter, let's jump straight to it.

```
public void Init(IReadMessage view)
{
    _view = view;
    _view.LoadMessage(_messageRepository.GetMessageByMessageID(_
webContex
                t.MessageID,_userSession.CurrentUser.AccountID));
}
```

As you can see here, we are populating the UI based on a call into the `MessageRepository.GetMessageByMessageID()` method. This method sends a `MessageWithRecipient` into the view, which then loads the message for display. Now that is simple!

For the **Reply** button, we will bubble up the click event into the presenter. The presenter then makes a call to the `Redirector` class that passes the current `MessageID` to the `NewMessage` page. Simple again!

```
public void Reply()
{
    _redirector.GoToMailNewMessage(_webContext.MessageID);
}
```

Summary

In this chapter, we have built an entire messaging facility. This section has gone over extending the framework to allow for the creation and retrieval of messages and all the related items of a message. We then covered creating a UI to allow users to create and send messages to the other users of the system. Next, we covered how to receive and read those messages.

This chapter will not only allow our users to create messages to send to each other but also provide our system with a way to communicate with our user base efficiently. This is not only a good feature to have in your community site but also a base requirement for it.

7
Media Galleries

In this chapter we will go over the concept of allowing people to share files. We will specifically be focused on sharing images, but will build the system so that we can easily set it up to share videos, audio files, resume, or any other type of binary file. In addition to that we will build the concept of having user-specific sets of files as well as content that can be shared among many users.

In order to create the file management software for our website, we need to consider topics such as a single or multi-file upload, file system management, and image manipulation in the case of photos. In addition to this we will cover creation of pages for displaying the user's photo albums, their friends' photo albums, as well as a few data management pages. This chapter will create a basic framework from which you can easily grow to suit the file management needs of just about any community site.

Problem

Apart from the standard infrastructure issues that we have to consider when building a system such as this, one of the core issues in any web-based file management system is file upload. As we all know, most server side technologies allow only one file to be uploaded at a time. ASP.NET is no different here. And while we could easily buy a third-party plug-in to handle multiple files at once, I figured we could dig into creating a multi-file upload system using a little client side script (Flash in our case) in order to fool our backend.

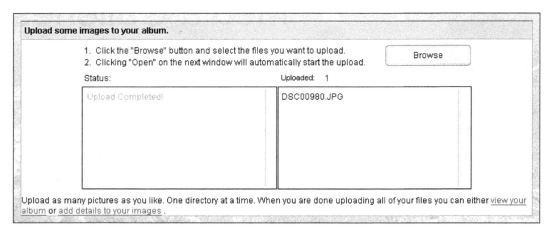

Once we get our file upload process working we are only one-third of the way there! As we are going to be mostly concerned with uploading images, we need to consider that we will need to provide some image manipulation. With each file that is uploaded to our system we need to create a handful of different sizes of each image to be used in various scenarios across our site. To start with, we will create a thumbnail, small, medium, large, and original size photos.

20d0d209-37a3-417e-bc2e-c0a7bf3a23e8__L.JPG

20d0d209-37a3-417e-bc2e-c0a7bf3a23e8__M.JPG

20d0d209-37a3-417e-bc2e-c0a7bf3a23e8__O.JPG

20d0d209-37a3-417e-bc2e-c0a7bf3a23e8__S.JPG

20d0d209-37a3-417e-bc2e-c0a7bf3a23e8__T.JPG

Now while creating different size files is technically working with the file storage system, I wanted to take an extra breath with regards to the file storage concepts. As we had discussed in the earlier chapters, we could choose to store the files on the file system or in a database. For avatars it made sense to store each with the profile data whereas for image galleries it makes more sense to store the file on the file system. While storing files to the file system we need to be very cautious as to how the file structure is defined and where and how the individual files are stored. In our case we will use system-generated GUIDs as our file names with extensions to define the different sizes that we are storing. We will dig into this more as we start to understand the details of this system.

Name	Date taken	Tags	Size	Rating
20d0d209-37a3-417e-bc2e-c0a7bf3a23e8__L.JPG			84 KB	☆☆☆☆☆
20d0d209-37a3-417e-bc2e-c0a7bf3a23e8__M.JPG			29 KB	☆☆☆☆☆
20d0d209-37a3-417e-bc2e-c0a7bf3a23e8__O.JPG	3/22/2008 9:32 PM		3,386 KB	☆☆☆☆☆
20d0d209-37a3-417e-bc2e-c0a7bf3a23e8__S.JPG			8 KB	☆☆☆☆☆
20d0d209-37a3-417e-bc2e-c0a7bf3a23e8__T.JPG			2 KB	☆☆☆☆☆

Once we have uploaded the files to the server and they are ready for our use across the system, we will take up the concept of user files versus system files. If we build the system with some forethought regarding this topic we can have a very generic file management system that can be extended for future use. We will build a personal system in this chapter. But as you will see with some flags in just the right places, we could just as easily build a system file manager or a group file manager.

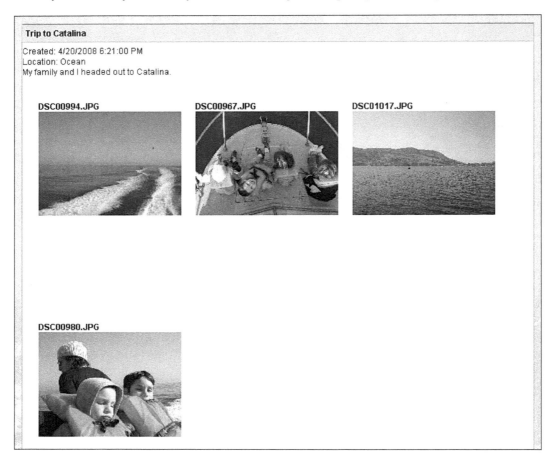

Design

Let's take a look at the design for this feature.

Files

In this case, as we are not storing our files in the database, we need to take a closer look at what actually needs to be managed in the database so as to keep track of what is going on in the file system. In addition to standard file metadata, we need to keep a close eye on where the file actually lives—specifically which file system folder the file will reside in. We also need to be able to maintain which accounts own which files, or in the case of system files, which files can be viewed by anyone.

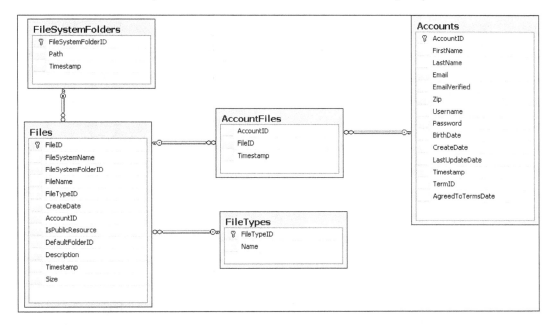

Folders

You may be wondering why I have a separate section regarding folders when we just touched upon the fact that we will be managing which file system folder we will be storing files in. In this section we are going to discuss folder management from a site perspective rather than a file system perspective—user folders or virtual folders if you desire.

Very similar to file storage, we will be storing various metadata about each folder. We will also have to keep track of who owns which folder, who can see which folder, or in the case of system folders whether everyone can see that folder. And of course as each folder is a virtual container for a file, we will have to maintain the relationship between folders and files.

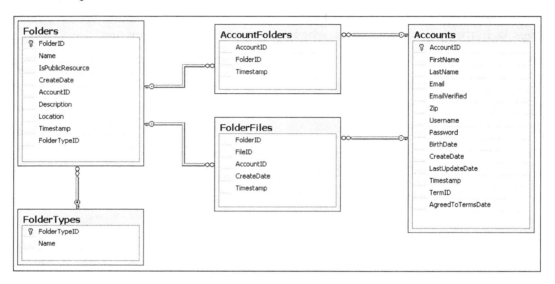

File upload

The file upload process will be handled by a Flash client. While this is not really a book about Flash I will show you how simple it is to create this Flash client, which is really just providing a way to store many files that need to be uploaded, and then uploading them one at a time in a way that the server can handle each file.

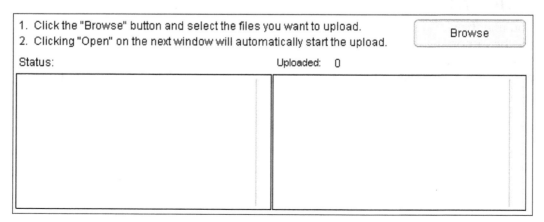

File system management

Managing the file system may seem like a non-issue. However, keep in mind that for a community site to be successful we will need at least 10,000 or so unique users. Given that sharing photos and other files is such a popular feature of most of today's community sites, this could easily translate into a lot of uploaded files.

While you could technically store a large number of files in one directory on your web server, you will find that over time your application becomes more and more sluggish. You might also run into files being uploaded with the same name using this approach. Also, you may find that you will have storage issues and need to split some of your files off to another disk or another server.

Many of these issues are easily handled if we think about and address them up front. In our case we will use a unique file name for each uploaded file. We will store each file in subdirectories that are also uniquely named based on the year and month in which the file was uploaded. If you find that you have a high volume of files being uploaded each day, you may want to store your files in a folder with the year and month in the name of the folder and then in another subdirectory for each day of that month.

In addition to a good naming convention on the file system, we will store the root directory for each file in the database. Initially you may only have one root for your photos, one for videos, and so on. But storing it now will allow you to have multiple roots for your file storage — one root location per file. This gives you a lot of extensibility points over time meaning that you could easily relocate entire sections of your file gallery to a separate disk or even a separate server.

Data management screens

Once we have all of the infrastructure in place we will need to discuss all the data management screens that will be needed — everything from the UI for uploading files to the screens for managing file metadata, to screens for creating new albums. Then we will need to tie into the rest of the framework and allow users to view their friends' uploaded file albums.

Solution

Let's take a look at our solution.

Implementing the database

First let's take a look at the tables required for these features.

Files

The most important thing to consider storing in the database first is of course our primary interest files. As with most other conversations regarding a physical binary file we always have to consider if we want to store the file in the database or on the file system. In this case I think it makes sense to store the file (and in the case of a photo, its various generated sizes) on the file system. This means that we will only be storing metadata about each file in our database.

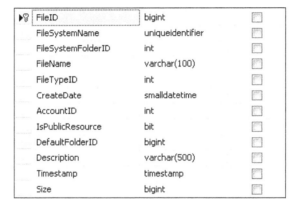

The most important field here to discuss is the **FileSystemName**. As you can see this is a GUID value. We will be renaming uploaded files to GUIDs in addition to the original extension. This allows us to ensure that all the files in any given folder are uniquely named. This removes the need for us to have to worry about overwriting other files.

Then we see the **FileSystemFolderID**. This is a reference to the `FileSystemFolders` table, which lets us know the root folder location where the file is stored.

Next on our list of items to discuss is the **IsPublicResource** flag. By its name it is quite clear that this flag will set a file as public or private and can therefore be seen by all or by its owner (**AccountID**).

We then come to a field that may be somewhat confusing: **DefaultFolderID**. This has nothing to do with the file system folders. This is a user created folder. When files are uploaded initially they are put in a virtual folder. That initial virtual folder becomes the file's permanent home. This doesn't mean that it is the file's only home. As you will see later we have the concept that files can live in many virtual folders by way of subscription to the other folders.

File system folders

As mentioned previously, the `FileSystemFolders` table is responsible for letting us know where our file's root directory is. This allows us to expand our system down the road to have multiple roots, which could live on the same server but different disks, or on totally different servers.

	Column Name	Data Type	Allow Nulls
▶🔑	FileSystemFolderID	int	☐
	Path	varchar(100)	☐
	Timestamp	timestamp	☐

There is nothing super important here to see. Simply a key, the **Path** (URL), and a **Timestamp** for LINQ to work with.

File types

The `FileTypes` table will help us to keep track of what sort of files we are storing and working with. This is a simple lookup table that tells us the extension of a given file.

	Column Name	Data Type	Allow Nulls
▶🔑	FileTypeID	int	☐
	Name	varchar(50)	☐

This is simply the name of the file type being specified.

Folders

Folders are virtual in this case. They provide us with a way to specify a container of files. In our case we will be containing photos, in which case folders will act as photo albums.

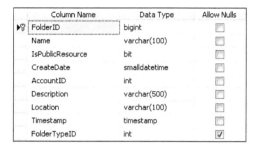

There isn't much here that can't be understood by its name. Do note though that we have another flag, **IsPublicResource**, which allows us to specify whether a folder and its resources are public or private, that is, viewable by all or viewable only by the owner.

Folder types

The `FolderTypes` table allows us a way to specify the type of folder. Currently this will simply be Name, photos, movies, and so on. However, down the road you may want to specify an icon for each folder type in which case this is the place where you would want to assign that specification.

Account folders

In the `AccountFolders` table we are able to specify additional ownership of a folder. So in the case that a folder is a public resource and external resources can own folders, we simply create the new ownership relationship here. This is not permanent ownership. It is still specified with the `Folders` table's **AccountID**. This is temporary ownership across many Accounts.

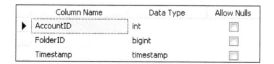

As you can see in the screenshot we have the owner (**AccountID**) and the folder that is to be owned (**FolderID**).

Account files

Similar to the `AccountFolders` table, the `AccountFiles` table allows someone to subscribe to a specific file. This could be used for purposes of **Favorites** or similar concepts.

The makeup of this table is identical to `AccountFolders`. You have the owner and the file being owned.

Folder files

The `FolderFiles` table allows an Account to not only subscribe to a file, similar to the Favorites concept, but it also allows a user to take one of my files and put it into one of their folders as though the file itself belonged to them.

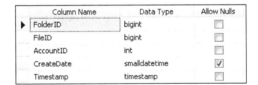

As you can see in the screenshot, this is primarily a table that holds the keys to the other tables. We have the **FolderID**, **FileID**, and **AccountID** for each file. This clearly specifies who is taking ownership of what and where they want it to be placed.

Creating the relationships

Once all the tables are created we can then create all the relationships.

For this set of tables we have relationships between the following tables:

- `Files` and `FileSystemFolders`
- `Files` and `FileTypes`
- `Files` and `Folders`
- `Files` and `Accounts`

- Folders and Accounts
- Folders and FolderTypes
- AccountFolders and Accounts
- AccountFolders and Folders
- AccountFiles and Accounts
- AccountFiles and Files
- FolderFiles and Accounts
- FolderFiles and Folders
- FolderFiles and Files

Setting up the data access layer

To set up the data access layer follow the steps mentioned next:

- Open the Fisharoo.dbml file.
- Open up your **Server Explorer** window.
- Expand your Fisharoo connection.
- Expand your tables. If you don't see your new tables try hitting the **Refresh** icon or right-clicking on tables and clicking **Refresh**.
- Then drag your new tables onto the design surface.
- Hit **Save** and you should now have the domain objects shown in the following screenshot to work with!

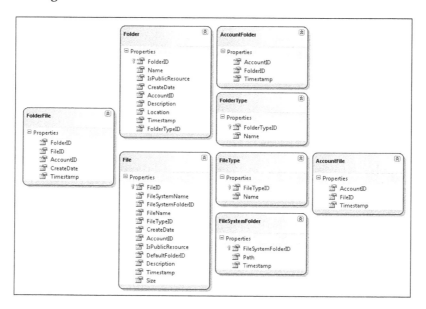

Keep in mind that we are not letting LINQ track our relationships. So go ahead and delete them from the design surface. Your design surface should have the same items that you see in the screenshot (though perhaps in a different arrangement!).

Building repositories

With the addition of new tables will come the addition of new repositories so that we can get at the data stored in those tables. We will be creating the following repositories to support our needs.

- FileRepository
- FolderRepository

Each of our repositories will generally have a method for select by ID, select all by parent ID, save, and delete. Once you have seen one repository you have pretty much seen them all. Review previous chapters, the appendices, or the included code for examples of a standard repository. However, I will discuss anything that varies from standard!

FileRepository

Other than the normal methods that all the XRepository classes have, the FileRepository also has a couple of additional more interesting methods.

- UpdateDescriptions
- DeleteFilesInFolder
- DeleteFileFromFileSystem

The UpdateDescriptions() method is an interesting concept. This method is the first example of performing multiple updates all at once rather than doing them one a time. This obviously will be much more performance oriented than individual update executions.

```
public void UpdateDescriptions(Dictionary<int,string>
fileDescriptions)
{
    using(FisharooDataContext dc = conn.GetContext())
    {
        List<Int64> fileIDs = fileDescriptions.Select(f =>
                        Convert.ToInt64(f.Key)).Distinct().ToList();
        IEnumerable<File> files = dc.Files.Where(f =>
                        fileIDs.Contains(f.FileID));
        foreach (File file in files)
        {
            file.Description =
                        fileDescriptions.Where(f=>f.Key==file.FileID)
                        .Select(f=>f.Value).ToString();
```

```
        }
        dc.SubmitChanges();
    }
}
```

As you can see, this method accepts a `Dictionary` collection, which contains a list of `FileID`s and `fileDescriptions`. We then open up the DataContext. Then off the `Dictionary` collection I get a list of unique `FileID`s. We then make one trip to the database to get all of the File objects we need using the `Contains()` method of the `FileID` collection. With the collection of appropriate files in hand we can then iterate through each of them setting the description to the value passed in via the `Dictionary` collection. Once all this leg work is done, we can call the `SubmitChanges` method. Keep in mind that we have one working DataContext for this entire operation. It is why this method of updation works!

The next method that is not a normal Repository method is the `DeleteFilesInFolder`. This method takes in a `Folder` object. With this `folder` object in hand we get a collection of related files. We then iterate over each file and call the `DeleteFileFromFileSystem` method. We then attach all the files to the current DataContext and then call the `DeleteAllOnSubmit` method to delete all the `File` records. We then call `SubmitChanges` to execute the changes.

Having mentioned the `DeleteFileFromFileSystem`, you probably understand what that method is responsible for. Essentially, it is responsible for removing the physical files that are stored on the file system. This is important as we have just allowed the data to be deleted, so we could end up with huge file stores of random unwanted files.

```
private void DeleteFileFromFileSystem(Folder folder, File file)
{
    string path = "";
    switch (file.FileTypeID)
    {
        case 1:
        case 2:
        case 7:
            path = "Photos\\";
            break;
        case 3:
        case 4:
            path = "Audios\\";
            break;
        case 5:
        case 8:
        case 6:
```

```
                path = "Videos\\";
                break;
        }
        string fullPath = _webContext.FilePath + "Files\\" + path +
                        folder.CreateDate.Year.ToString() +
                        folder.CreateDate.Month.ToString() + "\\";

        if (Directory.Exists(fullPath))
        {
            if (System.IO.File.Exists(fullPath + file.FileSystemName +
"__o." + file.Extension))
                System.IO.File.Delete(fullPath + file.FileSystemName +
"__o." + file.Extension);
            if (System.IO.File.Exists(fullPath + file.FileSystemName +
"__t." + file.Extension))
                System.IO.File.Delete(fullPath + file.FileSystemName +
"__t." + file.Extension);
            if (System.IO.File.Exists(fullPath + file.FileSystemName +
"__s." + file.Extension))
                System.IO.File.Delete(fullPath + file.FileSystemName +
"__s." + file.Extension);
            if (System.IO.File.Exists(fullPath + file.FileSystemName +
"__m." + file.Extension))
                System.IO.File.Delete(fullPath + file.FileSystemName +
"__m." + file.Extension);
            if (System.IO.File.Exists(fullPath + file.FileSystemName +
"__l." + file.Extension))
                System.IO.File.Delete(fullPath + file.FileSystemName +
"__l." + file.Extension);

            if(Directory.GetFiles(fullPath).Count() == 0)
                Directory.Delete(fullPath);
        }
}
```

This method starts off first by attempting to identify the `FileType` that we are dealing with, which gets us the root folder for that type of file.

 Keep in mind that if you want to store files in multiple locations and use the `FileSystemFolders`, then this will need to be tweaked a bit. The concept shown here is for a single root file folder!

With the root path identified we then create the `fullPath`. This variable is created by making a call into our `WebContext` class, which determines the root path on the server. We then add `Files`, which is the files' root folder. Then comes the path that we just configured. The next portion may seem odd at the moment. When we upload files (coming later) we upload to a directory with the name of the folder's creation date, year, and month.

With the `fullPath` configured appropriately we then check to make sure that the directory actually exists. Now we can step through each file that we created. We check to see if the file exists at the specified location and then call `System.IO.File.Delete`. We do this for each type of file we create in our upload process. Keep in mind that the upload and delete processes are fairly tied at the hip. So if we change something on one end we need to make changes to the other end too!

With the files deleted we take the file system beautification one step further. We need to check to see if the folder is now empty. If it is, then we delete the folder too!

FolderRepository

There are a couple of methods in the `FolderRepository` that are worth covering.

- `GetFoldersByAccountID`
- `GetFriendsFolders`

The `GetFoldersByAccountID` does just what it says! It takes in an `AccountID` and performs a search to get all the folders by the passed in `AccountID`. It does go a bit beyond that. It then iterates through each folder in the resulting list and generates the file system path for the folder's cover image. This determination is then assigned to the `FullPathToCoverImage`. If there is no cover image found then the default image is assigned. Once we have this taken care of, we return the list of folders.

```
public List<Folder> GetFoldersByAccountID(Int32 AccountID)
{
    List<Folder> result = new List<Folder>();
    using(FisharooDataContext dc = conn.GetContext())
    {
        var account = dc.Accounts.Where(a => a.AccountID ==
                                    AccountID).FirstOrDefault();
        IEnumerable<Folder> folders = (from f in dc.Folders
                                    where f.AccountID == AccountID
                                    orderby f.CreateDate
                                    descending
                                    select f);
        foreach (Folder folder in folders)
        {
            var fullPath = (from f in dc.Files
                                    join ft in dc.FileTypes on
```

```
                        f.FileTypeID equals ft.FileTypeID
                        where f.DefaultFolderID ==
                        folder.FolderID
                        select new {
                            FullPathToCoverImage =
                                f.CreateDate.Year.ToString() +
                                f.CreateDate.Month.ToString() +
                                "/" + f.FileSystemName + "__S." +
                                ft.Name}).FirstOrDefault();
                if(fullPath != null)
                    folder.FullPathToCoverImage =
                                        fullPath.FullPathToCoverImage;
                else
                    folder.FullPathToCoverImage = "default.jpg";
                if(account != null)
                    folder.Username = account.Username;
            }
            result = folders.ToList();
        }
        return result;
}
```

The next interesting method in this repository is the `GetFriendsFolders`. This method introduces a new LINQ to SQL concept— **Union**. The Union takes all the items from one collection and merges it with another collection of items. The items that are the same in both lists are merged so that the resulting list of items is unique.

```
public List<Folder> GetFriendsFolders(List<Friend> Friends)
{
    List<Folder> result = new List<Folder>();
    foreach (Friend friend in Friends)
    {
        if (result.Count < 50)
        {
            List<Folder> folders =
                    GetFoldersByAccountID(friend.MyFriendsAccountID);
            IEnumerable<Folder> result2 = result.Union(folders);
            result = result2.ToList();
        }
        else
            break;
    }
    return result;
}
```

In our method we take in a list of our `Friends`. We then iterate over this collection and with each pass we check to see if we have less than 50 folders (a random number of items I chose to show on our album homepage). If we have less than 50, then we get all the folders for the current friend and merge it into our result list using the `Union` method. We continue to do this until we are either out of `Friends` or have 50 folders to show on the homepage.

This method could be made better in a couple of ways. Firstly we could move the 50 to a configuration file or administration panel. Also, this method should return the folders that are the latest, or contain the latest files from our friends. And if we really want to be flexible this method should take into account that the user may have more friends than the current limitation. In this case we should really create pagination functionality allowing our user to see all their friends and their friends' folders. We can do that later though!

Now that we have a place for our data and ways to interact with it, let's move out one more layer closer to the UI. We will now discuss the services' layer to help us get the data out to the front of the application.

Implementing the services/application layer

Once all the repositories are built for a single serving purpose, we can begin to create the services' layer. Again, this layer is responsible for assembling aggregates and performing complex actions with our entities. We will create the following services.

- `FolderService`

FolderService

This service is fairly simple actually. It's sole responsibility for the time being is to interact with various repositories to get the list of `Friend`'s folders for display on the album homepage for our users.

```
public List<Folder> GetFriendsFolders(Int32 AccountID)
{
    List<Friend> friends =
            _friendRepository.GetFriendsByAccountID(AccountID);
    List<Folder> folders =
            _folderRepository.GetFriendsFolders(friends);
    folders.OrderBy(f => f.CreateDate).Reverse();
    return folders;
}
```

This method calls into the `FriendRepository` to produce a list of the user's `friends`. With that in hand we can then call into the `FolderRepository` to get all the folders for all of those friends. We then order the folders by their `CreateDate`. We then reverse the order so that the latest folder is on top.

That's it! We move on to the presentation layer.

Implementing the presentation layer

With the entire backend created and ready to go let's turn our attention to getting the presentation up and running. We will get started with building the file upload section first as it will be difficult to get the other sections to run successfully without uploaded files.

File upload

As you may already know ASP.NET is very handy at browsing to a file, selecting it, then uploading it. There are very few modifications that need to be made to your application to enable this functionality. Simply put your need to alter the form to include `enctype="multipart/form-data"`, add a file browse box to your page, and handle the uploaded file. Done!

What ASP.NET doesn't do well — or doesn't do at all — is handle multiple file uploads at once. There are many third-party providers that offer plug-ins to do this either in Java or Active-X. But this is not a good solution if we don't want to spend the money (though some are only a few hundred bucks!).

To get around the multi-file upload issue in ASP.NET we are going to build a simple Flash-based client. This client will be responsible for selecting a group of files on the local file system. It will then pass the files one at a time to our server side receiving page. When we discuss photo files (jpg, gif, and so on) we will also look at some basic image processing concepts.

Receiving files

Our file receiver will be able to receive multiple files at a time. In our case we will be primarily concerned with receiving image files. But we will set it up to receive other files as well. The receiver in our case will be housed inside a webpage in our `Files` directory. The beginning of our receiver will be responsible for spinning up some variables and objects.

```
public string ImageFolder = "";
Dictionary<string,int> sizesToMake = new Dictionary<string,int>();
private int sizeTiny = 50;
private int sizeSmall = 200;
```

```
private int sizeMedium = 500;
private int sizeLarge = 1000;
private IUserSession _userSession;
private IWebContext _webContext;
private IFileRepository _fileRepository;
private IAccountRepository _accountRepository;
int NewWidth = 0;
int NewHeight = 0;
string saveToFolder = "files";
```

The most interesting thing to note here is the `sizesToMake` collection. This will hold all the sizes, which we will generate further down the line. If we want to add an additional size or modify one of our existing sizes we would do that here.

We then step into the `Page_Load()` method and finish the initialization of our objects and our sizes collection.

```
protected void Page_Load(object sender, System.EventArgs e)
{
_userSession = ObjectFactory.GetInstance<IUserSession>();
_webContext = ObjectFactory.GetInstance<IWebContext>();
_fileRepository = ObjectFactory.GetInstance<IFileRepository>();
_accountRepository = ObjectFactory.GetInstance<IAccountRepository>();
sizesToMake.Add("T",sizeTiny);
sizesToMake.Add("S",sizeSmall);
sizesToMake.Add("M",sizeMedium);
sizesToMake.Add("L",sizeLarge);
```

We then interrogate a query string value to see what sort of file we are dealing with. In our case we will be working with photos, but we might deal with something else later.

```
//determine save to folder
switch (_webContext.FileTypeID)
{
    case 1:
        saveToFolder = "Photos/";
        break;
    case 2:
        saveToFolder = "Videos/";
        break;
    case 3:
        saveToFolder = "Audios/";
        break;
}
```

Once we have decided which folder we are working with, we would then need to check to make sure that that folder is actually on the file system. If not, then we may want to create it.

```
//make sure the directory is ready for use
saveToFolder += DateTime.Now.Year.ToString() +
                DateTime.Now.Month.ToString() + "/";
if (!Directory.Exists(Server.MapPath(saveToFolder)))
    Directory.CreateDirectory(Server.MapPath(saveToFolder));
```

We then have a few other variables that we want to set up. We need to get the Account that we are working with. We also need to receive the uploaded files. And finally we will need to get the full path to the folder that we are saving our files to.

```
Account account =
            _accountRepository.GetAccountByID(_webContext.AccountID);
HttpFileCollection uploadedFiles =  Request.Files;
string Path = Server.MapPath(saveToFolder);
```

Now that we have a collection of uploaded files we need to work with each file one at a time. To do this we will start a `for` loop. At the top of each iteration we will need to get a single file that we want to process.

```
for(int i = 0 ; i < uploadedFiles.Count ; i++)
{
    HttpPostedFile F = uploadedFiles[i];
```

We then need to initialize some more variables to be set up where we will store the files and how we will do it. We will get the folder ID from the query string. Notice that I am currently assuming that we are playing with image files with a static **fileType** of 1. If we were to create another page to upload say audio files, we would want to pass in the fileType. Next we attempt to get the uploadedFileName by parsing the end of the file name of the uploaded file. Once we have the file name we get the file extension. As we will be saving the files to the file system, we run the risk of overwriting files if we do not ensure that the file has a unique name. To do this, we create a new GUID string that will act as our file system's file name. With all this data in place we then have enough to create the final file name. We then create the domain object file.

```
string folderID = _webContext.AlbumID.ToString();
string fileType = "1";
string uploadedFileName =
            F.FileName.Substring(F.FileName.LastIndexOf("\\") + 1);
string extension =
    uploadedFileName.Substring(uploadedFileName.LastIndexOf(".") + 1);
Guid guidName = Guid.NewGuid();
```

```
string fullFileName = Path + "/" + guidName.ToString() + "__O." +
            extension;
bool goodFile = true;
//create the file
File file = new File();
```

Next, we look at the `fileType` that was set and determine the `File` object's `FileTypeID`. This is an enum that was set up in the File's partial class. Note that at the end of each inner switch statement we are setting a flag for `goodFile` to determine if we have successfully found our `FileTypeID`.

```
#region "Determine file type"
switch (fileType)
{
    case "1":
        file.FileSystemFolderID =
                        (int)FileSystemFolder.Paths.Pictures;
        switch (extension.ToLower())
        {
            case "jpg":
                file.FileTypeID = (int)File.Types.JPG;
                break;
            case "gif":
                file.FileTypeID = (int)File.Types.GIF;
                break;
            case "jpeg":
                file.FileTypeID = (int)File.Types.JPEG;
                break;
            default:
                goodFile = false;
                break;
        }
        break;
    case "2":
        file.FileSystemFolderID = (int)FileSystemFolder.Paths.Videos;
        switch (extension.ToLower())
        {
            case "wmv":
                file.FileTypeID = (int)File.Types.WMV;
                break;
            case "flv":
                file.FileTypeID = (int)File.Types.FLV;
                break;
            case "swf":
                file.FileTypeID = (int)File.Types.SWF;
```

```
            break;
        default:
            goodFile = false;
            break;
    }
    break;
case "3":
    file.FileSystemFolderID = (int)FileSystemFolder.Paths.Audios;
    switch (extension.ToLower())
    {
        case "wav":
            file.FileTypeID = (int)File.Types.WAV;
            break;
        case "mp3":
            file.FileTypeID = (int)File.Types.MP3;
            break;
        case "flv":
            file.FileTypeID = (int)File.Types.FLV;
            break;
        default:
            goodFile = false;
            break;
    }
    break;
}
```

Next, we attempt to populate the domain `File` object with all its properties such as the size of the uploaded file, the account that it belongs to, its file system name, and so on.

```
file.Size = F.ContentLength;
file.AccountID = account.AccountID;
file.DefaultFolderID = Convert.ToInt32(folderID);
file.FileName = uploadedFileName;
file.FileSystemName = guidName;
file.Description = "";
file.IsPublicResource = false;
```

Now we are ready to start the work. If the `goodFile` flag is still **true** then we can commit our file object to the database. We then save the actual uploaded file to the file system with its new file name. And finally if the `fileType` is a `Picture`, we scrub the file against our `Resize()` method to generate the various sizes of files we want to end up with.

```
if (goodFile)
{
    _fileRepository.SaveFile(file);
    F.SaveAs(fullFileName);
    if(Convert.ToInt32(fileType) == ((int)Folder.Types.Picture))
    {
        Resize(F,saveToFolder,guidName,extension);
    }
}
```

To get into the `Resize()` method we have to pass in the uploaded file that we are working with, the folder that we want to save the files to, the generated GUID for the file system name, and the extension of the uploaded file. Once in the `Resize()` method, we can create all the size variations that we need for our uploaded photo. We start off by setting up a `foreach` loop that will iterate through the dictionary in the class wide `sizesToMake` collection.

```
public void Resize(HttpPostedFile F, string SaveToFolder, Guid
                SystemFileNamePrefix, string Extension)
{
    //Makes all the different sizes in the sizesToMake collection
    foreach (KeyValuePair<string, int> pair in sizesToMake)
    {
```

Inside of our loop we will start up a new `System.Drawing.Image` and we will initialize it from the uploaded files input stream. We then move to creating a new `Bitmap` that is initialized from the newly created `Image`. With the `Bitmap` we can then create new variations on the size of that uploaded Image. First we look to see if the file that was uploaded is longer on the top or on the side so that we know how to appropriately determine the ratio of the image's height and width.

```
using(System.Drawing.Image image =
    System.Drawing.Image.FromStream(F.InputStream))
//determine the thumbnail sizes
using(Bitmap bitmap = new Bitmap(image))
{
    decimal Ratio;
    if(bitmap.Width > bitmap.Height)
    {
        Ratio = (decimal) pair.Value / bitmap.Width;
```

```
        NewWidth = pair.Value;
        decimal Temp = bitmap.Height * Ratio;
        NewHeight = (int)Temp;
    }
    else
    {
        Ratio = (decimal) pair.Value / bitmap.Height;
        NewHeight = pair.Value;
        decimal Temp = bitmap.Width * Ratio;
        NewWidth = (int)Temp;
    }
}
```

Once we have our sizes determined we can resize it and save it to the file system. We do this by again setting a reference to the uploaded file and reconstructing a new `Bitmap`. With this in hand we can then save the bitmap to the file system with its new dimensions. Do note though that in this case when we save the file to the file system, we are not adding a section to the name using the key name from the dictionary. This results in a file name that is made up of {GUID}__{key}.{extension}. This means that every file will be unique and will have uniquely named files of various sizes.

```
using(System.Drawing.Image image =
            System.Drawing.Image.FromStream(F.InputStream))
using(Bitmap bitmap = new Bitmap(image, NewWidth, NewHeight))
{
    bitmap.Save(Server.MapPath(SaveToFolder + "/" +
                        SystemFileNamePrefix.ToString() + "__"
                        + pair.Key + "." + Extension),
                image.RawFormat);
}
```

We continue to loop through all the different file sizes in our dictionary creating new files for each one. Once complete we will move to the next file that was uploaded. Let's now write a test page to test our receiving page.

Testing our receiver

Now that we have seriously cool uploading capabilities we need to write a test harness to make sure that it works. It is very good to have a simple way of testing complex logic. Remember that we are working with many aspects here. We could run into issues such as server-based security when we go on to save a file to the file system. We could run into configuration issues when we attempt to upload large files. Having a utility such as this will save you a lot of time down the road when you go to move your application out to a production box.

Let's get started by creating the super simple UI. To do this we will need to have a form. In the form we need to modify the enctype to a multipart/form-data and set the action path to point to our RecieveFiles.aspx file. Next we add a file input box so that we can browse out for a file. We will then add a simple HTML button to post a file to our receiver page.

```
<form method="post" action="ReceiveFiles.aspx?AccountID=1&AlbumID=1&F
ileType=1"
                           enctype="multipart/form-data">
<div>
    <input type="file" class="stdInput" id="file2" runat="server"
                       NAME="file2"/>
</div>
<input type="submit" value="test" />
</form>
```

This posting of a file to your receiver page will either put a file in the right location or it won't! It is quite likely that the first time you attempt to upload a file, you will get an error regarding file-level security—something along the lines of ASP.NET or Network service, which do not have rights to write a file to the specified location. To fix this you simply need to add those groups to the folder you are trying to write to with write access.

Another common configuration issue that you might come across is encountered when you attempt to upload large files. By default ASP.NET can only handle a 4MB file. Many images from today's digital cameras are much larger than that. To get around this limitation we can simply add a few lines to the web.config file. Either locate or add the following section to your web.config file. In the maxRequestLength property, change the 4MB limitation to whatever you like. I have an 8MB limitation defined here.

```
<httpRuntime
       executionTimeout="90"
       maxRequestLength="8192"
       useFullyQualifiedRedirectUrl="false"
       minFreeThreads="8"
       minLocalRequestFreeThreads="4"
       appRequestQueueLimit="100"
       />
```

Multi-file upload

Now that we have a way of receiving uploaded files and we have a way to test to be sure that our uploader works, let's create the UI to upload a handful of files. This is a Flash-based UI. You can either download a trial copy of Flash or look at alternatives in a product such as Swish or Flex.

As this is not so much a Flash book as it is an ASP.NET book, I will have to skim over this topic quickly. We will create a simple Flash UI that has a browse box, a couple of dynamic text boxes, and some labels.

We will build the entire UI on one frame.

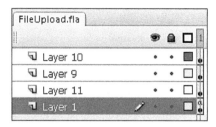

My UI looks something like this:

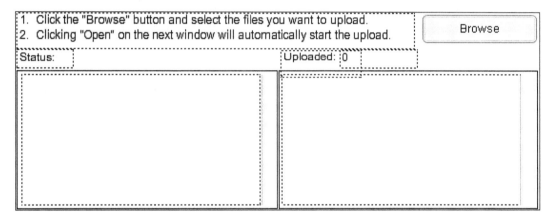

On the first layer we will add some action script that hooks up our UI and our `ReceiveFiles` page. The following code looks very much like C# code and should be fairly readable.

```
import flash.net.FileReferenceList;
import flash.net.FileReference;
stop();
//keep track of how many were loaded vs. uploaded
var fileLoadedCounter = 0;
var fileUpLoadedCounter = 0;
var listener:Object = new Object();
listener.onSelect = function(fileRefList:FileReferenceList) {
    status.text = "";
```

```
        uploaded.text = "";
        myTF = new TextFormat();
        myTF.color = 0x000000;
        status.setTextFormat(myTF);
        txtUploadCounter.text = "0";
        fileLoadedCounter = 0;
        fileUpLoadedCounter = 0;

        trace("onSelect");
        var list:Array = fileRefList.fileList;
        var item:FileReference;
        for(var i:Number = 0; i < list.length; i++) {
          //increment counter
          fileLoadedCounter ++;
          trace("fileLoadedCounter: " + fileLoadedCounter);
                item = list[i];
            trace("name: " + item.name);
          //sometext.text = "name: " + item.name + "\n" + sometext.text;
          AddToStatus("name: " + item.name);
                trace(item.addListener(this));
          //item.upload("http://localhost:56472/Files/ReceiveFiles.aspx?Al
                              bumID=1&FileTypeID=1&AccountID=1");
          item.upload(_root.SiteRoot+"Files/ReceiveFiles.aspx?AlbumID="+
             _root.AlbumID+"&FileTypeID="+_root.FileType+"&AccountID="+
                                          _root.AccountID);
        }
      trace("all done!");
    }
    listener.onCancel = function():Void {
        trace("onCancel");
    }
    listener.onOpen = function(file:FileReference):Void {
        trace("onOpen: " + file.name);
      //AddToStatus("onOpen: " + file.name);
    }
    listener.onProgress = function(file:FileReference,
        bytesLoaded:Number, bytesTotal:Number):Void {
        trace("onProgress with bytesLoaded: " + bytesLoaded + "
            bytesTotal: " + bytesTotal);
      AddToStatus("Bytes Loaded: " + bytesLoaded + " of Total: " +
                  bytesTotal);
    }
    listener.onComplete = function(file:FileReference):Void {
        trace("onComplete: " + file.name);
      AddToUploaded(file.name);
```

```
    //increment uploaded counter
    fileUpLoadedCounter ++;
    txtUploadCounter.text = fileUpLoadedCounter;
    trace("fileUpLoadedCounter: " + fileUpLoadedCounter);
    //did all files get uploaded?
    if(fileLoadedCounter == fileUpLoadedCounter)
    {
        status.text = "Upload Completed!";
        myTF = new TextFormat();
        myTF.color = 0xFF0000;
        status.setTextFormat(myTF);
    }
}
listener.onHTTPError = function(file:FileReference,
                    httpError:Number):Void {
    trace("onHTTPError: " + file.name + " httpError: " + httpError);
    AddToStatus("** The upload of " + file.name + " failed **");
}
listener.onIOError = function(file:FileReference):Void {
    trace("onIOError: " + file.name);
    AddToStatus("onIOError: " + file.name);
}
listener.onSecurityError = function(file:FileReference,
                        errorString:String):Void {
    trace("onSecurityError: " + file.name + " errorString: " +
        errorString);
    AddToStatus("onSecurityError: " + file.name + " errorString: " +
            errorString);
}
var fileRef:FileReferenceList = new FileReferenceList();
fileRef.addListener(listener);
Browse_btn.addEventListener("click", doBrowse);
function AddToUploaded(msg:String)
{
    uploaded.text = msg + "\n" + uploaded.text;
}
function AddToStatus(msg:String)
{
    status.text = msg + "\n" + status.text;
}
function doBrowse()
{
    fileRef.browse();
}
```

Once you have all this plugged in and working (or you can use the source from the books files), we will need to plug the Flash uploader onto a page. To do this, we will need to add the following code on a page that will house the uploader.

```
<object classid="clsid:d27cdb6e-ae6d-11cf-96b8-444553540000"
codebase="http://fpdownload.macromedia.com/pub/shockwave/cabs/flash/
swflash.cab#version=8,0,0,0" width="550" height="400" id="FileUpload"
align="middle">
    <param name="allowScriptAccess" value="sameDomain" />
    <param name="movie" value="../Files/FileUpload.
swf?SiteRoot=<%Response.Write(_webContext.RootUrl);%>&Al
bumID=<%Response.Write(_webContext.AlbumID.ToString());
%>&FileType=<%Response.Write(((int)Folder.Types.Picture).ToString());
%>&AccountID=<%Response.Write(_webContext.CurrentUser.AccountID.
ToString()); %>" />
    <param name="quality" value="high" />
    <param name="bgcolor" value="#ffffff" />
    <embed src="../Files/FileUpload.swf?SiteRoot=<%Response.Write(_
webContext.RootUrl);%>&AlbumID=<%Response.Write(_webContext.AlbumID.
ToString()); %>&FileType=<%Response.Write(((int)Folder.Types.Picture).
ToString()); %>&AccountID=<%Response.Write(_webContext.CurrentUser.
AccountID.ToString()); %>"
        quality="high"
        bgcolor="#ffffff"
        width="550"
        height="220"
        name="FileUpload"
        align="middle"
        allowScriptAccess="sameDomain"
        type="application/x-shockwave-flash"
        pluginspage="http://www.macromedia.com/go/getflashplayer" />
</object>
```

Most of this code is generated for you in Flash by going to the **File** menu and down to **Publish**. Open the resulting HTML file from the publishing process, and you are ready to go. Though in our file we are passing in (the names here are important and should match) some data to spin up the location of the upload appropriately. This is done with server-side script and some inline variables.

Once you have the UI showing on our upload page and have the appropriate variables plugged in you should be good to go. If for some reason you are not uploading files then make sure that your test script is working first. Make sure that your paths are appropriate and that there are no errors. If the Flash UI doesn't work, you can also run it in debug mode.

Now that we are uploading files, let's move on to discussing the display of those photos.

Photo albums

There are many things we can do now as we have files uploaded to the server in various sizes! I am going to show you the MyPhotos page, which will list all the galleries for the logged in account and link to the ViewAlbum page. This should demonstrate how to work with the photo albums and the photos. You can look at the other pages that are in the code to see how to create albums, link to the file uploader, and so on—basically all the data management tasks that surround the photo album concepts.

MyPhotos

In this page we will display all the photo albums that an account has. We will use a ListView to do this. In case you have not used a ListView before, we will cover some of the basics here.

```
<asp:ListView id="lvAlbums" runat="server"
               OnItemDataBound="lbAlbums_ItemDataBound">
    <LayoutTemplate>
        <ul class="albumsList">
            <asp:PlaceHolder ID="itemPlaceholder"
                             runat="server"></asp:PlaceHolder>
        </ul>
    </LayoutTemplate>

    <ItemTemplate>
        <li>
            <asp:HyperLink CssClass="albumsActionLink"
                           ID="linkEditAlbum" NavigateUrl="
                           ~/Photos/EditAlbum.aspx" Text="Edit"
                           runat="server"></asp:HyperLink>
            <asp:HyperLink CssClass="albumsActionLink"
                           ID="linkViewAlbum" NavigateUrl=
                           "~/Photos/ViewAlbum.aspx" Text="View"
                           runat="server"></asp:HyperLink>
            <asp:LinkButton CssClass="albumsActionLink"
                            ID="linkDeleteAlbum" Text="Delete"
                            OnClick="linkDeleteAlbum_Click"
                            runat="server"></asp:LinkButton><br />
            <asp:Label CssClass="albumsTitle" ID="lblName"
                       Text='<%#((Folder)Container.DataItem).Name %>'
                       runat="server"></asp:Label><br />
            <img src="<%#_webContext.RootUrl
```

```
                    %>files/photos/<%#((Folder)
                    Container.DataItem).FullPathToCoverImage %>" /><br />
            <asp:Label CssClass="albumsLocation" Text="in - "
                        runat="server"></asp:Label>
            <asp:Label CssClass="albumsLocation" ID="lblLocation"
                    Text='<%#((Folder)Container.DataItem).Location %>'
                    runat="server"></asp:Label><br />
            <asp:Label CssClass="albumsDescription"
                        ID="lblDescription" Text='<%#
                        ((Folder)Container.DataItem).Description %>'
                    runat="server"></asp:Label>
            <asp:Literal Visible="false" ID="litFolderID"
                        Text='<%#((Folder)Container.DataItem)
                        FolderID.ToString() %>'
                        runat="server"></asp:Literal>
        </li>
    </ItemTemplate>

    <EmptyDataTemplate>
        Sorry, you don't seem to have any albums at this time!
    </EmptyDataTemplate>
</asp:ListView>
```

Note that the `ListView` has an `OnItemDataBound="lbAlbums_ItemDataBound"` event hooked up. This will become important later on as it controls how we handle each item that is bound to the `ListView`.

The first item you will see inside of the `ListView` is the `LayoutTemplate`. This template defines the iterating items. In our case I have chosen to use an unordered list to display our albums. With some CSS we have full control over how each list item is rendered.

Inside the list you will see that we have a `PlaceHolder` defined with an ID of `itemPlaceholder`. You must use this ID as you see it here! This `PlaceHolder` is responsible for holding everything in the `ItemTemplate` as we do our iteration.

The next section you will see is the `ItemTemplate`. This template actually defines what goes into each item of our list. In our case we have some metadata about each album, the default image for the album, and some link to other functionalities.

Finally we have the `EmptyDataTemplate`. This template is responsible for showing something when there is no data to iterate through. In our case we are displaying a message stating that there are no albums to be displayed.

We can now turn to the code behind of this page (keep in mind that we are still using the MVP pattern). Most of our code behind is driven by our presenter file. In our code behind we have the LoadUI method, which is passed a list of Folder (Albums). This is the key DataSource for our ListView control.

```
public void LoadUI(List<Folder> folders)
{
    if (!IsPostBack)
    {
        lvAlbums.DataSource = folders;
        lvAlbums.DataBind();
    }
}
```

Next we have the lbAlbums_ItemDataBound. This is the method that we hooked up to in the ListView to handle each item as it is bound to our ListView. In this method we are referencing the controls in our ItemTemplate so that we can work with them. We make sure that the Album's description is not too long. If it is, we concatenate it to fit our current display. Then we are constructing our links so that they work as expected for each Album that we are binding.

```
protected void lbAlbums_ItemDataBound(object sender,
                                ListViewItemEventArgs e)
{
    if (e.Item.ItemType == ListViewItemType.DataItem)
    {
        HyperLink linkEditAlbum = e.Item.FindControl("linkEditAlbum")
                            as HyperLink;
        LinkButton linkDeleteAlbum =
                e.Item.FindControl("linkDeleteAlbum") as LinkButton;
        HyperLink linkViewAlbum = e.Item.FindControl("linkViewAlbum")
                            as HyperLink;
        Literal litFolderID = e.Item.FindControl("litFolderID") as
                        Literal;
        Label lblDescription = e.Item.FindControl("lblDescription")
                        as Label;
        if (lblDescription.Text.Length > 150)
        {
            lblDescription.Text = lblDescription.Text.Substring(0,
                                                        149);
            lblDescription.Text += "...";
        }
        linkEditAlbum.NavigateUrl += "?AlbumID=" + litFolderID.Text;
        linkDeleteAlbum.Attributes.Add("OnClick","javascript:
return(confirm('Are you sure you want to delete this album?'));");
        linkDeleteAlbum.Attributes.Add("FolderID",litFolderID.Text);
        linkViewAlbum.NavigateUrl += "?AlbumID=" + litFolderID.Text;
    }
}
```

And finally, we have a method to handle our delete link's click event. This method calls into our presenter to handle the deletion of an `Album`.

```
protected void linkDeleteAlbum_Click(object sender, EventArgs e)
{
    LinkButton linkDeleteAlbum = sender as LinkButton;
    _presenter.DeleteFolder(Convert.ToInt64(linkDeleteAlbum.Attributes
                    ["FolderID"]));
}
```

ViewAlbum

The `ViewAlbum` page is exactly the same as the `MyPhotos` page in that it uses the `ListView` to handle its rendering of the data.

```
<asp:ListView ID="lvGallery" runat="server"
            OnItemDataBound="lvAlbum_ItemDataBound">
    <LayoutTemplate>
        <ul class="albumsList">
            <asp:PlaceHolder ID="itemPlaceholder"
                runat="server"></asp:PlaceHolder>
        </ul>
    </LayoutTemplate>
    <ItemTemplate>
        <li>
            <asp:Label style="font-weight:bold;" ID="lblFileName"
                    Text='<%#((File)Container.DataItem).FileName
                %>' runat="server"></asp:Label>
            <asp:HyperLink ID="linkImage"
                NavigateUrl='<%#((File)Container.DataItem)
                CreateDate.Year.ToString() +
                ((File)Container.DataItem).
                CreateDate.Month.ToString() %>'
                runat="server"></asp:HyperLink>
            <asp:Literal Visible="false" ID="litImageName"
                        runat="server" Text='<%#((File)Container.
DataItem).FileSystemName.ToString()
    %>'></asp:Literal>
            <asp:Literal Visible="false" ID="litFileExtension"
                        runat="server" Text='<%# ((File)Container.
DataItem).Extension.ToString() %>'></asp:Literal><br
                                                    />
            <asp:Label ID="lblDescription" runat="server"
                    Text='<%#((File)Container.DataItem).
                    Description %>'></asp:Label>
        </li>
    </ItemTemplate>
```

```
    <EmptyItemTemplate>
        There are no photos in this gallery!
        <asp:HyperLink ID="linkAddPhotos" runat="server" Text="Click
                              here to add photos"></asp:HyperLink>.
    </EmptyItemTemplate>
</asp:ListView>
```

In the `ListView` there is a declaration for the `OnItemDataBound` so that we can handle each bit of data as it is bound. We then have the `LayoutTemplate` with its `PlaceHolder` named `itemPlaceholder`. There is also the `ItemTemplate` with its various controls (to show images in the Album in this case). And we have our `EmptyItemTemplate` to display a message when we have no data.

In the code behind we have a similar layout as the `MyPhotos` code behind. We load the photos for the given album. We also load some details about the album itself so that we can show things like the album's description and the like. There are a few controls that we have events hooked to so that we can handle things like navigation.

```
protected void lvAlbum_ItemDataBound(object sender,
                                     ListViewItemEventArgs e)
{
    if(e.Item.ItemType == ListViewItemType.DataItem)
    {
        HyperLink linkImage = e.Item.FindControl("linkImage") as
                              HyperLink;
        Literal litImageName = e.Item.FindControl("litImageName") as
                               Literal;
        Literal litFileExtension =
                e.Item.FindControl("litFileExtension") as Literal;
        string pathToImage = "~/files/photos/" +
            linkImage.NavigateUrl + "/" + litImageName.Text;
        linkImage.NavigateUrl = pathToImage + "__o." +
            litFileExtension.Text;
        linkImage.ImageUrl = pathToImage + "__s." +
            litFileExtension.Text;
    }
    if(e.Item.ItemType == ListViewItemType.EmptyItem)
    {
        HyperLink linkAddPhotos = e.Item.FindControl("linkAddPhotos")
                                  as HyperLink;
        linkAddPhotos.NavigateUrl =
                              "~/photos/AddPhotos.aspx?AlbumID=" +
                              _webContext.AlbumID.ToString();
    }
}

public void LoadAlbumDetails(Folder folder)
```

```
    {
        lblAlbumName.Text = folder.Name;
        lblLocation.Text = folder.Location;
        lblDescription.Text = folder.Description;
        lblCreateDate.Text = folder.CreateDate.ToString();
        if(folder.AccountID != _userSession.CurrentUser.AccountID)
        {
            btnEditPhotos.Visible = false;
            btnEditAlbum.Visible = false;
            btnAddPhotos.Visible = false;
        }
    }

    public void LoadPhotos(List<File> files)
    {
        lvGallery.DataSource = files;
        lvGallery.DataBind();
    }

    protected void lbEditPhotos_Click(object sender, EventArgs e)
    {
        _redirector.GoToPhotosEditPhotos(_webContext.AlbumID);
    }

    protected void lbEditAlbum_Click(object sender, EventArgs e)
    {
        _redirector.GoToPhotosEditAlbum(_webContext.AlbumID);
    }

    protected void btnAddPhotos_Click(object sender, EventArgs e)
    {
        _redirector.GoToPhotosAddPhotos(_webContext.AlbumID);
    }
```

Take a look in the photos folder of the website project. There are many other pages for editing photos, editing albums, and so on that demonstrate additional functionality with regards to interacting with our files and photo album data.

Summary

In this chapter we looked at the infrastructure and decisions that go into a media management application. We focused heavily on processing and storing images. But most of the principles that we looked at apply to all sorts of different files. The only real part that would need to be tweaked is how the file is processed once it is stored on the server. In the case of audio and video files you would most likely want to transfer them to a Flash format from a WAV or WMV format so that they become more accessible to your web users.

This chapter has added the ability to create photo albums. We then discussed the ability to upload and manipulate photos. We also discussed how to handle multiple file uploads and the most appropriate way to store them on the file system. Finally, we created a way for our users to interact with their albums and uploaded files.

8
Blogs

People join a community to either look for or provide information on a pre-specified topic. Often times this is performed by way of a blog. A blog allows people to freely express themselves by way of providing stories, articles, or quick blurbs generally on any topic with the community.

Building this key feature into your community is actually one of the easiest things to do. Having built so many features to this point, snapping in the blog module and its required components will go quite smoothly. We will cover not only creating a blog but also how to add friendly URLs to our blog posts. Once this is in place we will follow it up by attaching our blogging system to our alerts system.

Problem

In this chapter we will add the blogging feature to our site. This will handle creating and managing a post. It will also handle sending alerts to your friends' filter page. And finally we will handle creating a friendly URL for your blog posts.

Here we are making our first post to our blog.

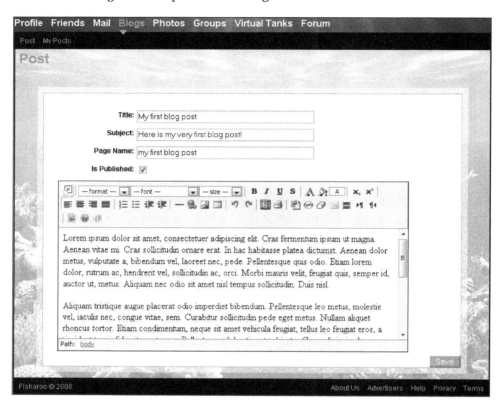

Once our post is created, we will then see it on the **Blogs** homepage and the **My Posts** section. From here we can edit the post or delete the post. Also, we can click into the post to view what we have seen so far.

The following screenshot shows what one will see when he/she clicks on the post:

I have the blog post set up to show the poster's avatar. This is a feature that you can easily add to or remove. Most of your users want to be able to see who the author is that they are currently reading!

Also, we will add a friendly URL to our blog post's pages.

Design

The design of this application is actually quite simple. We will only need one table to hold our blog posts. After that we need to hook our blog system into our existing infrastructure.

Blogs

In order for us to store our blog, we will need one simple table. This table will handle all the standard attributes of a normal blog post to include the title, subject, page name, and the post itself. It has only one relationship out to the Accounts table so that we know who owns the post down the road. That's it!

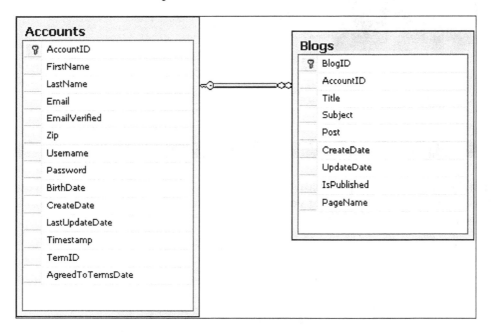

Solution

Let's take a look at the solution for these set of features.

Implementing the database

Let's take a look at the tables required by our solution.

Blogs

The blogs table is super simple. We discussed most of this under the Blogs section.

Column Name	Data Type	Allow Nulls
▶🔑 BlogID	bigint	☐
AccountID	int	☐
Title	varchar(200)	☐
Subject	varchar(500)	☐
Post	varchar(MAX)	☐
CreateDate	smalldatetime	☐
UpdateDate	smalldatetime	☐
IsPublished	bit	☐
PageName	varchar(200)	☐

The one thing that is interesting here is the **Post** column. Notice that I have this set to a **varchar(MAX)** field. This may be too big for your community, so feel free to change it down the road. For my community I am not overly worried. I can always add a UI restriction down the road without impacting my database design using a validation control. After that we will look at the **IsPublished** flag. This flag tells the system whether or not to show the post in the public domain. Next to that we will also be interested in the **PageName** column. This column is what we will display in the browser's address bar. As it will be displayed in the address bar, we need to make sure that the input is clean so that we don't have parsing issues (responsible for causing data type exceptions) down the road. We will handle that on the input side in our presenter later.

Creating the relationships

Once all the tables are created we can then create all the relationships.

For this set of tables we have relationships between the following tables:

* `Blogs` and `Accounts`

Setting up the data access layer

To set up the data access layer follow the steps mentioned next:

* Open the `Fisharoo.dbml` file.
* Open up your **Server Explorer** window.
* Expand your Fisharoo connection.

- Expand your tables. If you don't see your new tables try hitting the **Refresh** icon or right-clicking on tables and clicking **Refresh**.

- Then drag your new tables onto the design surface.

- Hit **Save** and you should now have the following domain objects to work with!

Keep in mind that we are not letting LINQ track our relationships, so go ahead and delete them from the design surface. Your design surface should have all the same items as you see in the screenshot (though perhaps in a different arrangement!).

Building repositories

With the addition of new tables will come the addition of new repositories so that we can get at the data stored in those tables. We will be creating the following repository to support our needs.

- `BlogRepository`

Our repository will generally have a method for select by ID, select all by parent ID, save, and delete. Once you have seen one repository you have pretty much seen them all. Review previous chapters, the appendices, or the included code for examples of a standard repository. I will discuss anything that varies from what is considered standard!

We will start with a method that will allow us to get at a blog by its page name that we can capture from the browser's address bar.

```
public Blog GetBlogByPageName(string PageName, Int32 AccountID)
{
    Blog result = new Blog();
    using(FisharooDataContext dc = _conn.GetContext())
```

```
    {
        result = dc.Blogs.Where(b => b.PageName == PageName &&
                        b.AccountID == AccountID).FirstOrDefault();
    }
    return result;
}
```

Notice that for this system to work we can only have one blog with one unique page name. If we forced our entire community to use unique page names across the community, we would eventually have some upset users. We want to make sure to enforce unique page names across users only for this purpose. To do this, we require that an AccountID be passed in with the page name, which gives our users more flexibility with their page name overlaps! I will show you how we get the AccountID later. Other than that we are performing a simple lambda expression to select the appropriate blog out of the collection of blogs in the data context.

Next we will discuss a method to get all the latest blog posts via the GetLatestBlogs() method. This method will also get and attach the appropriate Account for each blog. Before we dive into this method we will need to extend the Blog class to have an Account property.

To extend the Blog class we will need to create a public partial class in the Domain folder.

```
using System;
using System.Collections.Generic;
using System.Linq;
using System.Text;
namespace Fisharoo.FisharooCore.Core.Domain
{
    public partial class Blog
    {
        public Account Account { get; set; }
    }
}
```

Now we can look at the GetLatestBlogs() method.

```
public List<Blog> GetLatestBlogs()
{
    List<Blog> result = new List<Blog>();
    using(FisharooDataContext dc = _conn.GetContext())
    {
        IEnumerable<Blog> blogs = (from b in dc.Blogs
                                    where b.IsPublished
                                    orderby b.UpdateDate descending
                                    select b).Take(30);
        IEnumerable<Account> accounts =
```

```
                    dc.Accounts.Where(a => blogs.Select(b =>
                          b.AccountID).Distinct().Contains(a.AccountID));
            foreach (Blog blog in blogs)
            {
                blog.Account = accounts.Where(a => a.AccountID ==
                                   blog.AccountID).FirstOrDefault();
            }
            result = blogs.ToList();
            result.Reverse();
        }
        return result;
    }
```

The first expression in this method gets the top N blogs ordered by their UpdateDate in descending order. This gets us the newest entries. We then add a where clause looking for only blogs that are published.

We then move to getting a list of Accounts that are associated with our previously selected blogs. We do this by selecting a list of AccountIDs from our blog list and then doing a Contains search against our Accounts table. This gives us a list of accounts that belong to all the blogs that we have in hand.

With these two collections in hand we can iterate through our list of blogs and attach the appropriate Account to each blog. This gives us a full listing of blogs with accounts.

As we discussed earlier, it is very important for us to make sure that we keep the page names unique on a per user basis. To do this we need to have a method that allows our UI to determine if a page name is unique or not. To do this we will have the CheckPageNameIsUnique() method.

```
public bool CheckPageNameIsUnique(Blog blog)
{
    blog = CleanPageName(blog);
    bool result = true;
    using(FisharooDataContext dc = _conn.GetContext())
    {
        int count = dc.Blogs.Where(b => b.PageName == blog.PageName
                         && b.AccountID == blog.AccountID).Count();
        if(count > 0)
            result = false;
    }
    return result;
}
```

This method looks at all the blog entries except itself to determine if there are other blog posts with the same page name that are also by the same Account. This allows us to effectively lock down our users from creating duplicate page names. This will be important down the road when we start to discuss our pretty URLs.

Next, we will look at a private method that will help us clean up these page name inputs. Keep in mind that these page names will be displayed in the browser's address bar and therefore need not have any characters in them that the browser would want to encode. While we can decode the URL easily this conversation is more about keeping the URL pretty so that the user and search engine spiders can easily read where they are at. When we have characters in the URL that are encoded, we will end up with something like %20 where %20 is the equivelant to a space. But to read my%20blog%20post is not that easy. It is much easier to ready my-blog-post. So we will strip out all of our so called special characters and replace all spaces with hyphens. This method will be the CleanPageName() method.

```
private Blog CleanPageName(Blog blog)
{
    blog.PageName = blog.PageName.Replace(" ", "-").Replace("!", "")
        .Replace("&", "").Replace("?", "").Replace(",", "");
    return blog;
}
```

You can add to this as many filters as you like. For the time being I am replacing the handful of special characters that we have just seen in the code.

Next, we will get into the service layers that we will use to handle our interactions with the system. Unlike other chapters this chapter will not introduce any new service layers—we will add to the existing one.

Implementing the services/application layer

Once all the repositories are built for single serving purposes we can begin to create the services layer. Again, this layer is responsible for assembling aggregates and performing complex actions with our entities. We will not be creating any new services for this component but will need to add to the following existing service:

- AlertService

AlertService

The AlertService as we know from past chapters is responsible for sending out notifications to our users via their filter page. This is the page that shows new activity amongst your profile and your friends' profiles.

For blogs we added two methods to our `AlertService` class—one method to send out alerts for new blog posts and the other for alerts while updating our blog posts.

```
public void AddNewBlogPostAlert(Blog blog)
{
        alert = new Alert();
        alert.CreateDate = DateTime.Now;
        alert.AccountID = _userSession.CurrentUser.AccountID;
        alert.AlertTypeID = (int)AlertType.AlertTypes.NewBlogPost;
        alertMessage = "<div class=\"AlertHeader\">" +
                GetProfileImage(_userSession.CurrentUser.AccountID)
                + GetProfileUrl(_userSession.CurrentUser.Username)
                + " has just added a new blog post: <b>" +
                blog.Title + "</b></div>";
        alert.Message = alertMessage;
        SaveAlert(alert);
        SendAlertToFriends(alert);
}
```

If you have already read the chapter that included the `AlertService` you will know what goes into adding alerts. For those who are not aware, we will quickly take a look at this `AddNewBlogPostAlert()` method.

This method will take in the new Blog that was posted so that we can use some information about it in our alert. As soon as we get into the body of our method, we want to initialize a new Alert. We will then fill out some of the initial properties.

One of the properties that we will need to extend is the `AlertType` class that has the `AlertTypes` property. You will see that this `AlertTypes` property is really a representation of the record IDs we have stored in the `AlertTypes` table in the database. Open up the `AlertType` class and add a couple of new entries for the `NewBlogPost` and `UpdatedBlogPost`.

```
public partial class AlertType
{
    public enum AlertTypes
    {
        AccountCreated = 1,
        ProfileCreated = 2,
        AccountModified = 3,
        ProfileModified = 4,
        NewAvatar = 5,
        AddedFriend = 6,
        AddedPicture = 7,
        FriendAdded = 8,
        FriendRequest = 9,
```

```
            StatusUpdate = 10,
        NewBlogPost = 11,
        UpdatedBlogPost = 12

        }
    }
```

Then go into the `AlertTypes` table and create two new records `NewBlogPost` and `UpdatedBlogPost`. If the record IDs that are generated do not correspond to the numbers you see above, update the numbers you see in the enum to the ones that were created in the table.

Now we can look at the message that we want to show in our alert. This can consist of any standard HTML as it will be displayed on the alerts page or "the filter" as we will call it. Once the Alert is fully configured we can then save the Alert to the database. And in this case (but not all cases) we want this alert to show up on all of our friends' filters as well, to let them know that a new blog post was just created.

Here is the method for the updated blog post, which is almost identical to the one seen for updating the blog post:

```
public void AddUpdatedBlogPostAlert(Blog blog)
{
    alert = new Alert();
    alert.CreateDate = DateTime.Now;
    alert.AccountID = _userSession.CurrentUser.AccountID;
    alert.AlertTypeID = (int)AlertType.AlertTypes.NewBlogPost;
    alertMessage = "<div class=\"AlertHeader\">" +
                    GetProfileImage(_userSession.CurrentUser.AccountID)
                    + GetProfileUrl(_userSession.CurrentUser.Username)
                    + " has updated the <b>" + blog.Title +
                    "</b> blog post!</div>";
    alert.Message = alertMessage;
    SaveAlert(alert);
    SendAlertToFriends(alert);
}
```

With the repository and service layers completed we can now take a look at our UI.

Implementing the presentation layer

The presentation for this chapter is almost as simple as the infrastructure is. We will have a **Blog** link in the top navigation. When you click on this link you will be taken to a page where you see a list of the latest blog posts. From the Blog section you can then choose to either view a blog from the latest blogs page or you can choose to view your blogs or create a new blog. In addition to these four pages we will also address how fancy URLs come into play in the view post page.

Latest blog posts

Viewing the latest blog posts is a single call to the `BlogRepository`. In order for our UI to get to any repository though, it first has to hand off its control of all display interactions. It does this by initializing an instance of the `DefaultPresenter` and then passing a reference to itself into the `Init()` method of the presenter. Once in the `Init()` method of the presenter we can then make the call into the repository to get the latest blogs.

```
public class DefaultPresenter
{
    private IDefault _view;
    private IBlogRepository _blogRepository;
    public DefaultPresenter()
    {
        _blogRepository =
                ObjectFactory.GetInstance<IBlogRepository>();
    }
    public void Init(IDefault View)
    {
        _view = View;
        _view.LoadBlogs(_blogRepository.GetLatestBlogs());
    }
}
```

With the latest blogs in hand we are then able to pass them into the UI's code behind where the blogs are bound to a list view control in the `Default.aspx` page.

```
public partial class Default : System.Web.UI.Page, IDefault
{
    private DefaultPresenter _presenter;
    public Default()
    {
        _presenter = new DefaultPresenter();
    }
    protected void Page_Load(object sender, EventArgs e)
    {
        _presenter.Init(this);
    }
    public void LoadBlogs(List<Blog> Blogs)
    {
        lvBlogs.DataSource = Blogs;
        lvBlogs.DataBind();
    }
    public void lvBlogs_ItemDataBound(object sender,
                                ListViewItemEventArgs e)
    {
        Literal litBlogID = e.Item.FindControl("litBlogID") as
                        Literal;
```

```
        HyperLink linkTitle = e.Item.FindControl("linkTitle") as
                              HyperLink;
        Literal litPageName = e.Item.FindControl("litPageName") as
                              Literal;
        Literal litUsername = e.Item.FindControl("litUsername") as
                              Literal;
        //linkTitle.NavigateUrl = "~/Blogs/ViewPost.aspx?BlogID=" +
                              litBlogID.Text;
        linkTitle.NavigateUrl = "~/Blogs/" + litUsername.Text + "/" +
                              litPageName.Text + ".aspx";
    }
}
```

Also note that we have a `ItemDataBound()` method to handle each item that is
bound. This will allow us to configure all the controls in the UI for each set of objects.
Notice in particular that at the very end of our `ItemDataBound()` method, that we are
configuring the `NavigateUrl` property to display fancy URLs! This will be important
to remember when we start our discussion about the `ViewPost.aspx` page.

Out in the UI side we can see how all the data sections are bound to the container's
blog items.

```
<asp:ListView ID="lvBlogs" runat="server"
                OnItemDataBound="lvBlogs_ItemDataBound">
    <LayoutTemplate>
        <ul class="blogsList">
            <asp:PlaceHolder ID="itemPlaceholder"
                        runat="server"></asp:PlaceHolder>
        </ul>
    </LayoutTemplate>

    <ItemTemplate>
        <li>
            <h2 class="blogsTitle"><asp:HyperLink ID="linkTitle"
                            runat="server" Text='<%#((Blog)
                            Container.DataItem).Title %>'>
                            </asp:HyperLink></h2>
            <p class="blogsDescription">
            Created: <%#((Blog)Container.DataItem).CreateDate %> By:
                    <%#((Blog)Container.DataItem).
                    Account.Username %><br />
            <%#((Blog)Container.DataItem).Subject %><asp:Literal
                    ID="litBlogID" runat="server" Text='<%#((
                    Blog)Container.DataItem).BlogID %>'></asp:Literal>
            <asp:Literal ID="litPageName" runat="server"
                        Visible="false" Text='<%#((Blog)
                        Container.DataItem).PageName %>'></asp:Literal>
```

```
                    <asp:Literal ID="litUsername" runat="server"
                              Visible="false" Text='<%#((Blog)
                    Container.DataItem).Account.Username
                    %>'></asp:Literal>
              </p>
         </li>
    </ItemTemplate>

    <EmptyDataTemplate>
         Sorry, there are no blogs posted yet!
    </EmptyDataTemplate>
</asp:ListView>
```

If we had data in the system we would now see a list of the latest blogs!

My blog posts

The **My Blog Posts** section is 99.999% identical to the latest blogs post with the exception that they load their list of Blog objects via a different call into the same BlogRepository. In this case we get a list of Blogs by calling the GetBlogsByAccountID() method.

This method will get a list of our blog posts sorted by their create date.

Other than that they are identical.

Fancy URL support

Now that we have both the recent blog posts and the my posts pages created and out of the way we need to discuss handling the pretty URLs that we have our UIs currently displaying. At the moment we are sending people to domain.com/blogs/ username/pagename. As you may have guessed, this is a path to a resource that does not actually exist. In order to handle the unknown resources we will have to extend the UrlRewrite class that we have in the Handler's directory.

```
public class UrlRewrite : IHttpModule
{
    private IAccountRepository _accountRepository;
  private IBlogRepository _blogRepository;
    public UrlRewrite()
    {
        _accountRepository =
                    ObjectFactory.GetInstance<IAccountRepository>();
      _blogRepository =
                ObjectFactory.GetInstance<IBlogRepository>();
```

```
}

public void Init(HttpApplication application)
{
    //let's register our event handler
    application.PostResolveRequestCache +=
        (new EventHandler(this.Application_OnAfterProcess));
}

public void Dispose()
{

}

private void Application_OnAfterProcess(object source,
                                       EventArgs e)
{
    HttpApplication application = (HttpApplication)source;
    HttpContext context = application.Context;
    string[] extensionsToExclude = { ".axd", ".jpg", ".gif",
                        ".png", ".xml", ".config", ".css", ".
                        js", ".aspx", ".htm", ".html" };

    foreach (string s in extensionsToExclude)
    {
        if
         (application.Request.PhysicalPath.ToLower().Contains(s))
            return;
    }
    if (!System.IO.File.Exists(application.Request.PhysicalPath))
    {
     if
      (application.Request.PhysicalPath.
       ToLower().Contains("blogs"))
     {
        string[] arr =
        application.Request.PhysicalPath.
        ToLower().Split('\\');
        string blogPageName = arr[arr.Length - 1];
        string blogUserName = arr[arr.Length - 2];
        blogPageName = blogPageName.Replace(".aspx", "");
        if (blogPageName.ToLower() != "profileimage" &&
            blogUserName.ToLower() != "profileavatar")
        {
            Account account =
                    _accountRepository.
                    GetAccountByUsername(blogUserName);
```

```
                        Blog blog =
                                _blogRepository.GetBlogByPageName
                                (blogPageName, account.AccountID);
                        context.RewritePath("~/blogs/ViewPost.aspx?BlogID=" +
                        blog.BlogID.ToString());
                    }
                    else
                    {
                        return;
                    }
                }
                else
                {
                    string username =
                        application.Request.Path.Replace("/", "");
                    Account account =
                        _accountRepository.GetAccountByUsername(username);
                    if (account != null)
                    {
                        string UserURL =
                                "~/Profiles/profile.aspx?AccountID="
                                + account.AccountID.ToString();
                        context.Response.Redirect(UserURL);
                    }
                    else
                    {
                        context.Response.Redirect("~/PageNotFound.aspx");
                    }
                }
            }
        }
    }
```

In the `UrlRewrite` class just seen notice that I added a reference to the `BlogRepository` so that we can get the blog in question if that is indeed what this rewrite is for. Next, notice that I removed the `.aspx` extension from the list of extensions to exclude it from processing. This is because we want our pages to look like real pages even though they are actually dynamic (read non-existent) resources.

After that we test to see if we are working with a blog redirection. If we are, then we extract the user's username and the page name from the URL. With this information in hand we can locate the Blog that we need. From there we can easily do a redirection to the page as though the user had no idea. To them the pretty URL stays intact just as it was when they entered it or followed it.

Now when rewriting the URL on the server side you have to be aware that the local path "~" identifier may no longer work as expected. In my case it makes all images load as though the blog directory is the root directory. So for this reason you will notice that the `ViewPost.aspx` page has items in its UI with root level mappings in the standard HTML fashion `/images/resource` rather than `~/images/resource`. This fixes the issue without any problem. Everything else should work as expected.

View post

The `ViewPost.aspx` page is an amazingly straightforward page to build. It is extracting the page to be viewed from the URL by way of the rewritten URL, which contains the `BlogID` behind the scenes. The `ViewPostPresenter` gets to the `BlogID` through the `WebContext.BlogID` property.

```
_view.LoadPost(_blogRepository.GetBlogByBlogID(_webContext.BlogID));
```

Here is the UI that we are loading:

```
<h2><asp:Label ID="lblTitle" runat="server"></asp:Label></h2>
<asp:HyperLink ID="linkProfile" runat="server">
<asp:Image style="padding-bottom:5px;float:left;" Width="200"
        Height="200" ID="imgAvatar" runat="server" ImageUrl="/
images/profileavatar/profileimage.aspx" />
</asp:HyperLink>
Created: <asp:Label ID="lblCreated" runat="server"></asp:Label>
Updated: <asp:Label ID="lblUpdated" runat="server"></asp:Label><br
        /><br />
<asp:Label ID="lblPost" runat="server"></asp:Label>
```

The thing to be pay attention to, as I mentioned before, is that all the paths are in a fixed format off the root of the site. This way no matter where we are at, we know where to go to gain access to the specified resource.

Create or edit post

With all of this work out of our way we can now turn our attention to the dirty work of creating the actual blog post. This page will actually serve two purposes. We need to use it to create our blog post. But we will also repurpose the UI to edit already existing posts as well. Let's look at the presenter for this page.

```
public void Init(IPost View)
{
    _view = View;
    if(_webContext.BlogID > 0)
    {
        _view.LoadPost(_blogRepository.GetBlogByBlogID(
                            _webContext.BlogID));
```

```
        }
    }
    public void SavePost(Blog blog)
    {
        bool result = _blogRepository.CheckPageNameIsUnique(blog);
        if (result)
        {
            blog.AccountID = _webContext.CurrentUser.AccountID;
            _blogRepository.SaveBlog(blog);
        }
        else
        {
            _view.ShowError("The page name you have chosen is in use.
                        Please choose a different page name!");
        }
    }
}
```

In the first section of the Init method we are checking the WebContext.BlogID property to see if we have something to work with. If we do then we load the UI with the appropriate blog. The next item you see is the SavePost method that takes care of passing a loaded blog into the BlogRepository to be saved.

Next, we will take a look at the code behind that the presenter works with. Here we will see the LoadPost and btnSave_Click methods. There is nothing fancy to follow here. But the one aspect to pay attention to is that we keep track of the BlogID in the page so that we know what we are working with later.

```
    protected void btnSave_Click(object sender, EventArgs e)
    {
        Blog blog = new Blog();
        if (litBlogID.Text != "")
            blog.BlogID = Convert.ToInt64(litBlogID.Text);
        blog.IsPublished = chkIsPublished.Checked;
        blog.PageName = txtPageName.Text;
        blog.Post = txtPost.Text;
        blog.Subject = txtSubject.Text;
        blog.Title = txtTitle.Text;
        _presenter.SavePost(blog);
    }
    public void LoadPost(Blog blog)
    {
        txtTitle.Text = blog.Title;
        txtSubject.Text = blog.Subject;
        txtPost.Text = blog.Post;
        txtPageName.Text = blog.PageName;
        chkIsPublished.Checked = blog.IsPublished;
        litBlogID.Text = blog.BlogID.ToString();
    }
```

This takes care of the little details of data inputs and outputs. However, let's now take a look at what we need to do make the UI somewhat useable. You may recall that we used the Xinha WYSIWYG editor before. We will use it here too. All that is required to hook this up is a multiline text box control and a single line of JavaScript.

```
. . .
<asp:TextBox TextMode="MultiLine" ID="txtPost"
                    runat="server"></asp:TextBox>
. . .
<script type="text/javascript">
    xinha_editors[xinha_editors.length] = 'ctl00_Content_txtPost';
</script>
. . .
```

With this in place we should be ready to create a blog post!

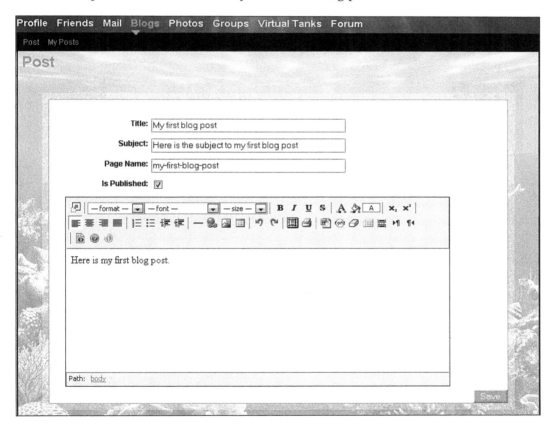

Summary

We now have a great way for our community members to share information with one another. This content will serve several purposes. It will not only provide a large repository of information for our community members to see value in our relationship but also a food source for our search engine spiders.

In this chapter we covered the creation of blog posts. We also went over the pages that are needed for people to see other users' posts as well as their own. And of course we provided a page to actually read a post. In addition to this we covered the concept of fancy or pretty URLs that are more user as well as search engine friendly. Finally, we added a touch more usability to our UI in the form of the Xinha WYSIWYG.

9
Message Boards

In this chapter we will be discussing message boards. A **message board** is a place where users can post messages to the community in a way that all the responses will be viewable no matter how much time passes between each post—think of it as a long running conversation. As the threads or topics and their posts get older, newer content will start to bury the older content. This makes this section of the site a very dynamic area that many users will want to watch. This is considered a somewhat sticky feature! Given the topic of our community—salt water fish—a message board is a perfect feature for our site. It will allow a user to post an issue that they are having with their aquarium in a way that the entire community can then read and interact with that user's issue. Over time your community will bubble up certain users as subject matter experts on specific topics. And eventually (you hope) your site's forum will become the place to go for your specific type of information. If nothing else, our dear friend Google will lead people your way.

Problem

To get started we should first discuss some proper terminology. A message board is really a set of containers for sorting data. On our board we will have the ability to first create categories. A **category** is the highest level of container and therefore will have a very generic topic. Each category can hold as many forums as is needed. The forum is related to the top level category's subject but is slightly more specific. In each forum we can have a number of threads. Each thread is a very specific subject that users can discuss. The discussion is performed with posts that are simply replies to the containing thread or a post on the thread.

Here is our message board landing page, which lists each category and its forums:

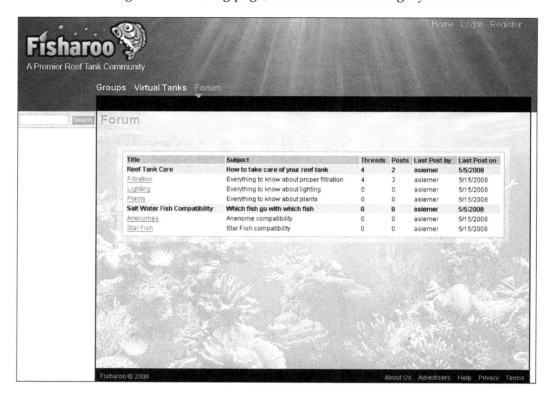

Here is our forum page, which lists all of the available threads for that forum:

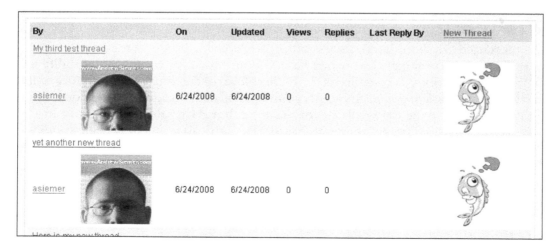

Here is a thread that would also have a list of its posts:

My third test thread

by: asiemer   on: 6/24/2008   updated: 6/24/2008   Reply

Here is my third test thread

As you may have guessed, the topic of a message board is a very large one. We will go over the basics of creating a message board with the ability to create categories, forums, threads, and posts. Each of these sections will be able to keep count of how much data lives beneath it. And all of the content will have the ability to be linked to in an SEO friendly manner (meaning we will support friendly URLs). Friendly URLs are also easier for our users to remember and work with. We will also tie in the ability to add alerts to our filters and our friends' filters so that they know when we have new content available.

> **SEO (Search Engine Optimization)** is generally defined as the process that optimizes organic search traffic. This generally translates to building your site in a search engine friendly manner that presents your site and its content in a way that makes the search engine's job easier to index your pages. Generally a long ugly query string such as `default.aspx?userid=324568` is less friendly than `domain.com/asiemer` would be. More information can be found on the topic here: `http://en.wikipedia.org/wiki/Search_engine_optimization`.

Obviously there are many features that are not yet supported by our application such as hot topics, private threads, ratings, and moderation. We will focus on building a solid framework in this chapter to which we can add these other features down the road.

Design

Let's take a look at the design for this feature.

Categories

Categories are the highest level container of board posts that we have in our system. It is responsible for grouping forums together in such a way that makes it easy for a user to locate what they are most interested in. At this level we will keep a count of how many threads and posts we have as well as who made the last post and when. The reason that we maintain counts at this level is to remove the need for us to perform the count each time we display the category data.

Forums

A **forum** is a container of threads. It is responsible for grouping together a more specific set of posts. This too keeps a count of thread and post counts so that we can see at this level how much data lies within, again without needing to sum the actual post and thread counts.

Threads and Posts

Threads and posts are technically identical with the exception that a post is not a container of anything. A **thread** is the next level container of data below a forum. It is a **post** that is marked as a thread and will act as the parent to many other posts. For the same performance reasons we will keep a reply count and a view count. Notice that we have a reference from **ThreadID** to **PostID**. All the posts in the system will have a parent post, which we will refer to as a Thread.

Friendly URLs

If you paid close attention to the previous tables, you must have noticed that there is a **PageName** in each table. In this system we will implement heavy use of friendly URLs. This will allow people to find the information not only in each post but also from the surrounding site as well. In addition to this it makes sharing information easier too.

Here are all the relationships:

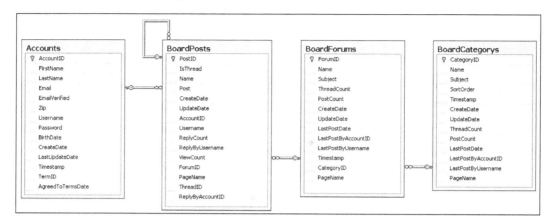

Alerts

Finally, we will extend our system to use our pre-existing alert system so that each time someone makes a post or creates a new thread, we will see an alert on both the creator's filter as well as one on the friends'. This will help us to promote the new content across the site.

Solution

Let's take a look at our solution.

Implementing the Database

Let's start our solution by first discussing the implementation of our database.

Categories

As we discussed before, the concept of a category is our top level container of data. Let's take a look at the table structure for categories:

Column Name	Data Type	Allow Nulls
CategoryID	int	☐
Name	varchar(100)	☐
Subject	varchar(250)	☐
SortOrder	int	☐
Timestamp	timestamp	☐
CreateDate	smalldatetime	☐
UpdateDate	smalldatetime	☐
ThreadCount	int	☐
PostCount	int	☐
LastPostDate	smalldatetime	☐
LastPostByAccountID	int	☐
LastPostByUsername	varchar(250)	☐
PageName	varchar(250)	☐

The **SortOrder** field is in charge of setting the display order in case we have multiple categories on one page. We already discussed the count fields earlier. The last X fields are to control who made the last post and when. **PageName** controls the friendly URLs that our system will use later.

Some of you may notice that the name of this table is `BoardCategorys` instead of `BoardCategories`. I have noticed that while dragging some spellings into the LINQ to SQL designer I get odd spellings for my object names. Where I could go in and rename the objects for each table I find that it is easier to just work with the issue in a way that LINQ to SQL will generate what I want in the first place. This way if I have to refresh the table later, I won't need to remember to rename it appropriately as well. As we get more and more tables in our system we are more prone to forgetting issues such as this.

Forums

Forums are the next level container that holds our entire individual user created threads.

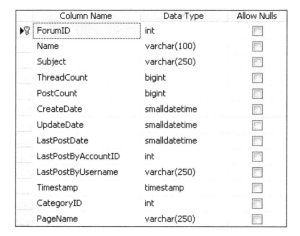

Column Name	Data Type	Allow Nulls
ForumID	int	☐
Name	varchar(100)	☐
Subject	varchar(250)	☐
ThreadCount	bigint	☐
PostCount	bigint	☐
CreateDate	smalldatetime	☐
UpdateDate	smalldatetime	☐
LastPostDate	smalldatetime	☐
LastPostByAccountID	int	☐
LastPostByUsername	varchar(250)	☐
Timestamp	timestamp	☐
CategoryID	int	☐
PageName	varchar(250)	☐

Similar to categories we maintain the counts of our low level posts and threads. We also maintain who created the last post and when. Notice that we have a foreign key reference to the `BoardCategorys` table.

Posts

As I stated earlier, the `BoardPosts` table is really a dual purpose table containing both posts and threads. I did this primarily because for most part each item has the same data in it with the exception of the parent **ThreadID** column.

Column Name	Data Type	Allow Nulls
PostID	bigint	☐
IsThread	bit	☐
Name	varchar(100)	☐
Post	varchar(3000)	☐
CreateDate	smalldatetime	☐
UpdateDate	smalldatetime	☐
AccountID	int	☐
Username	varchar(250)	☐
ReplyCount	int	☐
ReplyByUsername	varchar(250)	☑
ViewCount	int	☐
ForumID	int	☐
PageName	varchar(250)	☑
ThreadID	bigint	☑
ReplyByAccountID	int	☑

The field to note here is the **IsThread** field. This is the easiest way to know when a post is also a Thread. In addition to that we have the **ThreadID,** which also denotes the difference between a post and a thread in that a thread won't have a **ThreadID** — a thread is never part of a thread (at least not yet!). Also notice here that we have a foreign key for the forum that this thread is part of in the way of the **ForumID** foreign key. For threads, we also store the number of times it was viewed as well as how many replies it has.

A nice side effect to this post/thread structure is that any run-of-the-mill post can easily be moved off and treated as its own thread. Often times a moderator will find that a post within a thread is generating more traffic than the initial thread itself. In this case that post can easily be promoted to a thread in its own right!

Creating the Relationships

Once all the tables are created we can then create all the relationships.

For this set of tables we have relationships between the following tables:

- `BoardForums` and `BoardCategorys`
- `BoardPosts` and `Accounts`
- `BoardPosts` and `BoardForums`
- `BoardPosts` and `BoardPosts` (for post to thread reference)

Setting Up the Data Access Layer

To set up the data access layer follow the steps mentioned next:

- Open the `Fisharoo.dbml` file.
- Open up your **Server Explorer** window.
- Expand your Fisharoo connection.
- Expand your tables. If you don't see your new tables try hitting the **Refresh** icon or right-clicking on tables and clicking **Refresh**.

- Then drag your new tables onto the design surface.
- Hit **Save** and you should now have the following domain objects to work with!

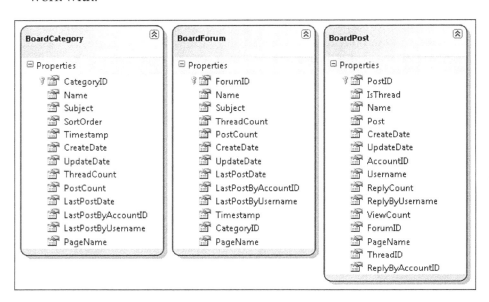

Keep in mind that we are not letting LINQ track our relationships, so go ahead and delete them from the design surface. Your design surface should have all the same items as you see in the screenshot (though perhaps in a different arrangement!).

Building Repositories

With the addition of new tables will come the addition of new repositories so that we can get at the data stored in those tables. We will be creating the following repositories to support our needs.

- `BoardCategoryRepository`
- `BoardForumRepository`
- `BoardPostRepository`

Each of our repositories will generally have a method for select by ID, select all by parent ID, save, and delete. Once you have seen one repository you have pretty much seen them all. Review previous chapters, the appendices, or the included code for examples of a standard repository. I will, however, discuss anything that varies from what is standard!

BoardCategoryRepository

One of the most important features of our message board that may be a bit different from other message boards is that it is very important for us to support friendly URLs. This means that we will need a method in each of our repositories to get the object by page name. Here is the method for this repository:

```
public BoardCategory GetCategoryByPageName(string PageName)
{
    BoardCategory category;
    using(FisharooDataContext dc = _conn.GetContext())
    {
        category = dc.BoardCategories.Where(bc => bc.PageName ==
                                        PageName).FirstOrDefault();
    }
    return category;
}
```

This is a fairly straightforward method that gets a board category by its page name. Nothing we haven't already covered here from a LINQ point of view!

BoardForumRepository

The `BoardForumRepository` also has a `GetForumByPageName` method but it is exactly the same as the previous method. Sorry!! nothing fun here to cover.

BoardPostRepository

Now this repository is full of interesting items to cover! To start, as our users will be creating posts and threads whereas they will not be allowed to create forums or categories, we need to be able to make sure that they don't create page names that are not unique. It is no good to try to get a thread by its name and end up getting several different threads instead of just the one we expected.

```
public bool CheckPostPageNameIsUnique(string PageName)
{
    bool result;
    using(FisharooDataContext dc = _conn.GetContext())
    {
        BoardPost bp = dc.BoardPosts.Where(p => p.PageName ==
                                        PageName).FirstOrDefault();
        if(bp != null)
            result = false;
        else
            result = true;
    }
    return result;
}
```

In this method we attempt to load a post by the `PageName` that was specified. If we return a null object then we know that the `PageName` is unique and we can return a true response. Otherwise we have to return a false result. Not fancy but it gets the job done.

The next method is responsible for getting all the posts for a given thread. This by itself is not that interesting. But as we know that we are only using this method on the page where a thread is viewed, we can insert some logic to increment the amount of times that a thread has been viewed.

 Keep in mind that this method will only be appropriate if we only use it for getting posts for a given thread and then displaying them. If we start to use this method for other tasks then our view count will be totally skewed!

```
public List<BoardPost> GetPostsByThreadID(Int64 ThreadID)
{
    List<BoardPost> result;
    using(FisharooDataContext dc = _conn.GetContext())
    {
        //increment the view count for this thread
        BoardPost thread = dc.BoardPosts.Where(p => p.PostID ==
                                        ThreadID).FirstOrDefault();
        if (thread != null)
            thread.ViewCount += 1;
        dc.SubmitChanges();
        IEnumerable<BoardPost> posts = dc.BoardPosts.Where(p =>
                            p.ThreadID == ThreadID && !p.IsThread)
                            .OrderBy(p=>p.CreateDate);
        result = posts.ToList();
    }
    return result;
}
```

We perform this task by getting the thread (really a board post) by its ID and then simply increment its `ViewCount` property. We then submit the changes on the DataContext to make sure that it is pushed back to the database.

We then move to get all the posts for that thread by its ID.

The next method, `SavePost`, is not only responsible for saving new posts and updating existing posts but also for taking care of incrementing counts at both the Forum and Category levels.

```
public Int64 SavePost(BoardPost boardPost)
{
    using(FisharooDataContext dc = _conn.GetContext())
    {
```

```
    if(boardPost.PostID > 0)
    {
        dc.BoardPosts.Attach(boardPost, true);
    }
    else
    {
        //get the parent containers when a new post is created
        // to update their post counts
        BoardCategory bc = (from c in dc.BoardCategories
                        join f in dc.BoardForums on
                        c.CategoryID equals f.CategoryID
                        where f.ForumID == boardPost.ForumID
                        select c).FirstOrDefault();
        BoardForum bf = (from f in dc.BoardForums
                        where f.ForumID == boardPost.ForumID
                        select f).FirstOrDefault();
        //update the thread count
        if(boardPost.IsThread)
        {
            bc.ThreadCount = bc.ThreadCount + 1;
            bf.ThreadCount = bf.ThreadCount + 1;
        }
        //update the post count
        else
        {
            bc.PostCount = bc.PostCount + 1;
            bf.PostCount = bf.PostCount + 1;
            //update post count on thread
            BoardPost bThread = null;
            if (boardPost.ThreadID != 0)
            {
                bThread = (from p in dc.BoardPosts
                        where p.PostID == boardPost.ThreadID
                        select p).FirstOrDefault();
            }
            if (bThread != null)
            {
                bThread.ReplyCount = bThread.ReplyCount + 1;
            }
        }
        dc.BoardPosts.InsertOnSubmit(boardPost);
    }
    dc.SubmitChanges();
    }
    return boardPost.PostID;
}
```

Notice that the first part of this method is just like every other save method. If the ID of the object being saved is greater than zero, we reattach the object to the data context as a new version of that object. We then call the `SubmitChanges()` method and persist it back to the database.

This is where everything else changes. If the item is a new post or thread then we have a whole bunch of things to do. The first thing that we want to do is get the parent objects. We get the `BoardCategory` and `BoardForum` off the post's related `ForumID`. We then check to see if the new post is also a thread. If it is, then we update the `ThreadCount` for our parent objects.

If the post is just a post then we update the `PostCount` for the parent objects. We also get that post's parent Thread. With the parent Thread in hand we update the reply count. We then perform the task that we are used to and insert the object. Finally we call the `SubmitChanges` method on the data context.

Finally we come to the `DeletePost` method. How could this be interesting? Remember that a post can also be a thread which means that it can have children. We can't delete a thread that has children as this will create a referential integrity issue (also called dirty data) for us.

```
public void DeletePost(BoardPost boardPost)
{
    using(FisharooDataContext dc = _conn.GetContext())
    {
        dc.BoardPosts.Attach(boardPost, true);
        //if this is a thread then we need to delete all of it's
          children
        if(boardPost.IsThread)
            dc.BoardPosts.DeleteAllOnSubmit(dc.BoardPosts.
                Where(bp=>bp.ThreadID == boardPost.PostID));
        dc.BoardPosts.DeleteOnSubmit(boardPost);
        dc.SubmitChanges();
    }
}
```

So, in order for us to address this issue we have to test the post that is up for deletion to see if it is also a thread with its `IsThread` property. If it is, then we also delete all of its children by passing a query that produces a list of items to the `DeleteAllOnSubmit()` method of the `BoardPosts` collection. Everything is business as usual from that point on!

Implementing the Services/Application layer

Once all the repositories are built for single serving purposes we can begin to create the services layer. Again, this layer is responsible for assembling aggregates and performing complex actions with our entities. We will create the following services:

- BoardService
- AlertService

BoardService

Our BoardService is actually not complex at all. It is responsible for providing us a way to get out the BoardCategory with an already hydrated list of BoardForum items. Before we look at the BoardService, we need to extend the BoardCategory object to contain a list of BoardForum objects. We do this by adding a BoardCategory class to our Domain directory. Then make this class a public partial class. And finally add a generic list of BoardForum objects.

```
public partial class BoardCategory
{
    public List<BoardForum> Forums { get; set; }
}
```

With this class extended we can now look at the BoardService.

```
[Pluggable("Default")]
public class BoardService : IBoardService
{
    private IBoardCategoryRepository _categoryRepository;
    private IBoardForumRepository _forumRepository;

    public BoardService()
    {
        _categoryRepository =
                ObjectFactory.GetInstance<IBoardCategoryRepository>();
        _forumRepository =
                ObjectFactory.GetInstance<IBoardForumRepository>();
    }
    public List<BoardCategory> GetCategoriesWithForums()
    {
        List<BoardCategory> categories =
            _categoryRepository.GetAllCategories();
        List<BoardForum> forums = _forumRepository.GetAllForums();
        for(int i = 0;i<categories.Count();i++)
        {
```

```
                    categories[i].Forums = forums.Where(f => f.CategoryID ==
                        categories[i].CategoryID).ToList();
                }
            return categories;
        }
    }
```

The first thing to notice is that this class, like all others in our solution, is marked up with attributes for StructureMap (Inversion of Control). Next, we declare our `BoardCategoryRepository` and `BoardForumRepository`. In the constructor for this class we then spin up instances of the two repositories.

This then brings us to the `GetCategoriesWithForums()` method. This is an optimized method that our message board homepage calls to get a list of categories and their forums. We are then able to iterate through each list and its child list without making a bunch of separate calls.

This method first gets a list of all Categories. It then gets a list of all the forums in the system. The method then iterates through all the Categories and selects a list of forums from the primary list of forums into the `BoardCategory.Forums` collection. It then returns the complete list of categories.

 This would be a great method to add to caching as both categories and forums are going to be a fairly static list of data in your site!

AlertService

The account service is pretty much complete from an infrastructure point of view. It is simply a matter of adding new service messages as we need additional functionality. In this case we want to post alerts when a new post or thread is created. Both of the methods that we want to add are very similar in that they initialize an alert, set the alert type, create a message, save the alert to the alert repository, and finally send the alert off to all of the user's friends.

```
    public void AddNewBoardPostAlert(BoardCategory category, BoardForum
                        forum, BoardPost post, BoardPost thread)
    {
        Init();
        alert.AlertTypeID = (int) AlertType.AlertTypes.NewBoardPost;
        alertMessage = "<div class=\"AlertHeader\">" +
                GetProfileImage(_userSession.CurrentUser.AccountID) +
                    GetProfileUrl(_userSession.CurrentUser.Username) +
                        " has just added a new post: <b>" +
                    post.Name + "</b></div>";
```

```
        alertMessage += "<div class=\"AlertRow\"><a href=\"" +
                    _webContext.RootUrl + "forums/" + category.PageName +
                    "/" + forum.PageName + "/" + thread.PageName +
                            ".aspx" + "\">" + _webContext.RootUrl +
                    "forums/" + category.PageName + "/" +
                            forum.PageName + "/" + thread.PageName +
                    ".aspx</a></div>";
        alert.Message = alertMessage;
        SaveAlert(alert);
        SendAlertToFriends(alert);
    }

    public void AddNewBoardThreadAlert(BoardCategory category, BoardForum
                            forum, BoardPost post)
    {
        Init();
        alert.AlertTypeID = (int)AlertType.AlertTypes.NewBoardThread;
        alertMessage = "<div class=\"AlertHeader\">" +
                    GetProfileImage(_userSession.CurrentUser.AccountID) +
                    GetProfileUrl(_userSession.CurrentUser.Username) +
                    " has just added a new thread on the board: <b>" +
                    post.Name + "</b></div>";
        alertMessage += "<div class=\"AlertRow\"><a href=\"" +
                    _webContext.RootUrl + "forums/" + category.PageName +
                    "/" + forum.PageName + "/" + post.PageName +
                            ".aspx" + "\">" + _webContext.RootUrl +
                    "forums/" + category.PageName + "/" +
                            forum.PageName + "/" + post.PageName +
                    ".aspx</a></div>";
        alert.Message = alertMessage;
        SaveAlert(alert);
        SendAlertToFriends(alert);
    }
```

Implementing the Presentation Layer

Now let's discuss the implementation of our presentation layer.

Default.aspx

With the entire infrastructure completed we can now move on to the more interesting part—displaying the data. We will start by looking at the homepage of the message board. This page will be responsible for displaying all of the categories and all of the forums for each category.

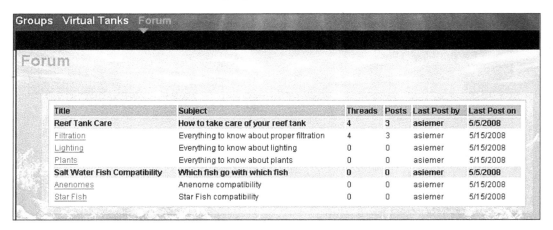

Other than the normal plumbing that is required by the model view presenter (MVP) pattern, this page is primarily made up of two repeaters—the first repeater displaying all the categories in the list of categories and the inner one displaying all the forums for each category.

The list of categories starts in the presenter for this page.

```
public class DefaultPresenter
{
    private IBoardService _boardService;
    private IDefault _view;
    private IRedirector _redirector;
    private IBoardForumRepository _forumRepository;
    private IBoardCategoryRepository _categoryRepository;
    public DefaultPresenter()
    {
        _boardService = ObjectFactory.GetInstance<IBoardService>();
        _forumRepository =
                ObjectFactory.GetInstance<IBoardForumRepository>();
        _categoryRepository =
                ObjectFactory.GetInstance<IBoardCategoryRepository>();
        _redirector = ObjectFactory.GetInstance<IRedirector>();
    }
```

```
public void Init(IDefault View)
{
    _view = View;
    _view.LoadCategories(_boardService.GetCategoriesWithForums());
}

public void GoToForum(string ForumPageName)
{
    BoardForum forum =
            _forumRepository.GetForumByPageName(ForumPageName);
    BoardCategory category =
            _categoryRepository.GetCategoryByCategoryID
            (forum.CategoryID);
    _redirector.GoToForumsForumView(forum.PageName,
                                category.PageName);
}
}
```

Once the page's code behind passes control from itself to the presenter by way of calling the presenter's init method, the presenter then passes a list of categories and forums (from the BoardService) back to the code behind via the LoadCategories method.

The code behind then loads the data source of the first repeater and binds it.

```
public partial class Default : System.Web.UI.Page, IDefault
{
    private DefaultPresenter _presenter;
    protected void Page_Load(object sender, EventArgs e)
    {
        _presenter = new DefaultPresenter();
        _presenter.Init(this);
    }

    public void LoadCategories(List<BoardCategory> Categories)
    {
        repCategories.DataSource = Categories;
        repCategories.DataBind();
    }

    public void repCategories_ItemDataBound(object sender,
                                        RepeaterItemEventArgs e)
    {
        if (e.Item.ItemType == ListItemType.Item || e.Item.ItemType
                        == ListItemType.AlternatingItem)
        {
            if (((BoardCategory) e.Item.DataItem).Forums != null)
```

```
                        {
                            Repeater repForums = e.Item.FindControl("repForums")
                                            as Repeater;
                            repForums.DataSource = ((BoardCategory)
                                            e.Item.DataItem).Forums;
                            repForums.DataBind();
                        }
                    }
                }
                public void repForums_ItemDataBound(object sender,
                                            RepeaterItemEventArgs e)
                {
                    if(e.Item.ItemType == ListItemType.Item || e.Item.ItemType ==
                                    ListItemType.AlternatingItem)
                    {
                        Literal litPageName = e.Item.FindControl("litPageName")
                                        as Literal;
                        LinkButton lbForum = e.Item.FindControl("lbForum") as
                                        LinkButton;
                        lbForum.Attributes.Add("ForumPageName",litPageName.Text);
                    }
                }
                public void lbForum_Click(object sender, EventArgs e)
                {
                    LinkButton lbForum = sender as LinkButton;
                    _presenter.GoToForum(lbForum.Attributes["ForumPageName"]);
                }
            }
```

In each iteration of the `repCategories_ItemDataBound` method, we then load the
`repForums` repeater with the list of forums for the given category and bind it. This
continues until the list of categories and forums is thrown on the page.

Also notice that when each forum item is bound, we also stuff the `PageName` into
our link button on the main page. This comes in handy when the user clicks a link
to navigate to the selected forum. Speaking of clicking the link!

Notice that we have a method `lbForum_Click` for the `LinkButton` click event.
In this method we are passing control again to the presenter and passing in the
`PageName` that we stored earlier in the `LinkButton`'s attribute collection.

This takes us back to the `GoToForum` method of our presenter. With the selected
forum's page name we are able to load both a `BoardForum` object and then a
`BoardCategory` object. With this information we are then able to use our redirector
to relocate our user.

Redirector

We are about to use the redirector class to relocate our user. Before we do this we need to add a method that will take us from our message board homepage to the selected forum. Rather than simply redirecting the person using a record ID, we will be using the category and forum page names.

```
public void GoToForumsForumView(string ForumPageName, string
                                CategoryPageName)
{
    Redirect("~/Forums/" + CategoryPageName + "/" + ForumPageName +
             ".aspx");
}
```

With the forum and category page name in hand we can construct a fictitious URL, which uses the category page name as a folder and the forum page name as a webpage. As this doesn't actually take the user anywhere, we will need to update our `UrlRewrite` handler.

But before we do that, and with the redirector file open, let's add one more method. This method will handle redirecting our user to view a post from the selected forum.

```
public void GoToForumsViewPost(string ForumPageName, string
                               CategoryPageName, string PostPageName)
{
    Redirect("~/Forums/" + CategoryPageName + "/" + ForumPageName +
             "/" + PostPageName + ".aspx");
}
```

This method effectively performs the same task with the exception that it also expects the post's page name (well, the thread's page name).

UrlRewrite

In order to support our fancy or pretty URLs (`http://www.domain.com/categoryname/forumname.aspx`) we will need to modify our `UrlRewrite` class to handle the additional functionality. Our additional code will be inserted between the blog's and profile's code.

```
...
else if (application.Request.PhysicalPath.ToLower().
Contains("forums"))
{
    string[] arr =
              application.Request.PhysicalPath.ToLower().Split('\\');
    int forumsPosition = 0;
    int itemsAfterForums = 0;
```

```
    string categoryPageName = "";
    string forumPageName = "";
    string postPageName = "";
    for (int i = 0; i < arr.Length;i++ )
    {
        if(arr[i].ToLower() == "forums")
        {
            forumsPosition = i;
            break;
        }
    }
    itemsAfterForums = (arr.Length - 1) - forumsPosition;
    if (itemsAfterForums == 2)
    {
        categoryPageName = arr[arr.Length - 2];
        forumPageName = arr[arr.Length - 1];
        forumPageName = forumPageName.Replace(".aspx", "");
        BoardForum forum =
                _forumRepository.GetForumByPageName(forumPageName);
        context.RewritePath("/forums/ViewForum.aspx?ForumID=" +
                forum.ForumID.ToString() +
                        "&CategoryPageName=" + categoryPageName +
                        "&ForumPageName=" + forumPageName, true);
    }
    else if (itemsAfterForums == 3)
    {
        categoryPageName = arr[arr.Length - 3];
        forumPageName = arr[arr.Length - 2];
        postPageName = arr[arr.Length - 1];
        postPageName = postPageName.Replace(".aspx", "");
        BoardPost post =
                _postRepository.GetPostByPageName(postPageName);
        context.RewritePath("/forums/ViewPost.aspx?PostID=" +
                post.PostID.ToString(), true);
    }
}
...
```

The very first thing we have to do is test to see if we are dealing with a forum's URL or not. If we are then we will work in this section of code. Next, we need to create an array of strings that is the result of splitting the PhysicalPath of the application on its back slashes. This produces an ordered array of items from front to back. So, in the case of http://www.domain.com/forums/category/forum/post we will get a collection of items that start with the drive letter and work their way through the directory tree including the directories that don't actually exist. The following screenshot shows an example of a working collection of items:

```
else if (application.Request.PhysicalPath.ToLower().Contains("forums"))
{
    string[] arr = application.Request.PhysicalPath.ToLower().Split('\\');
    int forumsP ⊟  ● arr | {string[10]}
    int itemsAfte    ● [0] | ℚ ▾ "p:"
    string catego     ● [1] | ℚ ▾ "projects"
    string forumP     ● [2] | ℚ ▾ "fisharoo"
    string postPa     ● [3] | ℚ ▾ "trunk"
                      ● [4] | ℚ ▾ "source"
                      ● [5] | ℚ ▾ "fisharooweb"
                      ● [6] | ℚ ▾ "forums"
    for (int i =      ● [7] | ℚ ▾ "reef-tank-care"
    {                 ● [8] | ℚ ▾ "salt-water-filtration"
        if(arr[i]     ● [9] | ℚ ▾ "my-third-test-thread.aspx"
        {
```

We then declare some items that we will use later on.

In the `for` loop, we will iterate through our collection of directories/folders to locate the position of the forum's item. With this in hand we can then determine how many items are left behind it. This will help us to determine if we are working with a category and forum or a category, forum, and thread. The difference is we have either two or three items in hand.

From there we test to see what we are working with based on the number of items behind the forum's item. We are now able to get the category page name and the forum page name (notice that we prune off the `.aspx` extension from our page name). We then load the `BoardForum` object for this request and rewrite the path to the `ViewForum.aspx` page passing in the requested forum's `ForumID`. We also pass along the category and forum page name for later use.

In the next segment we are working with three items, which means that a thread is being requested. Once again we load the category and forum page name as well as the post page name (again pruning off the `.aspx` extension). With this information we are able to load the board post and rewrite the path to the `ViewPost.aspx` page passing in the `PostID`.

ViewForum.aspx

The view forum page is responsible for displaying a single forum and all of its threads.

The view forum page is very similar to the homepage in that it accepts a collection of data from its presenter. With this collection in hand it then populates the display of the page. Upon each iteration of a forum the repTopics_ItemDataBound method loads the NavigateUrl property of the linkNewThread HyperLink control with the path to the post.aspx page. Part of this path is the IsThread=1 variable. The reason for this is that this is a dual purpose page for both creating a post and a thread.

```
public void LoadDisplay(List<BoardPost> Threads, string
                CategoryPageName, string ForumPageName, Int32 ForumID)
{
    litCategoryPageName.Text = CategoryPageName;
    litForumPageName.Text = ForumPageName;
    linkNewThread.NavigateUrl =
        "/forums/post.aspx?IsThread=1&ForumID=" + ForumID.ToString();
    repTopics.DataSource = Threads;
    repTopics.DataBind();
}
protected void repTopics_ItemDataBound(object sender,
                                RepeaterItemEventArgs e)
{
```

```
if(e.Item.ItemType == ListItemType.Item || e.Item.ItemType ==
                    ListItemType.AlternatingItem)
{
    HyperLink linkViewTopic = e.Item.FindControl("linkViewTopic")
                            as HyperLink;
    linkViewTopic.NavigateUrl = "/forums/" +
                            litCategoryPageName.Text + "/"
                            + litForumPageName.Text + "/" +
                            ((BoardPost)
                             e.Item.DataItem).
                            PageName + ".aspx";
}
}
```

Something that you might not expect this page to do is that it loads the navigation for each thread's HyperLink directly. This is one HyperLink that we do not pass through the Redirector class. The reason for this is that I would normally use a LinkButton. When you click the LinkButton, it would cause a post back, and in the Click method, we would make our call to the Redirector. Unfortunately as we got to this page through a rewritten URL, the post back doesn't go to the right place and causes us some pain. It is difficult to capture correctly. So I elect to use a real HyperLink and link directly to my fictitious fancy URL.

ViewPost.aspx

The view post page is most likely the easiest of all the pages. It expects a ThreadID and displays the thread and all of its posts.

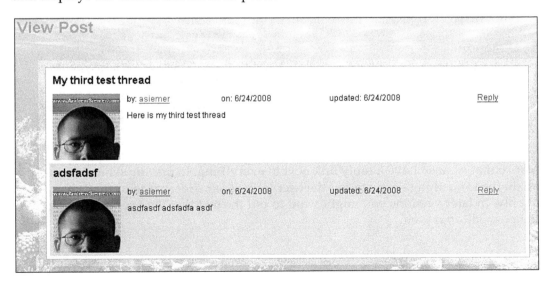

This too is done through a fancy URL something like `forums/reef-tank-care/ salt-water-filtration/my-third-test-thread.aspx`.

 We have already covered the translation of this in our section on the UrlRewrite.

This page is also handled by its presenter and is passed the Thread object and a list of Posts. With this data in hand the code behind is able to loads its UI and bind its list of posts. Both the posts and the thread are loaded identically.

```
public void LoadData(BoardPost Thread, List<BoardPost> Posts)
{
    linkUsername.Text = Thread.Username;
    linkUsername.NavigateUrl = "~/" + Thread.Username;
    lblUpdateDate.Text = Thread.UpdateDate.ToShortDateString();
    lblCreateDate.Text = Thread.CreateDate.ToShortDateString();
    lblSubject.Text = Thread.Name;
    lblDescription.Text = Thread.Post;
    imgProfile.ImageUrl =
                "/images/profileavatar/profileimage.aspx?AccountID="
                + Thread.AccountID.ToString();
    linkReply.Text = "Reply";
    linkReply.NavigateUrl = "/forums/post.aspx?PostID=" +
                            Thread.PostID.ToString();
    repPosts.DataSource = Posts;
    repPosts.DataBind();
}

public void repPosts_ItemDataBound(object sender,
                                    RepeaterItemEventArgs e)
{
    if(e.Item.ItemType == ListItemType.Item || e.Item.ItemType ==
                    ListItemType.AlternatingItem)
    {

    }
}
```

Notice that we also have a reply link next to everything. In our implementation they all do the same thing—navigating the user to the `Post.aspx` page to create a post or a reply. In later versions you might want to put the text that the user is replying to in the post editor as well.

Post.aspx

The post page is the one page that the message board actually requires you to be logged in so that you can interact with it. Once logged in you are able to create a new thread or reply to an existing thread or post.

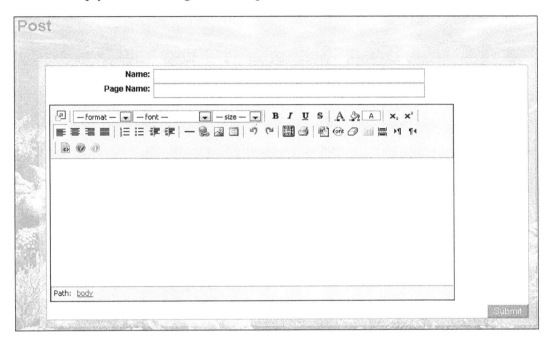

The only thing you might miss about this page is that it is dual purpose. This means that we need to be able to handle creating threads and posts. The difference here is that a post does not have a page name. So if the URL states that this post is to be a thread, the page name text box is enabled. If it is a post, then it is disabled.

The next feature to understand (covered many times before) is the WYSIWYG editor. This is mostly handled in the master page with a Xinha WYSIWYG editor. To get it to come to life though you need to have a text box with its **TextMode** set to **MultiLine**. You also need a snippet of JavaScript.

```
<script type="text/javascript">
        xinha_editors[xinha_editors.length] =
                                    'ctl00_Content_txtPost';
</script>
```

Once all of the UI is functioning correctly we then need to wire up the **Save** button. This is done to some degree in the code behind with the `btnSubmit_Click` method where we capture all the data from the UI. We then attempt to pass the data in the form of a `BoardPost` to the presenter to actually persist the data into the database.

```
protected void btnSubmit_Click(object sender, EventArgs e)
{
    BoardPost post = new BoardPost();
    post.Name = txtName.Text;
    post.PageName = txtPageName.Text;
    post.Post = txtPost.Text;
    _presenter.Save(post);
}
```

Now the `Save` method in the presenter is something a bit heftier than the rest of this code has been.

```
public void Save(BoardPost post)
{
    //is new thread
    if(_webContext.ForumID > 0)
    {
        post.ForumID = _webContext.ForumID;
        post.IsThread = _webContext.IsThread;
        if(!_postRepository.CheckPostPageNameIsUnique(post.PageName))
        {
            _view.SetErrorMessage("The page name you are trying to
                                    use is already in use!");
        }
    }
    //is reply post
    else
    {
        BoardPost postToReplyToo =
                    _postRepository.GetPostByID(_webContext.PostID);
        if (postToReplyToo.IsThread)
            post.ThreadID = postToReplyToo.PostID;
        else
            post.ThreadID = postToReplyToo.ThreadID;
        post.ForumID = postToReplyToo.ForumID;
    }
    post.CreateDate = DateTime.Now;
    post.UpdateDate = DateTime.Now;
    post.AccountID = _webContext.CurrentUser.AccountID;
    post.Username = _webContext.CurrentUser.Username;
```

```
    post.ReplyCount = 0;
    post.ViewCount = 0;

    post.PostID = _postRepository.SavePost(post);
    BoardForum forum = _forumRepository.GetForumByID(post.ForumID);
    BoardCategory category =
                    _categoryRepository.GetCategoryByCategoryID
                    (forum.CategoryID);
    BoardPost thread;
    if(post.IsThread)
        thread = _postRepository.GetPostByID(post.PostID);
    else
        thread = _postRepository.GetPostByID((long)post.ThreadID);
    //add an alert to the filter
    if(post.IsThread)
        _alertService.AddNewBoardThreadAlert(category,forum,thread);
    else
        _alertService.AddNewBoardPostAlert(category, forum, post,
                                    thread);
    _redirector.GoToForumsViewPost(forum.PageName,category.PageName,
                                    thread.PageName);
}
```

This method initially looks to determine if we are working with a post or a thread. If we are working with a new thread then we have to set the `ForumID` and `IsThread` properties. We then check to see if the page name that was provided is unique or not. If not we send out an error message to the UI and stop the Save processing.

If we are working with a post instead of a thread, then we get the post that we are replying to. With this in hand we check to see if it is a thread or itself is just a simple post as well. If it is a thread then we set our new post's `ThreadID` property to that post's `PostID`. Otherwise we set our post's `ThreadID` to that post's `ThreadID`. We also set the `ForumID` from the `postToReplyToo's ForumID` property.

With these determinations made and initial values set, we can then continue setting additional properties such as the create date, update date, accounted, and so on. We finally save the post and get the newly-created post's `PostID`.

With the post created, we then need to determine what type of alert to send out to our friends. If it is a thread then we send out a new thread alert. Otherwise we send out a new post alert.

Finally we can redirect the user to see their new post using the `Redirector.GoToForumsViewPost()`

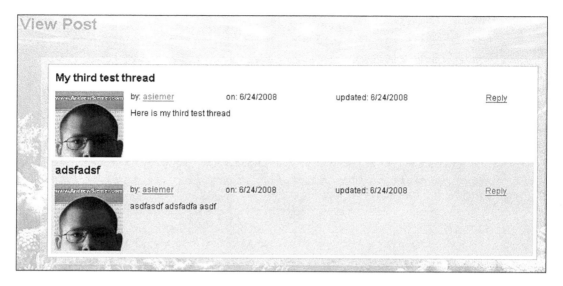

Summary

In this chapter we created the core features of a message board — categories, forums, threads, and posts. Along with these features we have also heavily implemented friendly URLs to help our content be more SEO friendly. This should feed the various search engine spiders effectively. In order to spread the word about our new content we have also integrated our message board section into our alert service. This takes each new post and broadcasts its arrival to homepages of friends of each of the posting user.

As discussed earlier, the subject of message boards is a large one. While we implemented a great foundation this section is by no means feature complete. If you look at the many options for forums and message boards on the market you will quickly notice that there are many other features that you could implement on top of what we built. This is a great start though!

10
Groups

What are Groups? In the social network context, **Groups** allow users of your community to interact with each other around a common topic. Groups start bringing together our other, already created concepts. Items such as forums, blogs, images, and many other features can be better utilized from the group point of view.

Take forums for example. As a user of our community you can interact with the pre-created forums and you are able to post topics or replies to any public forum in the system. You hope that other users who have similar interests as you, or those who have an answer for your posted question, will stumble upon your post. Many people will see your post, some will reply. There is no guarantee that the right person will see it and even less guarantee that the right person will give you the response that you are seeking. If you are able to post your topic to a forum that is somewhat related to your interest, then your chances go up a bit.

On the other hand, with a group-owned forum you know that there is a specific community, within the global community, paying extra close attention to your forum posts. In addition to that, when you post to a group-owned forum, you know that the entire user base of that group will be made aware of your post. This increases your odds of getting to the information that you are seeking. And you know that the majority of people looking at your post most likely have or know someone who has the information you are interested in.

Think of groups as sub-communities with special interests. Because they are sub-communities, they have the same life as a user in the system with the exception that they act on behalf of many users. By becoming part of a group you have taken on many new friends with common interests. You gain access to special interest forums and you could get to see the hidden image galleries!

Here is an example of what we will be building:

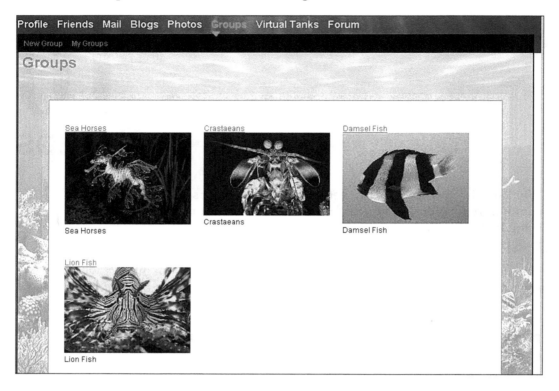

Problem

Given that there are so many features in our example site it is impossible for us to integrate them all with our group feature. Having said that, when you read through this chapter, keep in mind that just about anything that applies to a person in our community can be morphed to apply to a group of people. In this chapter, we will focus on creating the core framework for a group.

The framework we are building will allow us to create a group that will have both public and private presence in our site. A group will also be able to have a dedicated group page.

Here is the interface that will be built for group creation:

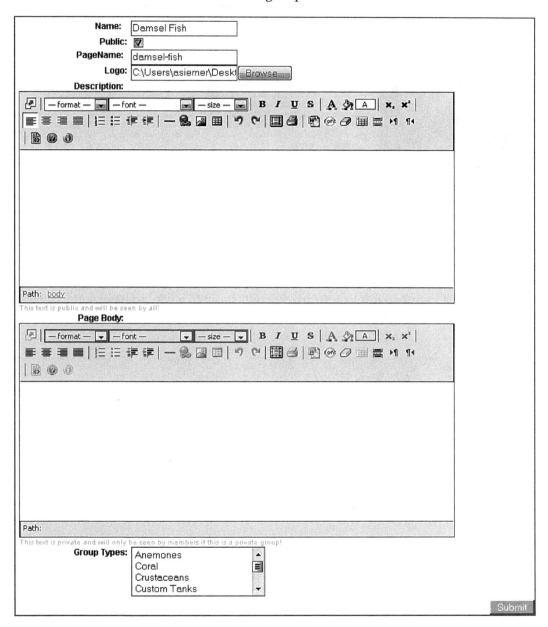

As we will have the concept of private groups, we will need to provide a way for people to join a group and be approved by the owner of the group. We will have a **Request Membership** link as shown in the following screenshot:.

This group is private! Request Membership

Created: 7/7/2008
Last Updated: 7/7/2008

Lorem ipsum dolor sit amet, consectetuer adipiscing elit. Mauris eget lacus. Maecenas enim nisl, fringilla vel, fermentum vel, tempor vel, leo. Mauris orci arcu, tincidunt vitae, rutrum non, cursus id, magna. Nullam velit. Nulla felis elit, faucibus ut, viverra et, blandit et, dui. Sed enim. Nunc tincidunt. Mauris semper justo nec tellus. Fusce nec felis eleifend metus aliquam vestibulum. Maecenas lorem lacus, bibendum vitae, lacinia vel, vestibulum vel, dolor. In mi sem, porttitor eu, dapibus in, accumsan vehicula, tortor. Fusce vel diam accumsan enim lobortis placerat. In faucibus dui vitae turpis. Quisque volutpat iaculis tellus. Nulla orci lectus, vehicula ac, facilisis et, laoreet sed, felis. Nunc luctus mollis velit. In condimentum ultricies urna.

Nam et arcu sed lacus convallis aliquam. Pellentesque sagittis consectetuer lorem. Vivamus pede felis, blandit sed, interdum in, adipiscing vitae, lorem. Fusce interdum varius lacus. In tortor nulla, eleifend ac, commodo vitae, auctor sit amet, est. Pellentesque habitant morbi tristique senectus et netus et malesuada fames ac turpis egestas. Cras hendrerit dolor quis sem. Pellentesque augue augue, consectetuer sit amet, facilisis a, mattis vitae, mauris. Phasellus sed lacus. Aenean mauris. Ut luctus vulputate quam. Fusce urna. Fusce vitae est sed tortor fermentum ultricies. Duis feugiat dolor sit amet sapien. Proin orci purus, luctus ut, varius semper, faucibus eu, massa. Nullam rhoncus lacus at velit. Sed sem nisl turpis duis.

In addition to a membership to a group, we will provide a way to have some of those members be considered owners or administrators of a group.

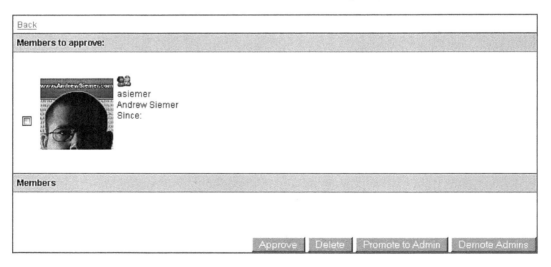

Once the foundation is in place, we will start to connect to some of our other features. We will allow each group to have its own forum.

This forum will have some differences in that when a user posts to the forum, the forum will not send alerts to their friends, but instead will send alerts to all the members of that group.

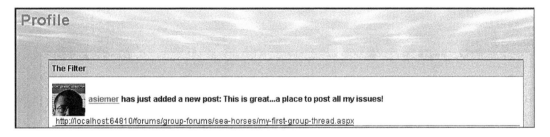

Down the road, we could also extend the group feature to have its own filter to catch user alerts to an account in a similar manner. We could also have related blog posts show up on the homepage of the group. We could also show the latest forum posts on the groups homepage. We could show the latest uploaded images. And many other things could be done off the group foundation.

Design

Let's take a look at the design for this feature.

Groups

In the same way that the `Accounts` table is the core hub for many items in our system, the `Groups` table could be built out to be an additional hub. For that reason, we will address the creation of this feature first. The table structure for a group is not overly complex.

Groups

	Column Name	Data Type	Allow Nulls
🔑	GroupID	int	☐
	Name	varchar(250)	☐
	CreateDate	smalldatetime	☐
	UpdateDate	smalldatetime	☐
	MemberCount	int	☐
	PageName	varchar(250)	☐
	Description	varchar(2000)	☐
	AccountID	int	☐
	Timestamp	timestamp	☐
	FileID	bigint	☐
	IsPublic	bit	☐
	Body	varchar(MAX)	☐
			☐

You are probably getting used to seeing the counts bubbled up at the parent level. I will explain again that we are doing this to remove the need to run aggregate queries. Instead, when we load the object we will automagically have the count in hand already.

Something else that you are probably used to seeing is the concept of a page name. As the group page will become a major center of information, we want to make sure that as far as Google or other search engine spiders are concerned, that this is a true page rather than some server-generated page. We do this in the hope of getting those cherished SEO points. Also it is much easier for the user to know where they are and it allows our user to send a human readable URL to their friends, which promotes sharing!

The last thing of importance to note is the `IsPublic` flag that we have in our group entry. This will be the key to tell us whether or not anyone can gain access to this group or only group members. We will touch upon this requirement a bit more down the road.

GroupMembers

Generally in a group there is more than one user who will help operate the group. We will therefore have an `AccountID` in the group, which will help us identify the owner of the group. But we will also need a method to track all the members of the group as well as the members who are also administrators.

	Column Name	Data Type	Allow Nulls
🔑	ID	bigint	☐
	GroupID	int	☐
	AccountID	int	☐
	CreateDate	smalldatetime	☐
	Timestamp	timestamp	☐
	IsAdmin	bit	☐
	IsApproved	bit	☐
			☐

GroupMembers

You can see from the structure in the screenshot that we are going to track the `GroupID` and the `AccountID` to create the relationship between `Groups` and `Accounts`. In addition to that information, we are also going to keep track of when the member requested membership, whether they are approved or not (`IsApproved`) and whether the account is also an administrator (`IsAdmin`). This gives us everything we need to create members for our groups.

GroupTypes

We will eventually have many different groups in our system. As an added feature we want an easy way for our users to locate groups that they may have some interest in. In order to provide this functionality, we will have a system to track the type a group is. Down the road we could use this system for searching groups or grouping them. Also this system will allow us to make the statement: "If you like this group you might also be interested in these related groups."

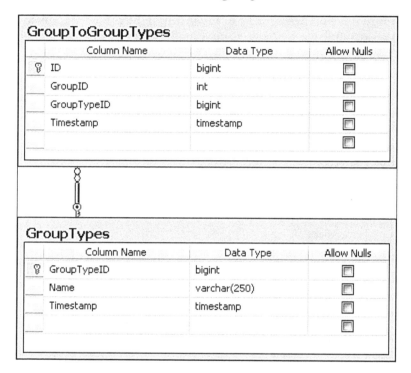

As you can see from the relationships in the screenshot, groups can be associated with many group types (and vice versa). The structure itself is very straightforward.

GroupForums

As we have covered earlier, when a user creates a group they also get a group-owned forum. In order to accomplish this, we have to create a link between the group and a new forum.

GroupForums			
	Column Name	Data Type	Allow Nulls
🔑	ID	bigint	☐
	GroupID	int	☐
	ForumID	int	☐
	CreateDate	smalldatetime	☐
	Timestamp	timestamp	☐
			☐

This is a simple many-to-many relationship that allows us to technically have many forums and many groups related to one another. I don't like to introduce limitations by design though. So just in case we need to have multiple forums for a group or one group with many forums, we can.

Schema

To see the bigger picture with regards to groups and the surrounding features, here is the groups schema:

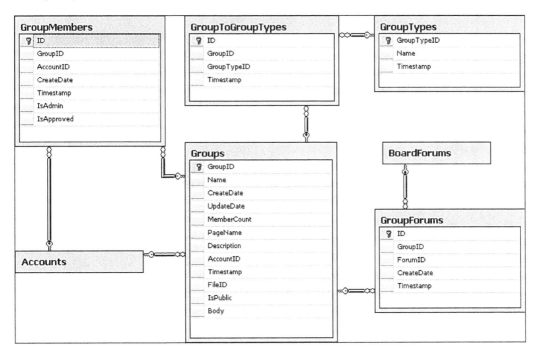

Solution

Now let's take a look at our solution.

Implementing the database

Let's take a look at what we need to implement the database.

Groups

Here is the Groups table structure:

	Column Name	Data Type	Allow Nulls
🔑	GroupID	int	☐
	Name	varchar(250)	☐
	CreateDate	smalldatetime	☐
	UpdateDate	smalldatetime	☐
	MemberCount	int	☐
	PageName	varchar(250)	☐
	Description	varchar(2000)	☐
	AccountID	int	☐
	Timestamp	timestamp	☐
	FileID	bigint	☐
	IsPublic	bit	☐
	Body	varchar(MAX)	☐

The majority of this table is self-explanatory. However, one thing to be very aware of is the **Body** field, which is **varchar(MAX)** here. This means that people could technically put any amount of text that they want here. If this is not the functionality that you want to provide, either make this field smaller or put some form of client-side validation on this field to restrict its size.

You may also be wondering why we have a large **Description** field and an even larger **Body** field. The primary reason for this is so that we have public and private fields of text. A description could simply be the first paragraph of the Groups' page text, or it could be a brief synopsis. This totally depends on how you structure your output. I have set it up so that the description and body show up together, with the description on top.

Another item worth noting is that we are tracking a **FileID** with each group. This reference will allow us to upload a photo to the system to be used as the group's avatar or logo.

GroupMembers

The GroupMembers table allows us to define who can be our group members. In addition to defining membership, this table will allow us to accept or reject members. Once we have members, we can also use this structure to define additional administrators in the group.

	Column Name	Data Type	Allow Nulls
▶🔑	ID	bigint	☐
	GroupID	int	☐
	AccountID	int	☐
	CreateDate	smalldatetime	☐
	Timestamp	timestamp	☐
	IsAdmin	bit	☐
	IsApproved	bit	☐

The structure is very simple and self-explanatory:

GroupTypes

This table allows us to define the different group types that we want provided by our system. If you wanted to allow your users to provide their own group type, you could add an additional field to define whether it should be system-defined or user-defined. I would probably call this flag IsSystemType. This will help us to define our initial library.

	Column Name	Data Type	Allow Nulls
▶🔑	GroupTypeID	bigint	☐
	Name	varchar(250)	☐
	Timestamp	timestamp	☐

Once we have the `GroupTypes` table created, we can then turn our attention to capturing relationships between groups and their type(s). Keep in mind that the users will be able to associate their groups with more than one type, if appropriate.

	Column Name	Data Type	Allow Nulls
▶🔑	ID	bigint	☐
	GroupID	int	☐
	GroupTypeID	bigint	☐
	Timestamp	timestamp	☐

This is a simple many-to-many relationship definition table that tracks both the **GroupID** and **GroupTypeID**.

GroupForums

This table, like many of the others described earlier, is simply a many-to-many relationship table. This table allows each of our groups to also have a forum. We do this by tracking the **GroupID** and the **ForumID**.

	Column Name	Data Type	Allow Nulls
▶🔑	ID	bigint	☐
	GroupID	int	☐
	ForumID	int	☐
	CreateDate	smalldatetime	☐
	Timestamp	timestamp	☐

Creating the relationships

Once all the tables are created, we can then create all the relationships.

For this set of tables, we have relationships between the following tables:

- `Groups` to `Accounts`
- `GroupMembers` and `Accounts`
- `GroupMembers` and `Groups`
- `GroupToGroupTypes` and `Groups`
- `GroupToGroupTypes` and `GroupTypes`
- `BoardForums` and `GroupForums`
- `GroupForums` and `Groups`

Setting up the data access layer

Follow the steps mentioned next:

- Open the `Fisharoo.dbml` file.
- Open up your **Server Explorer** window.
- Expand your Fisharoo connection.
- Expand your tables. If you don't see your new tables try hitting the **Refresh** icon or right-clicking on the tables and clicking **Refresh**.
- Then drag your new tables onto the design surface.
- Hit **Save** and you should now have the domain objects to work with as shown in the following screenshot:

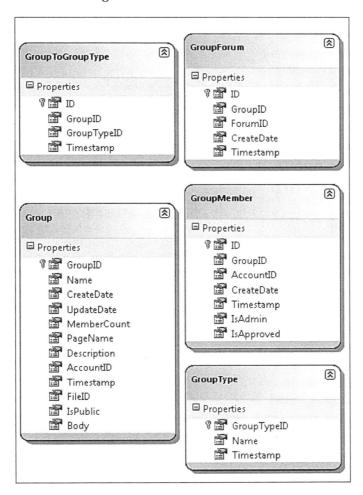

Keep in mind that we are not letting LINQ track our relationships, so go ahead and delete them from the design surface. Your design surface should have all the same items that you see in the screenshot (though perhaps in a different arrangement!).

Building repositories

With the addition of new tables will come the addition of new repositories so that we can get to the data stored in those tables. We will be creating or modifying the following repositories to support our needs:

- `GroupRepository`
- `GroupToGroupTypeRepository`
- `GroupMemberRepository`
- `GroupForumRepository`
- `GroupTypeRepository`
- `AccountRepository`

Each of our repositories will generally have a method for select by ID, select all by parent ID, save, and delete. Once you have seen one repository you have pretty much seen them all. Review previous chapters, the appendices, or the included code, for example, of a standard repository. However, in this chapter, I will discuss anything that varies from standard!

GroupRepository

The `GroupRepository` is possibly one of our largest repositories so far in the number of methods it provides. Here is the list of methods that we have to implement in this repository (extracted from this repositories interface definition).

- `bool CheckIfGroupPageNameExists(string PageName);`
- `List<Group> GetGroupsAccountIsMemberOf(Int32 AccountID);`
- `List<Group> GetGroupsOwnedByAccount(Int32 AccountID);`
- `Group GetGroupByID(Int32 GroupID);`
- `Group GetGroupByPageName(string PageName);`
- `Int32 SaveGroup(Group group);`
- `void DeleteGroup(Group group);`
- `List<Group> GetLatestGroups();`
- `bool IsOwner(int AccountID, int GroupID);`
- `Group GetGroupByForumID(int ForumID);`
- `void DeleteGroup(int GroupID);`

For the most part, all these method names are pretty much self-explanatory. And as simple as the functionality is the fact that the names described there isn't any magic performed by this repository. I will pick a couple of example methods though they demonstrate common tasks.

GetGroupByForumID

This group is responsible for going through the linking table `GroupForums` to get a Group by the passed in `ForumID`. This is performed by joining the `Groups` and `GroupForums` table on the `GroupID` field in each table. We then perform a `where` clause to get the appropriate group for this Forum.

```
public Group GetGroupByForumID(int ForumID)
{
    Group result = null;
    using(FisharooDataContext dc = conn.GetContext())
    {
        result = (from g in dc.Groups
                  join f in dc.GroupForums on g.GroupID equals
                  f.GroupID
                  where f.ForumID == ForumID
                  select g).FirstOrDefault();
    }
    return result;
}
```

Considering that our table structure technically allows multiple groups for multiple forums, you may need to pay attention if you add the logic that allows the user to create many relationships. The interface that we will create will allow only one forum to be created when a group is initially created. The restriction is strictly enforced through the limitation of the UI. If you intend to use the many-to-many structure on purpose, you will want to change the return type of this method to a `List<Group>`.

IsOwner

The `IsOwner` method is responsible for determining if the passed in `AccountID` is the owner of the group that is associated with the passed in `GroupID`. This is performed on the DataContext groups collection with a `where` clause to determine if we have ownership. If the item returned is not null, then we know that the user is indeed an owner; otherwise he/she is not.

```
public bool IsOwner(int AccountID, int GroupID)
{
    bool result = false;
    using(FisharooDataContext dc = conn.GetContext())
```

```
    {
        if (dc.Groups.Where(g => g.AccountID == AccountID &&
                        g.GroupID == GroupID).FirstOrDefault() != null)
            result = true;
    }
    return result;
}
```

CheckIfGroupPageNameExists

This method, while being almost identical to the method we just discussed, is very important as it determines if a Group's page name is in use yet or not.

```
public bool CheckIfGroupPageNameExists(string PageName)
{
    bool result = false;
    using (FisharooDataContext dc = conn.GetContext())
    {
        Group group = dc.Groups.Where(g => g.PageName ==
                                    PageName).FirstOrDefault();
        if(group == null)
            result = false;
    }
    return result;
}
```

DeleteGroup

In general, I would say that the DeleteGroup method is nothing fancy. However, in this method's case we have never performed a delete in this specific manner. Up to this point, so far we have passed in full objects for deletion using all LINQ to SQL concepts. We are not straying from that concept too much here—this is just a different way of doing the same thing. In a web world this may work better for you, as we don't tend to keep objects lying around, while we do almost always have object IDs in hand at all times.

```
public void DeleteGroup(int GroupID)
{
    using(FisharooDataContext dc = conn.GetContext())
    {
        Group group = dc.Groups.Where(g => g.GroupID ==
                    GroupID).FirstOrDefault();
        dc.Groups.DeleteOnSubmit(group);
        dc.SubmitChanges();
    }
}
```

This method takes in the `GroupID`. It then fetches the latest copy of that Group and passes it into the `DeleteOnSubmit` method of the DataContext. Another way to do the same thing is to pass the query into the `DeleteOnSubmit` method. Either way, it works!

GroupToGroupTypeRepository

Keep in mind that this particular repository is supporting an overly simple table structure—a lookup table so to speak. For this reason, the repository is fairly lightweight too. There are currently three methods in this repository.

- `void SaveGroupToGroupType(GroupToGroupType groupToGroupType);`
- `void DeleteGroupToGroupType(GroupToGroupType groupToGroupType);`
- `void SaveGroupTypesForGroup(List<long> SelectedGroupTypeIDs, int GroupID);`

SaveGroupTypesForGroup

We will now discuss the last method, `SaveGroupTypesForGroup`. This method is of interest in that it addresses a common problem that we have with lookup tables of this nature. The initial saving of items to a lookup table is simple. There are no other relationships defined, so we are doing a simple insert.

What happens when a user pulls up their UI again and attempts to save the same relationships with an additional relationship and one removed relationship? The easiest way to address this issue is to just toss away all the old relationships and then create the new relationships that we have in hand at that moment. This might be ok if we had no third column key (like we do to support LINQ to SQL). If we just had a clustered key with our two foreign keys, we could consider this. But do keep in mind that the "delete all" concept can thrash on your database a bit creating more traffic than is necessary.

Another way to manage this issue is to just remove deleted relationships and continue to throw new relationships into the system. This creates redundant data (and possibly data corruption). This method also thrashes on the database with more traffic than is necessary.

The third and the best way to handle this is to determine what is to be removed and what is to be added before we hit the database. This can be performed regardless of the additional columns that we have. And this method doesn't cause any extra data or hits on the database.

```
public void SaveGroupTypesForGroup(List<long> SelectedGroupTypeIDs,
int GroupID)
{
```

```
using (FisharooDataContext dc = conn.GetContext())
{
    //get a list of current selections
    List<long> currentTypes =
        dc.GroupToGroupTypes.Where(gt => gt.GroupID ==
                GroupID).Select(gt => gt.GroupTypeID).ToList();
    //make a list of items to delete
    List<long> itemsToDelete = currentTypes.Where(ct =>
                !SelectedGroupTypeIDs.Contains(ct)).ToList();
    //make a list of items to insert
    List<long> itemsToInsert =
        SelectedGroupTypeIDs.Where(s =>
                        !currentTypes.Contains(s)).ToList();
    //delete grouptogrouptypes
    dc.GroupToGroupTypes.DeleteAllOnSubmit(
        dc.GroupToGroupTypes.Where(g =>
                itemsToDelete.Contains(g.GroupTypeID)
                && g.GroupID == GroupID));
    //create the actual objects to insert
    List<GroupToGroupType> typesToInsert = new
                                    List<GroupToGroupType>();
    foreach (long l in itemsToInsert)
    {
        GroupToGroupType g = new GroupToGroupType() { GroupID =
                        GroupID, GroupTypeID = l };
        typesToInsert.Add(g);
    }
    //do the insert
    if (typesToInsert.Count > 0)
    {
        dc.GroupToGroupTypes.InsertAllOnSubmit(typesToInsert);
    }
    dc.SubmitChanges();
}
}
```

As you can see, we are pretty much only using standard LINQ statements to create unique lists of items for each purpose. We first get a list of the current relationships. We then make a list of the items to be deleted and then a list of items to be created. Next, we actually perform the delete on the relationships that need to be removed. And then we create the objects that represent the relationships. We then perform the insert of those objects. There is some work here in the extent of code to be created. But keep in mind that this results in minimal database thrashing and good clean data!

GroupForumRepository

The `GroupForumRepository` is even less interesting as compared to the last repository we considered. This repository is also supporting a standard many-to-many lookup table. It has the following methods.

- `void SaveGroupForum(GroupForum groupForum);`

- `void DeleteGroupForum(GroupForum groupForum);`

- `int GetGroupIdByForumID(int ForumID);`

- `void DeleteGroupForum(int ForumID, int GroupID);`

None of them is special as they all are implemented as we have seen before in the other repository examples.

GroupMemberRepository

Argh! Another many-to-many lookup table. Here are its methods:

- `List<int> GetMemberAccountIDsByGroupID(Int32 GroupID);`
- `void SaveGroupMember(GroupMember groupMember);`
- `void DeleteGroupMember(GroupMember groupMember);`
- `void DeleteGroupMembers(List<int> MembersToDelete, int GroupID);`
- `void ApproveGroupMembers(List<int> MembersToApprove, int GroupID);`
- `void PromoteGroupMembersToAdmin(List<int> MembersToPromote, int GroupID);`
- `void DemoteGroupMembersFromAdmin(List<int> MembersToDemote, int GroupID);`
- `bool IsAdministrator(Int32 AccountID, Int32 GroupID);`
- `void DeleteAllGroupMembersForGroup(int GroupID);`
- `bool IsMember(Int32 AccountID, Int32 GroupID);`

Wow! How can a simple lookup table be so complex? This particular repository provides many supporting type database lookups that allow us to do bulk executions, simple tasks such as promoting and demoting members to and from admin status, and tasks such as determining if a user is a member or an administrator.

GetMemberAccountIDsByGroupID

This particular method is not complex by any means. But you will notice that it is creating a list of members from two data sources. It first looks at all the members defined by the GroupMembers table. It then takes into account that the owner of the Group is not in that list, so it also extracts the owner to add to this list.

```
public List<int> GetMemberAccountIDsByGroupID(Int32 GroupID)
{
    List<int> result = new List<int>();
    using(FisharooDataContext dc = conn.GetContext())
    {
        result = dc.GroupMembers.Where(gm => gm.IsApproved &&
                                  gm.GroupID == GroupID).
                                  Select(gm => gm.AccountID).ToList();
        result.Add(dc.Groups.Where(g => g.GroupID ==
              GroupID).Select(gm => gm.AccountID).FirstOrDefault());
    }
    return result;
}
```

DeleteGroupMembers

This is a method that is performing a bulk-style action. We are selecting a list of members based on the IDs that were passed into the method. And we are then passing that list of GroupMembers into the DeleteAllOnSubmit method allowing us to perform a batch delete. This will support our multi-select page on the member management pages later.

```
public void DeleteGroupMembers(List<int> MembersToDelete, int
                              GroupID)
{
    using(FisharooDataContext dc = conn.GetContext())
    {
        IEnumerable<GroupMember> members =
            dc.GroupMembers.Where(gm =>
                              MembersToDelete.Contains(gm.AccountID)
                              && gm.GroupID == GroupID);
        dc.GroupMembers.DeleteAllOnSubmit(members);
        dc.SubmitChanges();
    }
}
```

GroupTypeRepository

The `GroupTypeRepository` has a handful of methods to perform the basic tasks. None of them is out of the ordinary, and their names are indicative and self-explanatory. Here is the list of methods:

- `GroupType GetGroupTypeByID(Int32 GroupTypeID);`
- `List<GroupType> GetGroupTypesByGroupID(Int32 GroupID);`
- `Int64 SaveGroupType(GroupType groupType);`
- `void DeleteGroupType(GroupType groupType);`
- `List<GroupType> GetAllGroupTypes();`

AccountRepository

This particular repository is the one that has grown over several chapters. In order to support Groups we had to add a couple of new methods to this class—`GetApprovedAccountsByGroupID` and `GetAccountsToApproveByGroupID`. These allow us to use our `GroupMembers` table to lookup an actual Account from a membership point of view. We will get users who would like to be a part of our group, and the members who are already a part of the group.

GetApprovedAccountsByGroupID

This method is of interest primarily for the reason that it supports server-side paging, that is to say, it has the ability to show a subset of records within the larger selection. This is accomplished using some standard LINQ expressions—`Skip()` and `Take()`.

"Why on earth do you need to write custom code to perform paging? Don't you know that the various grid type objects that are already provided to you in ASP.NET already perform this sort of logic out of the box?" Yes, they do. Should you use them in a production environment? Well, the answer is No. The way these controls work is they take your query and return all of the data from the database to your web server. The web server then caches this data on its end and sends a subset to the client that requested the data. This alone doesn't make a whole lot of sense in that the client may only care about the first page of data and you've selected the data for 100 pages! Now compound this problem further by putting this web server into the farm of web servers. If this is a popular page you are now sending huge chunks of data from your database to your web server for no reason! If you ever need to do paging, roll your own. You have to do a bit more work, but you get a great deal of performance and control out of it.

```
public List<Account> GetApprovedAccountsByGroupID(int GroupID, int
                                            PageNumber)
{
    List<Account> result = null;
    using(FisharooDataContext dc = conn.GetContext())
    {
        IEnumerable<Account> accounts = (from a in dc.Accounts
                                        join m in dc.GroupMembers on
                                        a.AccountID equals m.AccountID
                                        where m.GroupID == GroupID
                                        && m.IsApproved
                                        select
a).Skip((_configuration.NumberOfRecordsInPage*(PageNumber-1)))
                                            .Take(_configuration.
NumberOfRecordsInPage);
        result = accounts.ToList();
    }
    return result;
}
```

In this method, we are accepting the GroupID and PageNumber. This tells us the
set and also the subset of data that we are interested in. The LINQ query is very
standard up to the point of call to the Skip() method. This call allows us to tell the
query which record we want to start at in the set of data. Directly after that we call
the Take() method, which tells the query how many records from the starting record
we want to include in our returned set of data.

The easiest way to perform the skip logic is to take the number of records we want
our page size to be (stored in a config file somewhere) and multiply it by the page
number we are currently on (minus one as this is technically a zero based way of
doing things). The Take() method just wants to know how many records you are
interested in to make up your page set of data.

GetAccountsToApproveByGroupID

This method isn't anything more than a simple query around GroupMembers
and Groups.

```
public List<Account> GetAccountsToApproveByGroupID(int GroupID)
{
    List<Account> result = null;
    using (FisharooDataContext dc = conn.GetContext())
    {
        IEnumerable<Account> accounts = (from a in dc.Accounts
                                        join m in dc.GroupMembers on
```

```
                                        a.AccountID equals m.AccountID
                                        where m.GroupID == GroupID
                                        && !m.IsApproved
                                        select a);
               result = accounts.ToList();
           }
           return result;
       }
```

Implementing the services/application layer

Once all the repositories are built for single serving purposes we can begin to create the services layer. Again, this layer is responsible for assembling aggregates and performing complex actions with our entities. We will create and modify the following services.

- GroupService
- AlertService
- Redirector
- WebContext

GroupService

The GroupService is really just an abstraction layer from the GroupRepository for the most part. There are a couple of cases wherein we do something other than pass calls through to the repository layer. For the most part, it is there to be expanded later. This class has the following methods:

- int SaveGroup(Group group);
- bool IsOwnerOrAdministrator(Int32 AccountID, Int32 GroupID);
- bool IsOwner(Int32 AccountID, Int32 GroupID);
- bool IsAdministrator(Int32 AccountID, Int32 GroupID);
- bool IsMember(Int32 AccountID, Int32 GroupID);

IsOwnerOrAdministrator

This method is taking two methods—IsOwner and IsAdministrator—aggregating their result into one result.

```
public bool IsOwnerOrAdministrator(Int32 AccountID, Int32 GroupID)
{
    bool result = false;
    if (IsOwner(AccountID, GroupID) || IsAdministrator(AccountID,
                                                       GroupID))
```

```
        result = true;
    return result;
}
```

SaveGroup

Other than the `SaveGroup` method, all other methods are pretty much pass-through methods to a repository method. The `SaveGroup` method on the other hand does some pretty heavy lifting for us. It takes care of creating all the other data items that surround a group. It is currently creating a `BoardForum` and the `GroupForum` data that links this group to the new forum as well as saving the Group as normal.

```
public int SaveGroup(Group group)
{
    int result = 0;
    if(group.GroupID > 0)
    {
        result = _groupRepository.SaveGroup(group);
    }
    else
    {
        result = _groupRepository.SaveGroup(group);
        BoardForum forum = new BoardForum();
        forum.CategoryID = 4; //group forums container
        forum.CreateDate = DateTime.Now;
        forum.LastPostByAccountID =
                            _webContext.CurrentUser.AccountID;
        forum.LastPostByUsername = _webContext.CurrentUser.Username;
        forum.LastPostDate = DateTime.Now;
        forum.Name = group.Name;
        forum.PageName = group.PageName;
        forum.PostCount = 0;
        forum.Subject = group.Name;
        forum.ThreadCount = 0;
        forum.UpdateDate = DateTime.Now;
        int ForumID = _forumRepository.SaveForum(forum);
        //create relationship between the group and forum
        GroupForum gf = new GroupForum();
        gf.ForumID = ForumID;
        gf.GroupID = group.GroupID;
        gf.CreateDate = DateTime.Now;
        _groupForumRepository.SaveGroupForum(gf);
    }
    return result;
}
```

AlertService

In case you have not yet read the previous chapters, the AlertService is woven through all the other code in this site as it provides us with a way to let our users know that something has happened in our site. With Groups this is no different—with an exception that a user doesn't actually do much with our groups. They do make posts in our group-owned forum though! The difference here though is that rather than sending an alert to all their friends about a post in the forum, we will send an alert to all the group owners.

To do this, we have three new methods added to the alert service.

```
void AddNewBoardThreadAlert(BoardCategory category, BoardForum forum,
                            BoardPost post, Group group)
void AddNewBoardPostAlert(BoardCategory category, BoardForum forum,
                          BoardPost post, BoardPost thread, Group group)
void SendAlertToGroup(Alert alert, Group group)
```

The first two methods are exactly identical to every other alert method with the exception that they make a call to the SendAlertToGroup() rather than SendAlertToFriends(). For this reason we will take a look at the third method.

```
private void SendAlertToGroup(Alert alert, Group group)
{
    List<int> groupMembers =
                       _groupMemberRepository.
                       GetMemberAccountIDsByGroupID(group.GroupID);
    foreach (int id in groupMembers)
    {
        alert.AlertID = 0;
        alert.AccountID = id;
        SaveAlert(alert);
    }
}
```

This method takes in the newly-created alert. It then gets a list of groupMembers for the specified group. With these items in hand, it iterates through each groupMember and adds their AccountID to the Alert and then sends the Alert.

 This could potentially be a performance bottleneck. A better way to possibly do this is to create all the alerts first and then create a new SaveAlert() method that takes in a list of Alerts to do a bulk insert.

Redirector

While the `Redirector` class is not that complex, but it is very important as it abstracts our redirection logic out of the pages and puts it higher up into the business layer. This means that if things change in our page structure we have one place to go and make changes. There are of course times when we can't fit redirection into the `Redirector` class—just be sure that you don't put your redirection logic in a page out of sheer convenience!

```
public void GoToGroupsManageGroup(int GroupID)
{
    Redirect("~/Groups/ManageGroup.aspx?GroupID=" +
            GroupID.ToString());
}

public void GoToGroupsMembers(int GroupID, int PageNumber)
{
    Redirect("~/Groups/Members.aspx?GroupID=" + GroupID.ToString() +
            "&PageNumber=" + PageNumber.ToString());
}

public void GoToGroupsViewGroup(int GroupID)
{
    Redirect("~/Groups/ViewGroup.aspx?GroupID=" +
            GroupID.ToString());
}

public void GoToGroupsMembers(int GroupID)
{
    Redirect("~/Groups/Members.aspx?GroupID=" + GroupID.ToString());
}

public void GoToGroupsViewGroup(string GroupPageName)
{
    Redirect("~/Groups/" + GroupPageName + ".aspx");
}
```

There is nothing complex happening in these methods. I just felt that it was important that you saw where this was happening as we will use these methods quite a bit when we start building the UI!

WebContext

Similar to the Redirector, the WebContext class is not all that complex. Its purpose is simple and the way it conforms to its purpose is equally simple. This class is responsible for acting as a gateway to all requests to the HttpContext class. This means that any time we are making a call to query string items, post form items, or anything directly represented by the HttpContext class such as application variables, we should be hitting this class rather than going to the source.

Similar to the Redirector purpose, if anything changes in our application as to where we get or store our data, we can easily (again for the most part) make a change in one place.

There are two additions made to this class — we now have a NewGroup property and a GroupID property.

```
public bool NewGroup
{
    get
    {
        bool result = false;
        if(!string.IsNullOrEmpty(GetQueryStringValue("NewGroup")))
        {
            if(GetQueryStringValue("NewGroup") == "1")
                result = true;
        }
        return result;
    }
}

public Int32 GroupID
{
    get
    {
        Int32 result = 0;
        if(!string.IsNullOrEmpty(GetQueryStringValue("GroupID")))
        {
            result = Convert.ToInt32(GetQueryStringValue("GroupID"));
        }
        return result;
    }
}
```

Implementing the presentation layer

With all the backend out of the way, let's get to building the front end. It is always difficult to decide where to begin when creating an application of this nature. Do you populate the database with some sample test data and build the display page first? Or do you start with the data creation pages first and then work on the display pages? I think this time we will work with the data creation pages first, and then work our way out to the display pages towards the end. With that in mind, let's get started.

ManageGroup

While we could have created two pages to manage our group data—one for new groups and the other to edit groups—I find it far easier to create one page and one UI that allows us to both create and edit groups. This particular page has a couple of interesting features in it that we are providing—a WYSIWYG editor as well as an image upload feature. These two topics are the features that we will work with the most in this discussion.

Before we get started, it is important to know that the page knows its different states by the presence of two query string variables. The first variable is newgroup=1. This obviously tells the page that we intend to create a new group. The second variable is GroupID={number}, which allows us to populate the page with a specified group's data.

WYSIWYG

Our WYSIWYG editor of choice is Xinha (which we have covered before in the previous chapters). To use this editor, all we have to do is drop a textbox with the **TextMode** set to **MultiLine**. Then further down the page, we have to pass the full control ID into the Xinha engine with the following code.

```
<script type="text/javascript">
    xinha_editors[xinha_editors.length] =
                                'ctl00_Content_txtDescription';
    xinha_editors[xinha_editors.length] = 'ctl00_Content_txtBody';
</script>
```

This creates the full-featured WYSIWYG that you see here (you can configure more or less options globally depending on what you need).

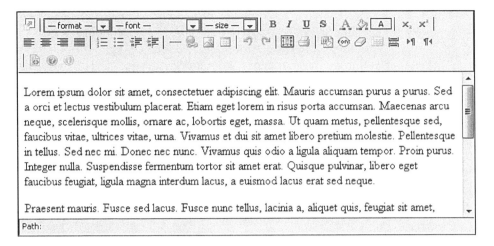

Image upload

While we cover the topic of file uploads in the chapter that covers files, folders, image galleries and the like I felt that we might want to recover some ground. In that chapter, we had the `FileUpload` logic stored in a helper page called `ReceiveFiles.aspx`. While this approach worked well when we had only one area of the site that required uploads, it no longer works when we have two areas of the site that require upload capabilities.

For that reason, we moved all the upload logic into a `FileService`. It is pretty much 100% duplicated from that file (so I won't recover it here). Then in the `ReceiveFiles` page, I removed all the old code and replaced it with a single call to the `FileService.UploadPhotos` method. Once this refactoring was completed, I was able to turn back to address the fact that I wanted the users to be able to upload a photo as their group's logo.

Here is the `SaveGroup` method from the `ManageGroupPresenter` (the rest of the code is standard plumbing code).

```
public void SaveGroup(Group group, HttpPostedFile file, List<long>
                 selectedGroupTypeIDs)
{
    if (group.Description.Length > 2000)
    {
        _view.ShowMessage("Your description is " +
                     group.Description.Length.ToString() +
                     " characters long and can only be 2000
                         characters!");
    }
    else
```

```
    {
        group.AccountID = _webContext.CurrentUser.AccountID;
        group.PageName = group.PageName.Replace(" ", "-");
        //if this is a new group then check to see if the page name
            is in use
        if (group.GroupID == 0 &&
         _groupRepository.CheckIfGroupPageNameExists(group.PageName))
        {
            _view.ShowMessage("The page name you specified is already
                             in use!");
        }
        else
        {
            if (file.ContentLength > 0)
            {
                List<Int64> fileIDs = _fileService.UploadPhotos(1,
                                _webContext.CurrentUser.AccountID,

                                _webContext.Files, 1);
                //should only be one item uploaded!
                if (fileIDs.Count == 1)
                    group.FileID = fileIDs[0];
            }
            group.GroupID = _groupService.SaveGroup(group);
            _groupToGroupTypeRepository.SaveGroupTypesForGroup(
                        selectedGroupTypeIDs,group.GroupID);
            _redirector.GoToGroupsViewGroup(group.PageName);
        }
    }
}
```

As you can see in the immediately preceding code, we are primarily performing
some data validation and clean up tasks. If we have a new group we verify that the
page name that was specified is unique to the system. If the page name is unique,
then we are able to process the save request. Prior to processing the save, we check
to see if a file is being uploaded. If it is, then we make a call to the FileService.
UploadPhotos method and pass in the upload files. From there, we perform
standard save operations. The rest of this page is a standard MVP event and
data plumbing.

Members

With a group successfully created, and with the ability to edit the group in place, we can turn our attention to managing membership. In the membership management page, we will be able to approve new membership requests. We can promote and demote existing members to the status of the administrator (allowing them to perform various tasks down the road). And we can delete members. This UI will have a multi-select checkbox type interface but not with the standard `CheckBoxList` control. In addition to that we will support pagination functionality in a custom manner.

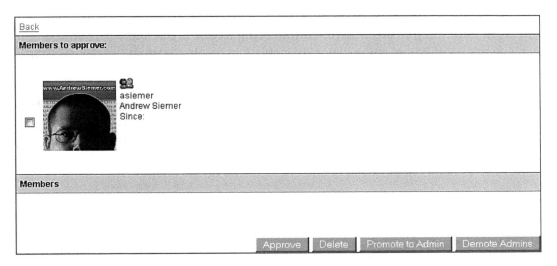

As we mentioned during the creation of our `AccountRepository.`
`GetApprovedAccountsByGroupID()` method—where we pass in the `GroupID` and `PageNumber`—the `PageNumber` input specifies which subset of data we want to see in our display. You will notice in the preceding image that we have a **Back** link (which takes us back to the group page). Next to that if we were on any page other than the first one, we would see **Previous**. Additionally, if we had approved members in the UI, we would also have a **Next** link.

Data pagination

These next and previous concepts are handled in the `MembersPresenter` with the following two methods:

```
public void Next()
{
    _redirector.GoToGroupsMembers(_webContext.GroupID,
                        (_webContext.PageNumber + 1));
```

```
    }

    public void Previous()
    {
        _redirector.GoToGroupsMembers(_webContext.GroupID,
                        (_webContext.PageNumber - 1));
    }
```

As you can see, with the pairing of the logic in the AccountRepository, we have a very simple pagination solution that can be performed with any set of data.

CheckBoxLists without the CheckBoxList control

The other easy thing to implement without being forced to use standard controls is the use of a Repeater and a CheckBox control to create a custom CheckBoxList, which is more preferred. This pairing is quite simply a Repeater control and a CheckBox. We can add any data that we need to capture for each selected checkbox to the CheckBox control as an attribute in the Repeater's OnItemDataBound event.

```
    public void repMembersToApprove_ItemDataBound(object sender,
                                        RepeaterItemEventArgs e)
    {
        if(e.Item.ItemType == ListItemType.AlternatingItem ||
                        e.Item.ItemType == ListItemType.Item)
        {
            ProfileDisplay p = e.Item.FindControl("Profile1") as
                        ProfileDisplay;
            CheckBox chkProfile = e.Item.FindControl("chkProfile") as
                        CheckBox;

            p.LoadDisplay(((Account)e.Item.DataItem));
            chkProfile.Attributes.Add("AccountID",
                    ((Account)e.Item.DataItem).AccountID.ToString());
        }
    }
```

We then have a method in the code behind to extract the selected values for use later.

```
    private List<int> ExtractMemberIDs(Repeater repeater)
    {
        List<int> result = new List<int>();
        foreach (RepeaterItem item in repeater.Items)
        {
            if(item.ItemType == ListItemType.AlternatingItem ||
                        item.ItemType == ListItemType.Item)
            {
```

```
                CheckBox chkProfile = item.FindControl("chkProfile") as
                                CheckBox;
            if(chkProfile.Checked)
                result.Add(Convert.ToInt32(chkProfile.Attributes[
                                        "AccountID"]));
        }
    }
    return result;
}
```

As you can see in the code, we are looking for the `AccountID` attribute that we added in the `OnItemDataBound` event. We do this by iterating through all the items in the `Repeater` and finding and casting our checkbox controls from each item. We can then work with the selected values no matter how many there are in the `Repeater`.

Default

The homepage of our Groups section, the `default.aspx` page, is responsible for listing all the groups in the system when a user first enters this section of the site. This page makes a call to the `GroupRepository` to get all the latest groups. It then bounds that collection of data to a `ListView` and outputs each group. Be aware that each of the group names has actual links to the custom group `PageName.aspx` (we will cover more on this in a moment). Nothing more to this page though.

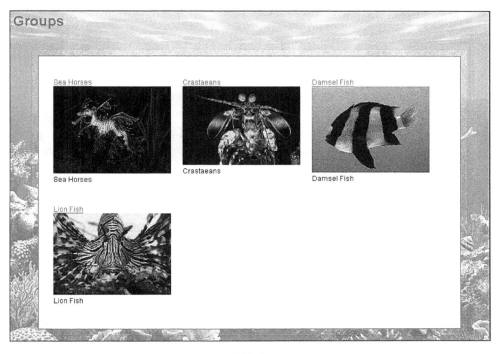

See the code for specific examples of how this works.

UrlRewrite

Before we dig too deep into data management, we find ourselves at a crossroads where we need to dig into our UrlRewrite class again. As we have a PageName field in our Groups we need to discuss how to handle Group PageNames. Once this is complete, we can move on to pulling up and viewing a group.

```
else if
    (application.Request.PhysicalPath.ToLower().Contains("groups") &&
    _webContext.GroupID == 0)
{
    string[] arr =
            application.Request.PhysicalPath.ToLower().Split('\\');
    string groupPageName = arr[arr.Length - 1];
    groupPageName = groupPageName.Replace(".aspx", "");
    Group group = _groupRepository.GetGroupByPageName(groupPageName);
    context.RewritePath("/groups/viewgroup.aspx?GroupID=" +
                    group.GroupID.ToString());
}
```

This code, similar to the other Rewrite code, looks for specific keys in the URL to determine which section of the code it needs to work with. In this case, we are looking for the "groups" identifier to let us know that we are in the Groups section.

 As we are looking for specific works to simply exist in our URL, we are prone to some errors. Keep in mind that someone could write a blog with the page name what-fish-love-to-swim-in-groups.aspx. This technically could kick off the group's rewrite code. Be forewarned!

Once we locate the appropriate keyword, we can load up an instance of our group by the specified page name and do a rewrite to the ViewGroup.aspx page with a passed in GroupID. This one isn't all that complex.

ViewGroup

Now that we have a groups listings page (the homepage) and we have our UrlRewrite class up to speed and capable of handling fancy URLs for our Groups, we can discuss the ViewGroup.aspx page. This page is responsible for showing everyone our group. It will have a private and public viewing feature (which is managed when the group is created/edited). When we link into this page we have a custom URL that corresponds to our actual page. Other than the security concerns of this page and the custom URL, it is just a data display page. In addition to displaying data, it will act as our jumping off point for viewing and managing other sections that are related to the group—such as the group-owned forum.

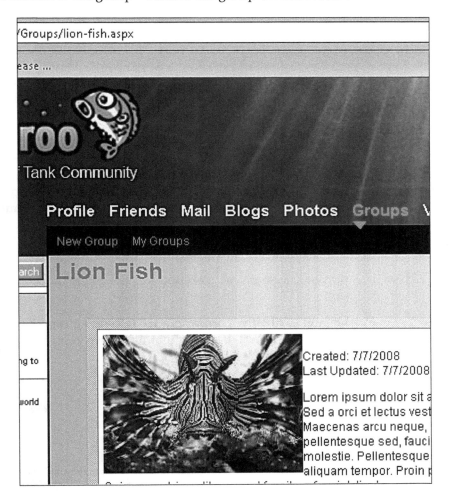

Private/Public

While determining whether a group is public or private is performed simply by checking a bit flag set in the database. Determining who can actually see a private group is a bit more complex.

```
//is this public or private data?
if (group.IsPublic)
{
    _view.ShowPrivate(true);
```

```
    _view.ShowPublic(true);
}
else if (ViewerIsMember())
{
    _view.ShowPrivate(true);
    _view.ShowPublic(true);
}
else
{
    _view.ShowPrivate(false);
    _view.ShowPublic(true);
}
```

Recall that we had created a few help functions to determine if a user was the owner of the group, a member of the group, or an administrator of the group. In our ViewGroupPresenter, we make a call to our ViewMembers method to determine where the user stands.

```
public void ViewMembers()
{
    _redirector.GoToGroupsMembers(_webContext.GroupID);
}
```

This lets us know quickly and easily if we can display the private group. If not, then the user is shown the appropriate message stating that the group is private (and they are prompted to request membership).

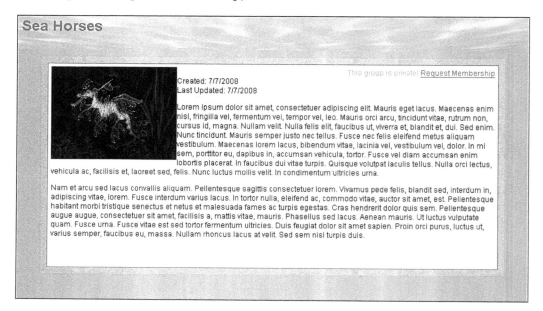

If you are part of the group or the owner of the group, you would see this instead:

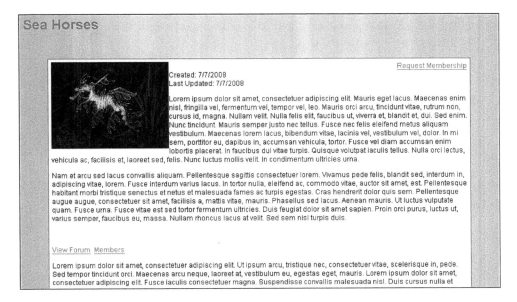

MyGroups

The MyGroups page is a duplication of the homepage in that it streams a bunch of groups. The immediate difference is that all the groups on this page belong to the viewer of the page. In addition to the security check and changed data source, we also offer a couple of additional features. From this page, we can delete the selected group. We also have the ability to link to the ManageGroup.aspx page.

The security comes in the form that this page requires the viewing party to be logged in. From the logged-in user's AccountID (stored in session), we then load the page with a call to the GroupRepository.GetGroupsOwnedByAccount() method from within the MyGroupsPresenter.

```
public void LoadData()
{
_view.LoadData(_groupRepository.GetGroupsOwnedByAccount(_webContext.
                                    CurrentUser.AccountID));
}
```

With each ItemDataBound event in the code behind, we pass in the GroupID to the attributes collection of our edit and delete buttons. We also add a bit of client-side JavaScript to confirm with the user that it is ok to actually perform the delete process on the selected group.

```
protected void lvGroups_ItemDataBound(object sender,
                                    ListViewItemEventArgs e)
{
    if (e.Item.ItemType == ListViewItemType.DataItem)
    {
        Image imgGroupImage = e.Item.FindControl("imgGroupImage") as
                            Image;
        Literal litImageID = e.Item.FindControl("litImageID") as
                            Literal;
        Literal litPageName = e.Item.FindControl("litPageName") as
                            Literal;
        LinkButton lbPageName = e.Item.FindControl("lbPageName") as
                            LinkButton;
        ImageButton ibDelete = e.Item.FindControl("ibDelete") as
                            ImageButton;
        Literal litGroupID = e.Item.FindControl("litGroupID") as
                            Literal;
        ImageButton ibEdit = e.Item.FindControl("ibEdit") as
                            ImageButton;
        ibDelete.Attributes.Add("GroupID", litGroupID.Text);
        ibEdit.Attributes.Add("GroupID", litGroupID.Text);
        ibDelete.Attributes.Add("onclick","return confirm('Are you
                            sure you want to delete this group?');");
        lbPageName.Attributes.Add("PageName", litPageName.Text);
        imgGroupImage.ImageUrl = "/files/photos/" +
                            _presenter.GetImageByID
                (Convert.ToInt64(litImageID.Text), File.Sizes.S);
    }
}
```

Forum enhancements

We discussed earlier that we would have Group-owned-and-operated Forums. To pull this off, we had to add a new category to the board system called specifically **group-forums**. I then restricted that category from the board categories display (the forum homepage). The forum homepage still looks like this:

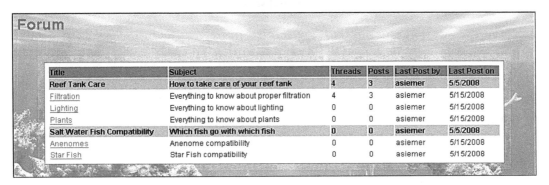

Title	Subject	Threads	Posts	Last Post by	Last Post on
Reef Tank Care	**How to take care of your reef tank**	**4**	**3**	**asiemer**	**5/5/2008**
Filtration	Everything to know about proper filtration	4	3	asiemer	5/15/2008
Lighting	Everything to know about lighting	0	0	asiemer	5/15/2008
Plants	Everything to know about plants	0	0	asiemer	5/15/2008
Salt Water Fish Compatibility	**Which fish go with which fish**	**0**	**0**	**asiemer**	**5/5/2008**
Anenomes	Anenome compatibility	0	0	asiemer	5/15/2008
Star Fish	Star Fish compatibility	0	0	asiemer	5/15/2008

No group category exists here! Also note that there isn't a **sea-horses** present in the display whereas we can clearly link to the **sea-horses** forum from the **sea-horses** group.

```
0/Forums/group-forums/sea-horses.aspx
```

Recall that earlier we discussed that when a group is created by the `GroupService`, we also create a new forum and attach it to the **group-forums** category (category 1). With this in place, when we load up the `ViewGroup` page, we can also load in the forum link for that group.

In addition to this, recall that we added a couple of methods to the `AlertService`. These methods allowed us to send alerts to all the members of the group rather than the friends of the poster. The only thing that we haven't covered up to this point to pull off this integration is how the posting forum page knows if it is a group-owned forum or not.

The only part of the forum system that was modified to create this addition is in the `PostPresenter.Save()` method (covered last chapter). At the very bottom of this method we added a bit of code to determine if we could load a group based on the `ForumID` or not.

Recall that this logic is valid only if we specify that a group can own only one forum (and vice versa). We currently do that by only creating the link at the time that the group is created. However, if you provide other tools for forum or group creation, you will need to keep in mind that some form of validation will need to be put in place, or this group/forum validation that we are currently discussing will need to be changed!

```
if(post.IsThread)
    thread = _postRepository.GetPostByID(post.PostID);
else
    thread = _postRepository.GetPostByID((long)post.ThreadID);
//is this forum part of a group?
Group group = _groupRepository.GetGroupByForumID(forum.ForumID);
    //add an alert to the filter
    if (post.IsThread)
    {
    //is this a group forum?
    if (group != null)
        _alertService.AddNewBoardThreadAlert(category, forum, thread,
                                             group);
        else

            _alertService.AddNewBoardThreadAlert(category, forum,
                                                 thread);
}
    else
    {
    //is this a group forum?
    if (group != null)
        _alertService.AddNewBoardPostAlert(category, forum, post,
                                           thread, group);
        else
            _alertService.AddNewBoardPostAlert(category, forum, post,
                                               thread);
}
    _redirector.GoToForumsViewPost(forum.PageName,category.PageName,
                                   thread.PageName);
```

With this code in place, our forum is not only aware that it is part of a group but is also able to send alerts to group members other than friends.

Summary

With this core framework in place you can see how groups can be used to bring many different systems together in a way that you start to create sub-communities. Obviously, this section has many other features which could be added to it. From the top of my mind I can think of integration in terms of the following features that might make some interesting additions to the group section:

- Messaging
    - You could create a "send to group" WYSIWYG section that sends messages to all the group members, the group's administrators, and/or the group owner.
    - Additionally, you could integrate all the groups that a user is a member of into the messaging system so that the group name could be used as a contact name to blast messages directly from the mail section.
    - To expand on the last bullet, you could also show all the group members as a separate section of their contacts area.

- Friends
    - Group members can be integrated easily as friends.
    - Not only you can specify public, private, friends' areas in your user profiles but also have a filter such as `members of groups I am part of`.

You obviously don't have to think only about how you can bring groups out to your other community features. You could also bring some of your features into the group. Some examples of that are as follows:

- Blogs
    - Any blog posts that a member of the group creates could be flagged and shown on the groups homepage.
    - You could have a top N blog posts section on the group's homepage.

- Forum
  - ○ Rather than force people to read into the forum, you could also post the latest threads (or flaming threads) on the homepage of the group.
  - ○ You could have sticky threads (threads that never get pushed off the board — think memos or news) in the group forums that show up as bulletins on the group's homepage.

- Group Filter
  - ○ In the same way that a user profile has all the alerts posted on the filter, the group homepage could have group alerts posted on it.

Finally, the number of items that can be integrated into your group's homepage is limited to the number of features offered by your site.

11
Comments, Tags, and Ratings

Giving our users the ability to comment, tag, and rate the various content in our site, provides them a level of interactivity that will make them want to come back again and again. There are mainly two reasons for these features to arouse the curiosity of users. First, it is human nature to want to provide their opinions about anything available to them. Once a group of users has offered its opinion on everything, you will find that a second group of users will rear their heads to look at and interact with the highest rated, most heavily commented and tagged content.

In this chapter, we will delve into what it takes to create a flexible system that will allow us to tag, rate, and comment any object in our system (at the database level). We will apply all these three systems to our photo gallery section. Tagging and commenting will be somewhat straightforward in that they will simply take raw user input and tie it to the various content areas. The rating system on the other hand will use the ASP.NET AJAX library to provide multiple attributes in a modal window with the rating control, which when aggregated will provide us with an average score for that item.

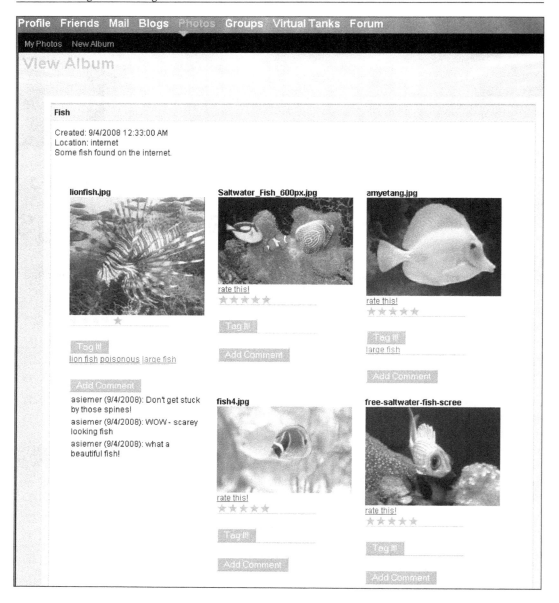

Problem

Let's take a look at the problems discussed in this chapter:

Ratings

The rating system included in the package of the ASP.NET AJAX controls works very well for a flat rating system. It has no issues with showing five stars horizontally or vertically, providing simple mouse over capabilities, capturing click events, and providing several properties to capture the selected input. What it doesn't do well is provide you with a way to capture multiple subratings for a piece of content. That is what we will build here! Clicking on the **rate this** link will throw up a modal window.

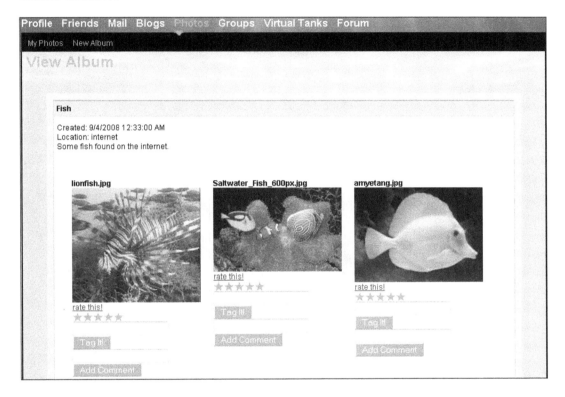

In the modal window, the user will have several dynamically generated attributes to apply individual ratings to. All these ratings are then aggregated to provide the final rating for that item.

Once we have received the rating for an item, we will thank the user for his/her input.

With the next view of this item, we will display the average rating.

Tagging

Tagging is a feature that allows us to attach keywords to an object. Each keyword has a score attached to it that allows us to build a tag cloud with the largest tags sifted to the top showcasing the keywords that have the most use in the system. This particular control will be created in a flexible manner that allows us to capture new tags, display the tags that are attached to an object, display tags that are attached to a section and those attached to the entire site.

Here we add a tag to an image:

With the tags in place showing a subcloud for that item, we can click through to see other content for the same tag words.

Selecting the **large fish** tag will then take us to a page that lists not only other related images but also any other content in the site with the same tag. In this case, selecting the **big fish** tag shows us three other resources with the same tag.

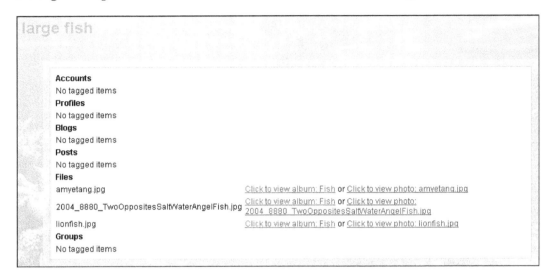

Also note that this page appears to be a resource in our site in the **Tags** directory. This will help us feed the search engine spiders, which in turn should get more users to our site!

Finally, we can go out to the homepage to see a site-wide tag cloud. This tag cloud displays tags with a higher tag count, that is, the tags that are attached to more items, and having a larger font. This quickly identifies the most popular tags to the site's users.

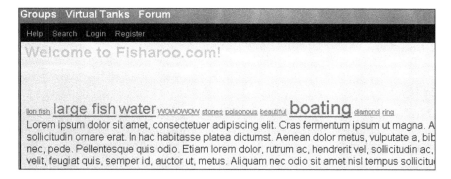

We will fully cover the algorithm used to determine the font size dynamically as well as some of the flexibilities that are baked into this control.

Commenting

Commenting allows our users to give more specific input about a resource. This can be integrated later into our search features to also help us get our content to our users. In addition to this, it allows our users to comment back and forth about a resource, generating curiosity from other users.

Design

Let's take a look at the design for this feature.

Ratings

The ASP.NET AJAX Control Toolkit provides you with a fair amount of flexibility when it comes to creating the standard five-star ratings that you can see scattered around on the Internet. You are able to create horizontal or vertically positioned stars, stars that can be run from left to right, and right to left. You can even swap out the stars for any other image such as happy faces, if you really want to.

 More information regarding the toolkit can be found here: `http://www.codeplex.com/AjaxControlToolkit` and `http://www.asp.net/ajax/ajaxcontroltoolkit/`.

The one thing that the control in the toolkit does not do is allow you to show multiple attributes to be rated for an item. It also does not allow you to aggregate those ratings to be rolled up into one global rating. It is this more flexible control, which we will discuss and build here.

Before we discuss rating attributes of an item, we need to discuss what an item is. In our community site, we may want to rate just about anything that is awfully vague and generally hard to work with. So we will say that our definition of "anything" is any table in the database (you will see more use of this object concept when we discuss comments and tags). In order to keep track of our objects, we will need to create a container that we can use as a hard reference.

For this, we will create a `SystemObjects` table. This will hold the name and `SystemObjectID` for each of the tables that we want to add ratings to. If we add more tables to our system that could benefit from ratings, we can easily extend our rating tool to work with the next object.

Now that we know what our objects are, we can discuss our attributes that will actually get individual ratings. For this, we will need the ability to have a flexible system that allows each unique object to have its own attribute definitions. We will create a `SystemObjectRatingOptions` table to manage these attributes. Here you will see the name of the attribute and its description. We will show the name in our display and add the description to a tooltip. In addition to this, we will create the relationship to our `SystemObjects` table. This will allow us to have custom attributes for something like images—as many as we like.

From there, we will need the ability to capture the actual end user feedback in the form of a rating. Each rating will apply to each attribute of a given SystemObject (or table). As individuals will be rating a unique item (an actual record) of the defined type of SystemObject, we will also need to track the record ID of the rated item in question. This will allow us to know that we are rating a specific record in the Files or Photos table so that we can easily query the data that we need.

With each rating we will also capture a score (1-5 in our demo). This will allow us to have an aggregate rating for each attribute. It will also allow us to have an aggregated rating for the actual rated item. We will simply average all scores collected for an item to provide us with a high-level, generic rating. With this system, we will also have the data that we would need for more sophisticated reports and displays as time permits.

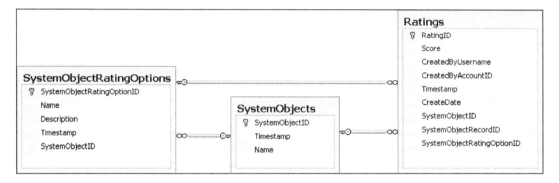

Tags

Tagging allows the users of your community to provide keywords that categorize your content. This in turn helps other users to locate the appropriate content in your site. The more the number of people who apply for a specific keyword to the content of your site, the larger the keywords displayed in the cloud.

This system will be built using the same SystemObjects concept. This will allow us to apply tags to any object defined in our system. In addition to the SystemObjects table, we will also have a Tags table. This will allow us to keep track of all of the unique tags that we collect over time. And this is where we will maintain our aggregated tag counts. While we could sum the count on the fly, it is easier and more efficient to build the sum as we collect new tags.

In addition to collecting new tags and maintaining the definition of our SystemObjects, we also need to maintain the relationship between our tags and the SystemObjects. We will do this with our SystemObjectTags table. This table will also keep track of who applied the tag and when.

With the tables defined, we should keep in mind that we want to build a flexible control. In our case, we will build a control that will not only collect tags for an object, but will also display the tags for a given item (a mini tag cloud if you will). We will also be able to keep track of all the tags for a parent (in the case that we are tagging images, we can have a tag cloud for our image gallery). And finally, we will add functionality to our control that will allow us to build a high-level global tag cloud that could be used on your site's homepage. This cloud will display the most popular tags for all of the collected tags.

The final complexity is what completes the tag cloud. We will have the tables in place to hold the data appropriately. We will have the control to capture and display the data. But the real kicker to a tag cloud is how it is displayed. A **tag cloud** displays each tag (a keyword or words) with a size relative to its own ranking in the overall popularity of the cloud. This means that the more the tags used in your cloud, the larger the tags will be in the cloud. On the other hand, the lesser the tags used, the smaller the tags will be in the cloud. We will fully discuss the algorithm behind this sorting when the time comes.

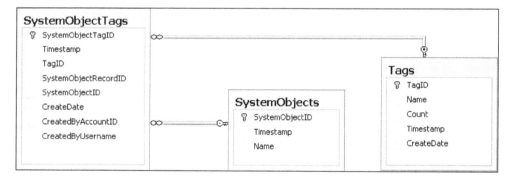

Comments

Compared to our fancy ratings and tagging controls, the commenting control is not very cool. Though it is not cool, it still fits this chapter in that this is another method for your users to provide very specific content about your content. The comments will come in handy later when you integrate the gathered content into your site's search results. Also, our friendly search engines will love to eat up your new content-specific comments.

This system, like the other two, will be built around the `SystemObject` table. In addition to that table, we will have a `Comments` table. The `Comments` table will not only gather all the normal data but also the body of the comment. That's it!

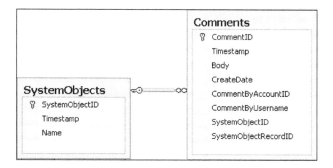

Solution

Let's take a look at our solution.

Implementing the database

Let's take a look at what is needed in the database.

SystemObjects

The `SystemObjects` table is at the center of this chapter's list of features. Having said that, this table is the easiest part of this equation. It simply keeps track of all the tables in the system. Specifically, it keeps track of the table names and maintains an ID for each name.

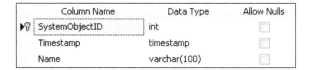

Ratings

The Ratings table is responsible for holding all the end user ratings. As you can see each rating ties back to the SystemObjects table and also directly to the record within the specified table. In addition to that, we are also tracking the Option that was rated. The most important part of this table though is the **Score** field. The **Score** tracks the selected number of stars (in our case) that the end user has selected.

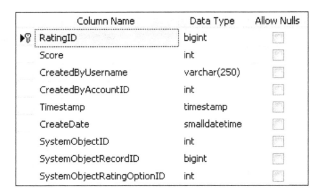

Column Name	Data Type	Allow Nulls
RatingID	bigint	
Score	int	
CreatedByUsername	varchar(250)	
CreatedByAccountID	int	
Timestamp	timestamp	
CreateDate	smalldatetime	
SystemObjectID	int	
SystemObjectRecordID	bigint	
SystemObjectRatingOptionID	int	

System object rating options

In addition to the ratings table we also have the SystemObjectRatingOptions table. This table tracks all the options that are available for each of our system objects.

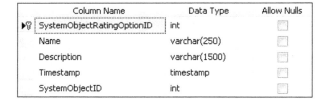

Column Name	Data Type	Allow Nulls
SystemObjectRatingOptionID	int	
Name	varchar(250)	
Description	varchar(1500)	
Timestamp	timestamp	
SystemObjectID	int	

Here is the SQL:

```
CREATE TABLE [dbo].[SystemObjectRatingOptions](
    [SystemObjectRatingOptionID] [int] IDENTITY(1,1) NOT NULL,
    [Name] [varchar](250) COLLATE SQL_Latin1_General_CP1_CI_AS NOT
    NULL,
    [Description] [varchar](1500) COLLATE SQL_Latin1_General_CP1_CI_AS
    NOT NULL,
    [Timestamp] [timestamp] NOT NULL,
    [SystemObjectID] [int] NOT NULL,
 CONSTRAINT [PK_SystemObjectRatingOptions] PRIMARY KEY CLUSTERED
 (
```

```
    [SystemObjectRatingOptionID] ASC
)WITH (PAD_INDEX  = OFF, IGNORE_DUP_KEY = OFF) ON [PRIMARY]
) ON [PRIMARY]
```

Tags

The Tags table is responsible for holding all the textual tags that our users attach to the various objects in our system. Knowing that we intend to collect a number of the same tags for multiple objects in our system, it is important that we maintain a unique list of tags with counts rather than a single entry for every tag entered into the system and then having to sum up the tags to get a count. Performance-wise, maintaining the aggregate value as we collect tags will easily outperform determining the summed value each time we need the count.

Column Name	Data Type	Allow Nulls
TagID	bigint	☐
Name	varchar(200)	☐
Count	int	☐
Timestamp	timestamp	☐
CreateDate	smalldatetime	☐

System object tags

This then brings us to our SystemObjectTags table. It is responsible for maintaining details of which tag is connected to which record of a certain type of object. This table simply maintains various record IDs to keep track of the relationships.

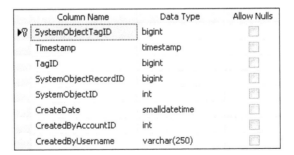

Column Name	Data Type	Allow Nulls
SystemObjectTagID	bigint	☐
Timestamp	timestamp	☐
TagID	bigint	☐
SystemObjectRecordID	bigint	☐
SystemObjectID	int	☐
CreateDate	smalldatetime	☐
CreatedByAccountID	int	☐
CreatedByUsername	varchar(250)	☐

Comments

This finally brings us to the Comments table. Of the three features, this is by far the easiest to implement as this table keeps track of everything for us directly. Each comment in this case is assumed to be unique and is therefore directly tied to an object and a record within that object. We also keep track of the user who left the comment (**CommentByAccountID**) and when (**CreateDate**) he/she did. The current size of the comment can be up to 2,000 characters. But if your community requires large comments, you can of course increase this number.

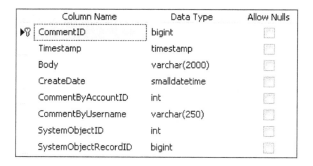

Column Name	Data Type	Allow Nulls
CommentID	bigint	
Timestamp	timestamp	
Body	varchar(2000)	
CreateDate	smalldatetime	
CommentByAccountID	int	
CommentByUsername	varchar(250)	
SystemObjectID	int	
SystemObjectRecordID	bigint	

Creating the relationships

Once all the tables are created, we can create all the relationships.

For this set of tables, we have relationships between the following tables:

- Ratings and Accounts
- Ratings and SystemObjectRatingOptions
- Ratings and SystemObjects
- SystemRatingOptions and SystemObjects
- SystemObjectTags and Accounts
- SystemObjectTags and SystemObjects
- SystemObjectTags and Tags
- Comments and Accounts
- Comment and SystemObjects

Setting up the data access layer

To set up the data access layer, follow the steps mentioned next:

- Open the `Fisharoo.dbml` file.
- Open up your **Server Explorer** window.
- Expand your Fisharoo connection.
- Expand your tables. If you don't see your new tables try hitting the **Refresh** icon or right-clicking on the tables and clicking **Refresh**.
- Then drag your new tables onto the design surface.
- Hit **Save** and you should now have the domain objects to work with, as shown in the following screenshot:

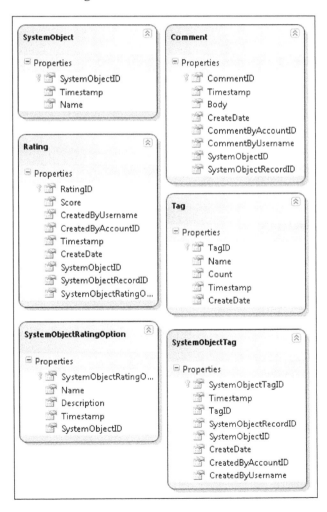

Keep in mind that we are not letting LINQ track our relationships. So go ahead and delete them from the design surface. Your design surface should have the same items that you see in the screenshot (though perhaps in a different arrangement!).

Building repositories

With the addition of new tables will come the addition of new repositories so that we can get at the data stored in those tables. We will be creating the following repositories to support our needs:

* `RatingRepository`
* `SystemObjectRatingOptionRepository`
* `TagRepository`
* `SystemObjectTagRepository`
* `CommentRepository`

Each of our repositories will generally have a method for select by ID, select all by parent ID, save, and delete. Once you have seen one repository you have pretty much seen them all. Review previous chapters, the appendices, or the included code, for example, of a standard repository. However, I will discuss anything that varies from standard!

RatingRepository

Let's take a look at the `RatingRepository`.

HasRatedBefore()

The `HasRatedBefore()` method takes in a `SystemObjectID`, `SystemObjectRecordID`, and `AccountID` to perform a check against the account to determine if that account has already provided a rating for the specified object. If it has, then the `HasRatedBefore()` method returns `true`, otherwise `false`.

```
public bool HasRatedBefore(int SystemObjectID, long
                           SystemObjectRecordID, int AccountID)
{
    bool result = false;
    using(FisharooDataContext dc = conn.GetContext())
    {
        if (dc.Ratings.Where(r => r.SystemObjectID == SystemObjectID
                                                    &&
            r.SystemObjectRecordID == SystemObjectRecordID &&
            r.CreatedByAccountID == AccountID).Count() > 0)
            result = true;
    }
    return result;
}
```

In this method, we instantiate a result variable as Boolean and assign it a `false` value. From there, we are performing a LINQ query against the collection of `Ratings` in the DataContext object. In this query, we will locate the specific record with three property checks against the `SystemObjectID`, `SystemObjectRecordID`, and `CreatedByAccountID`. We will then perform a `Count()` on the result of our query. If the count is greater than 0, then we know that we have already received a rating from this user for this specific item. We will therefore set our result variable to `true`. We will then return the result.

GetCurrentRating()

The `GetCurrentRating()` method is responsible for determining the average rating across all the rated options for a specific object in the system.

```
public int GetCurrentRating(int SystemObjectID, long
                            SystemObjectRecordID)
{
    double result;
    using(FisharooDataContext dc = conn.GetContext())
    {
        if (dc.Ratings.Where(r => r.SystemObjectID == SystemObjectID
                    && r.SystemObjectRecordID ==
                    SystemObjectRecordID).Count() > 0)
            result =
                dc.Ratings.Where(
                    r => r.SystemObjectID == SystemObjectID &&
                    r.SystemObjectRecordID == SystemObjectRecordID).
                    Select(r => r.Score).Average();
        else
            result = 0;
    }
    return Convert.ToInt32(result);
}
```

This method instantiates the result as a double (the `Average()` method, which we will call in a second, returns double). We then perform a check against the system to see if we have any ratings for the specified object. If we do, then we perform a query against our `Ratings` collection looking for our specified object. We are only interested in returning the average score for our object, so that we can locate our ratings and then call the `Select()` method. The `Select()` method fetches the **Score** field from all the objects. From there, we can call `Average()` to get our average across all the scores for all the ratings we have received. This value is then applied to our result variable. If we did not have any ratings, then we set the result to 0. Finally, we cast the result to an `int` and then return the result.

SaveRatings()

We are used to building a repository with a single object save method. This is fairly straightforward. Here we are going to focus on building a method that can handle more than one rating at a time.

```
public void SaveRatings(List<Rating> ratings)
{
    using(FisharooDataContext dc = conn.GetContext())
    {
        //get a list of items that have been rated before
        List<long> previouslyRatedSystemObjectRecordIDs =
                    dc.Ratings.Where(r => r.CreatedByAccountID ==
                                    ratings[0].CreatedByAccountID).
                    Select(r=>r.SystemObjectRecordID).ToList();
        foreach (Rating rating in ratings)
        {
            //be sure that this user has not already rated this
            // particular system object before
            if
                (!previouslyRatedSystemObjectRecordIDs.
                Contains(rating.SystemObjectRecordID))
                dc.Ratings.InsertOnSubmit(rating);
        }
        dc.SubmitChanges();
    }
}
```

This method is not really that complex. It simply takes advantage of LINQ to SQL's bulk insert capability. First, it takes in a generic list of `Rating` objects. Once it has opened a connection and got the DataContext, we determine which ratings the user has previously rated (as we don't want more than one rating per user, per object!). We then iterate through all the passed in ratings. Once we have made sure that the user has not already rated the option in question, we attach the rating to the DataContext. With all the appropriate ratings attached, we submit our changes with a bulk insert.

SystemObjectRatingOptionRepository

This particular repository has only three methods, `GetSystemObjectRatingOptionsBySystemObjectID()` (now that is a mouth full), `SaveSystemObjectRatingOption()`, and `DeleteSystemObjectRatingOption()`. These are all very standard methods that do just what they say. Looking at the code for this repository is a good example of a standard repository!

You will find code similar to this to select a record:

```
result = dc.SystemObjectRatingOptions.Where(soro =>
                                    soro.SystemObjectID ==
                                    SystemObjectID).ToList();
```

And code similar to this to save a record:

```
if(systemObjectRatingOption.SystemObjectRatingOptionID > 0)
{
    dc.SystemObjectRatingOptions.Attach(systemObjectRatingOption,
                                 true);
}
else
{
    dc.SystemObjectRatingOptions.InsertOnSubmit(systemObjectRatingOpt
ion);
}
dc.SubmitChanges();
```

And code similar to this to delete a record:

```
dc.SystemObjectRatingOptions.Attach(systemObjectRatingOption, true);
dc.SystemObjectRatingOptions.DeleteOnSubmit(systemObjectRatingOption);
dc.SubmitChanges();
```

TagRepository

This repository is used heavily in the building of our tag clouds. We have several methods to look at here.

GetTagByName()

The GetTagByName() method is responsible for looking for a tag by its name.

```
public Tag GetTagByName(string Name)
{
    Tag result = null;
    using(FisharooDataContext dc = conn.GetContext())
    {
        result = dc.Tags.Where(t => t.Name == Name).FirstOrDefault();
    }
    return result;
}
```

GetTagByID()

The `GetTagByID()` method is the same as the `GetTagByName()` with the exception that it looks for an item by its ID:

```
public Tag GetTagByID(int TagID)
{
    Tag result = null;
    using(FisharooDataContext dc = conn.GetContext())
    {
        result = dc.Tags.Where(t => t.TagID ==
                                 TagID).FirstOrDefault();
    }
    return result;
}
```

GetTagsGlobal()

The `GetTagsGlobal()` method is responsible for getting tags at the site level. It looks at all the tags for all the defined objects and returns a specified number. It orders the tags by their count in descending order and then uses the `Take()` method to specify how many tags to return. This method is used to build the site-level tag cloud.

```
public List<Tag> GetTagsGlobal(int TagsToTake)
{
    List<Tag> results = null;
    using(FisharooDataContext dc = conn.GetContext())
    {
        results = (from t in dc.Tags
                  select t).Distinct().OrderByDescending(t =>
                                  t.Count) Take(TagsToTake).ToList();
    }
    return results;
}
```

GetTagsBySystemObject()

This method is similar to the `GetTagsGlobal()` method in that it gets all the tags for a cloud. This method is a little different in that it gets the tag only for a specified object type. It only returns a specified number of tags by their count in descending order. Note that we use a `join` to get the tags through the `SystemObjectTags` table:

```
public List<Tag> GetTagsBySystemObject(int SystemObjectID, int
                                       TagsToTake)
{
    List<Tag> results = null;
    using(FisharooDataContext dc = conn.GetContext())
```

```
    {
        results = (from t in dc.Tags
                    join sot in dc.SystemObjectTags on t.TagID equals
                    sot.TagID
                    where sot.SystemObjectID == SystemObjectID
                    select t).Distinct().OrderByDescending
                    (t=>t.Count).Take(TagsToTake).ToList();
    }
    return results;
}
```

GetTagsBySystemObjectAndRecordID()

Finally, we come to the method that gets all the tags for a specified object down to the record level. This is for a specific item of a certain type of object. This method is used to display all the tags next to the item that was tagged.

```
public List<Tag> GetTagsBySystemObjectAndRecordID(int SystemObjectID,
                                        long SystemObjectRecordID)
{
    List<Tag> results = null;
    using (FisharooDataContext dc = conn.GetContext())
    {
        results = (from t in dc.Tags
                    join sot in dc.SystemObjectTags on t.TagID equals
                    sot.TagID
                    where sot.SystemObjectID == SystemObjectID &&
                       sot.SystemObjectRecordID == SystemObjectRecordID
                    select t).Distinct().OrderBy(t =>
                                            t.CreateDate).ToList();
    }
    return results;
}
```

SystemObjectTagRepository

There are three methods in this repository, GetSystemObjectByTagID(), SaveSystemObjectTag(), and DeleteSystemObjectTag(). We will discuss the GetSystemObjectByTagID() method here.

GetSystemObjectByTagID()

This is a rather large method. It is used to get all the objects that a tag is related to. This method is used when we display the tag and its links by clicking on a tag link.

This method allows for only one tag to be loaded currently. But that restriction is only on the method input side. All the internals of this method will work with more than one tag though.

```
public List<SystemObjectTagWithObjects> GetSystemObjectsByTagID(int
                                                             TagID)
{
    List<SystemObjectTagWithObjects> result = new
                            List<SystemObjectTagWithObjects>();
    List<SystemObjectTag> tags = new List<SystemObjectTag>();
    List<Account> accounts = new List<Account>();
    List<Profile> profiles = new List<Profile>();
    List<Blog> blogs = new List<Blog>();
    List<BoardPost> posts = new List<BoardPost>();
    List<File> files = new List<File>();
    List<FileType> fileTypes = new List<FileType>();
    List<Folder> folders = new List<Folder>();
    List<Group> groups = new List<Group>();
    using(FisharooDataContext dc = conn.GetContext())
    {
        tags =
            dc.SystemObjectTags.Where(sot => sot.TagID == TagID).
            OrderByDescending(sot => sot.CreateDate).ToList();
        accounts =
            dc.Accounts.Where(
                a =>
                tags.Where(t => t.SystemObjectID == 1).Select(t =>
                        t.SystemObjectRecordID).Contains(a.AccountID))
                .Distinct().ToList();
        profiles =
            dc.Profiles.Where(
                p =>
                tags.Where(t => t.SystemObjectID == 2).Select(t =>
                        t.SystemObjectRecordID).Contains(p.ProfileID))
                .Distinct().ToList();
        blogs =
            dc.Blogs.Where(
                b =>
                tags.Where(t => t.SystemObjectID == 3).Select(t =>
                        t.SystemObjectRecordID).Contains(b.BlogID))
                .Distinct().ToList();
        posts =
            dc.BoardPosts.Where(
                bp =>
```

```
                   tags.Where(t => t.SystemObjectID == 4).Select(t =>
                         t.SystemObjectRecordID).Contains(bp.PostID))
            .Distinct().ToList();
        files =
            dc.Files.Where(
                f =>
                tags.Where(t => t.SystemObjectID == 5).Select(t =>
                         t.SystemObjectRecordID).Contains(f.FileID))
            .Distinct().ToList();
        fileTypes = dc.FileTypes.ToList();
        for (int i = 0; i < files.Count();i++)
        {
            files[i].Extension =
                fileTypes.Where(ft => ft.FileTypeID ==
                         files[i].FileTypeID).Select(ft => ft.Name)
                    .FirstOrDefault();
        }
        folders =
                dc.Folders.Where(folder => files.Select(f =>
                         f.DefaultFolderID).
                         Contains(folder.FolderID)).ToList();
        groups =
            dc.Groups.Where(
                g =>
                tags.Where(t => t.SystemObjectID == 6).Select(t =>
                         t.SystemObjectRecordID).Contains(g.GroupID))
            .Distinct().ToList();
    }
    foreach (SystemObjectTag tag in tags)
    {
        switch(tag.SystemObjectID)
        {
            case 1:
                result.Add(new SystemObjectTagWithObjects()
                {SystemObjectTag = tag,Account = accounts.Where
                (a=>a.AccountID == tag.SystemObjectRecordID).
                FirstOrDefault()});
                break;
            case 2:
                result.Add(new
                        SystemObjectTagWithObjects()
                        {SystemObjectTag = tag, Profile = profiles
                        .Where(p=>p.ProfileID ==
                        tag.SystemObjectRecordID).FirstOrDefault()});
                break;
            case 3:
```

```
                result.Add(new SystemObjectTagWithObjects() {
                        SystemObjectTag = tag, Blog = blogs.
                Where(b => b.BlogID == tag.SystemObjectRecordID)
                        .FirstOrDefault() });
                break;
            case 4:
                result.Add(new SystemObjectTagWithObjects() {
                        SystemObjectTag = tag, BoardPost = posts.
                Where(p => p.PostID == tag.SystemObjectRecordID).
                        FirstOrDefault() });
                break;
            case 5:
                //need to get the file for use in getting the folder
                  as well
                File file = files.Where(f => f.FileID ==
                        tag.SystemObjectRecordID).FirstOrDefault();
                result.Add(new SystemObjectTagWithObjects() {
                        SystemObjectTag = tag, File = file , Folder =
                folders.Where(f=>f.FolderID ==
                        file.DefaultFolderID).FirstOrDefault()});
                break;
            case 6:
                result.Add(new SystemObjectTagWithObjects() {
                        SystemObjectTag = tag, Group = groups.
                Where(g => g.GroupID == tag.SystemObjectRecordID).
                        FirstOrDefault() });
                break;
        }
    }
    return result;
}
```

Though this method appears to be big and complex, it's not really. Initially, we get a list of tags by the `TagID` that was passed in. We then get a list of all the objects that the tag is attached to. Currently, in addition to Accounts, Profiles, Blogs, Posts, Files, and Groups, we also get `FileTypes` and `Folders`.

Once we have all this information uploaded, we can iterate through each tag and load the `SystemObjectTagWithObjects` object, which we have created especially for this purpose. It carries the `Tag` and the objects that are related to it.

```
public class SystemObjectTagWithObjects
{
    public SystemObjectTag SystemObjectTag { get; set; }
    public Account Account { get; set; }
    public Profile Profile { get; set; }
```

```
public Blog Blog { get; set; }
public BoardPost BoardPost { get; set; }
public File File { get; set; }
public Folder Folder { get; set; }
public Group Group { get; set; }
}
```

We then return a list of `SystemObjectTagWithObjects`, which we can then bind to a `Repeater` on the display side.

CommentRepository

This repository is pretty close to a standard repository. Other than the normal `get` and `delete` method, we also have a `GetCommentsBySystemObject()` method.

GetCommentsBySystemObject()

This method gets a list of comments for the object they are attached to.

```
public List<Comment> GetCommentsBySystemObject(int SystemObjectID,
                                        long SystemObjectRecordID)
{
    List<Comment> results = null;
    using(FisharooDataContext dc = conn.GetContext())
    {
        results =
            dc.Comments.Where(
                c => c.SystemObjectID == SystemObjectID &&
                    c.SystemObjectRecordID == SystemObjectRecordID).
                OrderByDescending(c => c.CreateDate).
                ToList();
    }
    return results;
}
```

Implementing the services/application layer

Once all the repositories are built for single-serving purposes, we can begin to create the services layer. Again, this layer is responsible for assembling aggregates and performing complex actions with our entities. We will create and modify the following services:

- `TagService`
- `Configuration`
- `WebContext`
- `Extensions`

TagService

The `TagService` has a few things that are responsible for adding tags and calculating font sizes.

AddTag()

We have the `AddTag()` method that takes care of adding Tags to our database. You may ask why we can't just take care of that in our `TagRepository`. In this case, we are doing more than just shoving a new record into the system. Here we need to see if we already have the tag or not. If we don't, then we need to create a new tag. If we do have the tag already, then we need to increment the count for that tag. Then we can save the tag back into the system.

In addition to adding a tag into the system, we also need to create the relationship for that tag and the object it is related to. This is a straightforward job. We simply spin up a new `SystemObjectTag` with the appropriate `TagID`. Then we can toss that into the database.

```
public void AddTag(string TagName, int SystemObjectID, long
                SystemObjectRecordID)
{
    Tag tag = _tagRepository.GetTagByName(TagName);
    if (tag == null)
    {
        tag = new Tag();
        tag.CreateDate = DateTime.Now;
        tag.Name = TagName;
        tag.Count = 1;
    }
    else
    {
        tag.Count += 1;
    }
    tag = _tagRepository.SaveTag(tag);
    SystemObjectTag sysObjTag = new SystemObjectTag();
    sysObjTag.CreateDate = DateTime.Now;
    sysObjTag.CreatedByAccountID = _webContext.CurrentUser.AccountID;
    sysObjTag.CreatedByUsername = _webContext.CurrentUser.Username;
    sysObjTag.SystemObjectID = SystemObjectID;
    sysObjTag.SystemObjectRecordID = SystemObjectRecordID;
    sysObjTag.TagID = tag.TagID;
    _systemObjectTagRepository.SaveSystemObjectTag(sysObjTag);
}
```

CalculateFontSize()

The `CalculateFontSize()` method is responsible for taking a collection of `Tags` and calculating the font size for each one. There is a bit to this calculation in that some tags may have a count as large as 389,654,980 (perhaps in a very popular site!) while other tags may only have been applied to a couple of items. If those were the numbers we used to calculate the font size, we may end up with a tag that is larger than the page or one that is so small that you can't read it. For this reason, we need to get the numbers to fit between something more reasonable. This is the calculation that we will discuss.

Before we look at the method in its entirety, let's discuss some of the variables that we will be working with:

- `MinimumRange`: This variable will hold the smallest count in our set of tags. This will form the lower bound of our collection. It is global to the calculation.

- `MaximumRange`: This variable will hold the largest count in our set of tags. This will form the upper bound of our collection. It is global to the calculation.

- `Delta`: This variable will hold the difference between our `MinimumRange` and our `MaximumRange`. It is global to the calculation.

- `Tag.InitialValue`: This will hold a copy of the `Count` for each tag.

- `Tag.MinimumOffset`: This is the `InitialValue`- `MinimumRange`.

- `Tag.Ranged`: This value is the `MinimumOffset` divided by the Delta.

- `Tag.PreCalculatedValue`: This is the `Ranged` value multiplied by the difference of the largest font size and the smallest font size subtracted by one (largest-smallest-1).

- `Tag.FinalCalculatedValue`: This is the `PreCalculatedValue` plus one.

- `Tag.FontSize`: This is the `FinalCalculatedValue` plus the smallest font size.

The result of all of these calculations is a set of tags that grow smoothly regardless of the difference between your smallest tag count and your largest tag count and regardless of the difference between your smallest font size and your largest font size.

The next complexity to this method is how we want to sort the tags in our cloud. Shall we sort them from small to tall, or from tall to small, or randomly? We will leave this up to a configuration value. If we want to sort the tags small to tall, we can use the `OrderBy()` method on the `Tags` collection. If we want to sort the tags tall to small, we can use the `OrderByDescending()` method. What do we do if we want to sort the tags randomly? We will add a new method to our `Extensions` class that will extend a Generic List of type Tag called `ShuffleList()`, which will handle shuffling the items in the collection. We will discuss that shortly.

```
public List<Tag> CalculateFontSize(List<Tag> Tags)
{
    decimal MinimumRange;
    decimal MaximumRange;
    decimal Delta;
    //get the smallest count in this list
    MinimumRange = (Tags.OrderBy(t => t.Count).Take(1).Select(t =>
                            t.Count).FirstOrDefault()) * 100;
    //get the largest count in this list
    MaximumRange = (Tags.OrderByDescending(t =>
                    t.Count).Take(1).Select(t => t.Count).
                    FirstOrDefault()) * 100;
    //determine the difference between the minimum and the maximum
    Delta = MaximumRange - MinimumRange;
    if (Tags.Count > 1)
    {
        for (int i = 0; i < Tags.Count(); i++)
        {
            //set a working value
            Tags[i].InitialValue = Tags[i].Count*100;
            //calculate the minimum offset
            Tags[i].MinimumOffset = Tags[i].InitialValue -
                            MinimumRange;
            //calculate the ranged value
            Tags[i].Ranged = Tags[i].MinimumOffset/Delta;
            //calculate the pre calculation
            Tags[i].PreCalculatedValue = Tags[i].Ranged*
                        ((_configuration.TagCloudLargestFontSize -
                        _configuration.AddToTagCloudFontSize) - 1);
            //calculate the final value
            Tags[i].FinalCalculatedValue = Tags[i].PreCalculatedValue
                            + 1;
            //calculate the font size
            Tags[i].FontSize =
                Convert.ToInt32(Tags[i].FinalCalculatedValue +
                            _configuration.AddToTagCloudFontSize);
        }
    }
}
```

```
//if a standard sort is not what you require, you can call
  Tags.Sort
//  The Tags.Sort() method (in the Domain/Tag.cs partial class)
    can be
//  modified to use different properties to sort by
if (_sortOrder == CloudSortOrder.Ascending) //small to tall
{
    Tags = Tags.OrderBy(t => t.FinalCalculatedValue).ToList();
}
else if (_sortOrder == CloudSortOrder.Descending) //tall to small
{
    Tags = Tags.OrderByDescending(t =>
                            t.FinalCalculatedValue).ToList();
}
else
{
    Tags.ShuffleList(); //randomize!
}
return Tags;
}
```

Extensions

We will add one extension method to our `Extensions` class called `ShuffleList()`, which is responsible for shuffling the items in our list of Tags. I found this snippet on Experts-Exchange.com at `http://www.experts-exchange.com/Programming/Languages/C_Sharp/Q_22571864.html`

ShuffleList()

```
public static List<Tag> ShuffleList(this List<Tag> listToShuffle)
{
    Random randomClass = new Random();
    for (int k = listToShuffle.Count-1; k > 1; --k)
    {
        int randIndx = randomClass.Next(k); //
        Tag temp = listToShuffle[k];
        listToShuffle[k] = listToShuffle[randIndx]; // move random
                                            num to end of list.
        listToShuffle[randIndx] = temp;
    }
    return listToShuffle;
}
```

WebContext

The `WebContext` class is responsible for handling anything that comes and goes between the `Session`, the `QueryString`, and the `Form` collections and anything else that we might want to deal with in the `HttpContext`.

SelectedRatings

The `SelectedRatings` property handles a `Dictionary<int, int>` collection that is stored in the `Session`. This collection is responsible for handling ratings that are collected for various options attached to an object. The first `int` is the `RatingOptionRecordID` and the second `int` is the `Rating` (score) that was applied to that `SystemObjectRatingOptionID`. This collection is built up prior to the user saving their rating options. What I mean to say is that every time a user adds a dictionary item to the `SelectedRatings` property, it adds the item to a collection stored in the Session rather than resetting the value all together. We will see how this plays out once we start to build our `Ratings` control.

If you are wondering about how this collection is handled — if it continues to grow — you should know that there is another method (coming up next) that handles the clearing of this collection.

```
public Dictionary<int, int> SelectedRatings
{
    get
    {
        Dictionary<int, int> result = new Dictionary<int, int>();
        if(GetFromSession("SelectedRatings") != null)
        {
            result = GetFromSession("SelectedRatings") as
                    Dictionary<int, int>;
        }
        return result;
    }
    set
    {
        //make sure that we add to the existing rating store rather
        //than creating a new one
        Dictionary<int, int> result = new Dictionary<int, int>();
        if (GetFromSession("SelectedRatings") != null)
        {
            result = GetFromSession("SelectedRatings") as
                    Dictionary<int, int>;
            foreach (KeyValuePair<int, int> pair in value)
            {
```

```
                    if (!result.ContainsKey(pair.Key))
                        result.Add(pair.Key, pair.Value);
                }
                SetInSession("SelectedRatings", result);
            }
            else
                SetInSession("SelectedRatings", value);

        }
    }
```

ClearSelectedRatings

ClearSelectedRatings()? That is a pretty clear statement. This method simply clears out the Dictionary<int, int> collection that is stored in the session behind the SelectedRatings.

```
public void ClearSelectedRatings()
{
    SetInSession("SelectedRatings", null);
}
```

TagID

TagID is a QueryString value that we pass in a UrlRewrite process when viewing the Tags.aspx page.

```
public int TagID
{
    get
    {
        int result = 0;
        if (GetQueryStringValue("TagID") != null)
        {
            result = Convert.ToInt32((GetQueryStringValue("TagID")));
        }
        return result;
    }
}
```

Configuration

The `Configuration` class is responsible for reading the values in our `config` files. In this last round of coding features we have added the following properties:

- `TagCloudLargestFontSize`: This value sets the largest font size for display in the tag cloud.

- `TagCloudSmallestFontSize`: This value sets the smallest font size for display in the tag cloud.

- `CloudSortOrder`: This value sets the sort order of the tags in the cloud.

- `NumberOfTagsInCloud`: This value sets the number of tags to be displayed in the cloud.

```
public int TagCloudLargestFontSize
{
    get { return (int)getAppSetting(typeof(int),
                        "TagCloudLargestFontSize"); }
}

public int TagCloudSmallestFontSize
{
    get { return (int)getAppSetting(typeof(int),
                        "TagCloudSmallestFontSize"); }
}

public string CloudSortOrder
{
    get { return getAppSetting(typeof (string),
                        "CloudSortOrder").ToString(); }
}

public int NumberOfTagsInCloud
{
    get { return (int) getAppSetting(typeof (int),
                        "NumberOfTagsInCloud"); }
}
```

Implementing the presentation layer

This chapter is all about creating three controls—`Comments`, `Ratings`, and `Tags`. In addition to the `Tags` control, we also have a `Tags.aspx` page that is responsible for displaying all the linked items for a specified Tag.

Comments Page

Let's get started by looking at the comments page.

Comments.ascx

The comment control is responsible for taking in a user's comment for an object in the system. This control is relatively simple, if compared to the others that we will be creating. It has a text box and a button to take in the comment. It also has a `PlaceHolder` to contain all the comments that we collect over time.

```
<asp:UpdatePanel runat="server">
    <ContentTemplate>
        <asp:Panel runat="server" ID="pnlComment">
            <asp:TextBox ID="txtComment" runat="server"></asp:
                    TextBox><asp:Button Text="Add Comment"
                    ID="btnAddComment" runat="server"
                    OnClick="btnAddComment_Click" />
            <asp:PlaceHolder ID="phComments"
                    runat="server"></asp:PlaceHolder>
        </asp:Panel>
    </ContentTemplate>
</asp:UpdatePanel>
```

Comments.ascx.cs

First, note that we are initializing the control in the overriden `OnInit()` Method. This allows us to get the control's output into the `ViewState` so that we can access everything down the road.

There are two properties for this class— `SystemObjectID`, and `SystemObjectRecordID`. They allow us to know what data to save and load.

When the page is initialized, we check the state of the current user to see if they are logged in or not. We do not allow unauthorized users to post comments. If the user is logged in, we show the comment text box and button. If they are not, we hide those controls.

Next, we load the page. To load the page, we load the comments from the presenter.

Then we have the event handler for capturing the added comments.

We also have a method to toggle the visibility of the panel that shows the comments.

There is also a method for clearing the panel of comments.

The most complicated method in this whole class is the `LoadComments()` method. This method is responsible for taking in a collection of comments, iterating through them, and adding them to the panel for display.

```
public partial class Comments : System.Web.UI.UserControl, IComments
{
    private CommentsPresenter _presenter;
    public int SystemObjectID { get; set; }
    public long SystemObjectRecordID { get; set; }

    protected override void OnInit(EventArgs e)
    {
        _presenter = new CommentsPresenter();
        _presenter.Init(this, IsPostBack);
    }

    protected void Page_Load(object sender, EventArgs e)
    {
        _presenter.LoadComments();
    }

    protected void btnAddComment_Click(object sender, EventArgs e)
    {
        _presenter.AddComment(txtComment.Text);
        txtComment.Text = "";
    }

    public void ShowCommentBox(bool IsVisible)
    {
        pnlComment.Visible = IsVisible;
    }

    public void ClearComments()
    {
        phComments.Controls.Clear();
    }

    public void LoadComments(List<Comment> comments)
    {
        if(comments.Count > 0)
        {
            phComments.Controls.Add(new LiteralControl("<table
                            width=\"100%\">"));
            foreach (Comment comment in comments)
            {
                phComments.Controls.Add(new LiteralControl("<tr><td>"
                        + comment.CommentByUsername + " (" +
```

```
                comment.CreateDate.ToShortDateString() + "):
                " + comment.Body + "</td></tr>"));
            }
            phComments.Controls.Add(new LiteralControl("</table>"));
        }
    }
}
```

CommentsPresenter.cs

The CommentsPresenter is responsible for handling all the logic behind this control. It determines whether or not to show the control based on whether or not the user who is viewing the control is logged in or not. It also handles loading the comments for the specified SystemObject and SystemObjectRecordID. Finally, there is a method for adding a Comment.

```
public class CommentsPresenter
{
    private IComments _view;
    private ICommentRepository _commentRepository;
    private IWebContext _webContext;
    public CommentsPresenter()
    {
        _commentRepository =
                ObjectFactory.GetInstance<ICommentRepository>();
                _webContext = ObjectFactory.GetInstance<IWebContext>();
    }
    public void Init(IComments view, bool IsPostBack)
    {
        _view = view;
        if(_webContext.CurrentUser != null)
            _view.ShowCommentBox(true);
        else
            _view.ShowCommentBox(false);
    }
    public void LoadComments()
    {
        _view.LoadComments(_commentRepository.
        GetCommentsBySystemObject(_view.SystemObjectID,_view.
        SystemObjectRecordID));
    }
    public void AddComment(string comment)
    {
        Comment c = new Comment();
```

```
        c.Body = comment;
        c.CommentByAccountID = _webContext.CurrentUser.AccountID;
        c.CommentByUsername = _webContext.CurrentUser.Username;
        c.CreateDate = DateTime.Now;
        c.SystemObjectID = _view.SystemObjectID;
        c.SystemObjectRecordID = _view.SystemObjectRecordID;
        _commentRepository.SaveComment(c);
        _view.ClearComments();
        LoadComments();
    }
}
```

Ratings Page

Now let's take a look at the ratings page.

Ratings.ascx

The `Ratings` control is responsible for displaying a modal pop up that contains the various options that can be rated. It then captures those ratings and saves them away to the database. In addition to handling the user interaction, it also displays the overall rating average for that particular object.

In order to use the rating control or the modal pop up, we need to register the `AjaxControlToolkit`. Once this is added, we can hook up the modal pop up to our `pnlModalPopup`. This panel contains a repeater that will show all the ratings that are available for this object. Outside of the modal pop up, we also have a rating control that displays the average rating for the object.

```
<%@ Import Namespace="Fisharoo.FisharooCore.Core.Domain"%>
<%@ Control Language="C#" AutoEventWireup="true" CodeBehind="Ratings.
ascx.cs" Inherits="Fisharoo.FisharooWeb.UserControls.Ratings" %>
<%@ Register Assembly="AjaxControlToolkit" Namespace="AjaxControlToolk
it" TagPrefix="cc1" %>
<asp:Panel ID="pnlRating" runat="server">
    <asp:UpdatePanel runat="server">
        <ContentTemplate>
            <asp:LinkButton ID="lbRateThis" runat="server" Text="rate
                this!" OnClick="lbRateThis_Click"></asp:LinkButton>
            <asp:Label ID="lblThankYou" runat="server" Text="Thank
                            you!" Visible="false"></asp:Label>
            <cc1:Rating ID="Rating1" Enabled="false" ReadOnly="true"
                runat="server"
                MaxRating="5"
                EmptyStarCssClass="ratingStarEmpty"
                FilledStarCssClass="ratingStarFilled"
```

```
            StarCssClass="ratingStar"
            WaitingStarCssClass="ratingStarSaved">
        </cc1:Rating>

    <asp:Panel ID="pnlModalPopup" runat="server"
        BackColor="White" ScrollBars="Vertical">
        <asp:Literal ID="litSelectedRatings" Visible="true"
                runat="server"></asp:Literal>
        <asp:Repeater ID="repRatingOptions" runat="server">
            <HeaderTemplate>
                <table>
                    <tr><td> </td><td> </td></tr>
            </HeaderTemplate>
            <ItemTemplate>
                    <tr>
                        <td>
                            <cc1:Rating id="Rating1"
                                    runat="server"
                                MaxRating="5"
                            EmptyStarCssClass="ratingStarEmpty"
                            FilledStarCssClass="ratingStarFilled"
                            StarCssClass="ratingStar"
                            WaitingStarCssClass="ratingStarSaved"
                                OnChanged="rating_Changed"
                                Tag='<%# ((SystemObjectRatingO
ption)Container.DataItem).SystemObjectRatingOptionID.ToString() %>'>
                                </cc1:Rating>
                        </td>
                        <td>
                            <asp:Label ID="lblOptionName"
                                ToolTip='<%# ((SystemObjectRat
ingOption)Container.DataItem).Description %>'
                                Text='<%# ((SystemObjectRating
Option)Container.DataItem).Name %>'

                                runat="server"></asp:Label>
                        </td>
                    </tr>
            </ItemTemplate>
            <FooterTemplate>
                </table>
            </FooterTemplate>
        </asp:Repeater>
```

```
            <asp:Button ID="btnSave" UseSubmitBehavior="false"
                 OnClick="btnSave_Click"
                    runat="server" Text="Save" />
            <asp:Button ID="btnCancel" runat="server"
                    Text="Cancel" />
        </asp:Panel>

        <cc1:ModalPopupExtender ID="ModalPopupExtender1"
            runat="server"
            TargetControlID="lbRateThis"
            PopupControlID="pnlModalPopup"
            DropShadow="true"
            OkControlID="btnSave"
            CancelControlID="btnCancel"></cc1:ModalPopupExtender>
            </ContentTemplate>
        </asp:UpdatePanel>
    </asp:Panel>
```

There are two things that are very important to notice in this UI. The first is the line that assigns the `SystemObjectRatingOptionID` to the Tag of property of the `Rating` control.

```
Tag='<%# ((SystemObjectRatingOption)Container.DataItem).
        SystemObjectRatingOptionID.ToString() %>'
```

When a `Rating` is selected, it fires an event that contains the `Rating` control and the selected value (the star that was selected). We are passing the `SystemObjectRatingOptionID` in the `Tag` property of the `Rating`.

The second important thing to notice is the property in our `btnSave` button. The `UseSubmitBehavior` property turns off the submit behavior of the `btnSave` button. If we don't disable this property, then the modal pop up will disappear when you click the button and you will not be able to capture the `btnSave_Click` event. When you do turn this behavior off, we are able to capture the event.

Ratings.ascx.cs

In this class, we have two properties— `SystemObjectID`, and `SystemObjectRecordID`. These allow us to load and capture the data for the appropriate object. Next, we initialize our presenter. In doing this, we load the current options, set the display, and set the current rating.

Next, we have the event handler that captures when a user selects a rating in our modal pop up. This is a straight through to the presenter.

Then we have the `btnSave_Click` event handler. This method not only sends the event upstream to the presenter but also sets the visibility of the `pnlModalPopup` to `false`, thus effectively hiding the pop up. (If this is not done, the `ModalPopup` seems to break and display itself in the page rather than above the page.) We also hide the label that acts as the link to show the `ModalPopup` and the `Rating` control that shows the average rating for the control. Finally, we thank the user for his/her input!

We then get to the `lbRateThis_Click` method, which shows the modal popup panel `pnlModalPopup`.

Finally, we have a method that sets the `lbRateThis` (link to show modal popup) and the `pnlModalPopup` visibility. This method is interacted with directly from the presenter:

```
public partial class Ratings : System.Web.UI.UserControl, IRatings
{
    public int SystemObjectID { get; set; }
    public long SystemObjectRecordID { get; set; }
    private RatingsPresenter _presenter;
    private IWebContext _webContext;
    protected void Page_Load(object sender, EventArgs e)
    {
        _presenter = new RatingsPresenter();
        _presenter.Init(this, IsPostBack);
    }

    public void SetCurrentRating(int CurrentRating)
    {
        Rating1.CurrentRating = CurrentRating;
    }

    public void LoadOptions(List<SystemObjectRatingOption> Options)
    {
        repRatingOptions.DataSource = Options;
        repRatingOptions.DataBind();
    }

    protected void rating_Changed(object sender, RatingEventArgs
                                  args)
    {
        _presenter.rating_Changed(sender, args);
    }

    protected void btnSave_Click(object sender, EventArgs e)
```

```
    {
        _presenter.btnSave_Click(sender, e, SystemObjectID,
                        SystemObjectRecordID);
        pnlModalPopup.Visible = false;
        lbRateThis.Visible = false;
        Rating1.Visible = false;
        lblThankYou.Visible = true;
    }

    protected void lbRateThis_Click(object sender, EventArgs e)
    {
        pnlModalPopup.Visible = true;
    }

    public void CanSetRating(bool Visible)
    {
        lbRateThis.Visible = Visible;
        pnlModalPopup.Visible = Visible;
    }
}
```

RatingsPresenter.cs

In the `RatingsPresenter`, we have started off with the `Init()` method. This method loads all the options for our `Ratings` control. It then moves on to determine if the user is logged in or not. If they aren't, then we disable the ability to set a rating. If the user is logged in, we check to see if the user has provided a rating for this control before or not. If they have, then we also disable the ability to set a rating. Otherwise, we allow the user to provide the ratings. Finally, we set the current rating for this control.

Next, we have our `LoadOptions()` method, which populates the display with all the available options. It does this by getting the properties from the view for `SystemObject` and the `SystemObjectRecordID`, and passing them to the `SystemObjectRatingOptionRepository.GetSystemObjectRatingOptionsBySystemObjectID()` method.

Then comes the `rating_Changed()` method, which captures the event from the display. We create a new `Dictionary<int, int>` object and add the `SystemObjectRatingOptionID` and the selected rating to it. We then add this to the `Session` for that user via the `WebContext.SelectedRatings` property. (Recall that this adds the rating to a collection stored in the session.)

Finally, we get to the `btnSave_Click()` method, which captures the `Save` button click passed up from the code behind. In this method, we load up the `Dictionary<int, int>` collection of ratings stored in the session. We then create a new list of Generic List of Ratings. If we have ratings in hand, we iterate through the list of `KeyValuePairs`. With each iteration, we spin up a new `Rating` and add it to the collection of Ratings. We then save all the ratings to the `RatingRepository`. `SaveRatings()` method. Then we clear the session using the `WebContext`. `ClearSelectedRatings()`.

```
public class RatingsPresenter
{
    private IRatings _view;
    private IWebContext _webContext;
    private ISystemObjectRatingOptionRepository
            _systemObjectRatingOptionRepository;
    private IRatingRepository _ratingRepository;
    public RatingsPresenter()
    {
        _webContext = ObjectFactory.GetInstance<IWebContext>();
        _systemObjectRatingOptionRepository =
                        ObjectFactory.GetInstance
                        <ISystemObjectRatingOptionRepository>();
        _ratingRepository =
                        ObjectFactory.GetInstance<IRatingRepository>();
    }
    public void Init(IRatings view, bool IsPostBack)
    {
        _view = view;
        LoadOptions(_view.SystemObjectID,
                    _view.SystemObjectRecordID);
        //not logged in? Can't add ratings
        if(_webContext.CurrentUser == null)
            _view.CanSetRating(false);
        //already rated this? Can't add ratings
        else if
            (_ratingRepository.HasRatedBefore
            (_view.SystemObjectID, _view.SystemObjectRecordID,
            _webContext.CurrentUser.AccountID))
            _view.CanSetRating(false);
        //ok ok...go ahead and rate this
        else
            _view.CanSetRating(true);
        _view.SetCurrentRating(_ratingRepository.GetCurrentRating(
            _view.SystemObjectID, _view.SystemObjectRecordID));
```

```csharp
    }
    public void LoadOptions(int SystemObjectID, long
                        SystemObjectRecordID)
    {
        _view.LoadOptions(_systemObjectRatingOptionRepository.
        GetSystemObjectRatingOptionsBySystemObjectID(SystemObjectID));
    }
    public void rating_Changed(object sender, RatingEventArgs args)
    {
        AjaxControlToolkit.Rating rating = sender as
                                AjaxControlToolkit.Rating;
        //add slected ratings to the session handler and make it a
                    dictionary object instead or a custom structure
        Dictionary<int, int> newRating = new Dictionary<int, int>();
        newRating.Add(Convert.ToInt32(rating.Tag),
                    Convert.ToInt32(args.Value));
        _webContext.SelectedRatings = newRating;
    }
    public void btnSave_Click(object sender, EventArgs e, int
                        SystemObjectID, long SystemObjectRecordID)
    {
        Dictionary<int, int> selectedRatings =
                        _webContext.SelectedRatings;
        List<FisharooCore.Core.Domain.Rating> ratings = new
                        List<FisharooCore.Core.Domain.Rating>();
        if(selectedRatings != null)
        {
            foreach (KeyValuePair<int, int> pair in selectedRatings)
            {
                FisharooCore.Core.Domain.Rating rating = new
                        FisharooCore.Core.Domain.Rating();
                rating.CreatedByAccountID =
                        _webContext.CurrentUser.AccountID;
                rating.CreatedByUsername =
                        _webContext.CurrentUser.Username;
                rating.CreateDate = DateTime.Now;
                rating.Score = pair.Value;
                rating.SystemObjectRatingOptionID = pair.Key;
                rating.SystemObjectID = SystemObjectID;
                rating.SystemObjectRecordID = SystemObjectRecordID;
                ratings.Add(rating);
            }
            _ratingRepository.SaveRatings(ratings);
        }
        _webContext.ClearSelectedRatings();
    }
}
```

Tags Page

Now let's take a look at the tags page.

Tags.ascx

From the client side, the tags control that we are creating appears to be very simple. This control has two panels—one to show the tags and the other to collect them.

```
<%@ Control Language="C#" AutoEventWireup="true"
            CodeBehind="Tags.ascx.cs" Inherits="Fisharoo.FisharooWeb.
UserControls.Tags" %>
<asp:UpdatePanel ID="UpdatePanel1" runat="server">
<ContentTemplate>
    <asp:Panel runat="server" ID="pnlTag" Visible="false">
        <asp:TextBox ID="txtTag" runat="server"></asp:TextBox>
        <asp:Button ID="btnTag" runat="server" Text="Tag It!"
                OnClick="btnTag_Click" />
    </asp:Panel>
    <asp:Panel runat="server" ID="pnlTagCloud" Visible="false">
        <asp:PlaceHolder ID="phTagCloud"
                        runat="server"></asp:PlaceHolder>
    </asp:Panel>
</ContentTemplate>
</asp:UpdatePanel>
```

Tags.ascx.cs

In this file we have defined both a class and an enum. The enum of `TagState` is defined to modify the various states of the tag control. We have the following entries defined:

- `ShowCloud`: This option shows only the cloud for the object that the control is configured for.

- `ShowTagBox`: This option shows the text box to collect tags. It does not show any cloud.

- `ShowCloudAndTagBox`: This option shows both the cloud and the text box.

- `ShowParentCloud`: This option shows the cloud for a parent. This option can be used to show all the tags for something like a photo album.

- `ShowGlobalCloud`: This option shows all the tags from the site's point of view.

The `Tags` class implements a `Display` property, which is of type `TagState` (our previously mentioned enum). In the `Page_Load()` method, we initialize our `TagsPresenter` and in doing so set the state of the control and load the tags that were already collected.

Next, we have some methods which the presenter uses to interact with the view — `ClearTagCloud()`, `ShowTagCloud()`, `ShowTagBox()`, and `AddTagsToTagCloud()`. These are all fairly self-explanatory! You do want to pay attention to the `AddTagsToTagCloud()` method though, because this is where we actually create the tags. Each tag is created as a `Hyperlink`. In building these tags, we set the size of the link by adding a style attribute to the control where we set the font-size property. Also note that we are linking to the `Tags/Tags.aspx` page (discussed shortly) where we display all the objects that have that particular tag linked to it.

Finally, we have a method that captures the click event of the `btnTag` Button `btnTag_Click`. This is a pass through to the presenter to save the new tag to the database. Once it has saved the tag, it clears the UI to capture another tag.

```
public enum TagState
{
    ShowCloud,
    ShowTagBox,
    ShowCloudAndTagBox,
    ShowParentCloud,
    ShowGlobalCloud
}
public partial class Tags : System.Web.UI.UserControl, ITags
{
    public TagState Display { get; set; }
    public int SystemObjectID { get; set; }
    public long SystemObjectRecordID { get; set; }
    private TagsPresenter _presenter;
    public Tags()
    {
        _presenter = new TagsPresenter();
    }
    protected void Page_Load(object sender, EventArgs e)
    {
        _presenter.Init(this, IsPostBack);
    }
    public void ClearTagCloud()
    {
        phTagCloud.Controls.Clear();
    }
```

```
public void ShowTagCloud(bool IsVisible)
{
    pnlTagCloud.Visible = IsVisible;
}

public void ShowTagBox(bool IsVisible)
{
    pnlTag.Visible = IsVisible;
}

public void AddTagsToTagCloud(Tag tag)
{
    HyperLink hlTag = new HyperLink();
    hlTag.Text = tag.Name;
    hlTag.NavigateUrl = "~/Tags/" + tag.Name.Replace(" ", "-");
    hlTag.Attributes.Add("style", "font-size:" + tag.FontSize +
                         "px;");
    phTagCloud.Controls.Add(hlTag);
    phTagCloud.Controls.Add(new LiteralControl(" "));
}

protected void btnTag_Click(object sender, EventArgs e)
{
    _presenter.Init(this,IsPostBack);
    _presenter.btnTag_Click(txtTag.Text);
    txtTag.Text = "";
}
}
```

TagsPresenter.cs

When the TagsPresenter is initialized, the DetermineClientState() method is called. This method looks at the various states of the user and the Display property to determine how to build the Tag control. It interacts with the view to show or hide various aspects of the control, from the text box to the tag cloud.

After that we have a few methods for building the different types of tag clouds based on the Display property. We can build the global tag cloud, a parent tag cloud, or a single object tag cloud. This is done by calling into the various methods of the TagRepository and getting the appropriate tags. The methods then iterate through the returned collection of tags and add each tag to the view through its AddTagsToTagCloud() method.

Finally, we have the `btnTag_Click()` method, which handles the passed through click event and captures the `TagName` of a new tag entry. This `TagName` is passed to the `TagService.AddTag()` method with the `SystemObjectID` and `SystemObjectRecordID`. We then determine if we have a cloud as part of our `Display` options. If we do, then we clear the cloud and rebuild it so that the new tag can be shown.

```
public class TagsPresenter
{
    private ITags _view;
    private ITagService _tagService;
    private IWebContext _webContext;
    private ITagRepository _tagRepository;
    private IConfiguration _configuration;
    public TagsPresenter()
    {
        _tagService = ObjectFactory.GetInstance<ITagService>();
        _webContext = ObjectFactory.GetInstance<IWebContext>();
        _tagRepository = ObjectFactory.GetInstance<ITagRepository>();
        _configuration = ObjectFactory.GetInstance<IConfiguration>();
    }
    public void Init(ITags view, bool IsPostBack)
    {
        _view = view;
        DetermineClientState();
    }

    public void DetermineClientState()
    {
        if (_webContext.CurrentUser != null && _view.Display ==
                                        TagState.ShowCloud)
        {
            _view.ShowTagCloud(true);
            BuildTagCloud();
        }
        else if (_webContext.CurrentUser != null && _view.Display ==
                TagState.ShowCloudAndTagBox)
        {
            _view.ShowTagBox(true);
            _view.ShowTagCloud(true);
            BuildTagCloud();
        }
        else if (_webContext.CurrentUser == null && _view.Display ==
                TagState.ShowCloudAndTagBox)
        {
```

```
            _view.ShowTagBox(false);
            _view.ShowTagCloud(true);
            BuildTagCloud();
        }
        else if (_view.Display == TagState.ShowCloud)
        {
            _view.ShowTagBox(true);
        }
        else if (_view.Display == TagState.ShowParentCloud)
        {
            _view.ShowTagCloud(true);
            _view.ShowTagBox(false);
            BuildParentTagCloud();
        }
        else if (_view.Display == TagState.ShowGlobalCloud)
        {
            _view.ShowTagCloud(true);
            _view.ShowTagBox(false);
            BuildGlobalTagCloud();
        }
        else
        {
            _view.ShowTagBox(false);
            _view.ShowTagCloud(false);
        }
    }

    public void BuildGlobalTagCloud()
    {
        List<Tag> tags = _tagRepository.GetTagsGlobal(
                _configuration.NumberOfTagsInCloud);
        tags = _tagService.CalculateFontSize(tags);
        foreach (Tag tag in tags)
        {
            _view.AddTagsToTagCloud(tag);
        }
    }

    public void BuildParentTagCloud()
    {
        List<Tag> tags =
            _tagRepository.GetTagsBySystemObject(_view.SystemObjectID,
                            _configuration.NumberOfTagsInCloud);
        tags = _tagService.CalculateFontSize(tags);
        foreach (Tag tag in tags)
```

```
        {
            _view.AddTagsToTagCloud(tag);
        }
    }

    public void BuildTagCloud()
    {
        List<Tag> tags =
                _tagRepository.GetTagsBySystemObjectAndRecordID
                (_view.SystemObjectID, _view.SystemObjectRecordID);
        tags = _tagService.CalculateFontSize(tags);
        foreach (Tag tag in tags)
        {
            _view.AddTagsToTagCloud(tag);
        }
    }

    public void btnTag_Click(string TagName)
    {
        _tagService.AddTag(TagName, _view.SystemObjectID,
                        _view.SystemObjectRecordID);
        if (_view.Display == TagState.ShowCloud || _view.Display ==
                        TagState.ShowCloudAndTagBox)
        {
            _view.ClearTagCloud();
            BuildTagCloud();
        }
    }
}
```

Installing the new user controls

Now that we have our controls built and ready for use, let's plug them into one of our existing pages. I am choosing the `ViewAlbum.aspx` page for this purpose. This page displays uploaded photos, which is fairly good content to collect ratings, comments and tags from our users.

To get started, we need to register our user controls to the page so that we have access to them. We do that by adding `Register` declarations to the top of the page.

```
<%@ Page Language="C#" EnableEventValidation="false"
        MasterPageFile="~/SiteMaster.Master" AutoEventWireup="true"
        CodeBehind="ViewAlbum.aspx.cs"
        Inherits="Fisharoo.FisharooWeb.Photos.ViewAlbum" %>
<%@ Import Namespace="Fisharoo.FisharooCore.Core.Domain" %>
```

```
<%@ Register Src="~/UserControls/Ratings.ascx" TagName="Ratings"
                TagPrefix="Fisharoo" %>
<%@ Register Src="~/UserControls/Tags.ascx" TagName="Tags"
                TagPrefix="Fisharoo" %>
<%@ Register Src="~/UserControls/Comments.ascx" TagName="Comments"
                TagPrefix="Fisharoo" %>
```

Once they are registered we are free to plug them in anywhere we like. I have chosen to add them just beneath the display of each photo.

```
<li>
    <asp:Label style="font-weight:bold;" ID="lblFileName"
                Text='<%#((File)Container.DataItem).FileName %>'
runat="server"></asp:Label>
    <asp:HyperLink ID="linkImage"
        NavigateUrl='<%#((File)Container.DataItem)
        .CreateDate.Year.ToString() +
        ((File)Container.DataItem).CreateDate.Month.ToString() %>'
        runat="server"></asp:HyperLink>
    <asp:Literal Visible="false" ID="litImageName" runat="server"
                Text='<%#((File)Container.DataItem).
                FileSystemName.ToString() %>'></asp:Literal>
    <asp:Literal Visible="false" ID="litFileExtension" runat="server"
            Text='<%# ((File)Container.DataItem).Extension.ToString()
            %>'></asp:Literal><br />
    <asp:Label ID="lblDescription" runat="server"
            Text='<%#((File)Container.DataItem).Description
            %>'></asp:Label>
    <asp:Literal Visible="false" ID="litFileID"
                Text='<%#((File)Container.DataItem).FileID %>'
                runat="server"></asp:Literal>
<Fisharoo:Ratings ID="Ratings1" runat="server" SystemObjectID="5"
        SystemObjectRecordID='<%#((File)Container.DataItem).FileID
        %>'></Fisharoo:Ratings>
<Fisharoo:Tags ID="Tags1" runat="server" SystemObjectID="5"
        SystemObjectRecordID='<%#((File)Container.DataItem).FileID
        %>' Display="ShowCloudAndTagBox" ></Fisharoo:Tags>
<Fisharoo:Comments ID="Comments1" runat="server"
        SystemObjectID="5"
        SystemObjectRecordID='<%#((File)Container.DataItem).
                FileID %>'></Fisharoo:Comments>

</li>
```

Once we have the controls physically plugged into the page, we would want to set their `SystemObjectID` to 5, which is the `File` object (in my database).

Table - dbo.SystemObjects			Table - dbo.Comments	Table -
SystemObjectID	Timestamp	Name		
1	<Binary data>	Accounts		
2	<Binary data>	Profiles		
3	<Binary data>	Blogs		
4	<Binary data>	BoardPosts		
5	<Binary data>	Files		
6	<Binary data>	Groups		

We would also want to set the `SystemObjectRecordID` to the `FileID` of the current iteration. Then for the `Tags` control we would want to set the `Display` property `ShowCloudAndTagBox`, which will allow our users to see already assigned tags and also add their own tags.

That's it! Your new user controls are officially ready for action.

UrlRewrite.cs

Before we can build the Tags page to display all the related objects for a tag, we need to translate the URL that is passed from our tag clouds. We currently have links in our tag clouds that look something like `http://www.someurl.com/tags/tag-name`. This doesn't map to any specific resource and will fail as is. For this reason, we will add another section to our `UrlRewrite` class that will handle this translation.

This code section shall be added to the `UrlRewrite.Application_OnAfterProcess()` that we are already using for URL rewriting in other places of the site. This particular snippet is looking for any URL that contains the word "tags". If it finds it, then it attempts to get the tag name after the "tags" bit. If it locates the tag name, it then attempts to load the tag by its name via the `TagRepository.GetTagByName()` method. If we find a tag, then we are able to rewrite the path via the `HttpContext.RewritePath()` method where we map our user to the `tags.aspx` page with the addition of the `TagID` in the `QueryString`.

```
#region TAGS
else if (application.Request.PhysicalPath.ToLower().Contains("tags"))
{
    Tag tag = null;
    int tagsPosition = 0;
    string tagName;
```

```
        string[] arr =
         application.Request.PhysicalPath.ToLowerInvariant().Split('\\');
        for(int i = 0;i<arr.Length;i++)
        {
            if(arr[i].ToLower() == "tags")
            {
                tagsPosition = i;
            }
            if(tagsPosition>0)
            {
                tagName = arr[i + 1];
                tag = _tagRepository.GetTagByName(tagName.Replace
                                                   ("-"," "));
                break;
            }
        }
        if(tag != null)
        {
            context.RewritePath("/tags/tags.aspx?TagID=" + tag.TagID);
        }
    }
#endregion
```

Tags page

Now that our user controls are built and plugged into our site, and we are able to translate our friendly URLs to something we can work with, we have one final thing to do. In our tag cloud, each Tag links to the tag name directly. In our `UrlRewrite` class, we translate the tag name to the tag ID and redirect our users to the `Tags.aspx` page so that we can see all the objects that share the same tag. This page is fairly straightforward as most of the heavy lifting is done behind the scenes. Let's take a look.

Tags.aspx

The display side of this page simply has a handful of repeaters—one repeater for each type of object to which we allow the tags to be attached. When we load our UI, the presenter sends the view a list of `SystemObjectTagWithObjects` objects. We iterate through this collection and for each object, we bind the specific collection of objects to its corresponding `Repeater`. In the case of `Files`, which is what we have plugged our controls into, we would take the `Files` collection and bind it to the `repFiles Repeater`. As we add our new user controls to other sections of the site, we can hook up to new sections in this page.

```
<asp:Repeater ID="repFiles" runat="server">
    <ItemTemplate>
        <tr>
```

```
            <td><%#((SystemObjectTagWithObjects)Container.DataItem).
    File.FileName
        %></td>
            <td>
                <asp:HyperLink runat="server" Text='<%# "Click to
                                        view album: " + ((SystemObjectTa
    gWithObjects)Container.DataItem).Folder.Name %>'
                    NavigateUrl='<%# "~/photos/ViewAlbum.aspx?AlbumID=" +
                    ((SystemObjectTagWithObjects)Container.DataItem).
                    File.DefaultFolderID %>'></asp:HyperLink> or
                <asp:HyperLink runat="server" Text='<%# "Click to
                                        view photo: " +
                                    ((SystemObjectTagWithObjects)
                                Container.DataItem).File.FileName %>
                            ' NavigateUrl='<%# "~/files/photos/" +
    ((SystemObjectTagWithObjects)Container.DataItem).File.CreateDate.Year.
    ToString() + ((SystemObjectTagWithObjects)Container.DataItem).File.
    CreateDate.Month.ToString() + "/" + ((SystemObjectTagWithObjects)Conta
    iner.DataItem).File.FileSystemName + "__O." + ((SystemObjectTagWithObj
    ects)Container.DataItem).File.Extension %>'></asp:HyperLink>
            </td>
        </tr>
    </ItemTemplate>
</asp:Repeater>
```

Tags.aspx.cs

All that this file does on its own is hook up to its presenter. When the presenter's `Init()` method is called, the presenter calls into the `LoadUI()` method of the view.

The `LoadUI()` method takes in a collection of `SystemObjectTagWithObjects`. It then proceeds in setting the data source for each repeater with a subset of the collection of `SystemObjectTagWithObjects` by specifying which `SystemObjectID` is to be used. Once all the lists are built, the repeater's `Items.Count` property is interrogated to see if we have any empty sections, and if we do, we add a "No tagged items" message.

The last method is the `SetTitle()` method, which allows the presenter to set the page title that is viewed as a header in our page as well as in the title bar of the browser (a property in the `Master` page).

```
    public partial class Tags : System.Web.UI.Page, ITags
    {
        private IWebContext _webContext;
        private TagsPresenter _tagsPresenter;
        protected void Page_Load(object sender, EventArgs e)
        {
            _webContext = ObjectFactory.GetInstance<IWebContext>();
            _tagsPresenter = new TagsPresenter();
```

```
            _tagsPresenter.Init(this, IsPostBack);
    }
    public void LoadUI(List<SystemObjectTagWithObjects>
                        tagWithObjects)
    {
        repAccounts.DataSource = tagWithObjects.Where(t =>
                        t.SystemObjectTag.SystemObjectID == 1);
        repAccounts.DataBind();
        repProfiles.DataSource = tagWithObjects.Where(t =>
                        t.SystemObjectTag.SystemObjectID == 2);
        repProfiles.DataBind();
        repBlogs.DataSource = tagWithObjects.Where(t =>
                            t.SystemObjectTag.SystemObjectID == 3);
        repBlogs.DataBind();
        repPosts.DataSource = tagWithObjects.Where(t =>
                            t.SystemObjectTag.SystemObjectID == 4);
        repPosts.DataBind();
        repFiles.DataSource = tagWithObjects.Where(t =>
                            t.SystemObjectTag.SystemObjectID == 5);
        repFiles.DataBind();
        repGroups.DataSource = tagWithObjects.Where(t =>
                            t.SystemObjectTag.SystemObjectID == 6);
        repGroups.DataBind();
        if (repGroups.Items.Count == 0)
            repGroups.Controls.Add(new LiteralControl("<tr><td
                        colspan=\"2\">No tagged items</td></tr>"));
        if (repFiles.Items.Count == 0)
            repFiles.Controls.Add(new LiteralControl("<tr><td
                        colspan=\"2\">No tagged items</td></tr>"));
        if (repPosts.Items.Count == 0)
            repPosts.Controls.Add(new LiteralControl("<tr><td
                    colspan=\"2\">No tagged items</td></tr>"));
        if (repBlogs.Items.Count == 0)
            repBlogs.Controls.Add(new LiteralControl("<tr><td
                    colspan=\"2\">No tagged items</td></tr>"));
        if (repProfiles.Items.Count == 0)
            repProfiles.Controls.Add(new LiteralControl("<tr><td
                    colspan=\"2\">No tagged items</td></tr>"));
        if(repAccounts.Items.Count == 0)
            repAccounts.Controls.Add(new LiteralControl("<tr><td
                    colspan=\"2\">No tagged items</td></tr>"));
    }
    public void SetTitle(string TagName)
    {
        ((SiteMaster)Master).Title = TagName;
    }
}
}
```

TagsPresenter.cs

The presenter for this file has one method: `Init()`. The `Init()` method sets the title by passing the `Name` property of the `Tag` that is loaded from the `TagRepository` using the `TagID` that is captured by the `WebContext.TagID` property. The presenter also calls the `LoadUI()` method of the view and sends it a collection of `SystemObjectTagWithObjects`. This collection is retrieved from the `SystemObjectTagRepository.GetSystemObjectsByTagID()` method, which is also passed the `TagID` property of the `WebContext`.

```
public class TagsPresenter
{
    private ITags _view;
    private ISystemObjectTagRepository _systemObjectTagRepository;
    private ITagRepository _tagRepository;
    private IWebContext _webContext;
    public TagsPresenter()
    {
        _systemObjectTagRepository =
            ObjectFactory.GetInstance<ISystemObjectTagRepository>();
        _tagRepository = ObjectFactory.GetInstance<ITagRepository>();
        _webContext = ObjectFactory.GetInstance<IWebContext>();
    }
    public void Init(ITags view, bool IsPostBack)
    {
        _view = view;
        _view.SetTitle(_tagRepository.GetTagByID(_webContext.TagID).
Name);
        _view.LoadUI(_systemObjectTagRepository.
GetSystemObjectsByTagID(_webContext.TagID));
    }
}
```

Summary

In this chapter, we have successfully created three controls to allow our users to express their opinions about various content areas of our site. We built a tagging control that allows us to take in tag keywords as well as display all the tags for various levels of our site from specific records all the way out to the entire site. We built a rating control that allows us to configure many options per system object for individual ratings which are then averaged across all ratings and displayed as a general score. Finally, we created a commenting control so that our users could express very specific opinions regarding any of our content items.

With these new user controls, we have created new avenues of interest for our users. We now have the ability to allow users to touch just about anything in our system. In addition to allowing users to provide input, we have also created another avenue of interest for our users who enjoy reading and seeing other users' inputs. We have come a long way in including our users in the community feel of our site.

12
Moderation

We are finally at a point where we have a community with pretty much every feature that represents a great community. To that point, a lot of the features that we allow our users to create are text-based or resource-based content such as images, movies, and so on. This is wonderful! Now all we have to do is deploy our site, invite some users, and watch our community grow. Prepare to rake in the money!

Not so fast! Allowing your user base to have complete freedom in filling your site with content is not a good idea. It means that you don't have any control over the destiny of your site. It also means that you will eventually have someone adding inappropriate material. You might even have a tech-savvy user attempting to steal some of your user's information for less than appropriate adventures. All these issues might eventually drive out all the good users leaving you only with bad users. Possibly, in the worst case, you might end up with legal issues on your hands due to the actions of your uncontrolled users.

I don't mean to scare you. I only mean to inform you that with a community driven by your user's content, you would need to take some responsibility and keep a tight grip on the reigns. This tight grip that I'm talking about is what this chapter is all about.

In this chapter, we will discuss various forms of moderation. With user-generated content, we can take advantage of user-generated moderation. After all, why not give the offended a method to report what offended them? We will also discuss about gagging users who are habitual offenders. And we will create a filter that will attack bad words, competitor's spams, and **Cross-site scripting attacks** (**XSS**).

Problem

The core problem in this chapter is that we do not want to give willy-nilly control to our user base. We should maintain as much control over our site as possible with regards to what goes into it and what is displayed on it. Let's discuss the core features.

Community moderation

The user moderation takes place with a simple AJAXed `ImageButton` that allows them to report inappropriate content inline along with the content.

The content that is flagged by the community will show up in the administration console under the **Moderation** section as shown in the following screenshot. Here you can approve or deny the content.

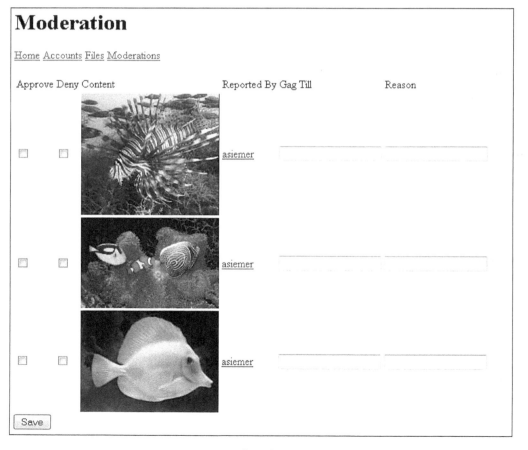

Gagging users

Once you have a list of moderated content, you will eventually start to notice some repeat offenders. For that reason, we need a way to slap the hands of those offenders. When viewing your flagged content, you will also see the owner of the content. If you find that you are seeing repeat offenders, you can apply a Gag to the user. A Gag will restrict the user from continuing to add content to the site as a form of punishment for bad behavior. Part of the Gag is to specify the reason and the date that the Gag order ends. It's shown in the following screenshot. If you don't want to specify an end data, you can apply a 20 year ban!

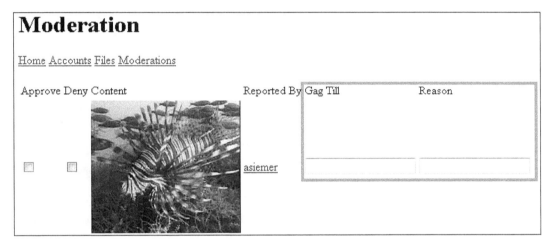

Dynamic filter

The dynamic filter will address a few issues. You can use it to effectively remove profanity from your site. You can also use it to intercept competitor postings or advertisements on your site. And most importantly, you can use it to restrict the types of scripting that you allow. This tool could block HTML, JavaScript, and just about anything else that you don't want on your site, which will aide you in dealing with Cross-site scripting issues.

As an example, I am posting to the forum, and I chose to use the offensive California term **dude** as shown in the following screenshot.

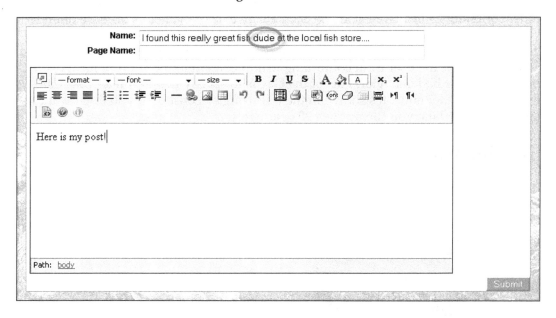

As shown in the following screenshot, I have added a filter entry to my ContentFilter list that disallows the word **dude** in my site and instead replaces it with **[filtered]**.

	ContentFilterID	StringToFilter	ReplaceWith	AccountID	CreateDate	TimeStamp
▶	1	dude	[filtered]	1	9/9/2008 12:00:...	\<Binary data\>
	2	<b>	\<b\>	1	9/9/2008 12:00:...	\<Binary data\>
	3	<i>	\<i\>	1	9/9/2008 12:00:...	\<Binary data\>
	4	</i>	\</i\>	1	9/9/2008 12:00:...	\<Binary data\>
	5	</b>	\</b\>	1	9/9/2008 12:00:...	\<Binary data\>
	6	<html>		1	9/9/2008 12:00:...	\<Binary data\>
	7	</html>		1	9/9/2008 12:00:...	\<Binary data\>

Tabs above table: Table - dbo.ContentFilters | Table - dbo.Moderations | Summary

So consequently, my post has been filtered and now shows **[filtered]** instead of dude in the following screenshot.

I found this really great fish [filtered] at the local fish store....

by: asiemer   on: 9/9/2008   updated: 9/9/2008   Reply

Here is my post!

Cross-site scripting (XSS)

Cross-site scripting (XSS) is a form of hacking that is performed on a webpage by injecting client-side code into the input of a webpage. This is done in an attempt to gain access to an unsuspecting user's personal information such as that stored in the cookies of most sites. With careful steps you can, for the most part, protect yourself from this issue by validating your site's input, encoding your site's output, and not trusting any data sources that are rendered on your site.

> This book is by no means meant to be authoritative on the subject of XSS issues or hacking webpages. Follow this link if you want to know more: `http://msdn.microsoft.com/en-us/library/ms998274.aspx`. Also search for ASP.NET XSS, SQL Injection, and web page hacking for further reading.

There is a common misnomer that the `ValidateRequest` flag of a page will protect you from this issue. That is not always the case. Also, in case you want to accept some HTML or JavaScript, you have to turn off the `ValidateRequest` feature. This leaves you pretty much unprotected. In our case, we have some pages that allow some HTML and JavaScript. If we do not take steps to protect ourselves, who will? We will use our filtering tool to address this concern.

Design

Let's take a look at the design for this feature.

Moderation

For us to enable Moderation, we will take advantage of the same concepts that we used in Chapter 11 for Rating, Tagging, and Commenting. This feature will be implemented as another `UserControl` that we can plug in wherever we need it. As it will tie into the **SystemObjects** table of objects, we are free to allow our users to moderate any database-oriented content—be it textual, image based, or just about anything else. As long as it has a record ID and a table associated to it, we can moderate it.

In addition to letting our users flag content for approval, we will need to create a page to manage what was flagged. We will implement a simple administration page that will show everything that is listed. For each listed item we can approve or deny the content. This page will also house our gagging capabilities, which we will discuss later.

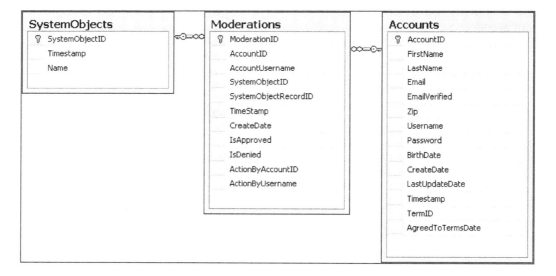

This structure is identical to our other users of the **SystemObjects** table. It has a **SystemObjectID** and a **SystemObjectRecordID**, which allow us to add a Moderation entry and see where it points to. When we build the administration page, you will see how we can use this data to get all the objects, regardless of type, for administration viewing purposes. In addition to the **SystemObjects** table, we are also linking to the **Accounts** table with the **AccountID** of the account that published the questionable content and the **AccountID** of the user that took action on the questionable content.

Gags

To gag a user — such as in a legal gag order — is to suppress them from being able to make comments publicly. We will extend this concept to say that we will not allow any user to publish content on our system if they have a gag order placed on them!

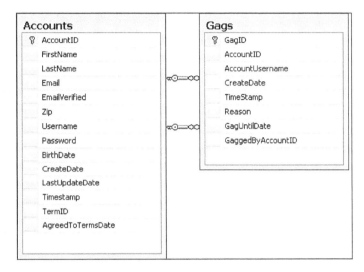

The most important thing to note in the **Gags** table is the **GagUntilDate** field as shown in the preceding screenshot. The date in this field is the date that the user can interact in the community again.

Filtering

The filtering system will provide us with the ability to map out content that we don't want, and swap it with the content that we actually need. We will first address this simple mapping issue with the concept that someone has used foul language on our site. We will be able to add the potty word that we don't like to our content filter list and insert a better word in its place so that our content is less offensive. In the case of my "dude" scenario we swapped in "[Filtered]".

While our filter can and should be used in this simple way, it can also be used to destroy a client-side script. To possibly destroy a script, you can add these text strings to our filter list (two different entries) `<script>` and `</script>` along with an empty string as the replacement value. This will effectively replace all `<script>` and `</script>` entries with an empty string. This will leave the code/text between the remaining script tags. That would effectively break the script — we think. It would still leave the script code intact, which could possibly be an issue. I could enter `<script >` and `</script >`, and it would not be caught!

In order to just use this concept of filtering, we would have to have an extensive database of possible entries to test for. Not only is this difficult, but would also be tremendously inefficient! Even if we had the greatest dictionary in the world, there is still a chance that we would miss something. And of course it would be fairly ugly as you would have all the code that we didn't catch displayed in the page. But at least they couldn't run the script at that point. It's a step in the right direction.

In order to address the issue of unaccounted for tags, and to bypass the need for a tag library, we will use `UrlEncode()` on the string to be filtered prior to filtering it. The first pass of `UrlEncode()` will convert the `<script>` and `</script>` tags into `&lt;script&gt;` and `&lt;/script&gt;`. It will also convert all the other special characters in the entry and make them encoded as well. This effectively renders all the HTML, CSS, and JavaScript code useless!

Now that we have killed all the possible markup and script in the text, what about the stuff that we want to allow on my site? We can make exceptions in our filter list by adding encoded words to be translated back to acceptable terms. In the case of a bold tag `<b>` the encode function would make it look like `&lt;b&rt;`. We can simply add the `&lt;b&rt;` to our list of words to be filtered with a replacement value `<b>`. Now we can build back what we want to accept. An acceptance list is much easier to manage than a database of possibilities for the content to be filtered.

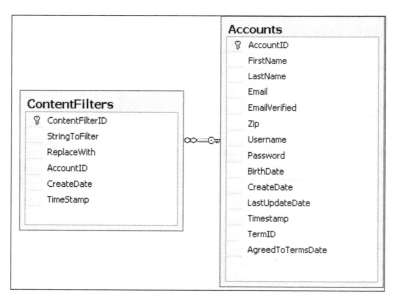

Solution

Now let's take a look at the solution.

Implementing the database

First let's take a look at what tables are needed:

Moderations

The moderation table shown in the following screenshot holds the **SystemObjectID** and **SystemObjectRecordID** as well as the Account that created the content in question. It also carries the Account that executed the resulting action as well as what that action is.

Column Name	Data Type	Allow Nulls
ModerationID	bigint	☐
AccountID	int	☑
AccountUsername	varchar(200)	☑
SystemObjectID	int	☐
SystemObjectRecordID	bigint	☐
TimeStamp	timestamp	☐
CreateDate	smalldatetime	☐
IsApproved	bit	☑
IsDenied	bit	☑
ActionByAccountID	int	☑
ActionByUsername	varchar(200)	☑

In addition to tables, we are going to need a way to quickly and easily determine if a bit of content has been flagged or not. I hate to say it boys and girls, but we are going to dip into the actual SQL for this one. We will create a function that will take a `SystemObjectID` and a `SystemObjectRecordID` and determine if that item is flagged or not.

```
create function [dbo].[IsFlagged]
(
    @SystemObjectID int,
    @SystemObjectRecordID bigint
)
returns bit

as
begin
    declare @result bit
    if exists (
            select 1
            from moderations
            where systemobjectid = @SystemObjectID and
```

```
                        systemobjectrecordid = @SystemObjectRecordID and
                        isdenied = 'true')
        begin
                set @result = 1
        end
        else
        begin
                set @result = 0
        end
        return @result
end
```

With this in place, we can simply make a call in our queries to determine when an item is flagged. We can then work with this information inside and outside of our queries quickly and easily.

Gags

The Gags table, as shown in the following screenshot, is responsible for determining if a user is on house arrest with regards to adding content to the community. It holds the gagged user's **AccountID**, their **AccountUsername**, when the gag was applied, why it was applied, who applied it, and when it is to be lifted.

Column Name	Data Type	Allow Nulls
GagID	bigint	
AccountID	int	
AccountUsername	varchar(200)	
CreateDate	smalldatetime	
TimeStamp	timestamp	
Reason	varchar(1000)	✓
GagUntilDate	smalldatetime	✓
GaggedByAccountID	int	

ContentFilters

Though the content filter has a great deal of responsibility, it is a relatively simple system. All it keeps track of is which pattern to filter, what to replace that pattern with, who created the filter, and when. The strength of the system is more in the implementation than in the storage!

Column Name	Data Type	Allow Nulls
ContentFilterID	int	☐
StringToFilter	varchar(500)	☐
ReplaceWith	varchar(500)	☐
AccountID	int	☐
CreateDate	smalldatetime	☐
TimeStamp	timestamp	☐

Creating the relationships

Once all the tables are created, we can create all the relationships.

For this set of tables we have relationships between the following tables:

- `Moderations` and `Accounts`
- `Moderations` and `SystemObjects`
- `Gags` and `Accounts`
- `ContentFilters` and `Accounts`

Setting up the data access layer

Follow the steps mentioned next:

- Open the `Fisharoo.dbml` file.
- Open up your **Server Explorer** window.
- Expand your Fisharoo connection.
- Expand your tables. If you don't see your new tables try hitting the **Refresh** icon or right-clicking on tables and clicking **Refresh**.

- Then drag your new tables onto the design surface.

- Hit **Save** and you should now have the following domain objects to work with!

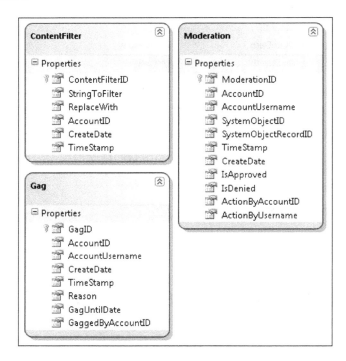

Keep in mind that we are not letting LINQ track our relationships. So go ahead and delete them from the design surface. Your design surface should have the same items that you saw in the preceding screenshot (though perhaps in a different arrangement!).

Building repositories

With the addition of new tables will come the addition of new repositories so that we can get at the data stored in those tables. We will create the following repositories to support our needs.

- `ModerationRepository`

- `GagRepository`

- `ContentFilterRepository`

Each of our repositories will generally have a method — for select by ID, select all by parent ID, save, and delete. Once you have seen one repository, you have pretty much seen them all. Review previous chapters, the appendices, or the included code for examples of a standard repository. However, I will discuss anything that varies from the standard!

ModerationRepository

For this repository, we have a standard `save` method that will take in one `ModerationRepository` at a time and deal with it appropriately. It essentially creates entries as our user's flag content. This is great for *one-at-a-time* record creation for our community users.

GetModerationsGlobal()

Once we have our `Moderation` records created, we need to be able to see the issues so that we can accept some content and deny the others. To do this, we have a method that gets all the moderations from a global point of view `GetModerationsGlobal()`.

```
public List<Moderation> GetModerationsGlobal()
{
    List<Moderation> result = new List<Moderation>();
    using(FisharooDataContext dc = conn.GetContext())
    {
        var groups = (from m in dc.Moderations
                      where m.IsDenied == null || m.IsApproved ==
                                              null
                      group m by m.SystemObjectRecordID
                      into g
                          select new { g, NumberOfReports = g.Count()
                                      }).OrderByDescending
                                      (g1 => g1.NumberOfReports);
        foreach (var v in groups)
        {
            result.Add(v.g.ToList()[0]);
        }
    }
    return result;
}
```

This method allows us to get all the moderations, grouped by the SystemObjectRecordID as many people could report the same bit of content. This reduced view is what we will see in our admin screens so that we can accept and reject content in a more streamlined fashion. There is no need to view every complaint!

In order to deal with this reduced view, initially we have to create a new struct that will hold our selected SystemObjectID, SystemObjectRecordID, and whether the item is approved or not.

```
public struct ModerationResult
{
    public int SystemObjectID { get; set; }
    public long SystemObjectRecordID { get; set; }
    public bool IsApproved { get; set; }
}
```

Our admin screen will be built similar to a web-based email client so that you can interact with several moderation records at a time. It will gather a collection of moderation records and package them up into a collection of ModerationResults. Once we have a collection of those items, we can pass them to our bulk save method SaveModerationResults().

```
public void SaveModerationResults(List<ModerationResult> results, int
                        ActionByAccountID,
                        string ActionByUsername)
{
    using(FisharooDataContext dc = conn.GetContext())
    {
        foreach (ModerationResult result in results)
        {
            List<Moderation> moderations =
                dc.Moderations.Where(
                    m =>
                    m.SystemObjectID == result.SystemObjectID &&
                    m.SystemObjectRecordID ==
                    result.SystemObjectRecordID).ToList();
            for (int i = 0; i < moderations.Count(); i++)
            {
                if (result.IsApproved)
                {
                    moderations[i].IsApproved = true;
                    moderations[i].IsDenied = false;
                }
                else
```

```
            {
                moderations[i].IsDenied = true;
                moderations[i].IsApproved = false;
            }
            moderations[i].ActionByAccountID = ActionByAccountID;
            moderations[i].ActionByUsername = ActionByUsername;
        }
        if(moderations.Count() > 0)
            dc.SubmitChanges();
    }
  }
}
```

This method is responsible for taking in a collection of ModerationResults, which is possibly a grouped result set of individual moderations. For this reason, with each iteration over the ModerationResults collection, we must first attempt to get a list of applicable Moderation records. We then set all the values for each of these records and save them back into the database.

We now have everything we need to get complaints from our users as well as the ability to respond to the complaints. What we are still missing is the ability to actually remove the content from our site based on the complaints. We can deal with this issue in two ways. We can add or delete content functionality that physically removes the offending content from the server entirely, or we can simply hide flagged content so that the user can possibly fix it. I personally would be very upset if a site administrator removed a ten page blog post just because I had one accidental dirty word! So we will stick with the concept that the content will simply be hidden from the site when it is flagged. This concept unfortunately doesn't have a magic bullet fix in C# or LINQ—at least not the right one! This is where that IsFlagged SQL function comes in. We will need to add our IsFlagged() call to our existing repositories where appropriate. Here is the FileRepository with an example highlighted:

```
public List<File> GetFilesByFolderID(Int64 FolderID)
{
    List<File> result = new List<File>();
    using (FisharooDataContext dc = conn.GetContext())
    {
        IEnumerable<File> files1 = (from f in dc.Files
                                    where f.DefaultFolderID ==
                                    FolderID &&
                                    dc.IsFlagged(5,f.FileID) !=
                                    true
                                    select f);
```

```
IEnumerable<File> files2 = (from f in dc.Files
                                join ff in dc.FolderFiles on
                                f.FileID equals ff.FileID
                                where ff.FolderID == FolderID &&
                                dc.IsFlagged(5,f.FileID) !=
                                true
                                select f);
IEnumerable<File> files3 = files1.Union(files2);
result = files3.ToList();
foreach (File file in result)
{
    var fileType = dc.FileTypes.Where(ft => ft.FileTypeID ==
                        file.FileTypeID).FirstOrDefault();
    file.Extension = fileType.Name;
}
    }
    return result;
}
```

This addition will effectively block the output of all the files that are flagged in our moderation system.

GagRepository

There are two methods in this repository that we will discuss:

1. One of them will give us the ability to get a listing of all the Gags in the system so that we can manage who is gagged, who is about to be ungagged, and possibly a user who may need a Gag extension.

2. The other method will allow us to check to see if a user is currently gagged. It will allow us to restrict a user from creating new content. We can also use it to make changes to the display such as hiding the new post button.

Our first method, GetActiveGags(), will allow us to get a list of all Gags that are still in effect.

```
public List<Gag> GetActiveGags()
{
    List<Gag> result = new List<Gag>();
    using(FisharooDataContext dc = conn.GetContext())
    {
        result = dc.Gags.Where(g => g.GagUntilDate >
                DateTime.Now).OrderBy(g => g.GagUntilDate).ToList();
    }
    return result;
}
```

The next method, `IsGagged()`, allows us to verify that a user is not currently under a gag restraint.

```
public bool IsGagged(Int32 AccountID)
{
    bool result = false;
    using(FisharooDataContext dc = conn.GetContext())
    {
        if(dc.Gags.Where(g=>g.AccountID == AccountID &&
                         g.GagUntilDate > DateTime.Now).
                         FirstOrDefault() != null)
        {
            result = true;
        }
    }
    return true;
}
```

ContentFilterRepository

The `ContentFilterRepository` currently only has one job. It returns a list of all the filters in the system.

```
public List<ContentFilter> GetContentFilters()
{
    List<ContentFilter> filters = new List<ContentFilter>();
    using (FisharooDataContext dc = _conn.GetContext())
    {
        filters = dc.ContentFilters.ToList();
    }
    return filters;
}
```

Implementing the services/application layer

Once all the repositories are built for single-serving purposes, we can begin to create the service layer. Again this layer is responsible for assembling aggregates and performing complex actions with our entities. We will create and modify the following services:

- `ContentFilterService`
- `Extensions`

ContentFilterService

The `ContentFilterService` is responsible for applying our `ContentFilters`. This method consolidates the call into the `ContentFilterRepository`, the `HtmlEncode()` of the string, and the actual work of applying the filters to the string being filtered.

```
public static string Filter(string StringToFilter)
{
    IContentFilterRepository _contentFilterRepository =
            ObjectFactory.GetInstance<IContentFilterRepository>();
    List<ContentFilter> _contentFilters = _contentFilterRepository.
GetContentFilters();
    StringBuilder sb = new StringBuilder(StringToFilter);
    //encode the final output for further security
    sb = new StringBuilder(HttpUtility.HtmlEncode(sb.ToString()));
    //replace all the dirty words and forbidden tags
    foreach (ContentFilter cf in _contentFilters)
    {
        sb.Replace(cf.StringToFilter, cf.ReplaceWith);
    }
    return sb.ToString();
}
```

Our initial entry into this method provides us with the string that we will be working with. Next, we get a list of `ContentFilters` to work with. In order to work with our string in a more efficient manner we are going to create a new `StringBuilder`. Our first pass of filtering our string will start with encoding our string using the `HttpUtility.HtmlEncode()` method. Once we have our base string to work with, we can begin iterating over our collection of `ContentFilters`. With each `ContentFilter`, we perform a `Replace()` where we swap out our `StringToFilter` for our `ReplaceWith` value. We then convert our `StringBuilder` back to a string prior to returning the result of our filtering process.

Extensions

The `Extensions` class is a pre-existing class that holds all our extension methods. In this case, we are going to add a new method to the `string` class. This will allow us to work with a string directly and apply the `Filter()` call directly to our string. Shorter syntax with the same results!

```
public static string Filter(this string s)
{
    return ContentFilterService.Filter(s);
}
```

To create our extension method, we declare a `static` method with a return type `string`. Next, we have the method name that we want to use. Here `this` references the `string` that the method is being applied to, while the next `string` specifies the type to apply the method to. In our method, `s` is our variable name to work with.

Implementing the presentation layer

The majority of our work in this chapter will be in the form of user controls and function calls. The changes that are made are more about how the content disappears rather than seeing new items.

Moderation

Now let's look at the feature of moderation.

The user control

Our moderation feature begins its life as a rather simple user control. This control is made up of an AJAX.NET `UpdatePanel`, one `Panel`, and one `ImageButton` for flagging our content. If the user is not logged in, we will hide the Panel. And once the user clicks the `ImageButton`, we will add the `Moderation` content to our table. Directly after the filter is captured, we will hide the button. From that point onwards when the users load their content they will no longer see the option to flag that content.

```
//UserControls/Moderations.ascx
<asp:UpdatePanel runat="server">
    <ContentTemplate>
        <asp:Panel ID="pnlFlagThis" runat="server" style="float:left;
padding-left:5px;padding-right:5px;">
            <asp:ImageButton ToolTip="Flag this content!"
ID="ibFlagThis" runat="server" ImageUrl="~/images/icon_flag.gif"
OnClick="ibFlagThis_Click" />
        </asp:Panel>
    </ContentTemplate>
</asp:UpdatePanel>
```

Note that we have a few properties. These are the same as our Tagging, Rating, and Commenting controls. These properties allow us to track the item that we are allowing our users to flag. Once we have the UI loaded for this control, we initialize our presenter and make a call to initialize our control.

```
public partial class Moderations : System.Web.UI.UserControl,
                                   IModerations
{
```

```
public int SystemObjectID { get; set; }
public long SystemObjectRecordID { get; set; }
public bool ShowFlagThis
{
    set
    {
        pnlFlagThis.Visible = value;
    }
}
ModerationsPresenter _presenter = new ModerationsPresenter();
protected void Page_Load(object sender, EventArgs e)
{
    _presenter.Init(this, IsPostBack);
}
protected void ibFlagThis_Click(object sender, EventArgs e)
{
    _presenter.SaveModeration(SystemObjectID,
                              SystemObjectRecordID);
}
}
```

Once the control is transferred to our presenter, we can set all the properties for our control and determine if we should show the control or not.

```
public class ModerationsPresenter
{
    private IModerations _view;
    private IWebContext _webContext;
    private IModerationRepository _moderationRepository;
    public ModerationsPresenter()
    {
        _webContext = ObjectFactory.GetInstance<IWebContext>();
        _moderationRepository =
                ObjectFactory.GetInstance<IModerationRepository>();
    }
    public void Init(IModerations view, bool IsPostBack)
    {
        _view = view;
        if (_webContext.CurrentUser == null)
            _view.ShowFlagThis = false;
        else if (_moderationRepository.HasFlaggedThisAlready(_
webContext.CurrentUser.
                                    AccountID, _view.SystemObjectID,
                                    _view.SystemObjectRecordID))
            _view.ShowFlagThis = false;
```

```
        else
            _view.ShowFlagThis = true;
    }

    public void SaveModeration(int SystemObjectID, long
                            SystemObjectRecordID)
    {
        if (_webContext.CurrentUser != null)
        {
            Moderation moderation = new Moderation();
            moderation.AccountID = _webContext.CurrentUser.AccountID;
            moderation.AccountUsername =
                                    _webContext.CurrentUser.Username;
            moderation.CreateDate = DateTime.Now;
            moderation.SystemObjectID = _view.SystemObjectID;
            moderation.SystemObjectRecordID =
                                    _view.SystemObjectRecordID;
            _moderationRepository.SaveModeration(moderation);
        }
        _view.ShowFlagThis = false;
    }
}
```

The last thing to be aware of is the button click event that is transferred from the code behind and into the presenter. From the presenter we create a new `Moderation` and save it to our database.

Once the user control is complete, we are able to plug it for all to use. The first thing that needs to be done is to register the new user control on the page where we intend to use it.

```
<%@ Register Src="~/UserControls/Moderations.ascx"
            TagName="Moderations" TagPrefix="Fisharoo" %>
```

Then we can locate the control where we need it. Remember that this is simply a link button that displays a small icon.

```
<ItemTemplate>
    <li>
    <Fisharoo:Moderations ID="Moderations1"
                            SystemObjectID="5"
                            SystemObjectRecordID='<%#((File)
                                                Container.
                                                DataItem).FileID
                                                %>'
                            runat="server">
    </Fisharoo:Moderations>
```

```
        <asp:Label style="font-weight:bold;"
                   ID="lblFileName"
                   Text='<%#((File)Container.DataItem).FileName %>'
                   runat="server">
        </asp:Label>
```

Note that we are loading the properties directly in the page. This may or may not work depending on when you load the repeater. You may need to locate and load the control in the OnItemDataBound event handler.

```
protected void lvAlbum_ItemDataBound(object sender,
                                     ListViewItemEventArgs e)
{
Fisharoo.FisharooWeb.UserControls.Tags Tags1 =
                        e.Item.FindControl("Tags1") as
                        Fisharoo.FisharooWeb.UserControls.Tags;
Fisharoo.FisharooWeb.UserControls.Moderations Moderations1 =
    e.Item.FindControl("Moderations1") as Fisharoo.FisharooWeb.
    UserControls.Moderations;
Moderations1.SystemObjectRecordID = Convert.ToInt64(litFileID.Text);
Tags1.SystemObjectRecordID = Convert.ToInt64(litFileID.Text);
```

Once this is complete, the community will be off and running to moderate content!

Moderating flagged content

Now that we have a working flagging system, it is time to stand up a page where we can manage the newly collected data. To achieve this, I have added a new section to our (sparse) administration area. This page has a quick repeater that shows some checkboxes to capture whether the item is to be approved or denied.

[There are also some Gagging tools here to capture the gagging of a user. We will discuss more of this later.]

```
<asp:UpdatePanel runat="server">
    <ContentTemplate>
        <table>
            <tr>
                <td>Approve</td>
                <td>Deny</td>
                <td>Content</td>
                <td>Reported User</td>
                <td>Gag Till</td>
                <td>Reason</td>
            </tr>
```

```
    <asp:Repeater ID="repModeration" runat="server"
                OnItemDataBound="repModeration_ItemDataBound">
    <ItemTemplate>
        <tr>
            <td><asp:CheckBox ID="chkApprove" runat="server"
            /></td>
            <td><asp:CheckBox ID="chkDeny" runat="server" /></td>
            <td><asp:PlaceHolder ID="phContent"
                    runat="server"></asp:PlaceHolder></td>
            <td>
                <asp:HyperLink runat="server" NavigateUrl='<%#
                        _configuration.WebSiteURL +
((Moderation)Container.DataItem).AccountUsername %>'
        Text='<%#((Moderation)
        Container.DataItem).AccountUsername %>'></asp:HyperLink>
                <asp:Literal ID="litSystemObjectID"
                    Visible="false" Text='<%#((Moderation)Cont
ainer.DataItem).SystemObjectID %>'
                    runat="server"></asp:Literal>
                <asp:Literal ID="litSystemObjectRecordID"
                    Visible="false" Text='<%#((Moderation)Cont
ainer.DataItem).SystemObjectRecordID %>'
                    runat="server"></asp:Literal>
                <asp:Literal ID="litAccountID" Visible="false"
                        Text='<%#((Moderation)
                        Container.DataItem).AccountID %>'
                        runat="server"></asp:Literal>
                <asp:Literal ID="litAccountUsername"
                    Visible="false" Text='<%#((Moderation)Cont
ainer.DataItem).AccountUsername %>'
                    runat="server"></asp:Literal>
            </td>
            <td><asp:TextBox ID="txtGagDate"
                        runat="server"></asp:TextBox></td>
            <td><asp:TextBox ID="txtReason"
                        runat="server"></asp:TextBox></td>
        </tr>
    </ItemTemplate>
    </asp:Repeater>
        </table>
        <asp:Button ID="btnSubmit" runat="server"
            OnClick="btnSubmit_Click" Text="Save" />
    </ContentTemplate>
</asp:UpdatePanel>
```

This is a very simple but efficient interface. It will show us the content that was flagged, who posted the content, and provide us with the opportunity to take the appropriate action.

With the UI created, we can take a quick look at the code behind. For the most part, the code in this page is a very normal loading and rendering of a `Repeater` control. The one place that may be a bit new to you though is in the `Save` button's `click` event. Here we will iterate through all the controls in the `Repeater` to extract the data that we need to work with.

```
protected void btnSubmit_Click(object sender, EventArgs e)
{
    List<ModerationResult> results = new List<ModerationResult>();
    foreach (RepeaterItem item in repModeration.Controls)
    {
        if(item.ItemType == ListItemType.AlternatingItem ||
            item.ItemType == ListItemType.Item)
        {
            CheckBox chkApprove = item.FindControl("chkApprove") as
            CheckBox;
            CheckBox chkDeny = item.FindControl("chkDeny") as
            CheckBox;
            Literal litSystemObjectID =
            item.FindControl("litSystemObjectID") as Literal;
            Literal litSystemObjectRecordID =
            item.FindControl("litSystemObjectRecordID") as Literal;
            TextBox txtGagDate = item.FindControl("txtGagDate") as
            TextBox;
            TextBox txtReason = item.FindControl("txtReason") as
            TextBox;
            Literal litAccountID = item.FindControl("litAccountID")
            as Literal;
            Literal litAccountUsername =
            item.FindControl("litAccountUsername") as Literal;
            if(chkDeny.Checked || chkApprove.Checked)
            {
                ModerationResult mr = new ModerationResult();
                mr.SystemObjectID =
                Convert.ToInt32(litSystemObjectID.Text);
                mr.SystemObjectRecordID =
                Convert.ToInt64(litSystemObjectRecordID.Text);
                if (chkApprove.Checked)
                {
                    mr.IsApproved = true;
                    results.Add(mr);
                }
```

```
                  //deny wins
                  if (chkDeny.Checked)
                  {
                      mr.IsApproved = false;
                      results.Add(mr);
                  }
              }
              if(!string.IsNullOrEmpty(txtGagDate.Text))
              {
                _presenter.GagUserUntil(Convert.ToInt32
                                     (litAccountID.Text),
                                     litAccountUsername.Text,
                                     DateTime.Parse(txtGagDate.Text),
                                     txtReason.Text);
              }
          }
      }
   if(results.Count() > 0)
       _presenter.SaveModerationResults(results);
}
```

There appears to be a lot going on here, but a fair amount of the code at the top of the method is dedicated to locating and loading the controls from the UI. Once we have the controls in hand, we can interrogate the state of each flagged item. When we find something with a checkbox selected for approving or denying, we add the item to our `List` of `ModerationResults` (recall that we created this earlier in the repository in the previous section).

[Also note that there is more gagging logic here!]

Once we have worked our way through the data, we then send our list of alterations through to the `ModerationRepository` where it is saved in bulk.

Gagging

In order to see how the Gagging feature works, you will need to have read the Moderation section explained previously in this chapter.

Now that we are here in the moderation pages UI, you can notice that we have two text box controls. We have one text box for capturing the reason why we have decided to gag a user. And the other text box is for providing the data, which indicates when the gag would ultimately be revoked for a user. You could accurately label that box "Grounded until..."

In the `btnSubmit_Click()` method (discussed previously), you will also see some code that interrogates the state of those text boxes. If we find something in the Repeaters control collection, then we call into the `GagUserUntil()` method of our presenter and effectively gag the user. The presenter creates a `new Gag` object and persists it out to our database.

```
public void GagUserUntil(int AccountID, string AccountUsername,
                         DateTime GagTillDate, string Reason)
{
    Gag gag = new Gag();
    gag.AccountID = AccountID;
    gag.CreateDate = DateTime.Now;
    gag.AccountUsername = AccountUsername;
    gag.GagUntilDate = GagTillDate;
    gag.Reason = Reason;
    gag.GaggedByAccountID = _webContext.CurrentUser.AccountID;
    _gagRepository.SaveGag(gag);
}
```

Filtering

Finally, we come to the meat and potatoes of our chapter. The filtering process is responsible for removing vulgar language, competitors' advertisments and bad mouthing, and XSS attacks. It is the almighty feature of features. Are you ready for it?

I have added this feature to our `ViewPost.aspx` page to demonstrate it. To get started, we need to add a reference to our implementation code where all our services live.

```
<%@ Import Namespace="Fisharoo.FisharooCore.Core.Impl" %>
```

Then we need to add a call to our `Filter()` extension method.

```
<tr style="background-color:#dddddd;">
        <td colspan="4"
            valign="top">
            <asp:Label ID="lblDescription"
            runat="server"
          Text='<%#((BoardPost)Container.DataItem).Post.Filter()
            %>'>
            </asp:Label>
        </td>
    </tr>
```

Done, finally! All the work for the implementation of this feature is in the backend — crucial for the feature of this nature. The easier it is to use, the more likely it will be used. Wherever possible we would actually be better off filtering the text in the presenter or even further up the chain. The closer this task is done to the actual data retrieval, the less likely it is to be forgotten! But as you can see, it is flexible enough to be used whenever and wherever you need it.

Summary

In this chapter we discussed how and why to implement some form of moderation. We looked at how our community provided content could be managed by the same community using a very simple flagging tool that is flexible enough to be added to any major entity on our site. We also looked at methods to deal with habitual rule breakers in the form of gagging them or suspending their content by adding privileges. Finally, we took a very high-level look at what Cross-site scripting is, and some measures that can be taken to address it. We then implemented a filtering system to automate the address of our XSS issues. This functionality has provided us with a way to remove inappropriate content as well as security issues.

Please do make a point of researching XSS more. At the very least take a look at the link provided by Microsoft regarding this topic!

13
Scaling Up

If you have made it this far then you must be the proud new owner of a community site that is ready to start accepting new community members. I know from experience that you did not go this far to start a community that will only ever have 100 users. You, like everyone else, would like very much to start building a social network that gets 100,000 or more active users. Ten thousand users is considered a success. One hundred thousand concurrent users and you might be able to sell your community to someone else. Hit a million and you can scream WOO HOO!

To get that many users to your site will require several things. It means that you will have to have a great new concept for your site. Something that really makes it stand out as different. It will require excellent marketing skills either by way of viral marketing or through a more traditional marketing campaign. It will also mean that your site will need to stand up under a heavy daily load of users continuously until you reach your goals. This last point is what this chapter is all about.

Problem

There are many aspects of a site with a large number of users that can bring the site to its knees. Some of this can be slowness of the features while others can be physically locking the system to a point that it is no longer responsive. In this chapter, I will do my best to address some of the possible issues that might come up with a community.

We will discuss issues at the database level in the form of indexing and partitioning our data. We will dive into how we can address application slowness by throwing more hardware at it and then load balancing that hardware. We will also discuss how to cache data dips and complex object creation so that we don't have to perform the queries or object manipulation every time. Next, we will speed up our search by creating highly optimized, indexed data sets. And finally we will look at reducing the number of systems our website speaks to directly so that our user experience is not directly impacted by infrastructure.

Design

Let's assume for this chapter that you have so many concurrent users on your site that you are starting to notice that the site and your servers are no longer able to keep up. What can we do? There are many approaches to this problem. You can simply leave the code unchanged and put the same code on many servers. You can address some performance in your code and stay on one server. You can even address some optimizations at the database level. Eventually though you will have to do all these to withstand the large loads of a successful community.

Database optimization

Up to this point we have not spent too much time discussing much at the database level. I will try to maintain that theme here as well, this book being more about ASP. NET and C# than it is about SQL! That being said, there are some things that we can do at the database level that we just can't do elsewhere.

Flagged for delete

Flagging content to be deleted rather than actually deleting it is not only going to be faster from the user's perspective but also from the database's perspective. When you attempt to delete a record, the database must lock that table prior to performing the delete. Also, with each deletion an entry must be made to the transaction log. And when a record is finally deleted, the database maintains the log sequence number and doesn't necessarily de-allocate the data pages for the deleted information. The bottom line—a delete statement is one of the most expensive commands that can be executed.

So, instead of deleting the record when the application says it needs an item deleted, we could set the FlaggedForDelete column to true. Then when our queries fetch data from this table, we could have a parameter in our WHERE clause checking that the data that we are selecting is not flagged for delete. We could then have an administrative process that runs however frequently is best for the current load that selects all the active data out of our table into a temp table, drops the table with our flagged for delete data, and then renames our temp table to the original name. When the table is truncated, the data pages are re-allocated to the system for re-use.

Keep in mind that with this method comes no "undo" feature. If you need your data to be persisted to the transaction logs for auditing purposes, this may not be the best method for you. Also, if you have any foreign key references to the table that you are truncating, you must drop those references prior to performing the truncate command. When you are through with your process, you will then have to recreate your keys.

Indexing

Indexing is a way of optimizing your database in such a way that the data is organized for fast searches. Without an index, various functions such as WHERE, ORDER BY, GROUP BY, TOP, and DISTINCT will have to perform a table scan, which will impact performance heavily. Without an index, when you are looking for a user's profile where ProfileID = 89734, SQL Server will have to look at every row to find the data that it is looking for. With an index in place, SQL Server will keep a list of ProfileIDs in a specific order so that locating the one we are interested in will be easy.

With an index in place, you will find that querying with a WHERE clause will be much faster. The downside to an index is that each time data is deleted from the index, the index must be recreated. The creation of an index can take time if the data set is large. This is a known downside and generally accepted as having an index is better than not having one.

Partitioning

Partitioning is the concept of splitting up a table's data into multiple tables. This can be done both vertically and horizontally. Both types of partitioning can be useful. I will explain both types, but we will go into further detail regarding horizontal partitioning.

Vertical partitioning is the concept of placing columns from one table into their own table. This data would remain in sync with the data from the other table. This process is sometimes referred to as **row splitting**. This action also occurs when normalizing a table. The performance gains from this type of partitioning is realized when you can quickly find data or static data and put it on one physical device and it becomes time consuming to find, or wider data, or more dynamic data, onto another device. Other than normalization, this type of partitioning is not used as frequently.

Horizontal partitioning is where you would take a physical set of data—the whole row—and store it in an identical table (schema wise). Each set is generally a ranged set of data. So for an ordering system you might put one quarter worth of data in table A, another quarter in table B, and so on. Generally, you would want to work with dates or numbers as your range set. However, in our case, we would only know the users by their usernames and passwords. So we might keep an indexed table of Usernames and UserIDs. Once we have the User's ID, we could then go to a partitioned table of user data partitioned on UserID in the range of 1-100,000, 100,001-200,000, and so on. Horizontal partitions speed up queries due to the fact that we are working with smaller sets of data. Also we can easily and quickly work with smaller sets of data in terms of adding to and deleting from those sets.

Web farming

Web farming (or load balancing) is the concept of spreading out your site's traffic over many servers. This addresses most of the performance problems whether in the application or on the server, by expanding your infrastructure and sharing the load across many servers. Generally, whoever is doing your load balancing will take a look at all the servers in your farm and route the user to the server with the lowest load. There are several ways to do this, and we will touch upon many of them lightly.

Caching

To cache in the terms of our application is to take some data or objects and store them in memory for later use. Later, when we need the stored item, we can simply retrieve it from memory. In terms of caching data from a database, we can take queried results and store them in memory. This means that when we go to get it again, we don't have to perform a server-to-server connection. We don't have to wait for the query to be executed, and we don't have to wait for the results to get sent back to us. We can just pluck the item from RAM. Take this one step further up the chain and we can enjoy further optimizations. We can take the data from the database, parse that data, build a list of fully hydrated objects, and then store that list in the cache. This means that in addition to skipping the database stuff we can also skip creation and hydration of our objects.

Caching, like indexing, comes with some downfalls. If we put data into our cache and then delete that data from the database, we may find our site using stale data. If we try to create blog entries with an account that no longer exists, we will get a database error. So while implementing a caching layer we must be very vigilant in making sure that our data is kept clean. Also, the problem can go the same way. If we have data in the cache that is stale but valid, we could show data that is incorrect to the user. It is important that we maintain this side of the clean data equation too!

Searching

Although a properly implemented set of indexes and caching layer can really add some serious performance to your site, it is not a fix all for everything. There is no reason to add search results to cache as a search is something that can literally be different for every search that is performed across all users. This would quickly fill our cache with bogus data. In addition to this shortcoming from cache, indexing doesn't fix everything up either. While an index can add some new legs to our search, it is not the best option for searching as people are generally interested in searching fields of text (not something we would want to index). And while we could implement FREETEXT search capabilities in SQL Server, there are better solutions out there.

In this section, we will discuss using Lucene.NET, which is a tool that allows you to index and search data efficiently. There are many big sites out that currently use Lucene for their search capabilities, and I will show you how to do it. While we won't be able to create a Google search engine, we can create all the fast searching features that any community site might need.

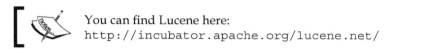
You can find Lucene here:
`http://incubator.apache.org/lucene.net/`

Email

How can sending email make the site slow? If you think about the normal emailing process, you will find that the web server has to, at the very least, connect to an SMTP server. This connection can take time. If you need to send hundreds of emails, then you need to possibly make the same amount of connections to an SMTP server.

To reduce this slowness, we will build a system that allows us to stuff our emails into a queue and send the email later from another system. This will greatly improve our users' experience as they will not have to wait for the web server to make a connection to SMTP and send an email. We will instead stuff the email into our queue and assume that the email will be delivered from another system.

Solution

Let's take a look at our solution.

Database optimization

The `FlaggedForDelete` concept is not one I am going to spend too much time on. You simply need to add `FlaggedForDelete` columns to each of your tables with `false` as the default value. As we are using LINQ to SQL, you would then need to update all the tables in your LINQ to SQL design surface. Then specify the default value of the `FlaggedForDelete` field as `false` in all your INSERT statements (you will need to set this value as objects come in to be inserted). With this in place, you would next need to update all your SELECT statements to check against the `FlaggedForDelete` field excluding items that are marked `true`. Don't forget that when you are running joined queries to check the `FlaggedForDelete` field on the linked tables as well. Last, you need to have a scheduled process that grabs all the rows that are flagged for deletion and removes them.

The process for removing rows that are flagged for delete is this:

- From table A, select the rows that are not flagged for deletion into a temp table
- Drop table A
- Rename the temp table as table A

Keep in mind that if there are foreign keys referencing the table that you want to run this process on, you will have to remove the keys. Then when the process is complete you will need to re-enable the keys.

Indexing

There are several types of indexes that can be created on a table — Unique, Clustered, Non-Clustered, and so on. A **Unique** index is one where the key of the index is unique across the entire table. Think of an auto-generated int value as a unique index. A clustered index keeps the sort of the table's data the same as the sort of the index. This makes for a very fast index. There can be only one clustered index on a table, as the table can have only one physical sort order! And then there is the non-clustered index. This index type keeps the indexed keys sorted logically, but this does not impact the physical sort of the table's data. An index can be made up of a single column such as the primary key of the int type. Or, you can create a composite key which is made of up to sixteen columns.

By default, when you create a table, the ID field or the primary key is established as the clustered index. If we wanted to create a new clustered index for the Accounts table using the Username field, we would first have to drop all the references to this primary key before we could remove the Clustered Index. We will focus on creating a unique non-clustered index on the Accounts table out of the Username field as the current Clustered Index will be used more often than the one we are going to create (as we frequently query on AccountID). To create this index, follow the steps given next.

- Go into the Accounts table details
- Select the Indexes folder
- Then right-click in the empty space and select **New Index...**

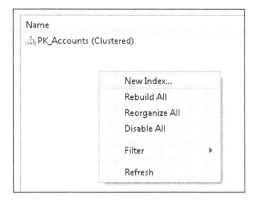

Then specify the **Index name** as **nci_Accounts_Username** (nci = non-clustered index), select **Unique** as we know that the **Username** field should be unique in our system, and then add the **Username** field to the columns that we want to build an index for.

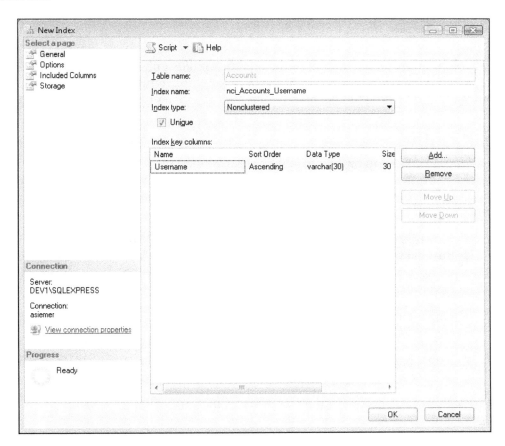

Then click **OK**, and we should have a **New Index** in place. If you have large amounts of data in the table that you created an index for, the index will be created right away. But SQL Server may need some time to generate the index.

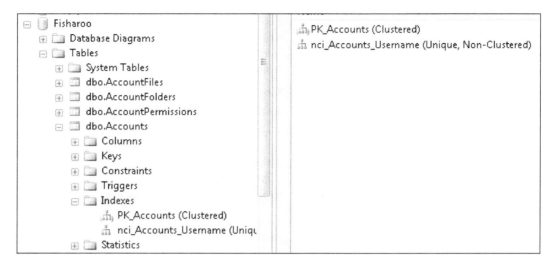

The use of an index is transparent to us. It is sort of like a phone book for SQL Server. Hence when we specify that we want the data for a user with the username of "asiemer", it knows how to find that data in a more efficient manner.

Partitioning

We will focus on how to build and utilize a partitioned table. Keep in mind that we only need to do this once the database has gotten to a point where it is starting to feel a bit sluggish (actually, you want to do this prior to feeling sluggish!). These are the general steps for creating the horizontal partition.

1. Create filegroups if you want to put the data on multiple physical disks. This is the best way to feel the most gain out of this particular performance hop up. This way when you are querying across the partition, the work is split up across multiple disks.

2. Create a partition function. This defines the range that we will be working with.

3. Create a partition scheme. This allows us to specify which partition sits on which filegroup.

4. With these steps out of the way, we can then start to create the partition tables.

FileGroups

To create a new filegroup, use this syntax.

```
Alter Database Fisharoo ADD FILEGROUP FG1
```

Once the filegroup is created, you can then add files to it.

```
ALTER DATABASE Fisharoo
ADD FILE
(
    NAME = FILE1,
    FILENAME = 'c:\Projects\Fisharoo\Trunk\DataBase\ FILE1.ndf',
    SIZE = 1MB,
    MAXSIZE = 10MB,
    FILEGROWTH = 1MB
)
TO FILEGROUP FG1;
```

You can add as many files to the file group as you think you will need. One file per disk per partition is the best thing you could do! You can always add to and modify this later.

Partition function

To create a partition function, use the following code:

```
CREATE PARTITION FUNCTION pfAccounts(int)
AS
RANGE LEFT FOR VALUES(10,000,20,000,30,000)
```

This partition function specifies that there will be three partitions. Each partition will hold 10,000 account records (you would probably want to define larger ranges). In the first partition, we will have accounts 1 through 10,000. The second partition will have 10,001 through 20,000. The third partition, that is, the final one will have accounts 20,001 through 30,000.

Partition scheme

To create a partition scheme use the following code (assuming that you made these file groups):

```
CREATE PARTITION SCHEME psAccounts
AS
PARTITION pfAccounts TO (FG1,FG2,FG3,[PRIMARY])
```

If you only have one file group defined then you can use this code:

```
CREATE PARTITION SCHEME psAccounts
AS
PARTITION pfAccounts ALL TO (FG1)
```

Partition tables

With these items in place we can then create the actual partition table.

```
CREATE TABLE Accounts
(
    AccountID INT,
    Username VARCHAR(20),
    ...
)
ON psAccounts(AccountID)
```

How does this affect our current system?

Unfortunately, this is not a behind-the-scenes fix all for your system like the indexes are. Querying a partitioned table requires a bit more syntax as you need to tell the SQL Server in which partition to look. This is not overly complex though. To get the account of a user with an AccountID of 25,000, you would run this query:

```
SELECT *
FROM Accounts
WHERE $PARTITION.pfAccounts(AccountID)  =
    (SELECT $PARTITION.pfAccounts(25,000))
```

The key here is the SELECT statement in the WHERE clause.

```
SELECT $PARTITION.pfAccounts(25,000)
```

This line returns the partition number to search for based on the range value that we build our partition function around. In this case, it knows that you are interested in the second partition. So it returns a 3 as partition 3 holds the account with AccountID 25,000. Beyond this querying, data is unchanged.

Take a look at this resource for further information regarding partitioned tables:

http://www.dotnetspider.com/resources/1082-Partitioning-Tables-SQL-SERVER.aspx

Gotchas

Do take note of the following points:

- Table partitioning, as described in the previous section, is available only in the Enterprise Edition (EE) of SQL Server. If you are working on something lower than EE, take a look at this post as it describes how to do a partitioned view instead of a partitioned table. This comes with some gotchas though so read it carefully! http://sqldev.wordpress.com/2008/03/16/sql-server-table-partitioning-without-enterprise-edition/

- LINQ to SQL and table partitions are not going to work as we would like (hopefully only for a while!). This means that for data that we are working with that is partitioned, we will have to work with it through stored procedures or table-valued user-defined functions.

Web farming

I am going to assume that we are interested in learning how to create a web farm in a windows environment.

 For those who need a Linux solution though you might try Ha Proxy (`http://haproxy.1wt.eu/`) or something similar.

Specifically, we are going to talk about setting up a web farm using Windows using the **Network Load Balancing** (**NLB**). This allows you to host a handful of servers behind one virtual IP address on your network as portrayed in the following diagram:

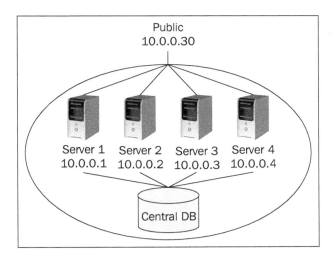

For this to work, each server in the farm needs to be configured identically so that any request that goes to any server will be handled in the same fashion. When a request comes to the virtual IP address, the packet will be routed to the least busy server. This configuration allows support of the concept of a reliable service. Meaning that if one server goes down, the farm will simply rebalance itself and route traffic to the servers that are still up.

To set this up, you need at least two machines running the Windows Server. Each machine will need to have one fixed IP address. While the machine can run on one network card, two cards are preferred — one card having the fixed IP address and the other using the virtual IP address. The IP addresses must be on the same class C network.

Open the **Network Load Balancing Manager** from **Administrative Tools**. Right-click on the **Network Load Balancing Clusters** and select **New Cluster**.

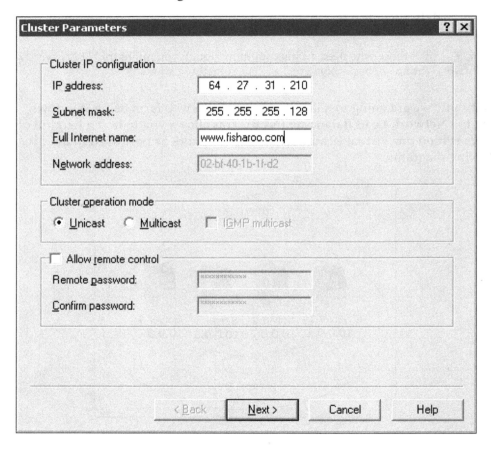

In **Cluster Parameters**, enter your virtual IP and your subnet mask (same subnet for all servers!). Then enter the domain name that points to this IP address (www.fisharoo.com). If you have more than one network card choose **Unicast**, for a single network card choose the **Multicast** option. Make sure that **IGMP multicast** is checked. Leave the **Allow remote control** unchecked. Click **Next**.

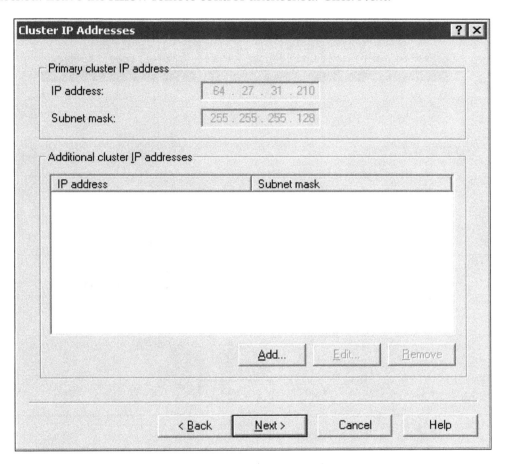

In the **Cluster IP Addresses** you can add additional virtual IP addresses. This allows you to host multiple websites from different IP addresses. We don't need this in our case. Click **Next**.

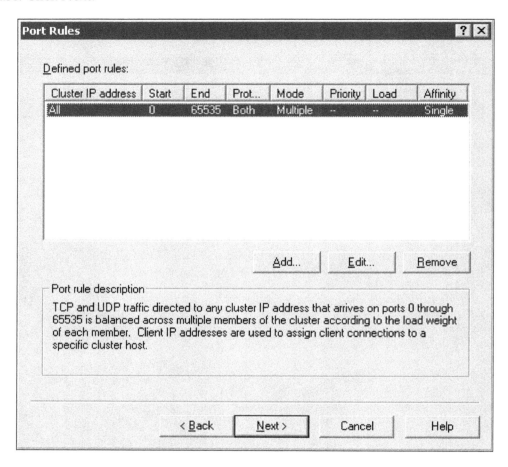

In the **Port Rules** table, we can define which ports our cluster will operate on. By default, the port that is configured handles traffic for all ports. This is a bit unsecure from my point of view. So we will remove the default configuration and configure port 443 for SSL and port 80 for web traffic. Select the default configuration and select **Remove**. Then to configure a new port 80 rule, click **Add...**

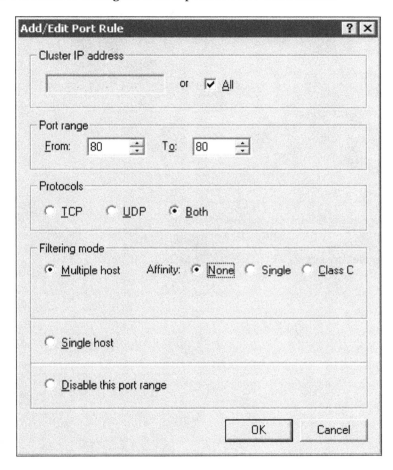

Make sure the **All** option is selected to make this rule apply to all IP addresses in the cluster. Then set the port range **From 80 To 80** (this effectively covers one port). Be sure that the **Both** option of **Protocols** is open to allow both **TCP** and **UDP** packets through this port. In the **Filtering mode** section, choose **Multiple host** and an **Affinity** of **None**. The second port, port 443, is exactly the same as the one before with the exception of a different port number. Click **Ok**. Then click **Next**.

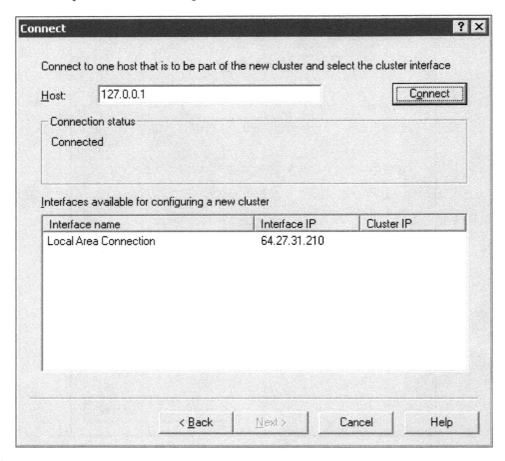

Now enter an IP address of one of the servers in the cluster. I entered the local host address for demo purposes. Then click **Connect**. You should then see the network address and IP address of that host. Select the IP address of the host that is part of the cluster and click **Next**.

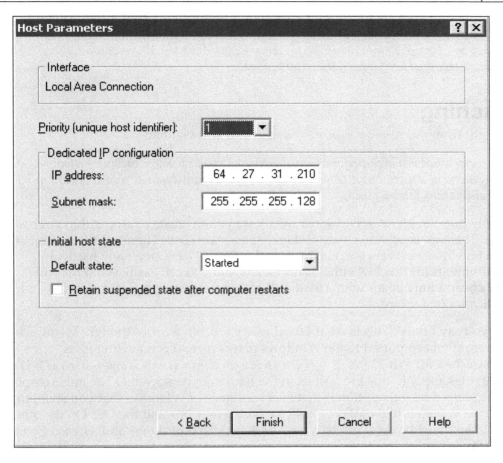

We will now configure the priority of each server in the cluster. Each server must have its own unique priority. The smaller the priority number, the higher the priority is for that server. 1 is the master server of the cluster. Once you hit **Finish**, you then have a new node in your cluster. You need to add all the servers that you want involved in your cluster.

Now you can configure your website's DNS to point to your network's virtual IP address for your web servers and the load should be transferred evenly across all the servers in the cluster. If one of the servers in your cluster goes down, your site should stay up. Keep in mind that with a clustered web farm, you will be able to service more requests. But don't forget to think about the other weak links in the chain. All the clustered servers are now pointing to a single data source. You might need to make that redundant as well if it is not already!

For more great information about setting up a network load balanced web farm in Windows Server, check out this great article from Rick Strahl at www.west-wind.com (http://www.west-wind.com/presentations/loadbalancing/networkloadbalancingwindows2003.asp).

Caching

Straight from www.danga.com/memcached you will see that:

> *memcached is a high-performance, distributed memory object caching system, generic in nature, but intended for use in speeding up dynamic web applications by alleviating database load.*

Simply put, the MemCached software allows you to create a farm within your web farm. This tool is used to create and manage a state farm. There aren't any limitations as to how many servers you can have in this farm. There aren't any hardware requirements for this tool either. This means that you can easily stand up some very cheap Linux boxes with a load of RAM, and expand your state farm as your application(s) require.

Did you say Linux? This is what I used to say too. No worries though. MemCached has recently been ported to the Windows platform, and is now offered as MemCached for Win32 (http://jehiah.cz/projects/memcached-win32/). The same rules apply to this product from the hardware perspective. The only reason I brought up the Linux option is that every instance of Windows that you stand up will cost you an initial outlay of cash for both a new box and the OS. On the other hand, the Linux boxes could be a farm of deactivated desktops and a free copy of your favorite Linux distro!

The reason that I use this over what is shipped with .NET is that there are lesser restrictions all around, and it seems to be better performing. Example: I can only have one .NET State Server or SQL Server whereas I can have as many nodes in my cache cluster as I want with MemCached. Moreover, the response time of MemCached over the standard State Server and SQL Server is also considerably better. I also don't have to worry about where my applications are physically running from as MemCache runs in its own world either on the same server as your application or on entirely different servers.

 You still need to set the machineKey or disable the MAC check as discussed to get your ASP.NET webpages to work. MemCached only takes care of caching and session handling!

This cache implementation can do for you exactly the same thing a State server can. You can point your session wrapper (or Context in our case) to your memcache implementation.

The server

Get the windows version of MemCached from the URL given in the *Caching* section. You can download the binaries or the source code. If you downloaded the source code, you need to build the solution. With the binaries in hand, you can unzip/put them into a directory on your local drive. Once you have the binaries installed, you can run these simple directions:

1. Unzip the binaries in your desired directory (eg. `c:\memcached`)
2. Install the service using the command:

   `c:\memcached\memcached.exe -d install`
3. Start the server from the Microsoft Management Console or by running the following command:

   `c:\memcached\memcached.exe -d start`
4. Use the server, by default listening to port 11211

You can run several instances of this program on each server if you need to. Also, you can change the port that you run the server(s) on. You could run a different instance per application if you like.

That's it!

The client

Once you have the server installed and running you will need a client. There are currently a few C# clients available.

- `https://sourceforge.net/projects/memcacheddotnet/`
- `http://code.google.com/p/beitmemcached/`
- `http://www.codeplex.com/EnyimMemcached`

There is also a host of other clients for other languages too.

- `http://www.danga.com/memcached/apis.bml`

In our implementation, we will use the `Enyim Memcached client`. I have used this client on several projects and have not seen it have any issues. This client comes in the form of a solution that you can get from `codeplex.com`. It has a test client, the actual code, and so on. I take the `Enyim.Caching` project from within the solution and plug it into my current project solution.

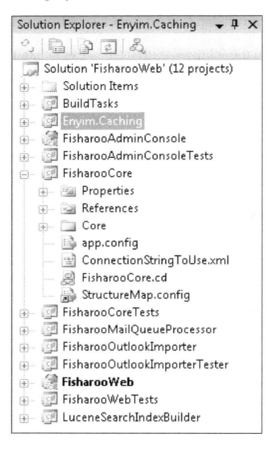

With this in place you can then add a reference to `Enyim.Caching` from your project.

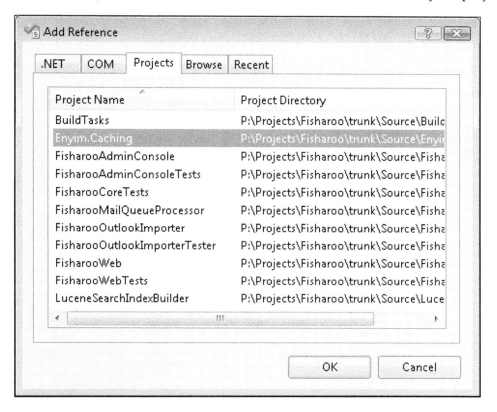

Using the client

With our new client in place we can then create a new cache wrapper that inherits from the same interface as our current cache wrapper.

```
public interface ICache
{
    object Get(string cache_key);
    List<string> GetCacheKeys();
    void Set(string cache_key, object cache_object);
    void Set(string cache_key, object cache_object, DateTime
            expiration);
    void Set(string cache_key, object cache_object, TimeSpan
            expiration);
    void Set(string cache_key, object cache_object, DateTime
            expiration, CacheItemPriority priority);
```

```
        void Set(string cache_key, object cache_object, TimeSpan
                expiration, CacheItemPriority priority);
        void Delete(string cache_key);
        bool Exists(string cache_key);
        void Flush();
}
```

We will call the new cache wrapper MemcachedCache. The big difference here is that we have a different Pluggable attribute of MemCached.

```
[Pluggable("MemCached")]
public class MemcachedCache : ICache
{
    private MemcachedClient cache;
    private TimeSpan _timeSpan = new TimeSpan(
        Settings.Default.DefaultCacheDuration_Days,
        Settings.Default.DefaultCacheDuration_Hours,
        Settings.Default.DefaultCacheDuration_Minutes, 0);
    public MemcachedCache()
    {
        cache = new MemcachedClient();
        List<string> keys = new List<string>();
        cache.Store(StoreMode.Add, "keys", keys);
    }

    public object Get(string cache_key)
    {
        return cache.Get(cache_key);
    }

    public List<string> GetCacheKeys()
    {
        return cache.Get("keys") as List<string>;
    }

    public void Set(string cache_key, object cache_object)
    {
        Set(cache_key, cache_object, _timeSpan);
    }

    public void Set(string cache_key, object cache_object, DateTime
                    expiration)
    {
        Set(cache_key, cache_object, expiration,
            CacheItemPriority.Normal);
    }
```

```
public void Set(string cache_key, object cache_object, TimeSpan
            expiration)
{
    Set(cache_key, cache_object, expiration,
        CacheItemPriority.Normal);
}

public void Set(string cache_key, object cache_object, DateTime
            expiration, CacheItemPriority priority)
{
    cache.Store(StoreMode.Set, cache_key, cache_object,
            expiration);
    UpdateKeys(cache_key);
}

public void Set(string cache_key, object cache_object, TimeSpan
            expiration, CacheItemPriority priority)
{
    cache.Store(StoreMode.Set, cache_key, cache_object,
            expiration);
    UpdateKeys(cache_key);
}

private void UpdateKeys(string key)
{
    List<string> keys = new List<string>();
    if (cache.Get("keys") != null)
    {
        keys = cache.Get("keys") as List<string>;
    }
    if (!keys.Contains(key.ToLower()))
    {
        keys.Add(key);
        cache.Store(StoreMode.Set, "keys", keys);
    }
}

public void Delete(string cache_key)
{
    if (Exists(cache_key))
        cache.Remove(cache_key);
}

public bool Exists(string cache_key)
{
    if (cache.Get(cache_key) != null)
        return true;
```

```
        else
            return false;
    }

    public void Flush()
    {
        cache.FlushAll();
    }
}
```

Starting the cache layer

Now that we have a class built to interact with our MemCached client, we need to plug it into our code base and use it. To do this, we will use our StructureMap tool to swap in the MemCached client instead of the standard HttpContext.Current.Cache in the System.Web.Caching namespace.

Open the structuremap.config file. Then enter the following code just after the Assembly entries:

```
<PluginFamily
    Assembly="Fisharoo.FisharooCore"
    Type="Fisharoo.FisharooCore.Core.ICache"
    DefaultKey="MemCached" />
```

This code tells StructureMap that although the cache object is wired as the default entry, we want to use the MemCached client instead. With this configuration complete, we can now wire our caching concepts into our existing data layer. For example, I am going to add it to the FolderRepository. We will take the GetFoldersByAccountID() specifically.

```
public List<Folder> GetFoldersByAccountID(Int32 AccountID)
{
    List<Folder> result = new List<Folder>();
    string cache_key = "GetFoldersByAccountID_" +
                        AccountID.ToString();
    Stopwatch sw = new Stopwatch();
    if (_cache.Exists(cache_key))
    {
        sw.Reset();
        sw.Start();
        result = XMLService.Deserialize<List<Folder>>
                (_cache.Get(cache_key).ToString());
        sw.Stop(); //46ms from cache
    }
    else
```

```
{
    sw.Reset();
    sw.Start();
    using (FisharooDataContext dc = conn.GetContext())
    {
        var account = dc.Accounts.Where(a => a.AccountID ==
                                    AccountID).FirstOrDefault();
        IEnumerable<Folder> folders = (from f in dc.Folders
                                    where f.AccountID ==
                                        AccountID
                                    orderby f.CreateDate
                                    descending
                                    select f);
        foreach (Folder folder in folders)
        {
            var fullPath = (from f in dc.Files
                            join ft in dc.FileTypes on
                            f.FileTypeID equals ft.FileTypeID
                            where f.DefaultFolderID ==
                            folder.FolderID
                            select new
                             {
                             FullPathToCoverImage =
                             f.CreateDate.Year.ToString() +
                             f.CreateDate.Month.ToString() +
                             "/" + f.FileSystemName + "__S." +
                             ft.Name}).FirstOrDefault();
            if (fullPath != null)
                folder.FullPathToCoverImage =
                fullPath.FullPathToCoverImage;
            else
                folder.FullPathToCoverImage = "default.jpg";
            if (account != null)
                folder.Username = account.Username;
        }
        result = folders.ToList();
    }
    sw.Stop(); //190ms from db

    _cache.Set(cache_key, XMLService.Serialize(result));
}
return result;
}
```

You will notice that we first build a cache_key, which is unique to the specific request. This can usually be done by using the method name and its input parameters to create a dynamic but unique cache key. With the key in hand, we can then do a lookup in our cache to determine if we have the item cached already or not. If we don't have the item cached in, we can do the normal work to get the item and then add it to the cache. This way, when we need this specific item again we can get it from the cache instead of rebuilding it.

I wrapped each call with a StopWatch to capture how long each process takes (one to the database and one to the cache). Note the time difference in this case between going to the database and going to the cache.

 One way to see the time for each process is to set a break point just after each StopWatch.Stop() method and mouse over each Stopwatch (sw) variable as the debugger completes each process.

Caching doesn't just take care of database calls. It is also worth wrapping complex code that does long processing to return a result set that doesn't change with every call. Places to consider wrapping with cache might be the database, file system access, web service results, and so on.

While implementing a caching layer, be very cautious that you take into account what happens when new data is added and more importantly when data is deleted. If data that is added is not in the cache, it may or may not be important to update the cached item. However, leaving deleted data in the cache is pretty much never a good idea! For that reason, we want to add some code to our delete method that will remove a deleted folder from cached entries.

```
public void DeleteFolder(Folder folder)
{
 string cache_key = "GetFoldersByAccountID_" + folder.AccountID;
 if(_cache.Exists(cache_key))
    _cache.Delete(cache_key);
    using(FisharooDataContext dc = conn.GetContext())
    {
        dc.Folders.Attach(folder, true);
        dc.Folders.DeleteOnSubmit(folder);
        dc.SubmitChanges();
    }
}
```

Now when a user deletes a folder we will remove it from the cache if it exists there. Then when a user goes to get a list of folders that used to contain a deleted folder, we will build the list again rather than find it in the cache.

Where do I start?

The easiest way to know where to put caching is to analyze the performance of your site and find the slowest parts. There are at times sections of code that may benefit from a tweak to squeeze out better performance. But frequently, there are highly optimized sections of code that just can't run any faster. These are the areas that may benefit from a cache wrapper. To get major gains from your caching you don't necessarily need to stow your items away in the cache for days on end. You can see gains by caching something for only a few seconds. The key is how frequently your data changes, and how frequently that data is accessed by your users. If the data changes constantly and it is accessed constantly, huge gains can be made from seconds of caching. If the data doesn't change much you can put it into cache and remove it only when your data changes.

Searching

So far we have talked about database optimizations from the point of view of creating indexes, streamlining our deletion process, and partitioning our data. It is apparent that the deletion process won't help us here. Let's discuss why the other two don't really help us either.

You might think that adding indexes to a table will help optimize our search process. But if you think about it, we need to search within the data of a column. Rarely will we have the full string that exactly matches the string that is found. In addition to that, we need to be able to support something more than wild card searches. We also want to support Boolean searches, multiphrase queries, and so on. For these reasons, indexing doesn't help us with searching.

Partitioning helps us deal with large amounts of data. It doesn't help us with searching that data though. Again, neither does this process help us make our search faster, nor does it allow us to support additional feature-rich forms of searching.

We have also discussed caching to help speed up our site. Unfortunately, caching search terms won't help us a whole lot either unless we cache the search terms for very long periods of time. For short term caching, we won't reap benefits here. And of course, there is the nagging issue that caching doesn't give us additional search capabilities.

This is where Lucene.NET comes in handy. The thing to know about Lucene.NET is that it works best searching already indexed data. So this is where we will start creating indexes.

Disclaimer: Lucene and Lucene.NET are huge tool sets. There is no way that I can completely cover this tool in one small section of a small book! Turn to Google if you have more questions after reading this!

Getting Lucene.NET

To get us started, we first need to download Lucene.NET. You can get that here: `http://incubator.apache.org/lucene.net/download/`

All that you really need are the `Lucene dll` and `config` files. Toss those somewhere on your hard drive and add a reference to your `FisharooCore` project. With this completed we can start to build an index builder.

Building indexes

We will start building our index builder by first creating a `LuceneSearchService` class. This class will contain everything from our index builders to our index searcher. Let's add a method called `BuildIndexes()`. This method should be locked so that it can be called only once (as building indexes could take a while with a lot of data).

```
private object _indexBuildLocker = new object();

...

private void BuildIndexes()
{
    lock (_indexBuildLocker)
    {

    }
}
```

Note that we have an object declaration at the top of the class called `_indexBuildLocker`. We can then place a lock on this object any time we call into the `BuildIndexes()` method. If the object is locked when another call is made to this method, the call will be blocked until the lock is released.

With this method in place as the gateway to our other methods that we will build to build our indexes, we can get started. Let's start by creating a `BuildBlogIndex()` method. This method will be responsible for building the index for our blog data. Here is the whole method for building an index:

```
private void BuildBlogIndex()
{
    int currentBlogPage = 1;
    bool moreRecords = true;
    //open up a new indexWriter
    IndexWriter indexWriter = new
                        IndexWriter(getCacheDirectory("Blogs"),
                        new StandardAnalyzer(), true);
    //keep track of how many records we have in the index
    int counter = 0;
    try
    {
        //as long as we have more records iterate through them
        while (moreRecords)
        {
            //get an updated list of profiles to add to the index
            List<Blog> blogs =
                        _blogRepository.GetBlogsForIndexing
                        (currentBlogPage);
            //get out of the loop once we run out of records
            if (blogs.Count() == 0)
                moreRecords = false;
            //with each profile we need to create a new record
            foreach (Blog blog in blogs)
            {
                Document doc = new Document();
                doc.Add(new Field("SystemObjectID", "3",
                        Field.Store.YES, Field.Index.NO,
                                Field.TermVector.NO));
                doc.Add(new Field("SystemObjectRecordID",
                        blog.BlogID.ToString(), Field.Store.YES,
                                Field.Index.NO,
                                Field.TermVector.NO));
                doc.Add(new Field("DisplayText",
                                blog.Title != "" ? blog.Title :
                                blog.Subject,
                                Field.Store.YES, Field.Index.NO,
                                Field.TermVector.NO));
                doc.Add(new Field("Content", blog.Title + " " +
                blog.Subject + " " + blog.Post + " " + blog.PageName,
                Field.Store.YES, Field.Index.TOKENIZED,
                                Field.TermVector.YES));
                doc.Add(new Field("URL",
                        "~/Blogs/default.aspx?BlogID=" +
                        blog.BlogID.ToString(),
```

```
                              Field.Store.YES, Field.Index.NO,
                              Field.TermVector.NO));
                doc.Add(new Field("Order", counter.ToString(),
                              Field.Store.YES, Field.Index.NO,
                              Field.TermVector.NO));
                doc.Add(new Field("AccountID",
                      blog.AccountID.ToString(), Field.Store.YES,
                              Field.Index.NO,
                              Field.TermVector.NO));
                indexWriter.AddDocument(doc);
                //RecordAdded!
                EventHandler handler = RecordAddedEvent;
                if (handler != null)
                {
                    handler(this, new EventArgs());
                }
                //increment the counter
                counter++;
            }
            currentBlogPage++;
        }
        //make sure we optimize the index after building it
        indexWriter.Optimize();
    }
    catch (Exception e)
    {
        //oops
        Log.Error(this, e.Message);
    }
    finally
    {
        //we need to make sure that we close this!
        if (indexWriter != null)
        {
            //close the index
            indexWriter.Close();
        }
    }
}
```

The first major step to build an index is to open an `IndexWriter`. This is done by passing in a `Directory` and a `StandardAnalyzer`. As we will have more than one index builder, I pulled out the `Directory` logic and put it into the `getCacheDirectory()` method to return the appropriate `Directory`.

```
private Directory getCacheDirectory(string SubFolder)
{
    if (!System.IO.Directory.Exists(_indexPath + "\\" + SubFolder))
    {
        System.IO.Directory.CreateDirectory(_indexPath + "\\" +
                                            SubFolder);
    }
    _directory = FSDirectory.GetDirectory(_indexPath + "\\" +
                                          SubFolder, false);
    return _directory;
}
```

The StandardAnalyzer is used to clean out the busy words from the index that is being created. This way, words like 'the', 'and', 'is', and so on, will be removed.

 It is important that if you clean the words going into your index, you also need to remove any busy words from your queries!

The next set of code allows us to work with smaller sets of data. We don't want to get a million records to work with as we build our index. Instead, we will work in smaller sets of data. So we are carefully watching to see if we have more records using the while (moreRecords) statement. Once we get the remaining records from our BlogRepository we will set the moreRecords variable to false.

```
//as long as we have more records iterate through them
while (moreRecords)
{
    //get an updated list of profiles to add to the index
    List<Blog> blogs =
                _blogRepository.GetBlogsForIndexing(currentBlogPage);
    //get out of the loop once we run out of records
    if (blogs.Count() == 0)
        moreRecords = false;
```

Once we manage to get all the records for building into our index, we need to iterate through each record to actually add to the index. A Lucene.NET index is made up of Documents. So with each new Blog record we want to create a new Document.

```
//with each profile we need to create a new record
foreach (Blog blog in blogs)
{
    Document doc = new Document();
```

Then for each Document we will add new fields. The thing to know about building an index is that you only need to put the data that is to be searched and the data that you need to link the search results back to the actual data, in your database. For this reason, we will track the SystemObjectID and the SystemObjectRecordID. This effectively lets us index just about anything in our system. Then we need to decide what we want to add to the Document to help us with our actual search. In this case we will have the DisplayText to show in our search results. We will also have a Content field to hold all the data that we want to search for each item. We will have a URL to get us to the item from within our search results. There will also be an Order field to contain any internal search orders. And finally, we will have an AccountID field so that we know who the content belongs to (in case we need to display a profile next to the results). With the Document created, we then need to add it to the IndexWriter.

```
doc.Add(new Field("SystemObjectID", "3", Field.Store.YES,
            Field.Index.NO,
            Field.TermVector.NO));
doc.Add(new Field("SystemObjectRecordID", blog.BlogID.ToString(),
            Field.Store.YES,
            Field.Index.NO, Field.TermVector.NO));
doc.Add(new Field("DisplayText",
            blog.Title != "" ? blog.Title : blog.Subject,
            Field.Store.YES, Field.Index.NO, Field.TermVector.NO));
doc.Add(new Field("Content", blog.Title + " " + blog.Subject + " " +
            blog.Post + " " + blog.PageName, Field.Store.YES,
            Field.Index.TOKENIZED,
            Field.TermVector.YES));
doc.Add(new Field("URL", "~/Blogs/default.aspx?BlogID=" +
            blog.BlogID.ToString(),
            Field.Store.YES, Field.Index.NO,
            Field.TermVector.NO));
doc.Add(new Field("Order", counter.ToString(), Field.Store.YES,
            Field.Index.NO,
            Field.TermVector.NO));
doc.Add(new Field("AccountID", blog.AccountID.ToString(),
            Field.Store.YES,
            Field.Index.NO, Field.TermVector.NO));
indexWriter.AddDocument(doc);
```

 There is some code in here that we don't need to worry about such as the counter and firing events. This is more for UI stuff than for building indexes!

Once we have iterated through all the pages of data and finally all the records, we then need to call the `Optimize()` method of the `IndexWriter`. This will make the index more efficient to work with.

```
//make sure we optimize the index after building it
indexWriter.Optimize();
```

In case you didn't notice that we had a `try` statement started at the top of the class, there was one! The reason I bring this up is that you are working with the file system. Any time you are working with the file system, it is very important that you clean up after yourself in the `finally` section. This is no exception.

```
finally
{
    //we need to make sure that we close this!
    if (indexWriter != null)
    {
        //close the index
        indexWriter.Close();
    }
}
```

Once the indexes are built, you should have some files similar to this:

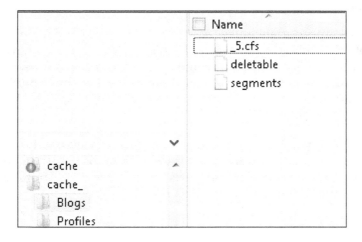

This is the Lucene.NET Index.

Building the search

Once we have an index built, we can then create a search process. The searching of Lucene is relatively easy compared to determining what you want to be represented in the index. Again, we want our process to be locked as this is a file-based process. So it is important that we have a method as a gateway that can be called externally.

```
public List<SearchResult> Search(string InputText)
{
    List<SearchResult> results = new List<SearchResult>();
    if (string.IsNullOrEmpty(InputText))
        return null;
    lock (_searchLocker)
    {
        results = SearchIndexes(InputText.ToLower());
    }
    return results;
}
```

Once we have a method to initialize our search, we can safely start the search process. In our case, we will be searching the `Profiles` and `Blogs` indexes (I created an index for both). Note that in the beginning of the search we have an array of indexes to search. Then we iterate through that list to perform searches on each index in the collection.

We then open the appropriate index. Also note that we are initializing a `Hits` object, which will hold the results of our search. In this implementation, I have created three types of searches. One is a wild card search, which will allow our user to specifiy an * as the wild card to search with. We then check to see if we have mutliple words in our search phrase, which to us will represent a `MultiPhraseQuery`. And finally, we have a simple `PhraseQuery`.

The wild card search will look for whatever you specify with anything else in place of the wild card. If I specify "Andrew*" as my search phrase, it should easily pick up "Andrew Siemer" or anything else that starts with Andrew. Be careful with this type of search as you might return a slew of data no different from `Select all` from SQL.

A `MultiPhraseQuery` query allows you to search for the first word in the phrase query, then search for the second word within the search results of the first word, and so on. This can be used to whittle down the search results with a fair amount of accuracy.

Finally, we have a simple `PhraseQuery`. This query takes in one word and searches the index for instances of that word.

With each search we are returned a collection of `Hits`. The `Hits` object holds all the documents that were found via your search. Each hit has a relavancy as well as the document so that you can use the record IDs of the found document and hence can get back to the data you have stored in your SQL table.

From there, we then iterate through each of our hits creating a new `SearchResult` (a custom structure that I made), which we can use to generically feed our UI.

```
private List<SearchResult> SearchIndexes(string InputText)
{
    List<SearchResult> result = new List<SearchResult>();
    string[] indexNames = {"Profiles", "Blogs"};
    foreach (string indexName in indexNames)
    {
        IndexReader reader =
                    IndexReader.Open(getCacheDirectory(indexName));
        IndexSearcher searcher = new IndexSearcher(reader);
        Hits hits = null;
        //are there any wild cards in use?
        if (InputText.Contains("*"))
        {
            WildcardQuery query = new WildcardQuery(new
                             Term("Content", InputText));
            hits = searcher.Search(query);
        }
            //is this a multi term query?
        else if (InputText.Contains(" "))
        {
            MultiPhraseQuery query = new MultiPhraseQuery();
            foreach (string s in InputText.Split(' '))
            {
                query.Add(new Term("Content", s));
            }
            hits = searcher.Search(query);
        }
            //single term query
        else
        {
            PhraseQuery query = new PhraseQuery();
            query.Add(new Term("Content", InputText));
            hits = searcher.Search(query);
        }
        for (int i = 0; i < hits.Length(); i++)
        {
            Document doc = hits.Doc(i);
```

```
                    SearchResult sr = new SearchResult();
                    sr.AccountID =
                              Convert.ToInt32(doc.GetField
                              ("AccountID").StringValue());
                    sr.DisplayText =
                            doc.GetField("DisplayText").StringValue();
                    sr.Content = doc.GetField("Content").StringValue();
                    sr.Order =
                        Convert.ToInt32(doc.GetField("Order").StringValue());
                    sr.SystemObjectID =
                Convert.ToInt32(doc.GetField("SystemObjectID").StringValue());
                    sr.SystemObjectRecordID =
                                    Convert.ToInt64(doc.GetField
                                    ("SystemObjectRecordID").StringValue());
                    sr.URL = doc.GetField("URL").StringValue();
                    result.Add(sr);
                }
            }
            return result;
        }
```

Here is what a `SearchResult` looks like. We use this structure to populate a grid or a repeater in our search result UI.

```
    public struct SearchResult
    {
        public int SystemObjectID { get; set; }
        public long SystemObjectRecordID { get; set; }
        public string DisplayText { get; set; }
        public string Content { get; set; }
        public string URL { get; set; }
        public int Order { get; set; }
        public int AccountID { get; set; }
    }
```

I did not plug this directly into the site, instead I created a simple webpage for you to see how it works. There is code to build the indexes from this page as well as to perform a search.

Here is the aspx code:

```
    <div>
        <asp:ScriptManager runat="server"></asp:ScriptManager>
        <asp:TextBox ID="txtSearch" runat="server"></asp:TextBox>
        <asp:Button ID="btnSearch" runat="server" Text="Search"
            OnClick="btnSearch_Click" />
```

```
<asp:Button ID="btnStart" runat="server" OnClick="btnStart_Click"
        Text="Build Lucene Search Indexes" />
<asp:UpdatePanel runat="server">
    <ContentTemplate>
        <asp:PlaceHolder ID="phResults"
                        runat="server"></asp:PlaceHolder>
    </ContentTemplate>
</asp:UpdatePanel>
</div>
```

Here is the code behind (sorry no MVP here!).

```
public partial class LuceneSearch : System.Web.UI.Page
{
    private ILuceneSearchService _luceneSearchService;
    protected void Page_Load(object sender, EventArgs e)
    {
        _luceneSearchService =
                ObjectFactory.GetInstance<ILuceneSearchService>();
        _luceneSearchService.RecordAddedEvent += new
                EventHandler(_luceneSearchService_RecordAddedEvent);
    }
    void _luceneSearchService_RecordAddedEvent(object sender,
                                                EventArgs e)
    {
        phResults.Controls.Add(new LiteralControl("<BR>Record
                                                    added"));
    }
    protected void btnStart_Click(object sender, EventArgs e)
    {
        phResults.Controls.Clear();
        _luceneSearchService.BuildIndexesThread();
    }
    protected void btnSearch_Click(object sender, EventArgs e)
    {
        phResults.Controls.Clear();
        foreach(SearchResult result in
            _luceneSearchService.Search(txtSearch.Text))
        {
            phResults.Controls.Add(new LiteralControl("<BR>" +
                    result.DisplayText + " " + result.Content));
        }

    }
}
```

As you can see, we take in the text from the UI and then perform a search on our LuceneSearchService. This returns the results, which we then bind to our repeater. There is also a button to click, to build the indexes.

Email

To this point we have discussed speeding up the site from a database point of view, a hardware point of view, an indexing point of view, and a caching point of view. I am sure that it didn't take you too much convincing that all these are wise places to look for eking that last bit of performance out of your site. Now we are going to look at speeding up the site from an infrastructure point of view. Specifically, we are going to look at a way to handle our email processing in such a way that we will reduce the number of network connections required to be made by the website directly.

> The concept of queuing up system-to-system communications is not a new one. This can be done with almost any communication that does not need real-time feedback. Any asynchronous communication is a prime candidate. And you don't necessarily need to employ a database as your queue. You can use MSMQ, the file system, or any other responsive local or semi-local resource. The concepts are mostly the same even though the technologies are vastly different.

Specifically, any time your website needs to connect to an external server—say FTP, HTTP, SMTP, TCP, and so on—the site takes a major hit in trying to establish a connection, and once connected, to actually perform its work with the third-party resource. Any time we can come up with a way to remove this connection, our users will be much happier. From the users' point of view, they want to create a message, click a button, and get feedback on whether their message was sent. We can simulate that by allowing them to create a message, stuff it in a database, and then telling the user that the message was sent. The connection to a database for a transaction is much quicker than the connection to the SMTP server. So we will store our messages in the database and have a third-party application process the outbound email at a later time.

Creating services to send email

We currently have an Email class, which handles the creation of email, the actual connectivity to the infrastructure, and finally the sending of the email. I think you will agree that this particular class is way overtasked. For this reason, we will move out the infrastructure and sending of email to an EmailService.

This service will have one method — Send() — to begin with. This method will be responsible for taking in a MailMessage, connecting to the mail server with a SmtpClient, and finally sending the email.

```
public void Send(MailMessage Message)
{
    Message.Subject = _configuration.SiteName + " - " +
                        Message.Subject;
    SmtpClient smtp = new SmtpClient();
    smtp.Send(Message);
}
```

We will then go into the Email class and remove its implementation of the Send() method. We will then need to update all the calls to the Send() method with the new call to the EmailService.Send() method.

```
public void SendEmail(string From, string Subject, string Message)
{
    MailMessage mm = new MailMessage(From,TO_EMAIL_ADDRESS);
    mm.Subject = Subject;
    mm.Body = Message;
    _emailService.Send(mm);
}
public void SendEmail(string To, string CC, string BCC, string
                    Subject, string Message)
{
    MailMessage mm = new MailMessage(FROM_EMAIL_ADDRESS,To);
    if(!string.IsNullOrEmpty(CC))
        mm.CC.Add(CC);
    if(!string.IsNullOrEmpty(BCC))
        mm.Bcc.Add(BCC);
    mm.Subject = Subject;
    mm.Body = Message;
    mm.IsBodyHtml = true;
    _emailService.Send(mm);
}

public void SendEmail(string[] To, string[] CC, string[] BCC, string
                    Subject, string Message)
{
    MailMessage mm = new MailMessage();
    foreach (string to in To)
    {
        mm.To.Add(to);
    }
    foreach (string cc in CC)
```

```
    {
        mm.CC.Add(cc);
    }
    foreach (string bcc in BCC)
    {
        mm.Bcc.Add(bcc);
    }
    mm.From = new MailAddress(FROM_EMAIL_ADDRESS);
    mm.Subject = Subject;
    mm.Body = Message;
    mm.IsBodyHtml = true;
    _emailService.Send(mm);
}

public void SendIndividualEmailsPerRecipient(string[] To, string
                                        Subject, string Message)
{
    foreach (string to in To)
    {
        MailMessage mm = new MailMessage(FROM_EMAIL_ADDRESS,to);
        mm.Subject = Subject;
        mm.Body = Message;
        mm.IsBodyHtml = true;
        _emailService.Send(mm);
    }
}
```

There are three overrides for the SendEmail() method, and one additional method SendIndividualEmailsPerRecipient() that makes a call to the old Send() method, which we updated with a call to the EmailService.Send() method instead.

Now that our infrastructure is separated out a bit, we can address the need for storing the email in some form of a queue rather than sending the email directly. To do this, we will start by first addressing our queue needs. We will use a queue in the database.

 We could just as easily use an MSMQ or the file system with some XML files. Rather than add something new to the project I figured we would build off our existing framework!

The database

We need to build three tables. Each table will have exactly the same structure, but a different purpose. We will have a receiving table that will take in new emails. This table can't be interrupted. We want to be able to receive new emails while also processing existing emails. To do this we will need to have a working table where we will put all the emails that need to be processed. And finally, as we have a log of all the communications that we have sent, we will also have a history table. This table will hold all the emails that we have processed over time.

Our tables will hold serialized email. This means that we will actually have the email, as sent, in its entirety. This means that we could easily re-serialize a batch of emails to be resent if we ever needed to.

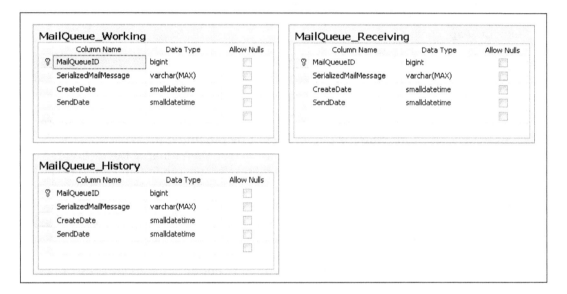

The only thing that is different about each of these tables is their names!

In order to process email that is received, we may have to go outside of what LINQ was designed for. For this reason, we will create a couple of stored procedures to help us out. We will have two procedures—one to essentially put the data from receiving into the working table, and the other to put the working data into the history table. This is just the idea, not the actual implementation!

Here is how we create the first procedure:

```
create procedure [dbo].[pr_MailQueue_SwapReceivingAndWorking_
GetWorking]
as
begin tran
--rename working to temp
execute sp_rename
    @objname = 'MailQueue_Working',
    @newname = 'MailQueue_Temp'
--rename receiving to working
execute sp_rename
    @objname = 'MailQueue_Receiving',
    @newname = 'MailQueue_Working'
--rename temp to receiving
execute sp_rename
    @objname = 'MailQueue_Temp',
    @newname = 'MailQueue_Receiving'
select * from MailQueue_Working
commit tran
```

This procedure moves the data from one table to another in a manner that is more efficient than actually moving the data. We start by renaming the working table (an empty table at this point) to MailQueue_Temp. We then rename the receiving table (a full table) to MailQueue_Working. And finally, we rename the temp table to MailQueue_Receiving so that we can continue to collect new emails. With this complete, we then return all the records in the working table. If this process is not run frequently enough, you might find that there is more data in this table than you can process in a single chunk. For that reason, you either need to process it more often, or modify the selection to select pages of data. Our implementation will assume that you process your queue frequently enough that the processor is never overloaded.

The next procedure, pr_MailQueue_MoveWorkingToHistory, cleans up after us when our email processor has completed its work.

```
create procedure [dbo].[pr_MailQueue_MoveWorkingToHistory]
as
begin tran
insert into MailQueue_History (SerializedMailMessage, CreateDate,
                                SendDate)
(select SerializedMailMessage, CreateDate, GetDate() from
                                MailQueue_Working)
truncate table MailQueue_Working
commit
```

This procedure inserts all the data from the working table into the history table. It then truncates the working table (which is why it was empty in the other procedure).

With the details worked out in the database, we can now drag these newly-created objects into our LINQ design surface so that we can work with them in our application.

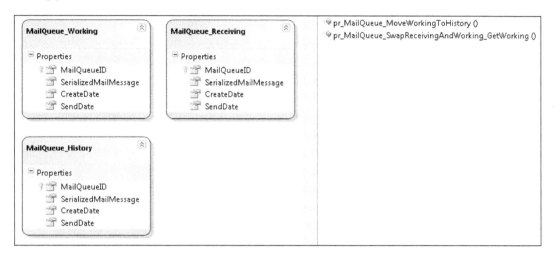

You should have the three new tables and the two new procedures similar to the ones shown in the screenshot. With these objects in place we can now create our new `EmailRepository`. This repository will have three methods — one to save a new email, the other to get all the email that needs to be processed, and the third one to copy the working table to the history table.

```
public void Save(MailQueue_Receiving MailQueue)
{
    using (FisharooDataContext dc = conn.GetContext())
    {
        dc.MailQueue_Receivings.InsertOnSubmit(MailQueue);
        dc.SubmitChanges();
    }
}

public List<pr_MailQueue_SwapReceivingAndWorking_GetWorkingResult>
        GetMailQueueToProcess()
{
    List<pr_MailQueue_SwapReceivingAndWorking_GetWorkingResult>
        results = new List<pr_MailQueue_SwapReceivingAndWorking_
GetWorkingResult>();
    using (FisharooDataContext dc = conn.GetContext())
```

```
    {
        results =
        dc.pr_MailQueue_SwapReceivingAndWorking_GetWorking().ToList();
    }
    return results;
}

public void MoveMailQueueWorkingToHistory()
{
    using (FisharooDataContext dc = conn.GetContext())
    {
        dc.pr_MailQueue_MoveWorkingToHistory();
    }
}
```

Services

With the repository and database out of the way, we need to create a new service. We already have an EmailService that directly sends email through an SMTP server. But what we need is a new service that can be swapped in place of the EmailService — the DBMailService. This service will need to conform to our IEmailService interface so that none of our application will need to know anything about how the email is sent.

Recall that our EmailService only had one method — Send(). We will have a Send() method that will deposit email into the new EmailRepository. But our DBMailService will also need a way for our email processor to process emails. So we need a second method of ProcessEmails().

```
public void Send(MailMessage Message)
{
    Message.Subject = _configuration.SiteName + " - " +
                        Message.Subject;
    MailQueue_Receiving mq = new MailQueue_Receiving();
    mq.CreateDate = DateTime.Now;
    mq.SerializedMailMessage = Message.SerializeEncrypted();
    mq.SendDate = Convert.ToDateTime("1/1/2000");
    _emailRepository.Save(mq);
}

public void ProcessEmails()
{
    //make sure we are only processing this in one thread!
    //otherwise we might lose emails
    lock (this)
    {
```

```
        try
        {
            List<pr_MailQueue_SwapReceivingAndWorking_
GetWorkingResult> results =
                new List<pr_MailQueue_SwapReceivingAndWorking_
GetWorkingResult>();
            results = _emailRepository.GetMailQueueToProcess();
            foreach (var result in results)
            {
                MailMessage mm =
                        XMLService.Deserialize<MailMessage>
                        (result.SerializedMailMessage);
                SmtpClient smtp = new SmtpClient();
                smtp.Send(mm);
            }
            _emailRepository.MoveMailQueueWorkingToHistory();
        catch(Exception e)
        {
            Log.Fatal(this, e.Message);
            return;
        }
    }
}
```

As you can see, the `Send()` method is fairly straightforward. We do need to Serialize our `MailMessage` prior to sticking it into our queue, which we will go over shortly. Otherwise, it is just an `EmailRepository` call.

The `ProcessEmail()` method on the other hand is a bit more involved. First and most important is the fact that this method should only be run one at a time. We don't want the method to be accessed by anything, so we need to lock it. Next, we need to get a list of emails to process. We then iterate through each email. Note that as we iterate over the email message, we are De-serializing each message (we will cover this shortly). We then connect to our mail server and send our email.

Rather than connect to an IIS SMTP server or some other non-bulk sending application, you could connect to something like PMTA or other bulk email delivery system. These systems would make this process even faster as they take in the email similar to the database and process the mail after receiving it. IIS SMTP attempts to send it straightaway, which can cause a delay in any application trying to send emails.

As we added a new method to our DBMailService, we will also want to update our IEmailService interface and the EmailService class (so that we can get our DBMailService and EmailService through StructureMap in all the cases). To do this, add a new method to your EmailService for the ProcessEmails() method. This method will throw up an error as we don't plan to implement it.

```
public void ProcessEmails()
{
    throw (new Exception("ProcessEmails is not implemented by this
                          class!"));
}
```

Serializing email

To start this section I have to rant a bit! We are trying to send a MailMessage through a queue process. This means that we need to be able to serialize the MailMessage. I think many people would need similar functionality either to stuff it into the database, or into an MSMQ, or onto the file system. The MailMessage is not serializable though!

There are two approaches to this issue. We can tap into the serialization of the MailMessage and specify how each of the objects in the MailMessage is to be serialized. Or we can fake the serialization. Hacking into and overriding the serialization could be a chapter in itself. So we are going to fake it.

To fake this process, I created a class called MyMailMessage with a subclass MailAddress. This encompasses all the features that I need to be represented in my emails at this point. We are avoiding the headers, attachments, and so on. At this point, we only care about the sender, the receivers, subject, body, and a few other things.

```
[Serializable]
public class MyMailMessage
{
    public MailAddress[] Bcc { get; set; }
    public MailAddress[] Cc { get; set; }
    public MailAddress[] To { get; set; }
    public string Body { get; set; }
    public MailAddress From { get; set; }
    public bool IsBodyHtml { get; set; }
    public MailAddress ReplyTo { get; set; }
    public MailAddress Sender { get; set; }
    public string Subject { get; set; }
    [Serializable]
    public class MailAddress
```

```
    {
        public string Address { get; set; }
        public string DisplayName { get; set; }
    }
}
```

Note that it is marked as Serializable!

With this in place, I was then able to create a few methods that effectively shuffle data in and out of the `MailMessage` class into and out of my new `MyMailMessage` object.

```
private static MailAddressCollection ConvertMyMailAddressesToMailAddre
sses(List<MyMailMessage.MailAddress>
                                    MyMailAddresses)
{
    MailAddressCollection mac = new MailAddressCollection();
    foreach(var a in MyMailAddresses)
    {
        mac.Add(ConvertMyMailAddressToMailAddress(a));
    }
    return mac;
}

private static MailAddress ConvertMyMailAddressToMailAddress(MyMailMes
sage.MailAddress
                                    MyMailAddress)
{
    MailAddress ma = null;
    if(MyMailAddress != null && MyMailAddress.Address != null &&
                    MyMailAddress.DisplayName != null)
        ma = new MailAddress(MyMailAddress.Address,
            MyMailAddress.DisplayName);
    return ma;
}

private static MyMailMessage.MailAddress[] ConvertMailAddressToMyMailA
ddress(MailAddressCollection
                                    MailAddresses)
{
    List<MyMailMessage.MailAddress> result = new
                                    List<MyMailMessage.MailAddress>();
    foreach (var a in MailAddresses)
    {
        result.Add(ConvertMailAddressToMyMailAddress(a));
    }
    return result.ToArray();
```

```
}
private static MyMailMessage.MailAddress
        ConvertMailAddressToMyMailAddress(MailAddress MailAddress)
{
    MyMailMessage.MailAddress ma = new MyMailMessage.MailAddress();
    if (MailAddress != null)
    {
        ma.Address = MailAddress.Address;
        ma.DisplayName = MailAddress.DisplayName;
    }
    return ma;
}
```

And finally, I was able to get to the meat and potatoes to build the `Serialize()` and `Deserialize()` methods that operate on the `MailMessage` with the helper methods just as seen in the code:

```
public static string Serialize(MailMessage MailMessage)
{
    string result = "";
    MyMailMessage mmm = new MyMailMessage();
    mmm.Bcc = ConvertMailAddressToMyMailAddress(MailMessage.Bcc);
    mmm.Body = MailMessage.Body;
    mmm.Cc = ConvertMailAddressToMyMailAddress(MailMessage.CC);
    mmm.From = ConvertMailAddressToMyMailAddress(MailMessage.From);
    mmm.IsBodyHtml = MailMessage.IsBodyHtml;
    mmm.ReplyTo =
            ConvertMailAddressToMyMailAddress(MailMessage.ReplyTo);
    mmm.Sender =
            ConvertMailAddressToMyMailAddress(MailMessage.Sender);
    mmm.Subject = MailMessage.Subject;
    mmm.To = ConvertMailAddressToMyMailAddress(MailMessage.To);
    result = XMLService.Serialize(mmm);
    return result;
}

public static MailMessage Deserialize(string SerializedMyMailMessage)
{
    MyMailMessage mmm =
                XMLService.Deserialize<MyMailMessage>
                (SerializedMyMailMessage);
    MailMessage mm = new MailMessage();
    foreach (var a in mmm.To)
    {
        mm.To.Add(ConvertMyMailAddressToMailAddress(a));
    }
```

```
        foreach (var a in mmm.Cc)
        {
            mm.CC.Add(ConvertMyMailAddressToMailAddress(a));
        }
        foreach (var a in mmm.Bcc)
        {
            mm.Bcc.Add(ConvertMyMailAddressToMailAddress(a));
        }
        mm.Body = mmm.Body;
        mm.IsBodyHtml = mmm.IsBodyHtml;
        mm.ReplyTo = ConvertMyMailAddressToMailAddress(mmm.ReplyTo);
        mm.Sender = ConvertMyMailAddressToMailAddress(mmm.Sender);
        mm.Subject = mmm.Subject;
        mm.From = ConvertMyMailAddressToMailAddress(mmm.From);
        return mm;
    }
```

As a great side effect of this class, I was also able to create the
`SerializeEncrypted()` and `DeserializeEncrypted()` methods that take
the returned string from the `Serialize()` method and wash them with our
`Cryptography.Encrypt()` and `Cryptography.Decrypt()` methods respectively.

```
    public static string SerializeEncrypted(MailMessage MailMessage)
    {
        string result = Serialize(MailMessage);
        result = Cryptography.Encrypt(result, "SomeSaltAndPepper");
        return result;
    }

    public static MailMessage DeserializeEncrypted(string
                                SerializedAndEncryptedMyMailMessage)
    {
        string result =
                Cryptography.Decrypt(SerializedAndEncryptedMyMailMessage,
                                "SomeSaltAndPepper");
        MailMessage mm = Deserialize(result);
        return mm;
    }.
```

Connecting the new DBMailQueueService

Now that we have this new service up and running and ready to be tested, how do we hook it into our existing system without changing much of our existing code? This is where the power of StructureMap comes in. We can open the `StructureMap.config` file and make this quick and simple change. Add the following to your `StructureMap.config` file:

```
<!--
    Use DefaultKey="Default" for sending the email
    in real time through the configured mail server
    or use DefaultKey="MailQueue" to send the mail
    in batches through another process
-->
<PluginFamily
    Assembly="Fisharoo.FisharooCore"
    Type="Fisharoo.FisharooCore.Core.IEmailService"
    DefaultKey="MailQueue" />
```

This will allow you to use the standard mail delivery system directly through an SMTP server in real-time as per your `web.config` settings by adding a `DefaultKey="Default"`. Or if you want to use the `MailQueue` that we just created you can add `DefaultKey="MailQueue"`. That's it! Remember that the keys that are specified here are in direct relationship to the `[Pluggable("MyInstanceName")]` attribute that you add to the top of all your classes. In the `[PluginFamily("MyInst anceName")]` that sits on top of your interfaces, you are specifying a default for that interface. This `config` entry overrides the default entry.

The queue

Now we are actually able to collect email from our site to be deposited into our `MailQueue`. As the implementation of this new feature is transparent to the site, all areas that send email will now deposit them into our queue.

 Keep in mind that you have the option of encrypting emails that are to be stored in the queue. This might be a good idea considering that you have emails that go out with users' passwords in them. Just something to think about!

Here is an example of an encrypted email sitting in our queue:

```
/o5aYaWlleVJuue+1T8my/hLqFRxWggAA1xCQOIrj17FbGtELANBBO7BufLeXQjN6HOzxw6V
8TRqaQeWJS5u/0CYhsGmd7/h+wsrAtqyxX1nA2oSpwdZoYZz6xAE8+k5Wc5L0n5OdEQA/832
24PNR99rDmQC8xewlDjR0f5RtASJIyS8nAooOPKIxYjhYOQ8+H9c/D3zhoET/9EG/jgFwUHe
3PBkbHZMewSfTP8hUD2Gngy+7Ck5pUZA6ucyZaO7VOtAsar5/JTdGcz8xDwPQa7YlKFvrNVW
HqHMYJqqTQLK6Kd3AXgPS2ryRXwBZD9vtAmOjwTTdA7/CTwwqA35u8WWqrWK2e103Cbb+kZE
V69PIDGjHLlCR20YRaJe2E3wmHkv13SH8hkihI1/2xRByg6DgCnNRF/9LQ+t5Mex4f/Q8DJn
eAlXg3qLVg9fngtRSty+pzPCFbCqu5dsm4A4JCEahjMZr8KJDWYRBnHSLduauXSQtLf7fjit
VssN8lCpzOrXAxHPtHb5ekJkO9DLjWcnvL4iDNzmcNDJou4D6BBN0eKK40hlgh/RkZGz+8YV
nZXgIIQz0GJWFki0+ooIWeY5AmSy7tU0/KpuP1Pokel4FBoPXrSrCp8L5mM97rzaNkgDTBFW
LfoEPKmrm11JMPont/jXqf79Itf7yr93kBLYAIaoOgmWEX7OY61q1py1RQIQwsMU9hTYC0DU
8wIsy62e6MPdPaYpTEqVjLXMtRtnvm8Zv5a1JFML1WcBu96HgIn5/e72qI97/eAuJi14MvFX
oYG8Taa76VLuV6UT5N4js4s54y1wSYN6FfQWbB84ro2qJ+VjGhangxTXMnJwd4MAmLI5vdxJ
EmPp9Zf3ae6iH70fhG60mLjhwk+vo82qgLpVDS0TwNhWdU6jut/uwZBAC00c9ArJU1YggMMt
+YsPon0zEDK+4509pAywsWNYWVZe8s/dZcSMveEDmHTLo5Y2Haj/14nxJPTW+1N6CVwqJpGb
9UT92GBdRO3arZkK0w9g0Q3JEiA14oCDZG/OT9qrcqU3jxnZYbD830f4EX4ogbdYeQ0mbehy
gw4+OCGfyLTRIRYsIqvH7qZzz8dU3XwLn5wGz1sKSXWHwstA3A3Gnx2WqNPI6mbYDkyMGxvs
P5MI7APaps2tgmLvTw89OV3Zqq4uAS4IP96F0f/p9j8i1qBBckFBGZp8gM6qeUL9X/KQp6JV
Q5qXgOyyUij1GSTZDqFZmyiLMd32X7pTsZshQCxHe6zqYuV+S1yYf8Y1eLKMURipp417Xc0g
xVHM/j17kkKUHjlPRdg6kPEIjZjbow+oXW/FDyVzsTi478ubS2qAlwowfp54s3pFm+NwE5V5
EFcfrVXuFXyZA/gtTv21e3FM56umFhWOP1khP2gziX7j3CskWegsQ3qOmlmP1mX9V6Ijj4Ui
hIt+25P6ffEbGEXmvdoqYTPcHgF6Z2vcXhWHvcLftJ212f+VgcAljsQ5io/btOywuAyfNX0G
RwkVgX4vDaPZrsyADfCxsZ8IkAfNybThePxUGfAOpAaZrk/HF/jw+eLel1DyQq53e/hSAAAW
MJN/Rs+53rXY4vjejXfQARtxxoE9ykFiAs8yIw==
```

Here is an example of the same message in an un-encrypted format:

```xml
<?xml version="1.0" encoding="utf-8"?>
<MyMailMessage xmlns:xsi="http://www.w3.org/2001/XMLSchema-instance"
xmlns:xsd="http://www.w3.org/2001/XMLSchema">
    <Bcc />
    <Cc />
    <To>
        <MailAddress>
            <Address>asiemer@hotmail.com</Address>
            <DisplayName />
        </MailAddress>
    </To>
    <Body>Here is the password you requested: [password]</Body>
    <From>
        <Address>website@fisharoo.com</Address>
        <DisplayName />
    </From>
    <IsBodyHtml>true</IsBodyHtml>
    <ReplyTo />
    <Sender />
    <Subject>Fisharoo - Password Reminder</Subject>
</MyMailMessage>
```

Notice that the password is technically not secure in this format. It is very easy to search all these entries for `password` and locate a list of users' passwords with a direct association to the users' accounts through their (also provided) email addresses!

Processing the queue

With a couple of emails in our queue, we can now focus on building a sample processor. I will build a quick console application to demonstrate this. Technically, you could take the console application and hook it up to your windows server as a scheduled task. But for production work, I would suggest that you convert this console application to a windows service, which is vastly more reliable (just not as easy to show demos of!).

To get started, I added a new console application project called **FisharooMailQueueProcessor** as shown in this screenshot:

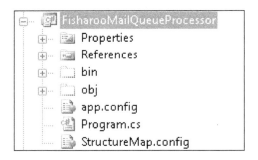

I added an **app.config** file and the project's own copy of the **StructureMap.config** file (not a reference to the solution version). The **app.config** file has a copy of all the properties that our `Configuration` class would expect to see, as well as an entry for the `system.net/mailSettings`, which points to our mail server.

```xml
<?xml version="1.0" encoding="utf-8" ?>
<configuration>
  <system.net>
    <mailSettings>
      <smtp>
        <network host="www.fisharoo.com" port="25"
            userName="admin@fisharoo.com" password="tm-es@as"/>
      </smtp>
    </mailSettings>
  </system.net>
  <appSettings>
    <add key="SiteName" value="Fisharoo"/>
```

```
      <add key="NumberOfRecordsInPage" value="20"/>
      <add key="NumberOfTagsInCloud" value="30"/>
      <!--
        CloudSortOrder - Possible options include the following:
          Random: randomly sorts the cloud each time
          Ascending: sorts the final value of the tag cloud from small
          to tall
          Descending: sorts the final value of the tag cloud from tall
          to small
      -->
      <add key="CloudSortOrder" value="Random"/>
      <add key="TagCloudSmallestFontSize" value="10"/>
      <add key="TagCloudLargestFontSize" value="30"/>
      <add key="RootURL" value="http://localhost:64810/"/>
      <add key="WebSiteURL" value="http://localhost:64810/"/>
      <add key="AdminSiteURL" value="http://localhost:64948/"/>
      <add key="DefaultCacheDuration_Days" value="0"/>
      <add key="DefaultCacheDuration_Hours" value="0"/>
      <add key="DefaultCacheDuration_Minutes" value="15"/>
      <add key="ToEmailAddress" value="website@fisharoo.com"/>
      <add key="FromEmailAddress" value="website@fisharoo.com"/>
    </appSettings>
  </configuration>
```

The `StructureMap.config` file specifies that the `IEmailService` should use the `MailQueue`. I added its own copy of the `config` file so that we don't depend upon the website's copy.

```
  <?xml version="1.0" encoding="utf-8" ?>
  <StructureMap>
    <Assembly Name="Fisharoo.FisharooCore" />
    <!--
    Use DefaultKey="Default" for standard cache
    or DefaultKey="MemCached" for memcached cache.
    -->
    <PluginFamily
        Assembly="Fisharoo.FisharooCore"
        Type="Fisharoo.FisharooCore.Core.ICache"
        DefaultKey="MemCached" />
    <!--
    Use DefaultKey="Default" for sending the email
    in real time through the configured mail server
    or use DefaultKey="MailQueue" to send the mail
    in batches through another process
    -->
```

```
    <PluginFamily
        Assembly="Fisharoo.FisharooCore"
        Type="Fisharoo.FisharooCore.Core.IEmailService"
        DefaultKey="MailQueue" />
</StructureMap>
```

Finally, we have the actual guts of the program:

```
public class Program
{
    static void Main(string[] args)
    {
        //you can use the InjectStub to tell ObjectFactory
        //to return a different type of class
        //other than the default type
        ObjectFactory.InjectStub(typeof(IEmailService), new
                            DBMailService());
        IEmailService _emailService =
                    ObjectFactory.GetInstance<IEmailService>();
            _emailService.ProcessEmails();
        //but make sure you reset it to your defaults
        //when you are done - this could be a source
        //of a bug if you forget!
        ObjectFactory.ResetDefaults();
    }
}
```

As we did most of our work in the DBMailService, we have very little work left to do to actually process our email queue. We inject a stub into StructureMap (this is another way to specify which type of class you want from the factory). We then get an instance of our IEmailService. Next, we call the ProcessEmails() method. And finally, we reset our StructureMap environment. You don't have to do the two StructureMap lines as this is technically handled in the config file. I just wanted to show you that this could be done. This means that the whole application that processes the email in our queue is two lines of code!

Summary

In this chapter, we discussed various areas of the application that might experience some growing pains over time. We addressed performance issues from a simple lack of resources to how they can be addressed by creating a web farm. Then we looked at possible inefficiencies in the database by discussing a better way to delete data, partition and index it. Next, we looked at a way to speed up data and object access on the site by implementing a caching layer using MemCached.NET. With these items addressed, we moved on to making our search capabilities better and faster. Finally, we looked at how network communications—emails in particular—could be speeded up a bit by adding a layer of abstraction between your website and the actual technology used to send emails.

The key to this chapter is looking at your site for possible pain points and addressing them with approaches that may not be ASP.NET or C# related. Frequently, your code may be optimized to a greater level, but may still appear to be slow. Poke around a bit to determine for yourself all the aspects that are involved with a problem, and learn to address it outside the box if that is best.

Index

T

tagging
  about 419
  data access layer, setting up 421
  database, implementing 419
  design 415, 416
  issues 410-413
  presentation layer, implementing 449, 457
  repositories, building 425
  services/application layer, implementing
    432
  solution 417
  system object tags 419, 420
Test-Driven Development. *See* **TDD**

U

user account
  business/domain layer, implementing
    111-113
  data access layer, implementing 87
  database, implementing 85
  design 79
  issues 78, 79
  logging in 84
  presentation layer, implementing 113
  registration 79
  security 82
  services/application layer, implementing
    106-110
  solution 85
user profiles
  avatar 160

data access layer, setting up 167, 168
database, implementing 163
design 158
issues 155-158
news feed 162
presentation layer, implementing 174
privacy 161, 162
profile 158
public profile 160, 161
services/application layer, implementing
  168
solution 162

V

view 34

W

web farming
  design 494
  solution 501-508
wrapper
  about 44
  cache wrapper 47-53
  configuring 44-47
  emails, sending 57-61
  redirection 56, 57
  session object 54-56

X

XSS 467

Thank you for buying
ASP.NET 3.5 Social Networking

About Packt Publishing

Packt, pronounced 'packed', published its first book "*Mastering phpMyAdmin for Effective MySQL Management*" in April 2004 and subsequently continued to specialize in publishing highly focused books on specific technologies and solutions.

Our books and publications share the experiences of your fellow IT professionals in adapting and customizing today's systems, applications, and frameworks. Our solution based books give you the knowledge and power to customize the software and technologies you're using to get the job done. Packt books are more specific and less general than the IT books you have seen in the past. Our unique business model allows us to bring you more focused information, giving you more of what you need to know, and less of what you don't.

Packt is a modern, yet unique publishing company, which focuses on producing quality, cutting-edge books for communities of developers, administrators, and newbies alike. For more information, please visit our website: www.packtpub.com.

Writing for Packt

We welcome all inquiries from people who are interested in authoring. Book proposals should be sent to author@packtpub.com. If your book idea is still at an early stage and you would like to discuss it first before writing a formal book proposal, contact us; one of our commissioning editors will get in touch with you.

We're not just looking for published authors; if you have strong technical skills but no writing experience, our experienced editors can help you develop a writing career, or simply get some additional reward for your expertise.

PUBLISHING

Building Websites with the ASP.NET Community Starter Kit

ISBN: 1-904811-00-0   Paperback: 268 pages

A comprehensive guide to understanding, implementing, and extending the powerful and freely available application from Microsoft

1. Learn .NET architecture through building real-world examples

2. Understand, implement, and extend the Community Starter Kit

3. Learn to create and customize your own website

4. For ASP.NET developers with a sound grasp of C#

Building Websites with VB.NET and DotNetNuke 4

ISBN: 1-904811-99-X   Paperback: 250 pages

A practical guide to creating and maintaining your own DotNetNuke website, and developing new modules and skins

1. Specially revised and updated version of this acclaimed DotNetNuke book

2. Create and manage your own website with DotNetNuke

3. Customize and enhance your site with skins and custom modules

4. Extensive coverage of the DAL and DAL+ for custom module development

5. Complete coverage of setup, administration, and development

Please check **www.PacktPub.com** for information on our titles

Elgg Social Networking

ISBN: 978-1-847192-80-6   Paperback: 179 pages

Create and manage your own social network site using this free open-source tool

1. Create your own customized community site

2. Manage users, invite friends, start groups and blogs

3. Host content: photos, videos, MP3s, podcasts

4. Manage your Elgg site, protect it from spam

5. Written on Elgg version 0.9

Drupal for Education and E-Learning

ISBN: 978-1-847195-02-9   Paperback: 380 pages

Teaching and learning in the classroom using the Drupal CMS

1. Use Drupal in the classroom to enhance teaching and engage students with a range of learning activities

2. Create blogs, online discussions, groups, and a community website using Drupal

3. Clear step-by-step instructions throughout the book

4. No need for code! A teacher-friendly, comprehensive guide

Please check **www.PacktPub.com** for information on our titles

www.ingramcontent.com/pod-product-compliance
Lightning Source LLC
Chambersburg PA
CBHW081450050326
40690CB00015B/2749